W9-AYQ-428

CARL CAMPBELL BRIGHAM LIBRARY
EDUCATIONAL TESTING SERVICE
PRINCETON, NJ 08541

Latent Variables Analysis

BVEW

Latent Variables Analysis

APPLICATIONS
FOR
DEVELOPMENTAL
RESEARCH

ALEXANDER VON EYE
CLIFFORD C. CLOGG

EDITORS

SAGE Publications
International Educational and Professional Publisher
Thousand Oaks   London   New Delhi

Copyright © 1994 by Sage Publications, Inc.

All rights reserved. No part of this book may be reproduced or utilized in any form or by any means, electronic or mechanical, including photocopying, recording, or by any information storage and retrieval systems, without permission in writing from the publisher.

For information address:

SAGE Publications, Inc.
2455 Teller Road
Thousand Oaks, California 91320

SAGE Publications Ltd.
6 Bonhill Street
London EC2A 4PU
United Kingdom

SAGE Publications India Pvt. Ltd.
M-32 Market
Greater Kailash I
New Delhi 110 048 India

Printed in the United States of America

Library of Congress Cataloging-in-Publication Data

Main entry under title:

Latent variables analysis: applications for developmental research /
edited by Alexander von Eye, Clifford C. Clogg.
  p.   cm.
  Includes bibliographical references (p.   ) and index.
  ISBN 0-8039-5330-5 (cloth).—ISBN 0-8039-5331-3 (pbk.)
  1. Latent structure analysis.   2. Latent variables.   I. Eye,
  Alexander von.   II. Clogg, Clifford C.
  QA278.6.L34   1994
  519.5'35—dc20   94-7962

94 95 96 97 98   10 9 8 7 6 5 4 3 2 1

Sage Production Editor: Susan McElroy

Contents

Acknowledgments

The editors are grateful to a number of special people, institutions, and societies that made this volume possible. Within the Pennsylvania State University, we would like to thank the College for Health and Human Development and Dean Anne Petersen for generous support. The same applies to the Department for Human Development and Family Studies, chaired in the Academic Year 1992/93 by Acting Department Head Steven Zarit. Our thanks go also to the Center for Developmental and Health Research Methodology, the Population Research Institute, and the State College Chapter of the American Statistical Association.

At the individual level, we would like to thank first the contributors to this volume. They all prepared excellent chapters and responded in a professional fashion to our requests for revisions. We would like to thank Tina Meyers, Administrative Assistant at the Center for Developmental and Health Research Methodology. Tina Meyers took care of coordination, correspondence, and contacts with authors and publishers, and much much more. She did all this in a masterful way. We would also like to thank Sage Publications, specifically C. Deborah Laughton and her most able staff.

Finally, we thank our families. They support us with enduring love. Without them, this book would not exist.

Preface

It is difficult to appreciate contemporary empirical research in the social and behavioral sciences generally, or in longitudinal and developmental research specifically, without a deep understanding of the role of latent variables. This is the case whether more theoretical research is considered (almost all of which is couched in terms of latent variables), whether routine empirical testing of behavioral theories is considered (much of which is based at least implicitly on analysis of latent variables as reported in most standard journals), or whether policy analysis or evaluation of program initiatives are considered (multiple measures of outcomes or even of "experimental" treatments are often combined by regarding them as indicators of one or more latent variables).

The fascination with latent variable concepts and with models involving latent variables is surely one of the distinctive characteristics of statistical method in social and behavioral research. But it is difficult to keep abreast of methodological developments pertaining to latent variables because this part of the language of social research is changing rapidly. The technology for building and diagnosing models with latent variables has become complex, and we need to find ways to translate this technology so that it becomes useable for application oriented researchers. There has been a proliferation in models having latent variables. Thus, the diversity is far greater than it was at a time when factor analysis dominated the area of latent variable analysis. Fortunately, we now have a better understanding of how models with latent variables relate to other models, and how ostensibly different latent-variable models relate to each other. These and related themes are intertwined in many of the chapters in this volume.

The purpose of the this book is to present current work on models with latent variables so that research workers can better understand the underlying logic of the techniques and so that methodological specialists and substantive researchers alike can better assess the suitability of particular methods for their own research contexts. This book covers conceptual and logical issues and problems common to all latent variable models. It also covers both models based on continuous latent variables and models based on discrete latent variables. Although the focus is on such tools for the analysis of change or development, virtually all of the material is relevant for other settings.

Latent variables come in many forms. Two examples will be considered briefly. The first example is when latent variables are regarded as *causal variables,* or, more generally, as predictors in some regression-type model. Whether latent variables are regarded as causal variables or merely as predictors, they are defined on the basis of two characteristics. First, they cannot be directly observed; rather, they must be inferred from observable or "manifest" variables which are sometimes called indicators of the latent variables. Second, the latent variables are responsible for systematic variation in the observables. For example, a researcher might assume that there is a causal entity (or, at least, a predictor) like *ability* or *intelligence* that affects (or predicts) such outcomes as job satisfaction, self esteem, performance on the job, occupational mobility, etc. In this setting, the analyst might use several available test items or responses on survey questions to summarize the latent variable *ability* and then consider one or more models that estimate the degree to which *ability* affects (or predicts) the outcomes of interest. This general research problem takes on a developmental or longitudinal aspect if we measure ability (using test items) at several points in time for the same individuals or if we observe the outcomes on several occasions. Of course, we might also posit latent variables for the outcomes of interest (e.g., self esteem), in which case we would model the degree to which one latent variable affects (or predicts) another latent variable.

The second example can be described as attempt at measurement, when *latent variable models serve to define the measurement process.* The research question might be *how well* a given set of indicators or observables actually measures an underlying construct. Or, the research question might be to determine the relationships between the observed measurements and the unobserved variables in some model in order to infer essential properties of both sets, such as "dimensionality." The basic idea here is to assess the quality of the observed measurements in terms of their consistency or reliability, perhaps even their validity as fundamental measures or indicators. The consideration of latent variable models as tools to assess the quality of measurements and their statistical and substantive content is very important, and it seems to us that such an assessment is important for causal analysis or regression-type modeling involving latent variables as well.

If individuals are followed over time so that multiple indicators are available on repeated occasions, developmental process or *change at the latent level* can be inferred from a variety of contemporary models, some of which are emphasized in this volume.

The chapters selected for this volume fall into four general topics:

(1) Theoretical Issues: Concepts in Latent Variables Analysis,

(2) Analysis of Latent Variables in Developmental Research: Continuous Variables Approaches,

(3) Analysis of Latent Variables in Developmental Research: Categorical Variables Approaches, and

(4) Testing in the Analysis of Latent Variables.

The first topic, Theoretical Issues, contains three chapters. In the first two chapters, Michael Sobel, Rolf Steyer, and Thomas Schmitt discuss statistical concepts of causality in non-experimental settings with latent variables. These chapters summarize the logic of causal inference with latent variables and give conditions or assumptions that must be maintained in order to draw causal inferences from statistical inferences. In the third chapter, Scott Hershberger discusses model equivalence. In many instances it may not be obvious in what respects ostensibly different latent variable models differ in fact for a given set of data. The notion of model equivalence provides a way to compare models.

The second section deals with *continuous variables approaches*. The first chapter, by Phillip Wood, links well-known regression models to latent variables analysis. Problems arising from unmeasured, latent variables and their effects on estimating regression parameters are discussed.

John Nesselroade delineates the relationship between exploratory, longitudinal factor analysis and latent variable concepts, thereby drawing on both Cattellean tradition of P-technique and modern longitudinal structural equation modeling. A formal generalization of this approach, including special models and procedures for hypothesis tests, is presented by Peter Molenaar in the following chapter. In tandem, these two chapters cover the history of longitudinal latent variable analysis from the beginnings of P-analysis to the latest developments in dynamic factor models.

A topic of much practical importance is taking account of missing data in models with latent variables, especially in longitudinal research. Michael Rovine presents methods for estimating models that fully exploit the information in the data, including the information in cases with incomplete information on one or more variables. These methods would be preferable to list-wise or case-wise deletion methods which can lead to possibly severe bias.

The third section concerns *categorical variables approaches* to latent variables analysis. The bridge between concepts of continuous and categorical latent variables approaches is established by Peter Molenaar and Alexander von Eye. Whether to define latent variables as categorical or continuous is largely determined by theory (or taste). The authors present a simulation that illustrates that, under specified conditions, solutions from these alternative definitions can be equivalent. This result turns the discussion of concepts of types (or latent classes) versus dimensions (number of continuous factors) in a new direction.

George Macready and C. M. Dayton present latent class models for longitudinal assessment of trait acquisition. Their chapter summarizes a long series of contributions by the authors on modeling dynamic trait development. One of the basic tenets in this chapter is that traits can be acquired and, thus, undergo change.

Christiane Spiel discusses latent trait models for measuring change from two perspectives. The first recasts latent trait models in terms that emphasize these models' formal similarities to Analysis of Variance. The second aims at parameter estimation. New designs are proposed that allow researchers to estimate parameters interesting from a developmental perspective. Still in the context of Rasch-type models, Anton Formann presents new approaches to measuring change. Unlike Christiane Spiel's chapter which focuses on latent trait models, Anton Formann's chapter focuses on latent class models.

Hoben Thomas discusses latent class models from a more general perspective. Latent class and log-linear models can be viewed as special cases of finite mixture models. This chapter presents finite mixtures of unknown componential form and applies them to developmental questions.

Log-linear models typically are estimated for manifest variables. In the next chapter, Jacques Hagenaars shows how to incorporate concepts of latent variables in log-linear analysis. The author gives log-linear models for the analysis of change in a categorical-data setting. These models can be viewed as generalizations of latent class models and regular log-linear models.

Allan McCutcheon shows, within a logit model framework, how latent variables concepts can be applied to dependent, categorical variables. Rolf Langeheine applies latent variable concepts to Markov-type models thus allowing researchers to model transition patterns at both the manifest and the latent levels. For example, one possible way to conceive of change in categorical variables is to suppose that a Markov process operates on latent states that are only indirectly observed.

The fourth section of this book presents papers dealing with *testing in latent variables contexts.* Testing is one of the areas in latent variables analysis that still provides ample space for development. This section contains two chapters. The first of these two chapters, authored by Albert Satorra and Peter Bentler, presents three corrections to three types of test statistics and a correction to the standard errors. These corrections improve the quality of the approximations of interest and possess desirable robustness characteristics. In the last chapter, Donald Rubin and Hal Stern discuss testing in latent class models using Bayesian methods and a predictive checking distribution. As one important step, this chapter shows how, for example, to directly test whether a latent class model with T latent classes is better than a model with either $T - 1$ or $T + 1$ latent classes.

Alexander von Eye   *Clifford C. Clogg*
Michigan State University   *The Pennsylvania State University*

PART 1

Theoretical Issues: Concepts in Latent Variables Analysis

1

Causal Inference in
Latent Variable Models

MICHAEL E. SOBEL

1. Introduction

Throughout history, scientists have referred to and debated the ontological status of unobserved entities. For instance, the ancient Greeks posited the existence of "atoms," conceptualized as minute particles of matter in constant motion. Surprisingly, the atomists fared better than 17th century physicists who propounded the phlogisten hypothesis and 19th century physicists who postulated the existence of ether; in modern physics, "atoms" are still around (though today's atom is endowed with properties that the Greeks did not even imagine) and atoms, as well as various subatomic particles and their properties, are commonly featured in physical explanations.

Social and behavioral scientists also refer to unobserved entities. Economists speak of utility, markets, permanent income, reservation wages, and the like; psychologists refer to intelligence, motivation, self-esteem, and attitude; and sociologists speak of social class, socioeconomic status, anomie, social structure, culture, and subculture. And like physicists, who do not observe the electrons that appear in physical explanations, social and behavioral scientists face the problem of making measurements that bear some relationship to the unobserved entities they invoke.

AUTHOR'S NOTE: For helpful comments on several previous drafts, I am grateful to
C. C. Clogg and P.C.M. Molenaar.

Typically economists do not try to measure utility or to say what it is: They usually treat utility as a primitive, using it, in conjunction with various axioms (about how utility works) and the principle of utility maximization, to get to the demand equations, which express, for a given consumer, the quantities of goods demanded (an observable) as a function of the prices of other goods and the consumer's income. Thus, utility (actually the utility function), though unobserved, appears useful in describing features of the observable world, and this is so whether the term refers to an entity the economist thinks actually exists or an entity that does not really exist (Phlips, 1974).

Similarly, psychologists cannot measure intelligence directly. But psychologists and other social and behavioral scientists typically take a different approach to their terms than the approach the economist takes to utility. For example, instead of treating intelligence as a primitive term, psychologists attempt to say something about its nature; having done so, they construct measurements (in this case ability tests) that are "indicative" of the "latent variable" intelligence. Then, in conjunction with a theory of measurement (e.g., classical test score theory), the indicators, a sample, and a statistical model (factor analysis for the case of classical test score theory) that expresses the relationship of intelligence to its indicators, the psychologist ascertains the fit of the model to the data, using this to argue that the ability tests in question are good (bad) measures of intelligence and/or that the notion of intelligence is adequate (inadequate). In some treatments, intelligence is regarded as a construct; here, no commitment to intelligence as a real entity need be made.

Sometimes unobserved entities are of interest more or less in and of themselves; for example, since Spearman (1904), psychologists have devoted much attention to the measurement of intelligence. But unobserved entities are often put to further use, appearing in explanations of various sorts. For example, in economics the permanent income hypothesis is invoked to explain household consumption over the life cycle. In psychology, attitudes are sometimes held to cause behavior (although the reverse is sometimes held as well), and intelligence appears as a cause of other phenomena. In sociology, a survey respondent's socioeconomic status is held to cause that respondent's level of anomie (Wheaton, Muthén, Alwin, & Summers, 1977), and education is held to cause occupational status (Blau & Duncan, 1967).

This chapter discusses the use of unobserved entities in causal inference in the social and behavioral sciences. Before proceeding further, it is useful to examine briefly the kinds of "things" that might be featured in causal accounts. Traditionally, philosophers have taken events to be the critical constituents. While this appears to exclude a number of other things (by ordinary language standards), the early 20th century philosophers, following physicists, took the concept of event to coincide with anything that could be given time and space coordinates (Emmet, 1984). A number of more recent accounts distinguish between events and other types of things, for example, factors, processes, conditions, states, and properties, invoking the latter types of entities in discussions of causation. For example, in Kim (1971) and Shoemaker (1980), events happen to one or more objects, and properties of the objects are involved in the causal relation.

Social and behavioral researchers often use statistics to make inferences, causal and noncausal. A typical setup is the case considered here, where a sample is drawn from a population of units and measurements on the sample units are taken. Within this context, it is natural to equate the concept of event with what happens to a unit (object), and to view the measurements (perhaps too simplistically) as measuring properties of these objects, thereby matching the setup to accounts (or portions thereof) of causation that focus on objects and their properties.

In the preceding setup, unobserved entities can enter in essentially two ways. First, the units (objects) might be unobserved. Although the units featured in the social and behavioral sciences are typically persons or other well-defined entities, such as counties, states, or countries, this is not always so. For example, sociologists speak of society, although they typically make measurements on countries. Thus, the units in sociological explanations may be unobserved entities, and in some instances, it may be more natural to think of these units as hypothetical, rather than actual. Second, the units may be observed entities (e.g., persons), but one or more (relevant) features of the unit are unobserved. One such type of unobserved entity, the subject of this chapter, is the latent variable.

The preceding themes (unobserved variables, causation, and probability), already linked together in Wright (1934), suggested the need for statistical procedures that allow the assessment of probabilistic causal relations among variables, with one or more unobserved (latent) variables. For metrical latent variables and indicators, the Jöreskog-Keesling-Wiley covariance structure model (Jöreskog, 1970, 1977), which merges linear simultaneous equation models from econometrics with factor analysis from psychometrics, seems to be such a procedure.

This model also used, at the estimation stage, the assumption (at least within groups) that the observed variables were drawn from a multinormal distribution. In the past decade various improvements have been made. Browne (1984) proposed the ADF (asymptotically distribution free) estimator, replacing the normality assumption with weaker assumptions. Muthén (1984) generalized the model form by allowing indicators of the metrical latent variables to be ordinal, as well as metric. A general nonlinear mean and covariance structure model for the metrical case has been discussed by Arminger & Sobel (1990). In other cases, the unobserved variables are categorical (e.g., latent class and latent profile models). Models with categorical unobserved variables have yet to be combined with simultaneous equation models in a general way, but work along such lines continues (e.g., Dayton & Macready, 1988).

The foregoing suggests that in the space of 100 years, appropriate statistical tools for the measurement of unobserved variables and the assessment of "probabilistic" causal relationships have been developed and these two lines of work successfully joined. This chapter argues against such a view. The discussion suggests two conclusions. The first, essentially implicit, is that latent variable models cannot substitute for careful explication and measurement of concepts; unexplicated and inexact (prescientific) concepts are not improved by a statistical model. The second, not unrelated to the first, is that causal models with latent variables have much less to do with causation (as implicitly conceptualized in the literature) than usually suggested: If researchers want to get serious about causal inference, more time at the drawing board and less time refining current procedures is in order.

The chapter proceeds as follows. Section 2 exposits an account of the causal relation and a corresponding approach to causal inference, for both experimental and nonexperimental (observational) studies. The approach, due primarily to Rubin (1974, 1977, 1978, 1980), also gives conditions under which causal inferences from nonexperimental studies coincide with those that would be obtained in a randomized experiment; these are used to examine the way social and behavioral scientists use the parameters of regression models and structural equation models to make causal inferences. Following Holland (1988) and Sobel (1990), the parameters (and functions of parameters) of such models, should not, in general, be interpreted as unit effects, as per the usual custom. In Section 3, latent variables are introduced and folded into the discussion. I argue that the typical conception of a latent variable as a hypothetical construct cannot be reconciled with the idea that latent variables are causes and effects. A better fit is obtained when latent variables are viewed Platonically; that is, given as a scale of measurement, the latent variable has a true value, independent of and not defined through our efforts to ascertain this value. Under this view, given a set of indicators, the usual assumptions in latent variable models may not hold for the Platonic latent variables, and the latent variable models we employ may not lead to reasonable causal inferences (even if all other conditions for valid causal inference were met), as demonstrated in the text. Section 4 concludes with a brief discussion of the problem of treating latent variables as causes.

2. Causal Inference With Directly Measured Variables

2.1. Causation and Causal Inference: General Considerations

Here, the term *causal inference* refers to the act of using evidence to make inferences about causation. Therefore, in the absence of a conception of the causal relation, it makes no sense to speak of causal inference. Further, the legitimacy of a causal inference depends, at least in part, on the relationship between the statements that the evidence and methods can support and the concept of causation under consideration. Thus, in this section, several notions of the causal relation are discussed; then some common approaches to causal inference are introduced and evaluated. For a more extended treatment of these and related issues, see Holland (1988), Rubin (1978), and Sobel (1990, in press). The treatment of unobserved variables is deferred to Section 3.

In the deterministic case, causation is sometimes equated with universal predictability. Social scientists who have followed this view tend to equate the causal relation with a looser form of predictability, stochastic dependence. For example, Basmann (1963) equated causality with the idea that a mechanism, isolated from external forces and repeatedly started from similar initial conditions, runs through the same approximate sequence of states. Granger (1969, 1980) equates causation with association that does not vanish by conditioning on the past. Zellner (1984) also takes this view, but argues, following Feigl (1953), that causation is predictability according to a law; Zellner does not define the notion of law but insists that inferences should only involve the observed data. Consequently, in contrast to recent philosophical treatments, he does not require that a law sustain a counterfactual conditional (a conditional statement with a premise that is contrary to fact). The foregoing notions of causation are most often featured in economics and employed in conjunction with problems of prediction in time series models.

A second account of the causal relation hinges on the idea of manipulating the cause, either in practice or hypothetically (Collingwood, 1940/1948; Cook & Campbell, 1979; Gasking, 1955; Sobel, in press; von Wright, 1971). Here, for example, a binary response is an event or state that is produced (prevented) by producing (preventing) an event or state called the cause (Collingwood, 1940/1948, p. 285); that is, the cause is simply the variable(s) subjected to manipulation, either hypothetical or actual. Thus, if X is a variable that is manipulated, Z a variable measured prior to the time of manipulation, and Y a variable measured subsequently, X is viewed as the cause of Y, and Z is part of the causal background; the effect of X on Y may vary across levels of Z. In another context, Z might be manipulated, in which case Z becomes the cause, and X becomes the background. Thus, as Collingwood stressed, causes are relative to the context under consideration.

The manipulative account fits well with the types of ideas many experimentalists hold about causation. The account also fits well with "singularist" (Ducasse, 1926/1975) and counterfactual notions of causation (Lewis, 1973). The idea that singular causal statements are meaningful in and of themselves, not only by virtue of being subsumable under a general law or class of instances, seems to be a natural one to employ in treatments of causation that relax the universality criterion. The notion that a causal statement should sustain a counterfactual conditional, which is generally held in modern philosophy, dates back at least to Mill. In Section 2.2, an account of the causal relation that is both singular and counterfactual is formalized. In previous work (Sobel, in press), such an account has been described as manipulative; I now think it is more appropriate to describe the account itself as counterfactual, viewing manipulation primarily as a means of fixing the meaning of the cause. Scientists who appeal to the idea of manipulation are typically advocating a counterfactual account of causation; because experimental researchers are forced to actually indicate the manipulation, the counterfactual is clear, while nonexperimental researchers often appeal to the notion of manipulating variables without stating how the values of the variables are changed, and consequently, the counterfactual is often not well specified.

Having introduced these two types of accounts, attention centers on the relation between these and causal inference in the social and behavioral sciences. If causation is equated primarily with prediction, it is natural for causal inference in the stochastic context to hinge on the concepts of statistical independence and dependence. In the simplest case, a variable X might be held to cause a variable Y if X were temporally prior to Y and X and Y were associated; often it is required that this hold when possible sources of spuriousness are taken into account. The most sophisticated uses of the predictive approach to causal inference in the social and behavioral sciences are in economics, where tests for Granger causality are featured (Geweke, 1984). It is important to note, contrary to some statements and to common use, that this approach will not typically sustain inferences that comport with a counterfactual account.

Psychologists and sociologists have traditionally taken two approaches to causal inference. The first is "experimental," with treatments either imposed by the investigator or naturally occurring. In one type of experiment, the units of study are thought to be subjected to multiple treatments and the responses of a unit are compared across the treatments received. For instance, consider the case where all subjects receive a particular treatment and a response (posttest measurement) is recorded; in addition, the subject's response is also measured prior to the imposition of the treatment, and this (pretest) measurement is viewed as a stand-in for the value of the response that would have been obtained in the absence of the treatment. Various types of effects may then be estimated by comparing the pretest and posttest measures. Sometimes a simple mean difference will suffice, but in other cases one might want to know these differences in various subgroups. Experiments of the type above are common in psychological and educational research and are often considerably more sophisticated than the foregoing presentation suggests. In a second type of experiment, each sample unit receives one treatment, from a set of treatments, and inferences about the relative effects of a particular treatment, say Treatment 1, as opposed to another, say Treatment 0, are made by comparing the responses of units that received Treatment 1 with the responses of units that received Treatment 0. Experiments of this kind are also common and often employ randomization, sometimes in conjunction with matching and/or statistical control. For treatment of various experimental designs and the substantive issues concerned with their use, see Cook and Campbell (1979), and for treatment of some basic statistical issues concerned with experimental design, see Winer (1971).

The second approach to causal inference is typically featured in nonexperimental studies and is common in disciplines where the relevant experiments cannot be or are not conducted, for example, economics and sociology. Here an investigator wants to study a particular effect and asks the question of how it comes about. The conventional answer consists of generating a list of variables (the independent variables) that are held to "explain" variation in the response. Typically, explanation is taken to be synonymous with causation, and thus the independent variables come to be viewed as causes of the response. Causal inference then consists of estimating an appropriate model, for example, a regression model in the case of a continuous response, a logit or probit model in the case where the response is categorical, and so on, and interpreting the model parameters ("effects"). When the response is vector valued, additional issues arise, but simultaneous equation models can often be used. Here, a set of variables is partitioned into subsets consisting of so-called exogenous and endogenous variables. The partitioning is a matter of substantive theory, perhaps in conjunction with temporal information on the variables. The endogenous variables are then "explained" by the exogenous variables and other endogenous variables with a parametric statistical model. The error terms of the model are assumed to be uncorrelated with the exogenous variables (this is the operational definition of *exogeneity*) and in line with everyday language usage (though not the preceding definition), the exogenous variables are viewed as determined outside the scope of the model. Parameters connecting the exogenous variables with endogenous variables, and parameters connecting endogenous variables with other endogenous variables are then interpreted as measures of effect (in a sense to be made precise subsequently).

The preceding approaches to causal inference are typically employed in conjunction with an unexplicated notion of the causal relation. Whereas the approach used in experimental work fits well with a counterfactual account of the causal relation, it is not so clear where the second approach fits. In the case of a univariate linear regression, for example, most social and behavioral scientists would include additional independent variables if the coefficients corresponding to these variables were statistically significant, arguing that their inclusion results in a better explanation. In turn, since explanation is typically equated with the notion of causal explanation, this suggests the view that prediction is the essence of causation. Typically, however, social and behavioral scientists do not interpret the parameters of a regression as regression coefficients, but as unit effects; for example, in the regression of Y on $X_1, \ldots, X_K$, the coefficient for X_1 would be interpreted as the amount the response would increase (decrease) if, for any unit, say with value x_1, the value of X_1 were increased to $x_1 + 1$, with the values of other variables held constant. Clearly, this interpretation (which is often unwarranted) hinges on the idea of a counterfactual, brought about by manipulation. Similar remarks apply to the interpretation of coefficients in simultaneous equation models (Holland, 1988; Sobel, 1990, in press). Thus, while the second approach to causal inference apparently fits better with causation as predictability, the interpretation of coefficients as effects entails an implicit commitment to a counterfactual account of the causal relation. Consequently, in this chapter, interest centers on the validity of such interpretations under a counterfactual account. The predictive account is not discussed further.

2.2. A Counterfactual Account: Formalization and Inference

Given the reliance of most social and behavioral research on a counterfactual account of causation, it is important to examine how causal inferences in these disciplines match up with this account. To address this issue, the account is formalized and conditions for valid causal inference are given. A number of the key developments are due to Rubin (1974, 1977, 1978, 1980); the intellectual origins of the account in the statistical literature date back at least to Neyman's work in the 1920s. Finally, the parameters researchers estimate are compared with the causal parameters of interest.

The setup here is similar to that in Pratt and Schlaifer (1988), which generalizes the treatment in Holland (1986). For a slightly more general setup, see Sobel (1993). The intuition behind these accounts is simple. For a population of interest, and a potential cause and effect, imagine that it is possible to apply all levels of the cause to any given element. For that element, record the values of the effect observed in conjunction with the different levels of the cause. If all values of the effect are the same, it is natural to say that the potential cause does not cause the effect for that element; otherwise the potential cause does cause the effect. The treatment is counterfactual, for in the real world, for any given element, only one level of the cause is actually observed. For this reason, without making some strong assumptions, it is not possible to make causal inferences at this elemental level, but remarkably it is possible, under the right conditions, to make inferences that hold on average. Details follow.

The three basic components of the account are: (a) a population $\mathcal{P}$, with elements i; (b) vectors X and Y, with values x in a subset Ω_1 of $\mathcal{R}^{K_1}$ and y in a subset Ω_2 of $\mathcal{R}^L$, where the set Ω_1 contains more than one element, (c) a function $F : \Omega_1 \times \mathcal{P} \to \Omega_2$, with values $y_{xi} = F(x,i)$. In this chapter, the value of the response when the cause has value x, y_{xi}, is regarded as the realization of a random vector Y_x, and responses are independent across units. The i.i.d. assumption is not necessary, but it simplifies the presentation and is natural to use in a comparison with latent variable models, which use similar types of assumptions.

Recall the idea behind the setup: For a population of units and a set of values that the vector called the cause can take, any value of the cause can be associated with the unit, and the response associated with each value recorded. This is why the function F is defined on the domain $\Omega_1 \times \mathcal{P}$; for every unit, this function records the outcomes when that unit is exposed to every level x of X. If, for any given element i of $\mathcal{P}$, F is constant (not constant) over all levels of the cause, that is, over Ω_1, it is natural to say that X does not cause (causes) Y for unit i of $\mathcal{P}$. Note that X may cause Y for unit i without causing Y for unit i', $i \neq i'$; for example, in the medical case where units are administered a drug or a placebo, unit i may get better only under the drug, and unit i' may get better with or without the drug. Note also that X may cause Y in "different" ways for different units; for example, suppose unit i behaves as before, but unit i' actually gets worse under the drug (relative to what would have happened without the drug).

In some contexts (e.g., the law) causation at the unit level is crucial, and as noted above, causal inference at the unit level relies on strong assumptions that stand in for the inability to observe the counterfactual observations. In other contexts, such as the medical experiment above, investigators (though certainly not the subjects) may be more interested in studying what happens on average; similar remarks apply to statistical studies in the social and behavioral sciences.

Two types of causation at the population level are now defined (for more general versions of these definitions, see Sobel, 1993):

Definition 1A. X causes Y in distribution in $\mathcal{P}$ if there exist x and x', two distinct elements in Ω_1, such that, $D(Y_x) \neq D(Y_{x'})$, where $D(Y_x)$ denotes the probability distribution associated with the random vector Y_x.

Definition 1B. X does not cause Y in distribution in $\mathcal{P}$ if, given $x' \in \Omega_1$, $D(Y_x) = D(Y_{x'})$ for all $x \in \Omega_1$.

Definition 2A. Suppose $E(Y_x)$ exists for all $x \in \Omega_1$ where E denotes expected value. X causes Y in mean in $\mathcal{P}$ if there exist x and x', two distinct elements in Ω_1, such that $E(Y_x) \neq E(Y_{x'})$.

Definition 2B. Suppose $E(Y_x)$ exists for all $x \in \Omega_1$. X does not cause Y in mean in $\mathcal{P}$ if, given $x' \in \Omega_1$, $E(Y_x) = E(Y_{x'})$ for all $x \in \Omega_1$.

The statistical literature focuses attention on causation in mean, where the average effect of x, relative to x', usually defined as

$$E(Y_x - Y_{x'}) , \qquad [1.1]$$

is the quantity of interest. It is important to note that a focus on (1.1) is nevertheless compatible with a singular account of the causal relation, as (1.1) is simply the mean of the unit effects. The key thing to note here is that were it possible to observe the actual unit differences $y_{xi} - y_{x'i}$, in a large sample the mean of these differences consistently estimates (1.1). This ties causation in mean to causation at the unit level and shows how the model dovetails with a singularist account of the causal relation.

The basic model can be extended in a number of directions. Often it is of interest to study how the average effects vary across subpopulations. The previous definitions can be extended by including a random vector of concomitants Z and conditioning on these concomitants (which are not viewed as causes) to obtain average conditional effects. For example, the average effect of x versus x' at level z of Z could be defined as:

$$E[(Y_x - Y_{x'}) \mid Z = z] . \qquad [1.2]$$

Similarly, the other definitions can be extended (Sobel, 1993).

2.3. Causal Inference With Directly Measured Variables:
Conditions for Consistent Estimation of Causal Parameters

To fix ideas, consider a simple case where a researcher wants to study the effectiveness of a drug and subjects can be assigned either to the control group ($X = 0$) or the treatment group ($X = 1$). The researcher takes a simple random sample of size n from $\mathcal{P}$ and assigns subjects to one of the two groups. The data obtained consist of observations (y_i, x_i), $i = 1, \ldots, n$, where x_i denotes the treatment unit i was assigned and y_i denotes the response of that unit. Typically, the difference between the sample means is the basis for causal inferences:

$$\bar{y}_1 - \bar{y}_0, \qquad [1.3]$$

where $\bar{y}_x = (n_x)^{-1} \sum_{(i|x_i = x)} y_i$, and n_x denotes the number of sample observations in group x, $x = 0, 1$. Under the model of Section 2.1, when $x_i = 0$, the response y_i is a drawing from the random variable Y_0, and when $x_i = 1$, the response is a drawing from the distribution of Y_1. Thus, $\bar{y}_x = (n_x)^{-1} \sum_{(i|x_i = x)} y_{xi}$ from which it is evident that $\bar{y}_x$ unbiasedly estimates $E(Y|X = x) = E(Y_x|X = x)$. Nevertheless, $\bar{y}_x$ is not a consistent estimate of $E(Y_x)$, as $E(Y_x|X = x) \neq E(Y_x)$ in general. However, under random assignment, defined as $Y_x \perp\!\!\!\perp X$ for $x = 0, 1$, where $\perp\!\!\!\perp$ denotes independence and $\not\perp\!\!\!\perp$ denotes dependence (Dawid, 1979), $E(Y_x|X = x) = E(Y_x)$ for $x = 0, 1$; in this case, (1.3) consistently estimates (1.1). Note that random assignment is a sufficient (but not necessary) condition for the equality of $E(Y_x|X = x)$ and $E(Y_x)$. The preceding example demonstrates the more general point that the vector analogue of (1.3) does not, in general, unbiasedly or consistently estimate (1.1). However, under random assignment of observations to treatments, $Y_x \perp\!\!\!\perp X$ for all Y_x, implying $E(Y_x|X = x) = E(Y_x)$. Therefore, when randomization is employed, $\bar{y}_x$ consistently estimates $E(Y_x)$, justifying the use of (1.3) to estimate the average effect (1.1).

The use of Rubin's model helps further to clarify the notion of causation experimentalists use. Given the preceding results, experimentalists (although they have not typically said so) must be trying to estimate (1.1). Under this hypothesis, it is easy to account for the emphasis on randomization (when possible) in experimental work and the warnings concerning the naive use of (1.3). Otherwise, the conditional expectation $E(Y|X = x)$ would appear to be of primary interest and the emphasis on randomization misplaced. When subjects are measured on the response prior to treatment, then given the treatment, after which the value of the response is recorded, the pretreatment response is typically viewed as a measure of the subject's response (at the time when the posttreatment response is measured), were the subject not given the treatment. This case is common in quasi-experimental work; under the preceding assumption about the pretreatment response, the unit effects $y_{1i} - y_{0i}$ can be observed, and, under random sampling from $\mathscr{P}$, the difference between the posttreatment average and the pretreatment average is a consistent estimate of (1.1). Note that the assumption on the pretreatment response allows correct inferences, even though randomization has not been employed; randomization is recent, dating back to Fisher, and a great deal of scientific progress prior to and during the 20th century was made by conducting experiments of the form just described. For further treatment of this and related cases, see Holland and Rubin (1983) and Holland (1986).

In some instances, researchers are more interested in the conditional average effects (1.2) than in the average effects (1.1). Conditioning on Z and varying the levels of the cause allows for assessment of how the average effects vary across a particular subpopulation, while varying Z, for fixed values x and x' of X, allows assessment of how a particular average effect of interest varies across subpopulations.

In other instances, a researcher might want to know how the average value of the response Y_x varies across subpopulations. For example, in our medical experiment, a researcher might want to know if the average response differs for men and women in the absence of treatment with the drug; to attempt to answer this question, the researcher might use analysis of covariance. In the framework here, questions of this nature involve comparison of $E(Y_x|Z = z)$ with $E(Y_x|Z = z^*)$, where x is a particular level of the causal variable, and z and z^* are two distinct levels of the concomitant vector, for example:

$$E(Y_x \mid Z = z) - E(Y_x \mid Z = z^*) .\qquad [1.4]$$

Such comparisons are often of great importance, but should not be interpreted as effects. This is not a defect of the model; Z is simply treated as part of the background and not as a cause.

To make inferences about the average conditional effects (1.2), researchers would usually compute (when possible) estimates of the form

$$\bar{y}_{x \mid Z = z} - \bar{y}_{x' \mid Z = z} ,\qquad [1.5]$$

where $\bar{y}_{x \mid Z = z} = (n_{xz})^{-1} \Sigma_{(i \mid x_i = x, z_i = z)} y_i$, and n_{xz} denotes the number of sample observations with $X = x$, $Z = z$. Analogous to the case of (1.3), $\bar{y}_{x \mid Z = z}$ unbiasedly estimates $E(Y_x|X = x, Z = z)$, and (1.5) does not, in general, unbiasedly or consistently estimate (1.2). However, under random assignment to the cause, $(Y_x, Z) \perp\!\!\!\perp X$ for all Y_x, which implies:

$$Y_x \perp\!\!\!\perp X \mid Z\qquad [1.6]$$

for all Y_x. It follows that $E(Y_x|X = x, Z = z) = E(Y_x|Z = z)$, so (1.5) unbiasedly and consistently estimates (1.2).

The preceding example also shows that random assignment to the cause is not needed to justify appropriate inferences about (1.2); the weaker assumption of random assignment to the cause, conditional on Z, given by (1.6) suffices. This assumption, in conjunction with the assumption that at all levels of Z, all values of the cause occur with positive probability, is referred to as "strongly ignorable treatment assignment" (Rosenbaum & Rubin, 1983) or adjustable treatment assignment (Rosenbaum, 1987).

The primary importance of the conditional random assignment assumption is not the fact that it is a weaker sufficient condition for estimation of (1.2). More importantly, in experiments, treatments are often assigned according to probabilistic rules that depend on Z, such that within levels of Z, assignment to treatments is random. In this case, the assumption of random assignment does not hold, but because the assumption of conditional random assignment holds, an investigator can estimate (1.2), or, if interest centers on (1.1), the investigator can first estimate (1.2), and then, if the marginal distribution of Z is known, average over this distribution to obtain (1.1). Finally, in the social and behavioral sciences, it is often impossible to conduct an experimental study. In this case, researchers who want to make causal inferences that accord with a counterfactual notion of causation should first decide on causes and responses, and then, insofar as neither randomization nor conditional randomization has been employed, imagine the covariates Z that determine the treatment assignment process and are relevant to the response. In that vein, note also that Z is not unique; that is, if Z_1 is a set of (nontrivial) covariates that satisfy (1.6), Z_2 could also be a set. While imagining a sufficient set of covariates is not a trivial exercise, Rubin's model at least provides a way for the nonexperimental scientist to think about how to make causal inferences that fit with a counterfactual account of the causal relation. Further, its use lends considerable clarity to the role of the variables (and hence interpretation of parameters) featured in statistical analyses in the social and behavioral sciences.

The preceding points are readily illustrated in linear regression, an important context for social and behavioral scientists. Here neither Z nor X is necessarily categorical, as was implicitly the case above; therefore, it will generally not be possible to calculate sample means for all the possible values these two variables may take, and it is necessary to make some assumptions concerning functional form. Suppose the causal regression model is:

$$Y_{xZ_{xi}} = \alpha_c + \Pi_{1c}x + \Pi_{2c}Z_{xi} + \epsilon_{xZ_{xi}} \qquad [1.7]$$

where α_c is an $L \times 1$ intercept vector, x a $K_1 \times 1$ vector of causes (fixed to one particular value for all i), Π_{1c} an $L \times K_1$ matrix of parameters, Z_{xi} a $K_2 \times 1$ vector of concomitants, Π_{2c} an $L \times K_2$ matrix of parameters, and $\epsilon_{xZ_{xi}}$ is an $L \times 1$ random term with conditional mean $E(\epsilon_{xZ_{xi}}|Z_{xi}) = 0$. Note that the concomitants are allowed to be affected by the cause and that the response is vector valued. The treatment of the response in this fashion is for purposes of future reference, and until the subject of simultaneous equation models is introduced, the reader may wish to think of the response as univariate. Under the setup above,

$$E(Y_{xi} \mid Z_{xi} = z) = \alpha_c + \Pi_{1c}x + \Pi_{2c}z , \qquad [1.8]$$

and substitution into (1.2) shows that

$$\Pi_{1c}(x - x') \qquad [1.9]$$

is the average conditional effect (for any particular value z) of x, relative to x'. The parameter matrix Π_{2c} describes how the response varies with Z but its elements should not be interpreted as effects. Finally, note that in the case where the error is constant across levels of the cause and the concomitants, (1.9) admits the interpretation of a unit effect.

To try to make inferences about the parameters of (1.7), the investigator considers:

$$Y_i = \alpha + \Pi_1 X_i + \Pi_2 Z_i + \epsilon_i , \qquad [1.10]$$

where $Y_i = Y_{X_i}$, $Z_i = Z_{X_i}$, and $E(\epsilon_i|X_i, Z_i) = 0$. For this case,

$$E(Y_i \mid X_i = x, Z_i = z) = E(Y_{xi} \mid X_i = x, Z_i = z) = \alpha + \Pi_1 x + \Pi_2 z . \qquad [1.11]$$

As in the case where Z and X were treated as categorical and sample means were used as estimates of population quantities, in general the conditional expectations in (1.8) and (1.11) are not equal, and the ordinary least squares (OLS) estimator for the parameters of (1.10) is not unbiased or consistent for the parameters of (1.7). Under conditional random assignment, however, $E[Y_{xi}|X_i = x, Z_i = z] = E[Y_{xi}|Z_i = z]$, and thus OLS unbiasedly and consistently (under mild conditions) estimates the parameters of (1.7).

Readers familiar with simultaneous equation models will immediately recognize (1.10) as the reduced form equation corresponding to the "structural" equation system:

$$Y_i = \nu + \Gamma_1 X_i + \Gamma_2 Z_i + B Y_i + \nu_i, \qquad [1.12]$$

where ν is an $L \times 1$ vector of intercepts, Γ_1 an $L \times K_1$ parameter matrix, Γ_2 an $L \times K_2$ parameter matrix, B an $L \times L$ parameter matrix with diagonal elements 0, and ν_i an $L \times 1$ vector of random terms with mean $E(\nu_i|X_i = x, Z_i = z) = 0$. Thus, the preceding results indicate that the reduced form parameters estimated in the simultaneous equations context do not, in general, coincide with the parameters of the causal reduced form (1.10). But researchers (under the condition $(I - B)$ is invertible) typically impart causal interpretations to the elements of both Π_1 and Π_2. That is, they do not distinguish between causes and covariates and each element π_{rs} is typically interpreted as a total effect (equilibrium multiplier in economics), that is, as the ultimate amount Y_{is} is changed when the value of X_{ir} is moved from x_{ir} to $x_{ir} + 1$. It should now be evident that such inferences (on average) fit with the account of Section 2.2 when (a) all the variables in the model are causes, and (b) treatment assignment is random. When (a) and (b) are not satisfied, which is the usual case in economics and the other social sciences, the model parameters do not generally warrant the usual interpretations.

Consideration of the parameters of the structural form (1.12) and their proper interpretation is even more difficult, because at least some of the dependent variables are typically treated as both causes and effects. Space limitations preclude further treatment here; further, the subsequent treatment of latent variables does not require the setup of a simultaneous equation system. For some further details on the difficulties associated with causal inference in simultaneous equation models, see Holland (1988) and Sobel (1990).

3. Latent Variable Models

In Section 2, I argued that different accounts of the causal relation privilege different approaches to causal inference. Attention focused on the relationship between a counterfactual account of causation and methods for causal inference in the social and behavioral sciences, for the case where causes, effects, and concomitants are directly measured. Matters become more complicated when one or more of these variables are not directly measured. One type of variable not directly measured is the omitted variable. Here, quantitative information on the value of a variable deemed relevant is missing; the variable itself is often taken to be directly measurable. The consequences of omitting such variables for parameter estimation are well known. Under a counterfactual account of the causal relation, omitted variables enter most naturally as concomitants. Concomitants, however, serve various purposes. In a randomized experiment, an investigator may want to use such variables to increase the precision of estimates of average effects; here, omitting a variable only decreases the precision with which these effects are estimated. But if the investigator wants to compare average effects at various levels of the concomitants, the concomitant must be observed. In a nonexperimental study, it is necessary, for estimation of average effects, to know the covariates that are sufficient for treatment assignment. If covariates of this nature are omitted, consistent estimates of the average effects typically cannot be constructed; often the best one can do is to make plausible assumptions about the omitted variable and see how sensitive conclusions are to different assumptions [for further material on such matters, see, e.g., Rosenbaum (1987, 1992) and the references cited therein, and Rosenbaum & Rubin (1983)].

A second type of variable (the subject of this chapter) not directly measured is the latent or unobserved variable. In this case, measured variables (typically called "observed") are viewed as indicators of one or more latent variables. In conjunction with a prior distribution for the latent variables, and a conditional distribution for the observed variables, given the latent variables, the posterior distribution of the latent variables can be determined. However, although the values of the latent variables can be estimated, these values cannot be determined for any given unit (Bartholomew, 1981). In addition to being unobserved, latent variables are sometimes said to be unobservable. It is worth noting, however, that latent variables that could have been directly measured, but were not, are sometimes featured in the literature (Bielby, 1986; Sobel & Arminger, 1986).

In the presence of latent variables, further assumptions and more complicated procedures are needed to bring the statistical analysis into line with the methods considered in Section 2; once this is accomplished, apparently the problem of causal inference can be handled as if the latent variables had actually been measured. For example, in simultaneous equation models with latent variables, coefficients attached to the latent variables in the so-called structural part of the model are treated just as coefficients attached to directly measured variables are treated in simultaneous equation models with directly measured variables. Indeed, this treatment is suggested in most of the statistical literature on covariance structure models (e.g., see Jöreskog (1977) and the manuals for the popular covariance structure analysis computer programs), and it is certainly the approach taken by empirical workers who use structural equation models with latent variables to draw causal inferences.

This chapter argues that the preceding approaches to causal inference in latent variable models are misguided. One reason, already brought out in Section 2, is that coefficients in linear models should not generally be interpreted as effects even when the variables are directly measured. There are other reasons as well. In Section 3.1, I examine the relationship between causal concepts and typical notions of latent variables, and conclude that it is often unreasonable to regard latent variables as either causes or effects. In Section 3.2, I argue that when it is reasonable to regard latent variables as causes or effects, the latent variables employed in statistical models for causal inference are not the latent variables that enter the causal relation. This implies that the parameters of such models cannot generally be endowed with a causal interpretation. To illustrate this point, elementary covariance structure models are used; however, the argument applies more generally to mean and covariance structure models and to other types of latent variable models as well.

3.1. What Are Latent Variables?

Psychometricians and others have espoused various opinions on the meaning of latent variables and their relevance to empirical inquiry. Some have argued that since latent variables are not directly measured, their meaning is not clear, and hence they are unimportant. A related view is that because a variable treated as latent cannot be meaningfully assigned a determinate value in the individual case, latent variables are unimportant. From either point of view, only the indicators (observed variables) are important.

The preceding views are not now dominant; the conventional wisdom is that latent variables are indispensable in social and behavioral theories (just as unobserved and unobservable entities are indispensable in the hard sciences), and by imposing enough structure on these entities, scientific theories that refer to these can be tested at the observed level (Clogg, 1992).

At least two types of latent variables are featured in social and behavioral research. The first refers to a directly measurable variable that was not directly measured. For example, a sociologist who wants to know how many years of schooling a survey respondent completed may have asked the respondent's wife and children instead of asking the respondent (or looking at the school records). Here, the relevant question is the properties of the measurement error in the indicators. The second type of latent variable is unobserved in the sense that direct measurement procedures could not even be devised, given the current state of affairs.

At least four views on the second type of latent variable are common. The first is that with large data sets, where many variables are measured and several variables might seem to have something in common, it is reasonable and/or necessary for human understanding to reduce the data by combining such variables into composite measures (Bartholomew, 1987). These can be used for "descriptive" purposes or put to further use, for example as independent variables in a regression Examples of composite measures include principal components, factor scores, and components (Bartholomew, 1987).

A second, dominant point of view, which fits well with various forms of empiricism, suggests, at the semantic level, latent variables are theoretical constructs that cannot be explicated precisely, but they do make sense and/or have commonsense appeal and enable us to make better sense of the complexities inherent in the observed world (Torgerson, 1958). Here, latent variables are typically treated as useful mental fictions, and the latent variables are often placed in a theoretical context, perhaps even in a network (a "causal" network according to some psychometricians) of relations among other latent variables. On this view, since latent variables are fictitious entities, theories incorporating such entities should be viewed as false; nevertheless, under some conditions, the use of latent variables has empirical consequences, and consequently these fictitious entities are useful in helping researchers summarize various features of the "observable" world. Further, these consequences can be used to adjudicate among two or more theories; even if theories are not true, some theories are more adequate empirically than others, and once it is decided how such adequacy ought to be assessed (not a trivial issue), a criterion for choice is provided (van Fraassen, 1980).

A third point of view is that latent variables are real entities, understood here as entities that exist in the physical world (see Nagel, 1961, on the notion of a real entity). To be sure, these latent variables are unobserved and may, depending on the view one adopts regarding the observability/unobservability distinction, be unobservable in some instances, but existence itself is not at issue. For contrasting views on the observability/unobservability distinction, compare, e.g., van Fraasen (1980) and Salmon (1984). Although a belief in existence does not entail the further belief that a theory is true or false, this view is often featured in conjunction with scientific realism. Here theories are regarded as true or false and the goal of empirical work is to assess the truth value of theoretical statements.

Finally, one can take various positions between the second and third views. One position is agnostic: Latent variables may or may not refer to real entities and it does not really matter, for their usefulness rests on the empirical consequences of these entities at the observable level. In van Fraasen (1980), this view of unobservable entities is espoused and defended.

In Section 2, two (broadly speaking) notions of the causal relation were discussed. Implicitly, it was assumed there is a correspondence between our notions of causation and causation as it is in the physical world; however, one might draw a distinction between these and admit the possibility that it is only the former that is of concern (or exists). In that case, it may be of interest to study how humans conceive of causation (White, 1990), and hypothetical, as opposed to actual, entities might figure prominently in such accounts. However, most scientists find such a view of the causal relation unappealing and would (even if they do not agree on exactly what constitutes causation) hold that the notions of causation they are employing pertain to the actual physical world. Under this view, the argument that the entities employed in the causal relation are either mental constructs or may or may not be real seems odd. Nevertheless, many empirical researchers and psychometricians who have readily embraced the idea that there are causal relations (networks of causal relations in some treatments) involving latent variables have also ascribed to the view that latent variables should not be reified; evidently, the causal relation is mental after all.

An alternative is to save the causal relation and risk the possibility of reification; if latent variables are regarded as causes and/or effects, these variables must be real entities. This raises some issues concerning the way latent variables are handled in statistical models for unobserved variables.

The idea that a latent variable is a real entity lends itself naturally to a Platonic conception of this entity. Such a conception has not sat well with psychometricians, who abandoned it as inappropriate for work with "unexplicated, inexact constructs" (Lord & Novick, 1968, p. 28). Thus, in most current work, latent variables and various properties of their distributions are defined by the measurement operations themselves, in conjunction with auxiliary assumptions. Latent variables defined in this manner are sometimes called "operational." A key assumption in latent variable models is the "axiom" of conditional (local) independence: for a vector of observed variables $W_1, \ldots, W_q$, and latent variables $T_1, \ldots, T_p$, with $p \leq q$, $(W_1, \ldots, W_q, T_1, \ldots, T_p)$ has a joint distribution satisfying the conditional independence relation:

$$D(W_1, \ldots, W_q \mid T_1, \ldots, T_p) = \prod_{j=1}^{q} D(W_j \mid T_1, \ldots, T_p) . \quad [1.13]$$

Although various rationales for the use of this "axiom" can be given, including convenience, the latent variables are generally held to "explain" the association among the observed variables. In turn, either the notion of "explanation" goes unexplicated or the latent variables are regarded as causes of the observed variables (Anderson, 1984; Bartholomew, 1987; Suppes & Zanotti, 1981). The latter view is essentially the principle of the common cause (Reichenbach, 1956; Simon, 1954): It is not the observed variables that are causing one another, but the latent variables that are causing the observed variables, thereby "explaining" the association among these. Note how this interpretation puts us back to square one: Either the causal relation is mental and latent variables do not refer to real entities or the causal relation is actual and the latent variables refer to real entities of some sort.

3.2. Causal Inference With Latent Variables

The place of Platonic and operational latent variables under the account of Section 2.2 is now considered. Latent variables that are presumed to refer to real entities are treated as Platonic. Several objections to the proposed treatment can be anticipated. The first is that operational latent variables are "measuring" (albeit imperfectly) the intended real entities. In this case, however, the operational latent variables are nothing more than proxies for their Platonic counterparts, implying the entities of interest are indeed Platonic. Second, one can hold that operational latent variables simply refer to whatever real entities the indicators, in conjunction with the conditional independence assumptions, indicate. This view leads to numerous problems. First, under this view, whenever the indicators are changed (or indicators added or omitted), the latent variable itself changes. It is difficult to see how scientific progress will be made with such latent variables. Further, there is a potential for vacuousness; latent variables satisfying the conditional independence assumption are not hard to come by. For example, Suppes and Zanotti (1981) show, for binary indicators, that a latent variable exists if and only if the indicators have a joint distribution. Holland and Rosenbaum (1986) state a generalization and discuss the implications for research practice; in particular, they argue for using stronger latent variable models that impose latent monotonicity criteria. Similarly, in the metrical case, Lord and Novick (1968) point out that for $p = q - 1$, there exist latent variables $T_1, \ldots, T_p$ that satisfy the assumptions of the factor analytic model.

A third objection is that when a latent variable is a well-defined entity and substantive knowledge of the measurement operations and conditions lead to the conclusion that the observed measures are independent, given the latent variable, the latent variable is operationally defined. But here it would be more accurate to say that the Platonic latent variable satisfies the axiom of conditional independence. Fourth, one could invoke the principle of the common cause and argue that the operational latent variable(s) that emerges from the analysis and "explain(s)" the association among the observed variables is (are) indeed the cause(s) that underlies the observed response and hence should coincide with the correct Platonic variable(s). Space considerations preclude further treatment of this argument here; in a separate paper, I shall show that such a view cannot be defended, except by fiat.

I now proceed, using several simple covariance structure models, to demonstrate the consequences for parameter estimation of using operational definitions for Platonic latent variables. The upshot of the demonstration is that (even in the case of a randomized experiment with a Platonic latent response) parameter estimates from the usual covariance structure models should not be endowed with a causal interpretation. Some previous (Magidson, 1977; Muthén & Jöreskog, 1983) attempts to use covariance structure analysis in conjunction with quasi-experimental or experimental designs have ignored this point (among others).

Suppose that T is a Platonic latent variable with three indicators W_1, W_2, W_3; suppose also that $E(T) = E(W_1) = E(W_2) = E(W_3) = 0$,

$$W_1 = \lambda_1 T + \delta_1$$

$$W_2 = \lambda_2 T + \delta_2 \qquad [1.14]$$

$$W_3 = \lambda_3 T + \delta_3$$

$E(\delta_j) = 0$, $E(T\delta_j) = 0$, $j = 1, 2, 3$. The covariance structure, Σ_{WW}, for $W = (W_1, W_2, W_3)'$ is then:

$$\Sigma_{WW} = \sigma_{TT} \lambda\lambda' + \Sigma_{\delta\delta}, \qquad [1.15]$$

where σ_{TT} denotes the variance of T, $\lambda = (\lambda_1, \lambda_2, \lambda_3)'$, and $\Sigma_{\delta\delta} = \{\sigma_{jk}\}$ is the covariance matrix of $\delta = (\delta_1, \delta_2, \delta_3)'$; in keeping with the Platonic conception of T, the axiom of local independence is not invoked, and thus the off-diagonal elements of $\Sigma_{\delta\delta}$ are not a priori constrained to 0. Of course, T, though Platonic, is not observed, and the model is not identified, but if T were observed, the 10 parameters (σ_{TT}, λ_j, $j = 1, 2, 3$, and the six parameters of $\Sigma_{\delta\delta}$) can be solved for using the moments σ_{TT}, σ_{TWj}, $j = 1, 2, 3$, and the six moments of Σ_{WW}.

The setup for the operational latent variable T^* is

$$W_1 = \lambda_1^* T^* + \delta_1^*$$

$$W_2 = \lambda_2^* T^* + \delta_2^* \qquad [1.16]$$

$$W_3 = \lambda_3^* T^* + \delta_3^*$$

with $E(\delta_j^*) = E(T^*) = 0$. In addition, local independence $[D(T, \delta_1^*, \delta_2^*, \delta_3^*) = D(T)\prod_{j=1}^{3} D(\delta_j^*|T)]$ is assumed, and the normalization $\lambda_1^* = 1$ is used to identify the model.

The covariance structure Σ_{WW} is:

$$\Sigma_{WW} = \sigma_{T^*T^*} \lambda^* \lambda^{*\prime} + \Sigma_{\delta^*\delta^*}, \qquad [1.17]$$

where $\sigma_{T^*T^*}$ denotes the variance of T^*, $\lambda^* = (1, \lambda_2^*, \lambda_3^*)'$, and $\Sigma_{\delta^*\delta^*} = \{\sigma_{jk}^*\}$ is the covariance matrix of $\delta^* = (\delta_1^*, \delta_2^*, \delta_3^*)'$; by virtue of the local independence assumption, the off-diagonal elements of this covariance matrix are 0 (in keeping with the operational conception of T^*).

From elementary algebra, the relationship between the parameters of (1.15) and (1.17) is easily derived (results given only for λ_2^*, λ_3^*, and $\sigma_{T'T'}$):

$$\lambda_2^* = \frac{\sigma_{TT}\lambda_2\lambda_3 + \sigma_{23}}{\sigma_{TT}\lambda_1\lambda_3 + \sigma_{13}} \tag{1.18}$$

$$\lambda_3^* = \frac{\sigma_{TT}\lambda_2\lambda_3 + \sigma_{23}}{\sigma_{TT}\lambda_1\lambda_2 + \sigma_{12}} \tag{1.19}$$

$$\sigma_{T'T'} = \frac{\sigma_{TT}(\lambda_1\lambda_2 + \sigma_{12}/\sigma_{TT})(\lambda_1\lambda_3 + \sigma_{13}/\sigma_{TT})}{\lambda_2\lambda_3 + \sigma_{23}/\sigma_{TT}}. \tag{1.20}$$

Using these equations, note also that in the special case where the Platonic latent variable satisfies the axiom of local independence, $\sigma_{12} = \sigma_{13} = \sigma_{23} = 0$, and thus, $\lambda_2^* = \lambda_2/\lambda_1$, $\lambda_3^* = \lambda_3/\lambda_1$, $\sigma_{T'T'} = \lambda_1^2\sigma_{TT}$.

Now suppose the Platonic latent variable T depends on the observed random vector $V = (X', Z')'$ as follows:

$$T = \Pi V + \varepsilon = \Pi_1 X + \Pi_2 Z + \varepsilon \tag{1.21}$$

where Π_1 is a row vector conformable to X, Π_2 a row vector conformable to Z, ε is a random variable with mean 0 and variance $\sigma_{\varepsilon\varepsilon}$, and $V \perp\!\!\!\perp \varepsilon$, $\delta \perp\!\!\!\perp \varepsilon$, $\delta \perp\!\!\!\perp V$. The covariance matrix Σ for the random vector $(V', W')'$ has components Σ_{VV}, Σ_{WW}, [as given by (1.15)], and

$$\Sigma_{WV} = \lambda \Pi \Sigma_{VV}. \tag{1.22}$$

As before, Equation (1.15) can be used to solve for λ; substitution into (1.22) then gives Π.

In the usual case, the latent variable is treated operationally; here the model consists of (1.16), (1.17), the relevant preceding assumptions, and the regression:

$$T^* = \Pi^* V + \varepsilon^*, \tag{1.23}$$

where the row vector $\mathbf{\Pi}^*$ conforms to V, ε^* is a random variable with mean 0 and variance $\sigma_{\varepsilon^* \varepsilon^*}$, and $V \perp\!\!\!\perp \varepsilon^*$. Additionally, suppose that $\delta^* \perp\!\!\!\perp \varepsilon^*$, $\delta^* \perp\!\!\!\perp V$.

Proceeding as before, (1.17) is used to solve for X; substitution into the equality

$$\Sigma_{WV} = \lambda^* \mathbf{\Pi}^* \Sigma_{VV} \qquad [1.24]$$

yields $\mathbf{\Pi}^*$. Clearly, $\mathbf{\Pi} \neq \mathbf{\Pi}^*$ in general; thus, use of the operational latent variable gives the wrong coefficients. In the special case where $\sigma_{12} = \sigma_{13} = \sigma_{23} = 0$, analogous elements of $\mathbf{\Pi}^*$ and $\mathbf{\Pi}$ are proportional.

As in Section 2, the key question is when the parameters $\mathbf{\Pi} = (\mathbf{\Pi}_1, \mathbf{\Pi}_2)$ of (1.21) correspond with the parameters of the explicitly causal model:

$$T_x = \mathbf{\Pi}_{1c} x + \mathbf{\Pi}_{2c} Z_x + \varepsilon_{xZ_x}. \qquad [1.25]$$

Paralleling the case there, the condition $(T_x \perp\!\!\!\perp X)|Z$ for all x is sufficient for $\mathbf{\Pi} = \mathbf{\Pi}_c = (\mathbf{\Pi}_{1c}, \mathbf{\Pi}_{2c})$ But even when this holds, $\mathbf{\Pi} \neq \mathbf{\Pi}^*$ in general, and thus the usual consistent estimates for $\mathbf{\Pi}^*$ are not consistent for $\mathbf{\Pi}_c$.

Fischer (1991 and references therein) has also considered the case where the effect is latent. He defines the effect as the change in the value of the latent trait before and after the outcome of the experiment (recall the discussion of this approach in Section 2). Fischer does not indicate whether or not the latent traits are Platonically or operationally conceived, and the parameters of interest in this approach are not defined as the parameters that are of interest in an explicitly causal approach. Nonetheless, the empirical examples appearing in this body of work are taken from experiments with random assignment. For further material on this approach, see Formann (Chapter 11, this volume) and Spiel (Chapter 10, this volume).

Now suppose the response and the cause are directly measured, the relevant causal model is given by (1.7), and the latent variable is a concomitant included in the vector Z_x of (1.7). If the latent variable is affected by the cause, then by the previous arguments, it is necessary to view this variable as referring to a real entity and natural to view this variable Platonically. When this latent variable is not affected by the cause, there is a role for both Platonic and operational latent variables.

In the case of random assignment, an investigator may wish to use (1.2) to make comparisons across subpopulations; here, if latent variables do not refer to real entities, it follows that the subpopulations are not real either. But one might also include the concomitant in (1.7) to increase the efficiency with which the causal parameters are estimated. In this case, without respect to whether the latent variable should be viewed as Platonic or operational, or real or fictitious, it is reasonable to include the operational latent variable T^* in the model; the only caveat is that the investigator should not confuse the version of (1.7) using T^* with the version using T.

Now consider the case where treatment assignment is not random and recall from Section 2 that treatment assignment might be conditionally random, given a set of covariates Z. In this case, (1.1) cannot be directly estimated, but if (1.7) holds and the distribution of the covariates is known, averaging (1.8) over this distribution gives (1.1). The case where treatment assignment is conditionally random, given the covariate vector Z, occurs in two ways. First, an experimenter might randomly assign observations within levels of Z; since the investigator cannot know the individual values of the latent variable, Z will not include latent variables. In the second case, the data come from a nonexperimental study and the investigator is attempting to account for the treatment assignment process. Fictitious entities would not appear to have much place in such an account. Thus, latent variables should be conceptualized as real entities and it is natural to treat these Platonically.

Finally, consider the case where the latent variable is viewed as a cause. The latent variable is now a component of the vector X; since fictitious entities do no causing, the latent variable must be considered a real entity. Under a counterfactual account, it is also necessary, for a given unit, that the value of the cause could be different, and in practice, as argued in Section 2, it is necessary to understand how the different values are produced. In a randomized experiment with an observed cause, different values of the cause are produced by the experimenter and randomization is employed. In the case where the cause is an unobserved variable, its value for particular units is not known, and the usual randomized experiment cannot even be implemented. Nevertheless, in principle the nonexperimental study in which one imagines the covariates sufficient for treatment assignment to the latent variable is conceivable, and under this scenario it is also possible (although additional assumptions will typically be needed) to estimate average effects. But note that in order to imagine the covariates sufficient for treatment assignment and to imagine how the unobserved cause could take different values on the same unit, a great deal of knowledge about the latent variable is needed. In this vein, the straightforward conclusion is that the operationally defined unexplicated and inexact (or prescientific) latent variables discussed in the literature should not be treated as causes.

As in the case of a latent response, the implications of using as an independent variable the operational latent variable T^* in place of the Platonic variable T can be obtained by examining the covariance structure for the observed variables. To that end, suppose Y is an observed random variable, let T be a component of the random vector V, let $\tilde{V} = (\tilde{V}_1', T)'$ be a rearrangement of V with last component T, and let

$$Y = \tilde{\Pi} V_1 + \tilde{\pi}_T T + \varepsilon,$$ [1.26]

where $E(\varepsilon) = 0$ and $V \perp\!\!\!\perp \varepsilon$. The factor analytic structure for T is described by Equations (1.14) and (1.15). With the usual independence assumptions, the covariance matrix for the observed vector $(\tilde{V}_1', W', Y)'$ has components $\Sigma_{\tilde{V}_1 \tilde{V}_1}$, Σ_{WW}, as given by (1.15),

$$\Sigma_{\tilde{V}_1 W} = \Sigma_{\tilde{V}_1 T} \lambda',$$ [1.27]

$$\Sigma_{\tilde{V}_1 Y} = \Sigma_{\tilde{V}_1 \tilde{V}_1} \tilde{\Pi}' + \tilde{\pi}_T \Sigma_{\tilde{V}_1 T},$$ [1.28]

$$\Sigma_{WY} = \lambda \Sigma_{T \tilde{V}_1} \tilde{\Pi}' + \pi_T \sigma_{TT},$$ [1.29]

$$\Sigma_{YY} = (\tilde{\Pi}, \pi_T) \Sigma_{\tilde{V}\tilde{V}} (\tilde{\Pi}, \pi_T)' + \sigma_{\varepsilon\varepsilon}.$$ [1.30]

These equations can be used to solve for the parameters of (1.26) as follows: first, use (1.15) to solve for λ; second, substitute this solution into (1.27) to solve for the unknown column vector $\Sigma_{\tilde{V}_1 T}$; third, substitute this solution in (1.28) to solve for $(\tilde{\Pi}', \pi_T)$; fourth, substitution of the solutions to Steps 2 and 3 into (1.20) gives $\sigma_{\varepsilon\varepsilon}$. For the case of an operational latent variable T^*, the components of the observed covariance matrix can be used in the same way to solve for the relevant parameters. But in this case, at the first step, (1.17) is used to solve for $\check{\lambda} \neq \lambda$; carrying out the remaining algebra shows that the parameter vector $(\tilde{\Pi}^*, \pi_T^{*\cdot})'$ obtained at Step 3 is not equal to the parameter vector $(\tilde{\Pi}, \pi_T)'$. Similar remarks apply to the error variance in the last step. As in Section 2, one wants to know when the parameter vector $(\tilde{\Pi}, \pi_T)'$ is equal to the parameter vector of (1.7); but as before, $(\tilde{\Pi}^*, \pi_T^*\cdot)'$ is not generally equal to $(\tilde{\Pi}, \pi_T)'$.

4. Discussion

This chapter considered the role of latent variables in causal inference. Section 2 set out a counterfactual account of the causal relation (that fits with notions of causation implicitly espoused by many social and behavioral researchers) and a corresponding approach to causal inference. Estimation of average effects and average conditional effects was discussed, and conditions for consistent estimation of these effects given. Section 3 extended the material from Section 2, which treated the case of directly measured variables, to the case where one or more variables were latent. Philosophical arguments about the nature of the causal relation and the status of latent variables proved important, and an appropriate mathematical treatment hinges on such arguments. In particular, matters were seen to be much more complicated than recognized in the literature, and causal inferences from so-called causal models with latent variables do not square with the concept of causation typically espoused in the literature. These points were illustrated using simple covariance structure models.

I also argued that latent variables can sometimes be viewed as causes, despite the fact that the values of these variables cannot be known (see also Holland, 1992, on this point), and for the case of covariance structure analysis, I showed how an analysis can be conducted that allows for inferences about average (conditional) effects of these variables.

A more general formulation of the problem of causal inference with latent causes is desirable. To that end, suppose that $X = (\tilde{X}', T')'$ is the cause vector, with observed component $\tilde{X}'$, where T takes values in a subspace Ω_0 of Ω_1; for simplicity, for any value $\tilde{x}$ of $\tilde{X}$, suppose that T can take any value in Ω_0. As before, let Y_x denote the response when the cause has value x, let W denote the vector of indicators of T, and let Z be a vector of covariates not affected by the cause vector. Suppose that $(Y', X', Z', W')'$ has joint distribution. Let A be any (Borel) subset of Ω_2; the conditional distribution of the observed data is:

$$\Pr(Y \in A \mid \tilde{X} = \tilde{x}, Z = z, W = w) =$$

$$\int_{\Omega_0} \Pr(Y \in A \mid X = x, Z = z, W = w) dP_{T \mid \tilde{X} = \tilde{x}, Z = z, W = w}(t), \qquad [1.31]$$

where $P_{T \mid \tilde{X} = \tilde{x}, Z = z, W = w}$ is the probability measure associated with the conditional distribution of T, given $\tilde{X} = \tilde{x}$, $Z = z$, $W = w$.

Now suppose Y depends on X and Z, but the indicators are redundant, once the latent variables are considered. This is the assumption $(Y \perp\!\!\!\perp W) \mid X, Z$; similar assumptions are typically featured in "causal models." Suppose also that the indicators are "sufficient" for the latent variables; by this I mean that the indicators contain all the probabilistic information about the latent variables, that is, $T \perp\!\!\!\perp (\tilde{X}, Z) \mid W$.

Under the preceding assumptions (1.31) reduces to:

$$\Pr(Y \in A \mid \tilde{X} = \tilde{x}, Z = z) = \int_{\Omega_0} \Pr(Y \in A \mid X = x, Z = z) dP_{T \mid W = w}(t) , \quad [1.32]$$

where $P_{T \mid W = w}$ is the probability measure associated with the posterior distribution of T, given $W = w$.

By definition,

$$\Pr(Y \in A \mid X = x, Z = z) = \Pr(Y_x \in A \mid X = x, Z = z) . \quad [1.33]$$

In the usual literature on causal modeling with latent variables, (1.33) is viewed as a description of the causal relationship between the response and the independent variables. But this is not correct; the conditional distribution of actual interest is

$$\Pr(Y_x \in A \mid Z = z) . \quad [1.34]$$

In general (1.33) and (1.34) are not identical, but if treatment assignment is random, conditional on the covariates, that is, $Y_x \perp\!\!\!\perp X \mid Z$ for all x, (1.33) and (1.34) are identical.

In principle, under conditional random assignment, the distribution of (1.34) can be obtained from (1.32), assuming some knowledge about the righthand side of the latter. Details are beyond the scope of the chapter; to close with a simple illustration, consider the simple case where the cause T is a binary latent variable taking values 0 and 1, and the covariate vector Z is finite; under the same assumptions used above, (1.32) is now:

$$\Pr(Y \in A \mid Z = z) = \sum_{t=0}^{1} \Pr(Y \in A \mid T = t, Z = z) \Pr(T = t \mid W = w) . \quad [1.35]$$

If treatment assignment is random, conditional on the covariates,

$$\Pr(Y \in A \mid T=t, Z=z) = \Pr(Y_t \in A \mid T=t, Z=z) = \Pr(Y_t \in A \mid Z=z)$$
[1.36]

and (1.35) reduces to

$$\Pr(Y \in A \mid Z=z) = \sum_{t=0}^{1} \Pr(Y_t \in A \mid Z=z)\Pr(T=t \mid W=w).$$ [1.37]

This is a finite mixture problem (Titterington, Smith, & Makov, 1985); typically, all the components of the mixture will be unknown.

References

Anderson, T. W. (1984). *An introduction to multivariate statistical analysis* (2nd ed.). New York: John Wiley.

Arminger, G., & Sobel, M. E. (1990). Pseudo maximum likelihood estimation of mean and covariance structures with missing data. *Journal of the American Statistical Association, 85,* 195-203.

Bartholomew, D. J. (1981). Posterior analysis of the factor model. *British Journal of Mathematical and Statistical Psychology, 34,* 93-99.

Bartholomew, D. J. (1987). *Latent variable models and factor analysis.* London: Griffin.

Basmann, R. L. (1963). The causal interpretation of non-triangular systems of economic relations. *Econometrica, 31,* 439-453.

Bielby, W. T. (1986). Arbitrary metrics in multiple-indicator models of latent variables. *Sociological Methods and Research, 15,* 3-23.

Blau, P. M., & Duncan, O. D. (1967). *The American occupational structure.* New York: John Wiley.

Browne, M. W. (1984). Asymptotically distribution-free methods for the analysis of covariance structures. *The British Journal of Mathematical and Statistical Psychology, 37,* 62-83.

Clogg, C. C. (1992). The impact of sociological methodology on statistical methodology (with discussion). *Statistical Science, 7,* 183-207.

Collingwood, R. G. (1948). *An essay on metaphysics.* Oxford: Clarendon Press. (Original work published 1940)

Cook, T. D., & Campbell, D. T. (1979). *Quasi-experimentation: Design and analysis issues for field settings.* Boston: Houghton Mifflin.

Dawid, A. P. (1979). Conditional independence in statistical theory (with discussion). *Journal of the Royal Statistical Society, Series B, 41,* 1-31.

Dayton, C. M., & Macready, G. B. (1988). A latent class covariate model with applications to criterion-referenced testing. In R. Langeheine & J. Rost (Eds.), *Latent trait and latent class models* (pp. 129-143). New York: Plenum.

Ducasse, C. J. (1975). On the nature and observability of the causal relation. In E. Sosa (Ed.), *Causation and conditionals* (pp. 114-125). London: Oxford University Press. (Original work published, 1926)

Emmet, D. (1984). *The effectiveness of causes.* London: Macmillan.

Feigl, H. (1953). Notes on causality. In H. Feigl & M. Brodbeck (Eds.), *Readings in the philosophy of science* (pp. 408-418). New York: Appleton-Century-Crofts.

Fischer, G. (1991). A new methodology for the assessment of treatment effects. *Psychological Assessment, 7,* 117-147.

Gasking, D. (1955). Causation and recipes. *Mind, 64,* 479-487.

Geweke, J. (1984). Inference and causality in economic time series models. In Z. Griliches & M. D. Intrilligator (Eds.), *Handbook of econometrics* (Vol. 2, pp. 1101-1144). Amsterdam: North-Holland.

Granger, C. W. (1969). Investigating causal relations by econometric models and cross-spectral methods. *Econometrica, 37,* 424-438.

Granger, C. W. (1980). Testing for causality: A personal viewpoint. *Journal of Economic Dynamics and Control, 2,* 329-352.

Holland, P. W. (1986). Statistics and causal inference (with discussion). *Journal of the American Statistical Association, 81,* 945-970.

Holland, P. W. (1988). Causal inference, path analysis, and recursive structural equation models (with discussion). In C. C. Clogg (Ed.), *Sociological methodology, 1988* (pp. 449-493). Washington, DC: American Sociological Association.

Holland, P. W. (1992). Comment on "The impact of sociological methodology on statistical methodology" by C. C. Clogg. *Statistical Science, 7,* 198-201.

Holland, P. W., & Rosenbaum, P. (1986). Conditional association and unidimensionality in monotone latent variable models. *The Annals of Statistics, 14,* 1523-1543.

Holland, P. W., & Rubin, D. B. (1983). On Lord's paradox. In H. Wainer & S. Messick (Eds.), *Principals of modern psychological measurement* (pp. 3-35). Hillsdale, NJ: Lawrence Erlbaum.

Jöreskog, K. G. (1970). A general method for analysis of covariance structures. *Biometrika, 57,* 239-251.

Jöreskog, K. G. (1977). Structural equation models in the social sciences: Specification, estimation and testing. In P. R. Krishnaiah (Ed.), *Applications of statistics* (pp. 265-287). Amsterdam: North-Holland.

Kim, J. (1971). Causes and events: Mackie on causation. *Journal of Philosophy, 68,* 426-441.

Lewis, D. (1973). Causation. *Journal of Philosophy, 70,* 556-567.

Lord, F. M., & Novick, M. R. (1968). *Statistical theories of mental test scores.* Reading, MA: Addison-Wesley.

Magidson, J. (1977). Toward a causal model approach for adjusting for preexisting differences in the nonequivalent control group situation. *Evaluation Quarterly, 1,* 399-420.

Muthén, B. (1984). A general structural equation model with dichotomous, ordered categorical, and continuous latent variable indicators. *Psychometrika, 49,* 115-132.

Muthén, B., & Jöreskog, K. G. (1983). Selectivity problems in quasi-experimental studies. *Evaluation Review, 7,* 139-174.

Nagel, E. (1961). *The structure of science.* New York: Harcourt, Brace & World.

Phlips, L. (1974). *Applied consumption analysis.* Amsterdam: North-Holland.

Pratt, J. W., & Schlaifer, R. (1988). On the interpretation and observation of laws. *Journal of Econometrics, 39,* 23-52.

Reichenbach, H. (1956). *The direction of time.* Berkeley: University of California Press.

Rosenbaum, P. R. (1987). The role of a second control group in an observational study (with discussion). *Statistical Science, 2,* 292-316.

Rosenbaum, P. R. (1992). Detecting bias with confidence in observational studies. *Biometrika, 79,* 367-374.

Rosenbaum, P. R., & Rubin, D. B. (1983). The central role of the propensity score in observational studies for causal effects. *Biometrika, 70,* 41-55.

Rubin, D. B. (1974). Estimating causal effects of treatments in randomized and non-randomized studies. *Journal of Educational Psychology, 66,* 688-701.

Rubin, D. B. (1977). Assignment to treatment groups on the basis of a covariate. *Journal of Educational Statistics, 2,* 1-26.

Rubin, D. B. (1978). Bayesian inference for causal effects: The role of randomization. *The Annals of Statistics, 6,* 34-58.

Rubin, D. B. (1980). Comment on "Randomization analysis of experimental data: The Fisher randomization test" by D. Basu. *Journal of the American Statistical Association, 75,* 591-593.

Salmon, W. C. (1984). *Scientific explanation and the causal structure of the world.* Princeton, NJ: Princeton University Press.

Shoemaker, S. (1980). Causality and properties. In P. van Inwagen (Ed.), *Time and cause* (pp. 109-135). Dordrecht, Holland: D. Reidel.

Simon, H. A. (1954). Spurious correlation: A causal interpretation. *Journal of the American Statistical Association, 49,* 467-492.

Sobel, M. E. (1990). Effect analysis and causation in linear structural equation models. *Psychometrika, 55,* 495-515.

Sobel, M. E. (1993). *Causation, spurious correlation and recursive structural equation models.* Unpublished manuscript. [Available from Michael Sobel, Department of Sociology, University of Arizona, Tucson, AZ 85721]

Sobel, M. E. (in press). Causal inference in the social and behavioral sciences. In G. Arminger, C. C. Clogg, & M. E. Sobel (Eds.), *A handbook for statistical modeling in the social and behavioral sciences.* New York: Plenum.

Sobel, M. E., & Arminger, G. (1986). Platonic and operational true scores in covariance structure analysis: An invited comment on Bielby's "Arbitrary metrics in multiple indicator models of latent variables." *Sociological Methods and Research, 15,* 44-58.

Spearman, C. (1904). General intelligence, objectively determined and measured. *American Journal of Psychology, 15,* 201-293.

Suppes, P., & Zanotti, M. (1981). When are probabilistic explanations possible? *Synthese, 48,* 191-199.

Titterington, D. M., Smith, A.F.M., & Makov, U. E. (1985). *Statistical analysis of finite mixture distributions.* New York: John Wiley.

Torgerson, W. S. (1958). *Theory and methods of scaling.* New York: John Wiley.

van Fraasen, B. C. (1980). *The scientific image.* Oxford: Clarendon Press.

von Wright, G. H. (1971). *Explanation and understanding.* Ithaca, NY: Cornell University Press.

Wheaton, B., Muthén, B., Alwin, D. F., & G. F. Summers. (1977). Assessing reliability and stability in panel models. In D. R. Heise (Ed.), *Sociological methodology, 1977* (pp. 84-135). San Francisco: Jossey-Bass.

White, P. (1990). Ideas about causation in philosophy and psychology. *Psychological Bulletin, 108,* 3-18.

Winer, B. J. (1971). *Statistical principles in experimental design* (2nd ed.). New York: McGraw-Hill.

Wright, S. (1934). The method of path coefficients. *The Annals of Mathematical Statistics, 5,* 161-215.

Zellner, A. (1984). Causality and econometrics. In A. Zellner (Ed.), *Basic issues in econometrics* (pp. 35-74). Chicago: University of Chicago Press.

2

The Theory of Confounding
and Its Application in Causal
Modeling With Latent Variables

ROLF STEYER
THOMAS SCHMITT

Causality has been an aversive issue for the vast majority of empirical researchers. For many of us, it is more convenient to pretend not to ask causal questions even in cases in which we cannot hide our real interest behind less suspicious terms such as *effect, influence, determination,* or *dependence.* However, the difficulty of the issue and its obvious relevance for empirical research (e.g., in epidemiology, in evaluation research, and in most other substantive fields of empirical science) have challenged many others.

How to convey something meaningful in a single chapter on a complex issue such as *causal modeling with latent variables*? The idea is to focus on a subclass of causal stochastic models, namely causal regression models. However, in this chapter, we will neglect all issues related to the dynamic (or process) aspects of a causal regression model (cf. Steyer, in press-c). Instead, we will focus on the core of the theory of causal regression models: the theory of confounding. *Confounding* refers to the phenomenon that the (population) regression coefficients change if additional variables are considered as regressors. Since these changes can be substantial, for example, changing a strong positive effect into a strong negative one, confounding will invalidate causal interpretations of the regression coefficients involved.

The organization of this chapter is as follows: We begin with a review and *some comments on some of the literature* (Section 1) and continue with presenting the *challenge of confounding* (Section 2) by (a) the well-known Simpson paradox and by (b) confounding in autoregression models with latent variables, a class of models often used, not only in developmental psychology. Next, we briefly describe the general theory of *regression models* (Section 3) and then turn to the theory of *confounding in regression models* (Section 4). We then illustrate the theory by some *applications* (Section 5), and in the *discussion* (Section 6) we hint at some important issues not treated in this chapter.

1. Some Comments on Some of the Literature

A thorough review of the different approaches to causality is far beyond the scope of this chapter. Some traditions in modern literature, however, should be mentioned and briefly be commented on before presenting our own approach. The interested reader is referred to Steyer (1992, chap. 2) for a more detailed review of the relevant literature.

Internal Validity. The *theory of internal validity* (e.g., Campbell, 1957; Campbell & Stanley, 1963; Cook & Campbell, 1979) has enriched us with many useful discussions related to the issue of causality, although one may not be content with the "somewhat primitive nature" (Cook & Campbell, 1986, p. 177) of this approach. There is no serious attempt to formalize the concepts. As a consequence, there are endless debates, for example, about the adequate analysis of nonequivalent control group designs (Kenny, 1975, 1979; Magidson, 1977; Reichardt, 1979; Rubin, 1973a, 1973b, 1974, 1977; Weisberg, 1979). Problems of statistical inference, practical problems of running a randomized experiment such as *systematic attrition,* and the problem of directness of a causal dependence are mixed up.

Path Analysis. The literature on *path analysis* originated by Sewall Wright (1918, 1921, 1923, 1934, 1960a, 1960b) has provided important concepts such as direct, indirect, and total effects. However, Wright failed to work out the formal differences between "functional relations" (Wright, 1934, p. 161) and relations that are characterized by ordinary regression models. How can we test whether a given regression equation describes a "functional" (or causal) relation or just an ordinary regression? Simply replacing the word *causal* by *functional* does not solve the problem.

Wold (1954, 1956, 1958, 1959, 1960, 1969) took considerable effort to overcome this problem. In 1954, he wrote: "The relationship is then defined as causal if it is theoretically permissible to regard the variables as involved in a fictive controlled experiment" (1954, p. 166). Although this definition meets the intuition of many experimentalists (including our own), it is not possible to derive empirically falsifiable propositions *outside* the controlled experiment. In nonexperimental studies, the empirical content of a causal hypothesis based on this definition is empty.

Structural Equation Modeling. The more up-to-date developments of path analysis in psychometrics and econometrics under the label of "structural equation modeling" or "simultaneous equation modeling," too, did not provide a clear distinction between causal and ordinary regression models. According to Goldberger (1973, p. 3) structural equation models—in contrast to least-squares regression—are intended to estimate "the fundamental parameters of the mechanism that generated the data." Again, how can we test whether or not the parameters of a given structural equation model describe the mechanism that generated the data? Goldberger provides some typical and useful examples in which they do not. Although these cases are certainly instructive, the more fundamental problem of a clear-cut definition remains unsolved by simply changing the labels from "functional" to "structural" or to "mechanism that generated the data."

The same strategy of changing the labels is followed by Bentler (1980, p. 420):

> Obviously it is not necessary to take a stand on the meaning of "cause" to see why the modeling process is colloquially called causal modeling (with latent variables). The word "cause" is meant to provide no philosophical meaning beyond a shorthand designation for a hypothesized unobserved process, so that phrases such as "process" or "system" modeling would be viable substitute labels for "causal" modeling.

Neither "causal modeling" nor "process modeling" nor "system modeling" have any empirical meaning. Again, how can we test whether or not a given system of regression equations describes a (causal) process?

Misspecification. There are a number of other important papers on the problem of misspecification of simultaneous equation models (e.g., Deegan, 1974; Hausman, 1978; Hausman & McFadden, 1984; Hocking, 1974; Holly, 1982; Kinal & Lahiri, 1983; Newey, 1985; White, 1980a, 1980b, 1981, 1982; White & Domowitz, 1984) and omitted variables

(Leamer, 1978; Mauro, 1990; Ramsey & Schmidt, 1976). However, these papers, too, fail to provide a formal definition of a *causal* model. Just as in Goldberger's paper mentioned above, the misspecified model is simply contrasted with the "true causal model" in order to study the consequences of the misspecification.

In the past decade some papers appeared explicitly warning about premature causal interpretations of structural equation models (e.g., Cliff, 1983; de Leeuw, 1985; Freedman, 1987; Mulaik, 1987; Rogosa, 1987). For instance, Cliff (1983, p. 125) writes:

> Correlational data are still correlational, and no computer program can take account of the variables that are not in the analysis. Causal relations can only be established through patient painstaking attention to all relevant variables, and should involve active manipulation as a final confirmation. *Post hoc non est propter hoc*, and a good fit for a causal model does not confirm it.

We may add that the goodness-of-fit test of a structural equation model should not be misunderstood as a test of causality. The reason for this caveat should be clear realizing that we may change a "causal hypothesis without changing fit" (Stelzl, 1985; see also Lee & Hershberger, 1990), because contradictory causal models may imply the same covariance matrix.

The Approach of Suppes, Stegmüller, and Spohn. The approach of Suppes, Stegmüller, and Spohn goes back to Suppes's (1970) book, *A Probabilistic Theory of Causality*. It has been improved by Stegmüller (1983) and especially by Spohn (1980, 1983, 1990, 1991, in press). The merits of this approach lie in the adequate and consequent use of probability theory. It is one of the few approaches in which only well-defined terms are used, at least in the papers of Spohn. A problematic point, however, at least from the point of view of empirical sciences, is that the guiding principle of the theory is John St. Mill's *Ceteris paribus* condition: Holding constant all potential disturbing variables and varying only X, you may observe the *effect* of X on Y. Although this leads to a well-defined concept of causality, its use in empirical work, especially in the social sciences, is limited. The simple reason is: There are so many potential disturbing variables that trying to hold them all constant is tantamount to Sisyphus's work.[1]

The Approach of Rubin, Holland, Rosenbaum, and Sobel. The approach of Rubin (1974, 1977, 1978, 1985, 1986, 1990) is inspired by Fisher's ideas of random assignment of observational units to experimental conditions. It has been adopted in a series of other papers such as Holland and Rubin (1983), Holland (1986, 1988), Rosenbaum and Rubin (1983a, 1983b, 1984, 1985a, 1985b), Rosenbaum (1984a, 1984b, 1984c), and Sobel (1992). The basic ideas of this approach will now briefly be described.

In his article, "Statistics and Causal Inference," Holland (1986, p. 946) writes (the indices t and c symbolize "treatment" and "control," respectively):

> For the model to represent faithfully this state of affairs we need not a *single* variable, Y, to represent a response, but *two* variables, Y_t and Y_c, to represent two potential responses. The interpretation of these two values, $Y_t(u)$ and $Y_c(u)$ for a given unit u, is that $Y_t(u)$ is the value of the response that would be observed if the unit were exposed to t and $Y_c(u)$ is the value that would be observed *on the same unit* if it were exposed to c.

Using this notation, Holland (1986, p. 947) then defines the difference $Y_t(u) - Y_c(u)$ as "the causal effect of t (relative to c) on u (as measured by Y)." [In Sobel's modification of Rubin's model (chapter 13, this volume) this "phenomenological approach" is supplemented by moving from the level of scores to the level of conditional distributions or conditional means (conditional on u).] Holland then mentions what he calls "the fundamental problem of causal inference": the impossibility "to *observe* the value of $Y_t(u)$ and $Y_c(u)$ on the same unit," which makes it impossible to *observe* the effect of t on u. An observational unit cannot simultaneously be assigned to the treatment *and* control conditions.

The solution to this problem within this approach is to define the average causal effect, T, of t (relative to c) over the set U of units as the expected value of the difference $Y_t - Y_c$ over the u's in U. The so defined average causal effect may then be estimated under certain conditions (such as random assignment of units to treatment conditions).

Other Approaches. An adequate and fair review even only of the literature on stochastic theories of causality is beyond the scope of this chapter. The books edited by Fetzer (1988) as well as by Skyrmes and Harper (1988), especially the paper by Davis (1988), give an impression about the diversity of the field. More literature may also be found in Steyer (1992, chap. 2), who also presents the most complete account of the theory of causal regression models (see also Steyer, 1984, 1985a, 1985b, 1985c, in press-a, in press-b).

2. The Challenge of Confounding

As noted above, this chapter focuses on the core of the theory of causal regression models: the theory of confounding. Before presenting the formal theory of confounding in regression models, we illustrate the challenge of confounding by two examples. The first one is analogous to *Simpson's paradox.* It deals with artificial data and with categorical variables. The second one, which is illustrated with empirical data, is an *autoregression model* with latent continuous variables.

2.1. Simpson's Paradox

In ordinary regression models we may often encounter the following paradox, sometimes referred to as *Simpson's paradox.* (For a more detailed description of this paradox, see Steyer, 1992, chap. 3; Novick, 1980; or Simpson, 1951). Suppose you are comparing a treatment ($X = 1$) to a control ($X = 0$) with respect to some criterion of success ($Y = 1$) or nonsuccess ($Y = 0$). In the total population the (conditional) probability (given $X = x$) for success is *lower* for the participants of the treatment than for the control subjects, that is, there is a *negative* "effect" of X on Y. However, for *each and every* sex subpopulation represented by the values of the variable W (e.g., $W = 0$ for men and $W = 1$ for women), the (conditional) probability (given $X = x$ and $W = w$) for success is *higher* for the participants of the treatment than for the control subjects. In other words, there is a *positive* "effect" of X on Y. Note that the total population consists of exactly those two subpopulations mentioned above. Tables 2.1 and 2.2 display data exemplifying such a case.

Such a situation is disastrous for every substantive interpretation: Our finding is a negative "effect" of X on Y in the total population. Hence, if we would ignore the finding in the subpopulations, our decision would be to cancel the rehabilitation program, although in *both* subpopulations, male *and* female, the "effect" of X on Y is positive. In less statistical terms: The treatment has a negative effect for *people,* but it has positive effects for both *men and women!*

One might think that this paradox is artificial. However, although it may be extreme in switching a negative effect into a positive one, it is merely an example of *the problem of confounding,* which may occur in *every* correlational study in which observational units are *not* randomly assigned to the treatment conditions. The problem of confounding is *not*

Table 2.1   Evaluation of a Rehabilitation Program for Parolees

Recidivism	Treatment		Total
	No (X = 0)	Yes (X = 1)	
Yes (Y = 0)	.200	.250	.450
No (Y = 1)	.300	.250	.550
Total	.500	.500	1.000

NOTE: Cf. Novick (1980). The numbers given are fictitious probabilities. Multiplied by 1,000, they may be interpreted as absolute frequencies in a sample of N = 1,000.

Table 2.2   Evaluation of a Rehabilitation Program for Parolees, Separately Analyzed for Men and Women

Recidivism	Treatment		Total
	No (X = 0)	Yes (X = 1)	
A. Men (W = 0)			
Yes (Y = 0)	.175	.450	.625
No (Y = 1)	.075	.300	.375
Total	.250	.750	1.000
B. Women (W = 1)			
Yes (Y = 0)	.225	.050	.275
No (Y = 1)	.525	.200	.725
Total	.750	.250	1.000

NOTE: Conditional probabilities $P(Y = y, X = x | W = w)$ given sex. Membership in one of the two sex groups is assumed to be equally probable.

limited to cases with categorical variables as evidenced in the following example for continuous latent variables.

2.2. Confounding in Autoregression Models

The class of autoregression models often used in longitudinal studies almost always suffers from confounding, at least if applied in psychology. Their application may be adequate in those cases where there are no differences in the general level of the attributes studied. However, in *psychological applications,* for instance, there are important interindividual differences between the subjects in the sample, differences in the general level of the attributes, which persist throughout all occasions of measurement.

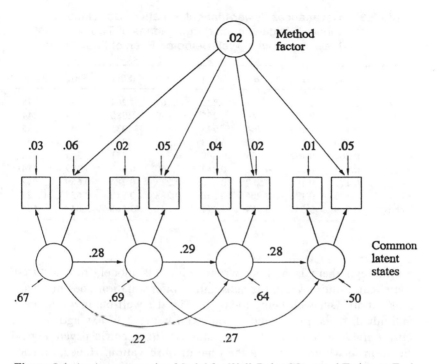

Figure 2.1. An Autoregression Model for Well-Being Measured Twice on Each of Four Occasions (There is only a single method factor because the variance of the other one is not significant. Goodness-of-fit statistics: $\chi^2_{18} = 25.94$, $p = 0.10$, adj. goodness-of-fit = .97.)

An example is the model depicted in Figure 2.1, representing two measurements of well-being on each of four occasions, 3 weeks apart, for a sample of 502 students and other persons (see Table 2.3). In this model, the state of well-being on Occasion 2, for instance, depends on the corresponding state on Occasion 1. The dependency is described by the (auto)-regression coefficient amounting to .28 that corresponds to a correlation of .27. (Aside from the four latent state variables, there is a method factor accounting for the correlations between the second test halves across the four occasions of measurement. This method factor represents the component of the second test half not shared with the first test half. A corresponding method factor for the first test half is not necessary in this data set: The variance of this factor was not significantly different from zero.)

Table 2.3   Covariances (lower triangular matrix), Correlations (upper triangular matrix), and Means of Two Measurements of Well-Being on Each of Four Occasions

	WB_{11}	WB_{21}	WB_{12}	WB_{22}	WB_{13}	WB_{23}	WB_{14}	WB_{24}
WB_{11}	0.702	.924	.247	.239	.263	.264	.264	.248
WB_{21}	0.669	0.745	.249	.265	.250	.280	.244	.244
WB_{12}	0.183	0.193	0.764	.948	.324	.331	.392	.355
WB_{22}	0.186	0.213	0.742	0.803	.326	.353	.356	.344
WB_{13}	0.201	0.197	0.255	0.260	0.794	.951	.373	.372
WB_{23}	0.201	0.220	0.260	0.283	0.760	0.803	.389	.414
WB_{14}	0.179	0.168	0.282	0.266	0.273	0.286	0.669	.942
WB_{24}	0.173	0.176	0.266	0.270	0.288	0.319	0.657	0.727
Means	3.759	3.537	3.774	3.611	3.741	3.568	3.847	3.685

Although there is nothing wrong with this model from a purely statistical point of view, the substantive interpretation does not make sense at all. Our well-being today, that is, the well-being within each individual, does *not* depend on our well-being 3 weeks ago. On the *intraindividual level* it rather depends on the specific psychological situation in which we are at the time of observation. Hence, on each occasion there must be a latent variable representing *occasion-specific effects.* On the *interindividual level,* the well-being at a specific occasion *k* of measurement additionally depends on the general tendencies of the subjects (the members of the sample) to feel well, that is, there will be a *latent trait variable,* the values of which represent this general tendency of well-being.

The model depicted in Figure 2.2, which, in latent state-trait theory (see, e.g., Schmitt & Steyer, 1990; Steyer, Ferring, & Schmitt, 1992; Steyer, Majcen, Schwenkmezger, & Buchner, 1989; Steyer, Schwenk-mezger, & Auer, 1990; Steyer & Schmitt, 1990a, 1990b) is called a *singletrait-multistate-multimethod model,* represents the substantive theory described in the last paragraph. According to this model, the autoregression effects are zero, once the common latent trait variable is introduced. Hence, within each subpopulation characterized by identical trait scores, the well-being on occasion *k* + 1 does *not depend* at all on the well-being on occasion *k.* Note that the reasons to prefer the singletrait-multistate-multimethod model (Figure 2.2) over the autoregression model (Figure 2.1) are not statistical in nature. Instead, it is the

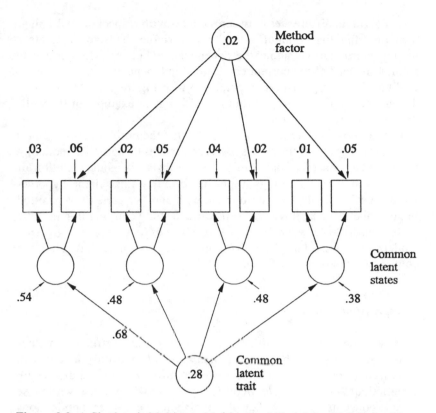

Figure 2.2. A Singletrait-Multistate-Multimethod Model for Well-Being Measured Twice on Each of Four Occasions (There is only a single method factor because the variance of the other one is not significant. Goodness-of-fit statistics: $\chi^2_{21} = 20.04$, $p = 0.52$, adj. goodness-of-fit = .98.)

substantive causal interpretation that makes sense for the model depicted in Figure 2.2 but not for the model in Figure 2.1. Nevertheless, there are also statistical reasons to prefer the model depicted in Figure 2.2, such as better fit, fewer parameters, and the nonsignificant autoregressive effects, once the common latent trait is introduced into the model (see Section 5).

Whereas in Simpson's paradox, controlling for the omitted sex variable W, a negative effect turned into a positive one, controlling for the omitted common latent trait variable turns a strong positive effect to zero (compare Figure 2.1 to Figure 2.2). Hence, if there are persisting interindividual differences between subjects with respect to well-being, then omitting the common latent trait variable leads to completely wrong interpretations about the dependencies between the constructs studied: Instead of the correct conditional independence, the erroneous finding is a strong positive dependence (see Figure 2.1). In fact, this dependency in the autoregression model is a nice example of the well-known *spurious correlation.*

The examples presented above suggest that the problem of confounding is probably one of the most serious challenges to statistical modeling in empirical observational studies. Any substantive interpretation of empirical statistical findings might be seriously false if the hypothesized causal variable X is confounded with another variable W omitted in the model. Hence, it seems worthwhile to study confounding in some more detail. Since we will only deal with confounding in regression models, we first clarify the concept of regression before studying confounding in regression models.

3. Regression Models

Most readers will be familiar with *linear regression* from elementary statistics, some with the *general linear model,* and only a few with *conditional expectations.* The first two are *statistical models* describing assumptions about a *sample.* In this chapter, we will not deal with these sample concepts, although they play their role in empirical applications of the theory presented. However, our substantive theories do not deal with dependencies in samples. Instead our hypotheses deal with the true means or *expected values* of random variables, with *true (i.e., population) correlation* between random variables, or with their *true regressive dependency,* for instance. Just as stochastic dependence or independence is defined in terms of *probability,* and not in terms of relative frequencies, we will define *unconfoundedness* in the context of *true (or population) regressive dependencies.* Hence, the central concept is the (population concept of a) *regression,* which will be used as a synonym for *conditional expectation* in the sequel.

A *regression* $E(Y|X)$ of a *regressand* Y on a *regressor* X is that random variable, the values of which are the *conditional expected values* $E(Y|X = x)$ (for a more precise definition see, e.g., Bauer, 1981; Feller, 1971; Steyer, 1988, 1992; or Steyer & Eid, 1993, Appendix G). In the definition of the regression it is presumed that X and Y have a *joint distribu-*

tion, that is, it must be possible that any pair $\langle x, y \rangle$ of values of X and Y occur together. Y has to be numerical, that is, the values y of Y are numbers, whereas X may take its values x in an arbitrary set. Hence, the values x of X may be qualitative, such as "experimental condition" or "control condition." The regressor X may also be a multidimensional variable or *random vector,* that is, $X = \langle X_1, X_2 \rangle$ may take values such as $x = \langle 4, 3.5 \rangle$.

Propositions about a regression are involved not only in simple and multiple regression analysis, but also in logistic regression, in the analysis of variance, in the general linear model,[2] in factor analysis, and in structural equation models. Propositions about regressions may be presented in different ways, for example, as:

a. a *regression curve* in a Cartesian coordinate system;

b. a *histogram* depicting conditional probabilities;

c. a *table* or a *bar diagram* containing conditional expected values;

d. a *path diagram;*

e. an *equation.*

The way of presentation should not be mixed up with the logical structure of the concept of a regression. In all cases (a) to (e), propositions are made about how the conditional expected values $E(Y|X = x)$ of a variable Y depend on the values of another (or of more than one other) variable(s) X (or $X_1, \ldots, X_m$), or about how strong the regressive dependency is, for example, as measured by the coefficient of *determination*

$$R^2_{Y|X} = \mathrm{Var}[E(Y|X)]/\mathrm{Var}(Y) . \qquad [2.1]$$

The concept of regression may be used to describe different kinds of dependencies of a regressand Y on a regressor X. *Regressive independence* of Y on X is defined by:

$$E(Y|X) = E(Y) . \qquad [2.2]$$

Otherwise we say that Y is *regressively dependent* on X.

Simple Regressive Dependence. If there is a regressive dependency of a regressand Y on a regressor X, it can be of many kinds. The simplest kind of regressive dependence is the *linear* one, which may occur if X is *numeric. Simple linear regressive dependence* is defined by $E(Y|X)$ being a *linear* function of X:

$$E(Y \mid X) = \alpha_0 + \alpha_1 \cdot X, \quad \text{where } \alpha_0, \alpha_1 \in \mathfrak{R}. \qquad [2.3]$$

We consider $\alpha_1 = 0$ to be a special case of linear regressive dependence in which we may also talk about *regressive independence*.

Simple Linear Quasi-Regressive Dependence. If the regression is *not* linear, we still may ask how well the dependence of Y on X can be described by a *linear* function, although this function will not be a regression in the sense defined above. Such a linear function representing the best linear predictor (in terms of the least squares criterion) between X and Y, will be called a *linear quasi-regression* in the sequel. (Müller, 1975, uses the term "regression of the 2nd kind.") The linear quasi-regression is that linear function $f(X) = \alpha + \beta \cdot X$ of X that minimizes the following function of the coefficients a and b:

$$LS(a, b) := E\{[Y - (a + b \cdot X)]^2\}, \qquad [2.4]$$

the least squares criterion. If $LS(a, b)$ has a minimum for the coefficients $a = \alpha$ and $b = \beta$, the function $f(X) = \alpha + \beta \cdot X$ may be denoted $\hat{Y}$. This linear quasi-regression $\hat{Y}$ is identical with the (true) regression $E(Y \mid X)$ only if $E(Y \mid X)$ is in fact a linear function of X. Otherwise the regression $E(Y \mid X)$ and the linear quasi-regression $\hat{Y}$ differ from each other.

Partial Linear Regressive Dependence. If *two* numeric regressors, X and W, are considered, there are several kinds of dependencies of the regressand Y on the two regressors X and W. The simplest kind can be described by the multiple regression equation:

$$E(Y \mid X, W) = \beta_0 + \beta_1 X + \beta_2 W, \quad \beta_0, \beta_1, \beta_2 \in \mathfrak{R}. \qquad [2.5]$$

It is well known that the *partial regression coefficient* β_1 need not be identical with the corresponding simple regression coefficient α_1 (see 2.3). In the case $\alpha_1 \neq \beta_1$, X and W are *confounded*. This definition will now be generalized.

4. The Theory of Confounding in Regression Models

We will first present a precise definition of the concept of *unconfoundedness* and then turn to the issue of interaction or *additive decomposability*. Note that, in the following definition, only Y has to be real-valued or numerical, whereas both X and W may take their values in arbitrary sets. Hence, X may take values "treatment" and "control," for example, and the values of W might be "male" and "female."[3] Note that, throughout the chapter, we refer to the "population concepts" or better, to the *theoretical concepts and not to sample concepts* (of probability, regression, independence, etc.).

Definition 1. Let X, Y, and W be random variables with a joint distribution and let $E(Y \mid X)$ and $E(Y \mid X, W)$ denote conditional expectations.

(i) X and W are called *additively unconfounded with respect to* $E(Y \mid X)$ if and only if:

(a) there exists a numerical function $f(W)$ of W such that

$$E(Y \mid X, W) = E(Y \mid X) + f(W).$$ [2.6]

(ii) X and W are called *unconfounded with respect to* $E(Y \mid X)$ if and only if

(b) for each value x of X:

$$E(Y \mid X = x) = \int E(Y \mid X = x, W = w) P^W(dw).$$ [2.7]

[Note that Equation 2.7 may be written

$$E(Y \mid X = x) = \sum_w E(Y \mid X = x, W = w) \cdot P(W = w)$$ [2.8]

if W is discrete. The summation is across all values w of W.]

(iii) X and W are called *confounded with respect to* $E(Y \mid X)$ if and only if neither (a) nor (b) holds.

(iv) If X and W are confounded with respect to $E(Y \mid X)$ we call W a *confounder* with respect to $E(Y \mid X)$.

Note that Condition (a) will not necessarily hold in the case of random assignment of observational units to treatment conditions (that might be represented by X), because it requires two things:

- the conditional expectation $E(Y \mid X, W)$ of Y given X and W is *additively decomposable* into a function $g(X)$ of X and a function $f(W)$ of W, such that $E(Y \mid X, W) = g(X) + f(W)$;
- $g(X) = E(Y \mid X)$.

Since additive decomposability is a more precise concept of "no inter-action in the analysis of variance sense" and it is well known that random assignment does not prevent such interactions, additive decom-posability will not necessarily hold in the case of random assignment.

Unconfoundedness has important consequences for the interpretation of the dependency described by the regression $E(Y \mid X)$. Presuming uncon-foundedness, the conditional expected values $E(Y \mid X = x)$ are the true means (over the distribution of W) of the conditional expected values $E(Y \mid X = x, W = w)$. This is much more than we can hope for in ordinary regression models as has been demonstrated by the two introductory examples in Section 2. If Equation 2.7 holds, the Simpson paradox cannot occur any more for the specific variables X, Y, and W. Furthermore, the equality of the corresponding simple and partial regression coefficients (see the last paragraph of Section 3) will hold, too (cf. the autoregression example in Section 2). This will be shown later on in Theorem 3.

4.1. Some Theorems on Unconfoundedness

The first theorem specifies two sufficient conditions for unconfound-edness:

Theorem 1. X and W are unconfounded with respect to $E(Y \mid X)$ if:

(a) X and W are stochastically independent, or
(b) Condition (a) of Definition 1 holds.

Proof. The fact that stochastic independence of X and W implies uncon-foundedness of X and W with respect to $E(Y \mid X)$ can easily be seen: If W is discrete, the equation

$$E(Y \mid X = x) = \sum_w E(Y \mid X = x, W = w) \cdot P(W = w \mid X = x) \qquad [2.9]$$

is always true, and $P(W = w \mid X = x) = P(W = w)$ if X and W are stochastically independent. Hence, Equation 2.8 follows, and the same argument holds in the case of W being continuous. However, Equation 2.7 also follows from Equation 2.6. This may be proved as follows:

$$E(Y \mid X = x) = E(Y \mid X = x) \cdot 1 = E(Y \mid X = x) \sum_w P(W = w)$$

$$= \sum_{w} E(Y \mid X = x) \cdot P(W = w)$$

$$= \sum_{w} [E(Y \mid X = x, W = w) - f(w)] \cdot P(W = w)$$

$$= \sum_{w} E(Y \mid X = x, W = w) \cdot P(W = w) - \sum_{w} f(w) \cdot P(W = w)$$

$$= \sum_{w} E(Y \mid X = x, W = w) \cdot P(W = w) . \qquad \text{[See Eq. 2.6]}$$

The last equation follows from $\sum_{w} f(w) \cdot P(W = w) = E[f(W)] = 0$, which is true because: $E(Y) = E[E(Y \mid X, W)] = E[E(Y \mid X) + f(W)] = E(Y) + E[f(W)]$.

According to Theorem 1, stochastic independence of X and W is sufficient for X and W to be unconfounded with respect to the regression $E(Y \mid X)$, but Condition (a) of Definition 1 is sufficient, too. Note that unconfoundedness is not necessarily fulfilled in an ordinary regression model. However, it *may* be true in special applications. We distinguish two cases:

- Unconfoundedness may hold because of the very nature of the empirical phenomenon studied.
- Unconfoundedness of X and W will *always* hold in experiments with random assignment of the observational unit to the experimental conditions (represented by X), provided that W characterizes some attribute of the observational unit *before* the assignment to one of the experimental conditions.

The reason for the second point is that *random assignment* is *defined* by stochastic independence between the treatment variable X and *all* variables representing an attribute of the observational unit *before* the assignment to one of the experimental conditions.

In our introductory examples, we have already given some reasons why it is important for the interpretability of a regressive dependency that unconfoundedness, and therefore Equation 2.7, hold. Here is another reason: Suppose that your substantive hypothesis postulates—other variables being constant—a *positive linear regressive effect* of X

on Y, and let those other variables be represented by the multidimensional random variable $W = \langle W_1, \ldots, W_m \rangle$. If W is observed, you may test this hypothesis. However, if, in the worst case, you did not observe any component of W at all, your hypothesis can still be tested in an indirect way, *provided that unconfoundedness and therefore Equation 2.7 hold* (e.g., guaranteed by random assignment of units to experimental conditions). How is this possible? The following theorem and its proof give the answer (see Erdfelder & Bredenkamp, in press).

Theorem 2. If X and W are unconfounded with respect to $E(Y \mid X)$ and

$$E(Y \mid X, W) = g_0(W) + g_1(W) \cdot X,$$

$$\text{where } g_1(w) > 0 \text{ for all values } w \text{ of } W, \qquad [2.10]$$

then

$$E(Y \mid X) = \alpha_0 + \alpha_1 \cdot X = E[g_0(W)] + E[g_1(W)] \cdot X,$$

$$\text{where } \alpha_1 = E[g_1(W)] > 0. \qquad [2.11]$$

Proof. Equation 2.10 implies $E(Y \mid X = x, W = w) = g_0(w) + g_1(w) \cdot x$, for all values x of X and w of W. Inserting this into Equation 2.7 yields

$$E(Y \mid X = x) = \sum_w [g_0(w) + g_1(w) \cdot x] \cdot P(W = w)$$

$$= \sum_w g_0(w) \cdot P(W = w) + \sum_w g_1(w) \cdot P(W = w) \cdot x$$

$$= E[g_0(W)] + E[g_1(W)] \cdot x, \qquad [2.12]$$

for all values x of X and w of W. Hence, the slope coefficient α_1 of the linear regression $E(Y \mid X) = \alpha_0 + \alpha_1 \cdot X$ is identical with the expectation $E[g_1(W)]$ of the function $g_1(W)$, the value $g_1(w)$ of which is the slope coefficient of the *conditional regression* $E_{W = w}(Y \mid X) = g_0(w) + g_1(w) \cdot X$ of Y on X given $W = w$. Since $g_1(W)$ has been assumed to take only *positive* values (see 2.10), its expectation must be positive, too.

According to this theorem, the substantive hypothesis of a positive effect of X on Y—all variables $W_1, \ldots, W_m$ constant—implies that the slope coefficient α_1 of the simple linear regression is positive, provided that X and W are unconfounded with respect to $E(Y \mid X)$. If, in a specific application, the slope coefficient is *not* positive and unconfoundedness has been secured (e.g., by random assignment), the substantive hypothesis can be rejected. Hence, unconfoundedness and its consequence, Equation 2.7, are not simply a matter of taste; instead they are of crucial importance if the substantive hypothesis of a positive effect of X on Y—all variables $W_1, \ldots, W_m$ constant—are to be tested empirically.

What can we do in studies in which—for ethical, economical, or other reasons—we cannot secure unconfoundedness by random assignment of units to experimental conditions? The general answer is: Whenever we have the hypothesis of unconfoundedness of X and a variable W with respect to $E(Y \mid X)$, we may try to *falsify* this hypothesis. In some cases this may easily be achieved. The following theorem is an example.

Theorem 3. If X and W are unconfounded with respect to $E(Y \mid X)$ and

$$E(Y \mid X, W) = \beta_0 + \beta_1 X + \beta_2 W, \qquad [2.13]$$

then

$$E(Y \mid X) = \alpha_0 + \alpha_1 \cdot X, \quad \alpha_0, \alpha_1 \in \Re, \qquad [2.14]$$

$$\alpha_1 = \beta_1, \qquad [2.15]$$

If, additionally

$$E(W \mid X) = \gamma_0 + \gamma_1 X, \quad \gamma_0, \gamma_1 \in \Re, \qquad [2.16]$$

holds, then

$$\gamma_1 \beta_2 = 0. \qquad [2.17]$$

Proof. We only give the proof for W being discrete. The general proof is analogous.[4] For all values x of X:

$$E(Y \mid X = x) = \sum_w E(Y \mid X = x, \, W = w) \cdot P(W = w) \qquad \text{[See Eq. 2.7]}$$

$$= \sum_w (\beta_0 + \beta_1 x + \beta_2 w) \cdot P(W = w) \qquad \text{[See Eq. 2.13]}$$

$$= \beta_0 + \beta_1 x + \beta_2 \cdot \left[\sum_w w \cdot P(W = w) \right]$$

$$= \beta_0 + \beta_1 x + \beta_2 E(W) = [\beta_0 + \beta_2 E(W)] + \beta_1 x . \qquad [2.18]$$

Hence, the constant α_0 of the linear regression $E(Y \mid X)$ is identical to $\beta_0 + \beta_2 E(W)$ and its slope coefficient α_1 is equal to β_1, which proves Equation 2.15.

Equation 2.17 may be derived as follows:

$$E(Y \mid X) = E[E(Y \mid X, \, W) \mid X]$$

$$= E(\beta_0 + \beta_1 X + \beta_2 W \mid X) \qquad \text{[See Eq. 2.13]}$$

$$= \beta_0 + \beta_1 X + \beta_2 E(W \mid X) .$$

The last equation shows that $E(Y \mid X)$ can only be of the form $\alpha_0 + \alpha_1 X$ (see Eq. 2.14) if $\beta_2 = 0$ or the regression $E(W \mid X)$, too, is a linear function of X, that is, if Equation 2.16 holds. Inserting Equation 2.16 into the last equation,

$$E(Y \mid X) = \beta_0 + \beta_1 X + \beta_2 E(W \mid X) = \beta_0 + \beta_1 X + \beta_2 (\gamma_0 + \gamma_1 X) , \qquad [2.19]$$

shows that Equation 2.17 follows, too, because of Equation 2.2.

According to this theorem, the simple and the partial regression coefficients α_1 and β_1 are identical if X and W are unconfounded with respect to $E(Y \mid X)$ and if the regression $E(Y \mid X, \, W)$ is a linear combination of X and W. Hence, provided that Equation 2.13 holds, the test of the hypothesis $\alpha_1 = \beta_1$ is also a test of the hypothesis that X and W are unconfounded with respect to $E(Y \mid X)$.

How should we test the hypothesis $\alpha_1 = \beta_1$? As far as we know, no direct test of this kind of hypothesis is available. Fortunately, however, a significance test of the hypothesis $\gamma_1\beta_2 = 0$ is available for large samples: Sobel (1982, 1986) used the δ method to obtain the asymptotic distribution and the large-sample standard error of $\gamma_1\beta_2$. Dividing the estimate of $\gamma_1\beta_2$ by its standard error yields a t-value that may serve as a test statistic. The product $\gamma_1\beta_2$ and its standard error may be computed by LISREL 8 (Jöreskog & Sörbom, 1993).

4.2. Implications of Additive Unconfoundedness

If not only unconfoundedness of X and W with respect to $E(Y \mid X)$ but also the more restrictive condition of additive unconfoundedness holds, there are additional advantages for the interpretation of the dependency of a variable Y on another one, X: In this case, the regression of Y on X given $W = w$ is the same as the (unconditional) regression $E(Y \mid X)$ except for an additive constant:

$$E_{W=w}(Y \mid X) = E(Y \mid X) + f(w) , \qquad [2.20]$$

that is, the dependency described by $E(Y \mid X)$ holds for each value w of W. The only differences between the conditional regressions $E_{W=w}(Y \mid X)$ lie in different additive constants $f(w)$. This means that the ($W = w$)-conditional regressions $E_{W=w}(Y \mid X)$ are parallel to each other and parallel to the (unconditional) regression $E(Y \mid X)$. Hence, ignoring W will not lead to a complete different dependency of Y on X.

The only problem is: There is no way to secure additive unconfoundedness by means of experimental design. Whether or not additive unconfoundedness holds depends only on the nature of the empirical phenomenon studied.

5. Applications

We may distinguish two different kinds of applications of the theory of confounding in regression models. The first one deals with *techniques of experimental design* aimed at securing stochastic independence between the treatment variable X and every *potential disturbing variable* W (i.e., every variable that may *not* be influenced by X; for more details, see the discussion section). The technique of random assignment of observational units to experimental conditions is an example. This technique is current practice in experimental research and needs no further illustration. Hence, we may concentrate on the second kind of applications, dealing with *falsification of a causal hypothesis in nonexperimental or observational studies* in which random assignment of observational units to treatment conditions is not possible. In this kind of studies, too, we often have the hypothesis that the regression $E(Y \mid X)$ describes the causal regressive dependence of Y on X, and unconfoundedness of X and W with respect to $E(Y \mid X)$ is a necessary (though not sufficient) condition for this causal hypothesis to hold, provided that we can exclude that W is influenced by X and therefore might be a *mediator* (see the discussion for more details). Hence, a test of causality can be made via the test of unconfoundedness. This will now be illustrated by the examples presented in Section 2. The first one deals with hypothetical, known probabilities, the second one with empirical data.

5.1. Simpson's Paradox

The dependency of *recidivism* (Y) on the *treatment variable* (X) (see Table 2.1) can be perfectly described by the linear regression equation

$$E(Y \mid X) = P(Y = 1 \mid X) = \alpha_0 + \alpha_1 \cdot X = .60 - .10 \cdot X . \qquad [2.21]$$

Inserting $X = 0$ and $X = 1$ into this equation yields the two conditional probabilities $P(Y = 1 \mid X = 0) = .60$ and $P(Y = 1 \mid X = 1) = .50$, which can easily be computed from the probabilities presented in Table 2.1.

In Section 2 we have argued that this dependency is misleading because X and the sex variable W are confounded with respect to $E(Y \mid X)$. In order to prove this proposition, consider the multiple regression

$$E(Y \mid X, W) = P(Y = 1 \mid X, W) = .30 + .40 \cdot W + .10 \cdot X . \qquad [2.22]$$

This equation perfectly describes the dependency of Y on X and W presented in Table 2.2. Inserting the four possible combinations of values of X and W into this equation yields the conditional probabilities $P(Y = 1 \mid X = 0, W = 0) = .30$, $P(Y = 1 \mid X = 0, W = 1) = .70$, $P(Y = 1 \mid X = 1, W = 0) = .40$, and $P(Y = 1 \mid X = 1, W = 1) = .80$, which may also be computed from the probabilities presented in Table 2.2. According to

Theorem 3, the regression coefficients of X in the last two equations have to be identical if X and W were unconfounded with respect to $E(Y \mid X)$. Since they are not, we have shown that X and W are in fact confounded. Hence, checking for confounding saves us from erroneous conclusions about the causal dependency of Y on X.

This example may also be used to illustrate the effect of random assignment of subjects to treatment conditions. In this case, applying this technique would yield stochastic independence of the treatment variable X and the sex variable W. The variables X and W would then no longer be confounded, and the coefficients of X in the regressions $E(Y \mid X)$ and $E(Y \mid X, W)$ would be identical (for details of this modified example, see Steyer, 1992, p. 58).

5.2. Confounding in Autoregression Models

Introducing the challenge of confounding in Section 2, we argued on more or less intuitive grounds that omitting the common latent trait variable W (see Figure 2.2) in the autoregression model depicted in Figure 2.1 leads to erroneous conclusions about the dependence of the variable Y (well-being on Occasion 2) on the variable X (well-being on Occasion 1). We may now reformulate this argument in more precise terms: X and W are confounded with respect to the regression $E(Y \mid X)$. The argument supporting this finding runs as follows: According to the model depicted in Figure 2.2,

$$E(Y \mid X, W) = \beta_0 + \beta_1 X + \beta_2 W, \qquad [2.23]$$

with $\beta_1 = 0$ and $\beta_2 = 1$. [Analyzing the singletrait-multistate-multimethod model with autoregressions between the latent states (see Figure 2.3) yields an autoregression coefficient $\beta_1 \approx .003$ (with the nonsignificant t-value .07) whereas the effect $\beta_2 = 1$ of W on Y is highly significant.] According to Theorem 3 (Equation 2.17), we may test for unconfoundedness of X and W with respect to the regression $E(Y \mid X)$ (see Figure 2.1) by testing the hypothesis

$$\gamma_1 \beta_2 = 0, \qquad [2.24]$$

where γ_1 is the slope coefficient of the regression

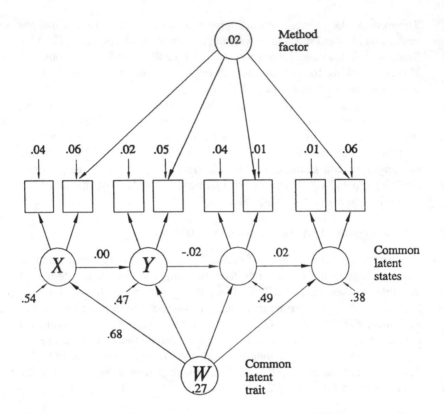

Figure 2.3. A Singletrait-Multistate-Multimethod Model With Autoregressions for Well-Being Measured Twice on Each of Four Occasions [The t-values for the autoregression effects are (from left to right): 0.07, −0.32, 0.29, all not significant. There is only a single method factor because the variance of the other one is not significant. Goodness-of-fit statistics: $\chi^2_{18} = 19.67$, $p = 0.35$, adj. goodness-of-fit = .98.]

$$E(W \mid X) = \gamma_0 + \gamma_1 X . \qquad [2.25]$$

(Note that this equation does *not* represent a *causal* regressive dependency. Nevertheless it may be correct as a regression equation. It is only used for technical reasons.) A LISREL analysis computes .28 as an estimate of $\gamma_1 \beta_2$ with a standard error of .04, which yields a t-value of

7. Hence the hypothesis $\gamma_1\beta_2 = 0$ has to be rejected and we can conclude that X and W are in fact confounded with respect to $E(Y \mid X)$.

We recommend the *singletrait-multistate-multimethod with autoregressions between the latent states* (see Figure 2.3) as a general model for longitudinal studies in psychology. It contains both the autoregression model (see Figure 2.1) and the singletrait-multistate-multimethod (see Figure 2.2) as special cases. If the attribute studied is changing only slowly compared to the interval between occasions of measurement, autoregression effects will be nonzero. If, however, the change is rapid, the latent trait may in fact explain all the covariance between the latent state variables. Omitting the latent trait will almost always—at least in psychology, where we usually have considerable interindividual differences in the trait components of the attributes considered—lead to an overestimation of the causal effects between the latent state variables.

6. Discussion

In this chapter, we focused on confounding, the core of the theory of causal regression models (see Steyer, in press-c, for a formal presentation). Although this considerably simplified the presentation, it should be noted that other important problems of causal modeling have been ignored so far in this chapter:

- The distinction between disturbers and mediators
- The asymmetry of a causal dependency
- The empirical phenomenon described by the model

These points will now be discussed in some detail.

6.1. Disturbers Versus Mediators

Confounders may be partitioned into two classes: *disturbers* and *mediators*. Examples of disturbers have already been given in Section 2: *Sex* is a disturber in the rehabilitation example, and the *well-being trait* is a disturber in the well-being example. *Disturbers*—by definition—are those confounders that cannot be influenced by the causing variable X considered. *Mediators,* however, are influenced by X and *mediate*—at least in part—the effect of X on Y. An example is the variable *social skills* (Z) in our rehabilitation example: The training (X)

may increase the social skills (Z), which themselves will decrease recidivism (Y). Hence, mediators transmit the (indirect) effects of X on Y. However, according to our concept of confounding, they are also confounders. This will now be shown.

Suppose, for simplicity, that the dependencies between X, Y, and Z may be described by the regression equations: $E(Y \mid X, Z) = \beta_0 + \beta_1 X + \beta_2 Z$ and $E(Z \mid X) = \gamma_0 + \gamma_1 X$. The algebra of conditional expectations (see, e.g., Steyer, 1988) then reveals that these two equations imply $E(Y \mid X) = (\beta_0 + \beta_2\gamma_0) + (\beta_1 + \beta_2\gamma_1) \cdot X$ (see 2.19). This equation shows that, in this case, the coefficient of the simple regression is the *total effect* $\alpha_1 = \beta_1 + \beta_2\gamma_1$ of X on Y which consists of the sum of the *direct effect* β_1 and the *indirect effect* $\beta_2\gamma_1$ of X on Y. It follows that, if $\beta_2\gamma_1 \neq 0$, the coefficients α_1 and β_1 are unequal and, according to Theorem 3, X and Z are confounded with respect to the regression $E(Y \mid X)$.

Hence, in some models, confounding poses a serious problem for causal interpretations, whereas in other models, in which the confounder is also a mediator, it does not. Obviously, it is necessary to refer to "time" or the "causal process" if we want to distinguish between these two types of confounding variables: A mediator must come *between* X and Y, whereas disturbers do not, and therefore cannot be influenced by X. (For a formal treatment of the issue, see Steyer, 1992, pp. 99-103, or Steyer, in press-c.)

6.2. Asymmetry of a Causal Regressive Dependency

The second point, namely the asymmetry of the causal dependency, is also related to the idea of "time" or the "causal process." It may be true that there is no confounding of X and any other variable W, but the regression $E(Y \mid X)$ still may not describe a causal dependency, because X "does not come before" Y. Hence, a causal model needs some formal representation of this preorderedness relation (see Steyer, 1992, chap. 6, or Steyer, in press-c). The regression itself—although an asymmetric concept—does not serve this purpose. In the rehabilitation example, for instance, there is a regressive dependence of Y (recidivism) on X (treatment). However, there is also a regressive dependence of X on Y.

In this example—as in many others—preorderedness of X to Y does not pose a serious practical problem. In other cases, however, in which there is no treatment variable, the difficulties might be considerable and may prohibit causal interpretations. Consider our well-being example! It is tempting to use the daily hassles and uplift scale (Lazarus & Cohen,

1977) as a cause (X) of well-being (Y). The problem is, however, that it would be the *self-reported* daily hassles and uplifts; and there is no way to guarantee that the number of daily hassles and uplifts *reported* does not depend on our state of well-being when the self-report is made.

Note that the borderline is not between *treatment variables* and purely *observational variables.* Other observational variables may pose no problem at all with respect to the preorderedness relation. All variables representing any aspect of the weather before the well-being is assessed are unproblematic in this respect (although they may be problematic with respect to confounding).

6.3. The Empirical Phenomenon

The third point, the empirical phenomenon described by the model, is also important, but has not been covered in this chapter. Talking in ordinary language terms about variables often seduces us into forgetting what, in fact, we are talking about. When we talk about *recidivism,* for instance, is it about recidivism within a given individual or across the individuals of a population? And what are the social and economic circumstances? Obviously, the training program may have another effect at a boom time than at a time of economic depression.

All three points mentioned above have to be represented in a causal model, but only the first two are specific for a causal model. The third one is important for *all* stochastic models. Representing the empirical phenomenon in a stochastic model may be achieved by making explicit the underlying *probability space.* Unfortunately, this is rarely done in regression models. It often seems that the (set of) equation(s) describing the dependence between the random variables considered are the model. However, a regression model consists of the underlying probability space (characterizing the empirical random experiment) *and* the regression(s) considered. A *causal* regression model has additional structure: the *process* with respect to which the preorderedness relation can be expressed, and the set of variables considered potential disturbing variables with respect to the regression to be studied (see Steyer, 1992, or in press-c, for formal details).

7. Conclusion

Causal modeling is a complex undertaking, especially in studies in which no random assignment of observational units to experimental conditions is possible. Nevertheless, in many cases *causal* modeling is necessary if statistical models should make sense at all. As has been shown by the two introductory examples, without the additional assumptions of a causal model, statistical models usually do not describe the dependencies of substantive interest between the variables studied. Of course, much has to be done before causal modeling will be routine work in nonexperimental research. What is still needed are not only an outline of practical steps (see Steyer, in press-a), but also illustrating and convincing examples, and last but not least the implementation of the tests of causality in convenient statistical software.

Notes

1. A more realistic and more useful guiding principle has been brought up in this century by Sir Ronald Fisher's work: the *Ceteris distributionibus paribus condition.* According to this principle the *distributions* of all potential disturbing variables should be held constant, which is easily achieved by the technique of random assignment of observational units to experimental conditions. This guiding principle is adhered to in the theory of causal regression models (Steyer, 1984, 1985a, 1985b, 1985c, 1992, in press-a, in press-b, in press-c).

2. In the general linear model (GLM), the design matrix X is considered a matrix of *constants* that, for instance, indicate to which treatment the jth unit of the sample has been exposed. Although the GLM does not represent this fact, the units may be *randomly* assigned to the treatment conditions. If we also consider the *sampling* of units and not only the measurement of the dependent variables, the indicators for the treatment conditions will be *random variables*, too. Also "organismic variables" such as "sex" or "race" will be *random variables* if we include the sampling of units in the random experiment considered.

3. For a definition of a random variable more general than those presented in most other English textbooks on probability theory, see, for example, Bauer (1981) or Dudley (1989), where all other concepts of probability theory used in the sequel such as *joint distribution, conditional expectation, measure integral,* and the *distribution P^W* of W (used in Equation 2.7) and so forth will be found, too. These general concepts are necessary if we do not want to restrict the theory to the case of numerical random variables W. However, the more special definitions presented in textbooks such as Billingsley (1986) or Feller (1971) will suffice for understanding the general ideas. The mathematician should also note that, for simplicity, we will ignore all refinements associated with the fact that the conditional expectation is uniquely defined only up to probability 1. Hence, the proofs of the theorems will be simplified. The exact proofs may be found in Steyer (1992).

4. See Note 3.

References

Bauer, H. (1981). *Probability theory and elements of measure theory.* New York: Academic Press.

Bentler, P. M. (1980). Multivariate analysis with latent variables: Causal modeling. *Annual Review of Psychology, 31,* 419-456.

Billingsley, P. (1986). *Probability and measure* (2nd ed.). New York: John Wiley.

Campbell, D. T. (1957). Factors relevant to the validity of experiments in social settings. *Psychological Bulletin, 54,* 297-312.

Campbell, D. T., & Stanley, J. C. (1963). Experimental and quasi-experimental designs for research on teaching. In N. L. Gage (Ed.), *Handbook on research on teaching* (pp. 171-246). Chicago: Rand McNally.

Cliff, N. (1983). Some cautions concerning the application of causal modeling methods. *Multivariate Behavioral Research, 18,* 115-126.

Cook, T. D., & Campbell, D. T. (1979). *Quasi-experimentation: Design and analysis issues for field settings.* Boston: Houghton Mifflin.

Cook, T. D., & Campbell, D. T. (1986). The causal assumptions of quasi-experimental practice. *Synthese, 68,* 141-180.

Davis, W. A. (1988). Probabilistic theories of causality. In J. H. Fetzer (Ed.), *Probability and causality* (pp. 133-160). Dordrecht: Reidel

Deegan, J. (1974). Specification error in causal models. *Social Science Research, 3,* 235-259.

de Leeuw, J. (1985). Reviews of confirmatory factor analysis: A preface to LISREL by J. S. Long; Covariance structure models: An introduction to LISREL by J. S. Long; An introduction to latent variable models by B. S. Everitt; and Causal modeling in nonexperimental research by W. Saris & H. Stronkhorst. *Psychometrika, 50,* 371-375.

Dudley, R. M. (1989). *Real analysis and probability.* Belmont, CA: Wadsworth/Brooks/Cole.

Erdfelder, E., & Bredenkamp, J. (in press). Hypthesenprüfung [Testing of hypotheses]. In W. H. Tack & T. Herrmann (Eds.), *Enzyklopädie der Psychologie. Themenbereich B: Methodologie und Methoden. Serie 1: Forschungsmethoden der Psychologie. Band 1: Methodologische Grundlagen der Psychologie.* Göttingen: Hogrefe.

Feller, W. (1971). *An introduction to probability theory and its applications.* New York: John Wiley.

Fetzer, J. H. (Ed.). (1988). *Probability and causality.* Dordrecht: Reidel.

Freedman, D. A. (1987). As others see us: A case study in path analysis. *Journal of Educational Statistics, 12,* 101-128.

Goldberger, A. S. (1973). Structural equation models: An overview. In A. S. Goldberger & O. D. Duncan (Eds.), *Structural equation models in the social sciences* (pp. 1-18). New York: Seminar Press.

Hausman, J. A. (1978). Specification tests in econometrics. *Econometrica, 46,* 1251-1271.

Hausman, J. A., & McFadden, D. (1984). Specification tests for the multinomial logit model. *Econometrica, 52,* 1219-1240.

Hocking, R. R. (1974). Misspecification in regression. *American Statistician, 28,* 39-40.

Holland, P. (1986). Statistics and causal inference (with comments). *Journal of the American Statistical Association, 81,* 945-970.

Holland, P. W. (1988). Causal inference in retrospective studies. *Evaluation Review, 13,* 203-231.

Holland, P. W., & Rubin, D. B. (1983). On Lord's paradox. In H. Wainer & S. Messick (Eds.), *Principles of modern psychological measurement* (pp. 3-25). Hillsdale, NJ: Lawrence Erlbaum.

Holly, A. (1982). A remark on Hausman's specification test. *Econometrica, 50,* 749-759.

Jöreskog, K. G., & Sörbom, D. (1993). *LISREL 8. User's reference guide.* Chicago: Scientific Software International.

Kenny, D. A. (1975). A quasi-experimental approach to assessing treatment effects in the nonequivalent control group design. *Psychological Bulletin, 82,* 345-362.

Kenny, D. A. (1979). *Correlation and causality.* New York: John Wiley.

Kinal, T., & Lahiri, K. (1983). Specification error analysis with stochastic regressors. *Econometrica, 51,* 1209-1219.

Lazarus, R. S., & Cohen, J. B. (1977). *Coping questionnaire. The hassles scale. The uplift scale.* Unpublished paper. University of California, Berkeley.

Leamer, E. E. (1978). *Specification searches.* New York: John Wiley.

Lee, S., & Hershberger, S. (1990). A simple rule for generating equivalent models in covariance structure modeling. *Multivariate Behavioral Research, 25,* 313-334.

Magidson, J. (1977). Toward a causal model approach for adjusting for preexisting differences in the nonequivalent control group situation: A general alternative to ANCOVA. *Evaluation Quarterly, 1,* 399-420.

Mauro, R. (1990). Understanding L.O.V.E. (Left Out Variables Error): A method for estimating the effects of omitted variables. *Psychological Bulletin, 108,* 314-329.

Mulaik, S. A. (1987). Toward a conception of causality applicable to experimentation and causal modeling. *Child Development, 58,* 18-32.

Müller, P. H. (Hrsg.) (1975). *Lexikon der Stochastik* [Lexicon of stochastics] (2nd ed.). Berlin: Akademie-Verlag.

Newey, W. K. (1985). Maximum likelihood specification testing and conditional moment tests. *Econometrica, 53,* 1047-1070.

Novick, M. R. (1980). Statistics as psychometrics. *Psychometrika, 45,* 411-424.

Ramsey, J., & Schmidt, P. (1976). Some further results on the use of OLS and BLUS residuals in specification error tests. *Journal of the American Statistical Association, 71,* 389-390.

Reichardt, C. S. (1979). The statistical analysis of data from nonequivalent group designs. In T. D. Cook & D. T. Campbell (Eds.), *Quasi-experimentation: Design and analysis issues for field settings* (pp. 147-205). Boston: Houghton Mifflin.

Rogosa, D. R. (1987). Casual models do not support scientific conclusions: A comment in support of Freedman. *Journal of Educational Statistics, 12,* 185-195.

Rosenbaum, P. R. (1984a). From association to causation in observational studies: The role of tests of strongly ignorable treatment assignment. *Journal of the American Statistical Association, 79,* 41-48.

Rosenbaum, P. R. (1984b). Conditional permutation tests and the propensity score in observational studies. *Journal of the American Statistical Association, 79,* 565-574.

Rosenbaum, P. R. (1984c). The consequences of adjustment for a concomitant variable that has been affected by the treatment. *Journal of the Royal Statistical Society, Series A, 147,* 656-666.

Rosenbaum, P. R., & Rubin, D. B. (1983a). Assessing sensitivity to an unobserved binary covariate in an observational study with binary outcome. *Journal of the Royal Statistical Society, Series B, 45,* 212-218.

Rosenbaum, P. R., & Rubin, D. B. (1983b). The central role of the propensity score in observational studies for causal effects. *Biometrika, 70*, 41-55.

Rosenbaum, P. R., & Rubin, D. B. (1984). Reducing bias in observational studies using subclassification on the propensity score. *Journal of the American Statistical Association, 79*, 516-524.

Rosenbaum, P. R., & Rubin, D. B. (1985a). The bias due to incomplete matching. *Biometrics, 41*, 103-116.

Rosenbaum, P. R., & Rubin, D. B. (1985b). Constructing a control group using multivariate matched sampling methods that incorporate the propensity score. *The American Statistician, 39*, 33-38.

Rubin, D. B. (1973a). Matching to remove bias in observational studies. *Biometrics, 29*, 159-183.

Rubin, D. B. (1973b). The use of matched sampling and regression adjustment to remove bias in observational studies. *Biometrics, 29*, 185-203.

Rubin, D. B. (1974). Estimating causal effects of treatments in randomized and nonrandomized studies. *Journal of Educational Psychology, 66*, 688-701.

Rubin, D. B. (1977). Assignment of treatment group on the basis of a covariate. *Journal of Educational Statistics, 2*, 1-26.

Rubin, D. B. (1978). Bayesian inference for causal effects: The role of randomization. *The Annals of Statistics, 6*, 34-58.

Rubin, D. B. (1985). The use of propensity scores in applied Bayesian inference. *Bayesian Statistics, 2*, 463-472.

Rubin, D. B. (1986). Which ifs have causal answers. *Journal of the American Statistical Association, 81*, 961-962.

Rubin, D. B. (1990). Comment: Neyman (1923) and causal inference in experiments and observational studies. *Statistical Science, 5*, 472-480.

Schmitt, M. J., & Steyer, R. (1990). Beyond intuition and classical test theory: A reply to Epstein. *Methodika, 4*, 101-107.

Schmitt, M. J., & Steyer, R. (1993). A latent state-trait model (not only) for social desirability. *Personality and Individual Differences, 14*, 519-529.

Simpson, E. H. (1951). The interpretation of interaction in contingency tables. *Journal of the Royal Statistical Society, Series B, 13*, 238-241.

Skyrmes, B., & Harper, W. L. (Eds.). (1988). *Causation, chance, and credence.* Dordrecht: Kluwer.

Sobel, M. E. (1982). Asymptotic confidence intervals for indirect effects in structural equation models. In S. Leinhardt (Ed.), *Sociological methodology (1982)* (pp. 290-312). San Francisco: Jossey-Bass.

Sobel, M. E. (1986). Some new results on indirect effects and their standard errors in covariance structure models. In N. A. Tuma (Ed.), *Sociological methodology (1986)* (pp. 159-186). San Francisco: Jossey-Bass.

Sobel, M. E. (1992). *Causation and spurious correlation: A reexamination.* Unpublished manuscript, University of Arizona, Tucson.

Spohn, W. (1980). Stochastic independence, causal independence, and shieldability. *Journal of Philosophical Logic, 9*, 73-99.

Spohn, W. (1983). Deterministic and probabilistic reasons and causes. *Erkenntnis, 19*, 371-396.

Spohn, W. (1990). Direct and indirect causes. *Topoi, 9*, 125-145.

Spohn, W. (1991). A reason for explanation: Explanations provide stable reasons. In W. Spohn, B. C. van Fraasen, & B. Skyrmes (Eds.), *Existence and explanation* (pp. 165-196). Dordrecht: Kluwer.

Spohn, W. (in press). On Reichenbach's principle of the common cause. In W. C. Salmon & G. Wolters (Eds.), *Proceedings of the First Pittsburgh-Konstanz Colloquium.* Pittsburgh, PA: Pittsburgh University Press.

Stegmüller, W. (1983). *Erklärung, Begründung, Kausalität* [Explanation, giving reason, causality] (Probleme und Resultate der Wissenschaftstheorie und Analytischen Philosophie, Band I.). Berlin: Springer-Verlag.

Stelzl, I. (1985). Changing a causal hypothesis without changing fit: Some rules for generating equivalent path models. *Multivariate Behavioral Research, 21,* 309-331.

Steyer, R. (1984). Causal linear stochastic dependencies: The formal theory. In E. Degreef & J. van Buggenhaut (Eds.), *Trends in mathematical psychology* (pp. 317-346). Amsterdam: North-Holland.

Steyer, R. (1985a). Causal regressive dependencies: An introduction. In J. R. Nesselroade & A. von Eye (Eds.), *Individual development and social change: Explanatory analysis* (pp. 95-124). Orlando, FL: Academic Press.

Steyer, R. (1985b). The conditionally randomized experiment and the concept of conditional weak causal regressive dependence. *Trierer Psychologische Berichte, 12*(9), 1-36.

Steyer, R. (1985c). The randomized experiment and the concept of weak causal regressive dependence. *Trierer Psychologische Berichte, 12*(5), 1-40.

Steyer, R. (1988). Conditional expectations: An introduction to the concept and its applications in empirical sciences. *Methodika, 2,* 1-26.

Steyer, R. (1992). *Theorie kausaler Regressionsmodelle* [Theory of causal regression models]. Stuttgart: Gustav Fischer Verlag.

Steyer, R. (in press-a). Principles of causal modeling: A summary of its mathematical foundations and practical steps. In F. Faulbaum (Ed.), *SoftStat '93. Advances in statistical software 4.* Stuttgart: Gustav Fischer Verlag.

Steyer, R. (in press-b). Stochastische Modelle [Stochastic models]. In W. H. Tack & T. Herrmann (Hrsg.), *Methodologische Grundlagen der Psychologie. (Enzyklopädie der Psychologie. Themenbereich B: Methodologie und Methoden, Serie 1: Forschungsmethoden der Psychologie, Band 1).* Göttingen: Hogrefe.

Steyer, R. (in press-c). The theory of causal regression models. I: The randomized experiment and causal regressive in/dependence. Paper submitted to *Journal of Mathematical Psychology.*

Steyer, R., & Eid, M. (1993). *Messen und Testen.* [Measurement and testing]. Berlin: Springer-Verlag.

Steyer, R., Ferring, D., & Schmitt, M. J. (1992). States and traits in psychological assessment. *European Journal of Psychological Assessment, 8,* 79-98.

Steyer, R., Majcen, A-M., Schwenkmezger, P., & Buchner, A. (1989). A latent state-trait anxiety model and its application to determine consistency and specificity coefficients. *Anxiety Research, 1,* 281-299.

Steyer, R., & Schmitt, M. J. (1990a). The effects of aggregation across and within occasions on consistency, specificity, and reliability. *Methodika, 4,* 58-94.

Steyer, R., & Schmitt, M. J. (1990b). Latent state-trait models in attitude research. *Quality and Quantity, 24,* 427-445.

Steyer, R., Schwenkmezger, P., & Auer, A. (1990). The emotional and cognitive components of trait anxiety: A latent state-trait anxiety model. *Personality and Individual
Differences, 11,* 125-134.

Suppes, P. (1970). *A probabilistic theory of causality.* Amsterdam: North-Holland.

Weisberg, H. I. (1979). Statistical adjustments and uncontrolled studies. *Psychological
Bulletin, 86,* 1149-1164.

White, H. (1980a). A heteroscedasticity-consistent covariance matrix estimator and a
direct test for heteroscedasticity. *Econometrica, 48,* 817-838.

White, H. (1980b). Nonlinear regression on cross-section data. *Econometrica, 48,* 721-
746.

White, H. (1981). Consequences and detection of misspecified nonlinear regression
models. *Journal of the American Statistical Association, 76,* 419-433.

White, H. (1982). Maximum likelihood estimation of misspelled models. *Econometrica,
50,* 1-25.

White, H., & Domowitz, I. (1984). Nonlinear regression with dependent observations.
Econometrica, 52, 143-161.

Wold, H.O.A. (1954). Causality and econometrics. *Econometrica, 22,* 162-177.

Wold, H.O.A. (1956). Causal inference from observational data. *Journal of the Royal
Statistical Society, Series A, 119,* 28-61.

Wold, H.O.A. (1958). A case study of interdependent versus causal chain systems. *Review
of the International Statistical Institute, 26,* 5-25.

Wold, H.O.A. (1959). Ends and means in econometric model building. In U. Grenander
(Ed.), *Probability and statistics. The Harald Cramér volume* (pp. 355-434). New York:
John Wiley.

Wold, H.O.A. (1960). A generalization of causal chain models. *Econometrica, 28,*
443-463.

Wold, H.O.A. (1969). Mergers of economics and philosophy of science. *Synthese, 20,*
427-482.

Wright, S. (1918). On the nature of size factors. *Genetics, 3,* 367-374.

Wright, S. (1921). Correlation and causation. *Journal of Agricultural Research, 20,*
557-585.

Wright, S. (1923). The theory of path coefficients—A reply to Niles' criticism. *Genetics,
8,* 239-255.

Wright, S. (1934). The method of path coefficients. *Annals of Mathematical Statistics, 5,*
161-215.

Wright, S. (1960a). Path coefficients and path regressions: Alternative or complementary
concepts? *Biometrics, 16,* 189-202.

Wright, S. (1960b). The treatment of reciprocal interaction, with or without lag, in path
analysis. *Biometrics, 16,* 423-445.

3

The Specification of Equivalent
Models Before the Collection of Data

SCOTT L. HERSHBERGER

Advances within structural equation modeling have provided researchers with a valuable device for confirming their theories or models. Yet a failure to disconfirm a hypothesized model is not conclusive evidence for the veracity of the model; indeed, other models may exist that fit the data as well or better. This chapter is concerned with equivalent models, models that fit the data as well as the hypothesized model, and how equivalent models may be identified prior to the collection of data. Before the process of data collection begins, it behooves the researcher to know exactly how many models are competing with the hypothesized model. If the competition is too great due to the existence of a multitude of equivalent models, consideration must be given to revising the hypothesized model to reduce the possible number of competing equivalent models. Importantly, the revision of the hypothesized model may necessitate the alteration of the original data collection design by, for example, requiring the collection of data on an additional set of variables. If reducing the number of equivalent models requires changing the design of the study, the researcher would be most benefited by knowledge of the equivalent models as early in the study as possible before effort has been expended in collecting incomplete data.

Equivalent models occur when the parameters estimated for the models imply identical expected correlation or covariance matrices. If there are two models, M1 and M2, and a sample covariance matrix, S, the parameters estimated for models M1 and M2 will imply covariance matrices $\tilde{\Sigma}_{M1}$ and $\tilde{\Sigma}_{M2}$, respectively. M1 and M2 are considered equivalent if and only if $\tilde{\Sigma}_{M1} = \tilde{\Sigma}_{M2}$, or more generally, $(S - \tilde{\Sigma}_{M1}) = (S - \tilde{\Sigma}_{M2})$. Models M1 and M2 are in this sense statistically equivalent, producing the same value for goodness-of-fit measures. On occasion two models will provide a statistically equivalent fit to the data without implying the same covariance matrix. This may occur simply through rounding of the chi-square goodness-of-fit value. When two models do not imply the same covariance matrix, they are not considered equivalent. Truly equivalent models should be predictable from the initially proposed model. The subject of this chapter is the identification of equivalent models before the stage of modeling where goodness-of-fit indices are calculated. While a nuisance in selecting a best-fitting model, numerically identical goodness-of-fit indices arrived at by happenstance result from the idiosyncracies of the sample covariance matrix and not generally through statistically indistinguishable models.

Equivalent models may imply very different conceptualizations of the data, and are thus differentiable at the theoretical level; but at the statistical level, there is a problem of indeterminacy in the selection of a "true" model. Due to this indeterminacy, parallels between the issues of model equivalence and identification can be drawn. When a model is unidentified, unique estimates of some or all of the parameters are unavailable; when equivalent models exist, a model cannot be specified to uniquely represent the data. Further, if a model is not identified, then models equivalent to it will also not be identified; on the other hand, the existence of equivalent models does not necessarily imply anything about the identification status of the equivalent models. It is generally true, however, that given two models with the same number of observed variables, the more restricted of the two will more likely be identified and will more likely have fewer equivalent models. Just-identified models present a worst case situation of model equivalence. Just-identified models may be perfectly fit to any covariance matrix, thus providing no test of a hypothesized model. Due to their parameter saturation, just-identified models will also have the greatest number of equivalent models, allowing for a number of parameter respecifications while still implying the same covariance matrix.

Although the existence of equivalent models is critical to the process of theory construction and testing, equivalent models appear to have been little acknowledged and investigated, a profound problem given their pervasively hidden presence in the psychological literature (Breckler,

1990; MacCallum, Wegener, Uchino, & Fabrigar, 1993). Equivalent models are common within the natural sciences as well. Glymour (1980) discusses the problems presented by a number of Newtonian models that make identical predictions from different equation systems. Model equivalence is also not specific to structural equation modeling with covariance structures; undoubtedly model equivalence exists for mean, kurtotic, and other moment structures, although I am unaware of any research directly addressing this issue. Equivalent models are certainly not specific to structural equation modeling as a technique. As MacCallum et al. (1993) point out, the multidimensional scaling models for three-way proximity data presented by Tucker (1972) and Carroll and Chang (1972) are very different representations of individual differences in judgment tasks, yet both models will equivalently fit a set of data.

An early example of the explicit specification of equivalent models occurs with the method of reverse paths commonly used in behavior genetic analyses (Wright, 1968). It is often of interest in behavior genetic research to incorporate the correlation between spouses for a trait in a path model. Because the trait is typically an endogenous variable that is a function of exogenous latent genetic and environmental variables, it is difficult to explicitly include the spousal correlation for the trait in the path model. The method of reverse paths literally reverses the functional relationship between the observed trait and latent variables, producing a model equivalent to the initial one. Two equivalent models are shown in Figures 3.1a and 3.1b. Another procedure that introduces the spousal correlation into the path model is the method of co-paths (part c of Figure 3.1) (Carey, 1986). This model will also be an equivalent model. Duncan (1969) also presented nine distinct models that were equally consistent with the data, arguing for the preeminence of substantive over statistical rationale for model selection.

These early examples illustrate an awareness of equivalent models, but the first systematic research concerned with equivalent models was performed by Stelzl (1986), who proposed four rules for the generation of equivalent recursive structural models. The four rules correspond to four types of revisions one could perform on the structural portion of a model to produce equivalent models: (1) the permutation of a causal sequence among a set of variables; (2) the addition or deletion of variables from a causal sequence; (3) the replacement of a directed path between two variables with their residual correlation; and (4) the replacement of correlated residuals with a directed path.

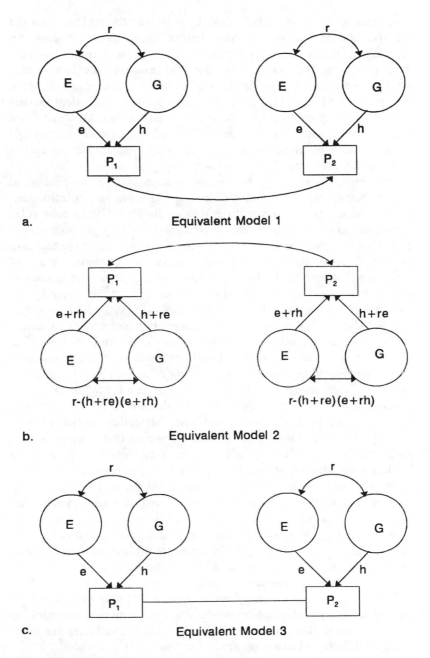

a.   Equivalent Model 1

b.   Equivalent Model 2

c.   Equivalent Model 3

Figure 3.1. Three Equivalent Models of Genetic and Environmental Influences on a Spousal Correlation

A critical aspect of Stelzl's (1986) work was the emphasis on the specification of equivalent models before the collection of data. An alternative approach to the identification of equivalent models occurs during the stage of model estimation. For example, Luijben (1991) gives the necessary and sufficient conditions for identical modification indices or Lagrange multiplier statistics to produce equivalent models upon the subsequent freeing of the relevant parameters. Although value lies in the detection of equivalent models during the data analysis stage of research, equivalent models are preferably detected at an earlier point in the research.

The emphasis in this chapter is on the identification of equivalent models before the collection of data. The *replacing rule* is introduced as a generalization and simplification of Stelzl's (1986) four rules applicable to the structural portion of a model with or without nonrecursive paths. The variables may be latent or observed. As in the case of Stelzl's rules, the replacing rule is predictive of the existence of models equivalent to the hypothesized model, not requiring data to discover the equivalent models at some later stage of the research. The basis for the replacing rule's ability to generate equivalent models is shown to be its respect for the partial correlation and tetrad constraints in the originally hypothesized model. Then, model equivalence within measurement models is discussed with reference to the *reversed indicator rule*. As in the case of the replacing rule, the reversed indicator rule relies upon model specifications and not data for the discovery of equivalent models. Three empirical examples are presented at the end of the chapter, illustrating the importance of detecting equivalent models and the ability of the replacing and reversed indicator rules to detect such models. The discussions of equivalent structural and measurement models have been separated, largely due to the general independence of parameter estimation in these two portions of a structural model (e.g., Anderson & Gerbing, 1988). Nonetheless, hypothesized models that produce equivalent models through the respecification of both the measurement and structural portions are certainly weaker theoretically than models that produce equivalent models through the alteration of only one of the two portions. In addition, the equivalent models discussed here all have the same number of parameters; Luijben (1991) cites a theorem from topology due to Brouwer (1911) that places the possibility of equivalent models with different numbers of free parameters into doubt. Throughout the chapter, measured variables are interchangeably referred to as "observed" or "indicator" variables.

Replacing Rule and Structural Models

The four rules developed by Stelzl (1986) for completely recursive structural models may be simplified and extended to models with nonrecursive relationships by use of the replacing rule (Lee & Hershberger, 1990). (Lee and Hershberger also formally demonstrate how the replacing rule subsumes Stelzl's four rules.) Before the replacing rule is defined, it is necessary to define several terms. A structural model may be divided into three sections or blocks: A *preceding block*, a *focal block*, and a *succeeding block*. The focal block includes the relationships we are interested in altering to produce an equivalent model; the preceding block consists of all the variables in the model that causally precede the variables in the focal block; and the succeeding block consists of all the variables in the model that causally succeed the variables in the focal block. Within the econometrics literature, the division of a structural model into blocks, where recursiveness obtains between and within blocks, is termed a block recursive system (Kmenta, 1971). For the application of the replacing rule, a fully recursive block model is not required. What the replacing rule does require may be termed *limited block recursiveness*. In a limited block recursive model, the relations between the blocks and within the focal block are recursive; however, relationships within the preceding and succeeding blocks may be nonrecursive. (Under certain conditions discussed below, relationships within the focal block may be nonrecursive. For now, we will assume a fully recursive focal block.)

The replacing rule may be defined as follows. Let X and Y represent two variables in a focal block, where X and Y within the focal block stand in the relationship $X \rightarrow Y$; X is a source variable and Y is an effect variable in the focal block. Both X and Y receive paths from other variables in the preceding and focal blocks, and they may also send paths to other variables in the succeeding block. Let U_X and U_Y represent the residuals of X and Y. According to the replacing rule, the directed path between X and Y (i.e., $X \rightarrow Y$) may be replaced by their residual covariance (i.e., $U_X \leftrightarrow U_Y$) if the predictors of the effect variable Y are the same as or include those of the source variable X. Thus, the directed path $X \rightarrow Y$ may be replaced by the residual covariance $U_X \leftrightarrow U_Y$ provided the specified conditions are satisfied. The reverse application of the replacing rule will also produce an equivalent model. A residual covariance, $U_X \leftrightarrow U_Y$, may be replaced by a directed path, $X \rightarrow Y$ or $X \leftarrow Y$, when the predictors of the effect variable are the same as or include those of the source variable following the replacement.

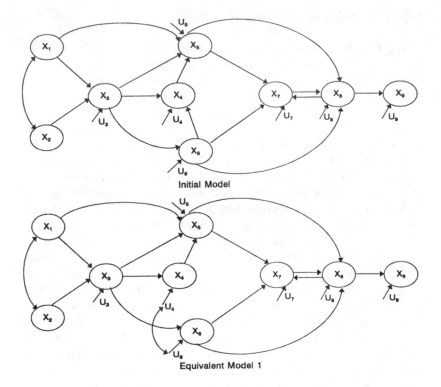

Figure 3.2a. An Example of the Generation of Equivalent Structural Models Using the Replacing Rule

An example of a model to which the replacing rule can be applied is shown in Figure 3.2.

In Figure 3.2, within the initial model, variables X_1, X_2, and X_3 will be defined as the preceding block, variables X_4 and X_6 as the focal block, and variables X_5, X_7, X_8, and X_9 as the succeeding block. Within the focal block, the directed path $X_6 \rightarrow X_4$ may be replaced by the residual covariance $U_6 \leftrightarrow U_4$: the predictor X_3 influences both the source (X_6) and effect (X_4) variables in the focal block. This application of the replacing rule is shown in Model 1, a model equivalent to the initial model. This example also illustrates an important special case of the replacing rule, wherein both the source and effect variables have the same predictors. In this situation, the variables in the focal block are symmetrically determined, and it is a matter of statistical indifference

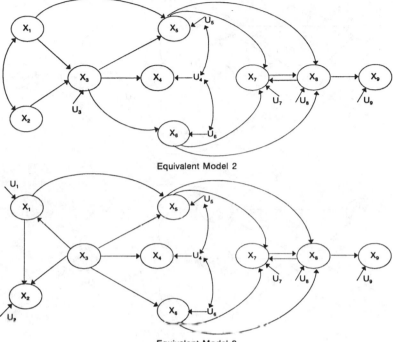

Equivalent Model 2

Equivalent Model 3

Figure 3.2b. An Example of the Generation of Equivalent Structural Models Using the Replacing Rule

if the directed path between the source and effect variables is reversed or replaced by a residual covariance. The source and effect variables are said to be in a *symmetric focal block.*

Frequently, applications of the replacing rule will give rise to additional opportunities to generate equivalent models, opportunities that were not present prior to the alteration produced by the replacing rule. For example, let a new focal block be defined as consisting of X_4 and X_5, with X_4 as the source variable and X_5 as the effect variable. Within the initial model, application of the replacing rule to this focal block is not possible because both X_4 and X_5 have one predictor not shared with the other. After the alteration to the relationship between X_4 and X_6 shown in Model 1, however, the effect variable X_5 has as one of its predictors the only predictor (X_3) of the source variable X_4. In equiva-

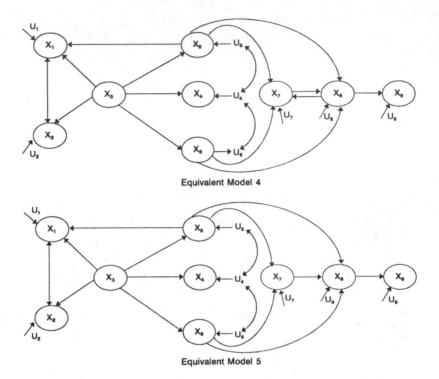

Figure 3.2c. An Example of the Generation of Equivalent Structural Models Using the Replacing Rule

lent Model 2, the directed path $X_4 \rightarrow X_5$ has been replaced by the residual covariance $U_4 \leftrightarrow U_5$. This example also illustrates that focal blocks are not invariantly defined within a structural model: Any two variables within the same model may be designated as part of a focal block if the focal block meets the requirements of the replacing rule. For instance, neither $X_3 \rightarrow X_4$, $X_5 \rightarrow X_7$, nor $X_6 \rightarrow X_7$ may be defined as a focal block for the application of the replacing rule: The source variable in all three cases has predictors not shared with the effect variable, and in addition, defining $X_5 \rightarrow X_7$ or $X_6 \rightarrow X_7$ as the focal block would necessitate defining a succeeding block (X_8 and X_9) nonrecursively connected to a focal block.

Another special case of the replacing rule occurs when a preceding block is completely saturated—all variables are connected by either directed paths or residual covariances. In this case, the preceding block is defined as a focal block, and any residual covariance/directed path replacement yields an equivalent model. The replacing rule may be applied whenever the necessary conditions are met; the existence of a preceding or a succeeding block is not absolutely necessary. In the initial model, variables X_1, X_2, and X_3 are designated as a focal block. The results of applying the replacing rule to this just-identified, saturated focal block are shown in Model 3. In Model 3, $X_1 \leftrightarrow X_2$ has been replaced by $X_1 \rightarrow X_2$, $X_1 \rightarrow X_3$ has been replaced by $X_1 \leftarrow X_3$, and $X_2 \rightarrow X_3$ has been replaced by $X_2 \leftarrow X_3$. Further, application of the replacing rule to this focal block has provided yet another heretofore unavailable opportunity to generate an equivalent model. Variables X_1 and X_5 now define a symmetric focal block, thus permitting the substitution of $X_1 \rightarrow X_5$ by $U_1 \leftrightarrow U_5$ or $X_1 \leftarrow X_5$, of which the latter substitution is shown in Model 4.

Symmetric focal blocks also provide a basis for generating equivalent models when two variables are nonrecursively connected. Whenever two nonrecursively connected variables define a symmetric focal block (have all their predictors in common), the nonrecursive path between them may be replaced by a single directed path or a residual covariance. Of course, initially, the nonrecursive paths are equated due to the impossibility of uniquely identifying each path when both variables have the same predictors. The converse of this rule holds as well: Directed paths or residual covariances within a symmetric focal block may be replaced by equated nonrecursive paths. In Model 4, let $X_7 \leftrightarrow X_8$ be a focal block where $X_7 \rightarrow X_8 = X_7 \leftarrow X_8$, then $X_7 \leftrightarrow X_8$ may be replaced by either $X_7 \rightarrow X_8$, $X_7 \leftarrow X_8$, or $U_7 \leftrightarrow U_8$. Model 5 presents a model equivalent to all the prior models, where now $X_7 \rightarrow X_8$. Thus, under the special circumstance of a symmetric focal block, the replacing rule can be applied to nonrecursive paths. The equivalence of equated nonrecursive paths to a single directed path or a residual covariance in a symmetric focal block provides a method by which the spousal correlation may be incorporated in a behavior genetic model. Referring back to Figure 3.1a, the variables P_1 and P_2 form a symmetric focal block, with predictors E and G. The covariance between P_1 and P_2, not permitted between endogenous variables within a structural model, may be replaced, with equated paths, by the equivalent specification, $P_1 \leftrightarrow P_2$. To a certain extent, the method of co-paths, shown in Figure 3.1c, implicitly exploits the equivalence of equated nonrecursive paths to a single directed path or residual covariance within a symmetric focal block, through its "double pass through" structure.

It is interesting to note that if, in Model 4, $X_8 \leftarrow X_9$ instead of $X_8 \rightarrow X_9$, X_7 and X_8 would not have defined a symmetric focal block, thus preventing application of the replacing rule. In the alternative circumstance where X_9 is an additional predictor of X_8, X_9 would have held the position of an instrumental variable allowing the nonconstrained estimation of the nonrecursive paths between X_7 and X_8. Instrumental variables are an example of a more general strategy within structural equation modeling for the reduction of equivalent models: To the degree that variables in a model do not share predictors, the number of equivalent models will be reduced. Symmetric focal blocks exemplify the model equivalence difficulties that arise when focal block variables share all their predictors, and just-identified preceding blocks illustrate the problem even more so. In general, constraining the number of free parameters within a model will have a salutary effect on the problem of model equivalence. For example, in the initial model, by not stipulating $X_1 \rightarrow X_4$, potential equivalent models were prevented from occurring (e.g., based on Model 3, such a specification would have allowed the generation of equivalent models from the directed path $X_3 \rightarrow X_4$). Conversely, the specification of a completely saturated focal block (i.e., the focal block of X_1, X_2, and X_3) produced a number of equivalent models. As it is, the equivalent models presented in Figure 3.2 do not describe all the possible equivalent models in the class of models equivalent to the initial model.

Partial Correlations and Equivalent Models

One reason why the replacing rule works as a method for discovering equivalent models is the retention of the partial correlation structure among both the observed and latent variables in the model. Although equivalent models can differ dramatically in how the set of variables hypothesized to affect an endogenous variable are configured, the same endogenous variable across the equivalent models must be influenced ultimately by the same set of variables. In the construction of equivalent models, a variable previously unassociated with an endogenous variable cannot be introduced as a source of variation in the endogenous variable.

For example, in order to show how the replacing rule substitutes a residual covariance for a directed path while maintaining the partial correlation structure of the initial model, assume $X \rightarrow Y$ within a focal block, with predictor variables $(P_1, \ldots, P_m)$ and $(Q_1, \ldots, Q_n)$ in a preceding block. Let the structural equations of X and Y be:

$$X = F(P_1, \ldots, P_m) + u, \qquad [3.1]$$

$$Y = G(P_1, \ldots, P_m) + H(Q_1, \ldots, Q_n) + bX + v, \qquad [3.2]$$

where u is the residual of X, v is the residual of Y, $u \leftrightarrow v$ is zero, and F, G, H, b represent path coefficients, and all variables are measured from their means. Deleting $X \rightarrow Y$ implies the following alteration for the structural equation for Y:

$$Y = G(P_1, \ldots, P_m) + H(Q_1, \ldots, Q_n) + b(P_1, \ldots, P_m + u) + v, \quad [3.3]$$

$$Y = J(P_1, \ldots, P_m) + H(Q_1, \ldots, Q_n) + b(u + v), \text{ or} \qquad [3.4]$$

$$Y = J(P_1, \ldots, P_m) + H(Q_1, \ldots, Q_n) + e, \qquad [3.5]$$

where J represents the changed values of the path coefficients. Removing the directed path $X \rightarrow Y$ induces a nonzero covariance between the residual covariance of X and Y:

$$\text{COV}(u, e) = \text{COV}(u, bu + v) = b\text{VAR}(u) + 0 \neq 0. \qquad [3.6]$$

Importantly, this replacement has not altered the partial correlation structure of the model; both X and Y have the same predictors both before and after application of the replacing rule. Further, the statistical equivalence of the parameter substitution is substantiated by the identical expectation for the covariance between X and Y that can be derived from either Equations 3.1 and 3.2, or Equations 3.1 and 3.5.

Note that the replacing rule was applicable to the above case because the predictors of Y included all the predictors of X $(P_1, \ldots, P_m)$. If this were not so, application of the replacing rule would alter the partial correlation structure of the initial model, producing a nonequivalent model. Specifically, again assume $X \rightarrow Y$ within a focal block, and now let the structural equations of X and Y be:

$$X = F(P_1, \ldots, P_m) + H(Q_1, \ldots, Q_n) + u, \qquad [3.7]$$

$$Y = G(P_1, \ldots, P_m) + bX + v, \qquad [3.8]$$

where all terms are as before and $u \leftrightarrow v$ is still zero. Deleting $X \to Y$ implies the following alteration for the structural equation for Y:

$$Y = G(P_1, \ldots, P_m) + b(P_1, \ldots, P_m + Q_1, \ldots, Q_n + u) + v, \qquad [3.9]$$

or

$$Y = J(P_1, \ldots, P_m) + K(Q_1, \ldots, Q_n) + e, \qquad [3.10]$$

where J and K represent the changed values of the path coefficients. Removing the directed path $X \to Y$ induces a nonzero covariance between the residual covariance of X and Y, as before (Equation 3.6 is still true), but it also induces a correlation between Y and the set of predictors $Q_1, \ldots, Q_n$. The initial model is no longer equivalent to the revised model, as can be shown by the inequality between the covariance of X and Y calculated by Equations 3.7 and 3.8, or 3.7 and 3.9. From the covariance algebra it is clear that for the replacing rule to produce equivalent models, the effect variable must have at least the same preceding block predictors as the source variable.

The importance of maintaining the partial correlation structure of the variables for the generation of equivalent models may further be demonstrated by evaluating the expectations for the correlations among the variables implied by the model of Figure 3.3.

If all variables are standardized, the path model in Figure 3.3 implies the following expectations for the correlations:

$$\text{Corr}_{A,B} = c. \qquad [3.11]$$

$$\text{Corr}_{A,Y} = a_2 + bc. \qquad [3.12]$$

$$\text{Corr}_{A,X} = a_1. \qquad [3.13]$$

$$\text{Corr}_{B,Y} = b + a_2 c. \qquad [3.14]$$

$$\text{Corr}_{B,X} = a_1 c. \qquad [3.15]$$

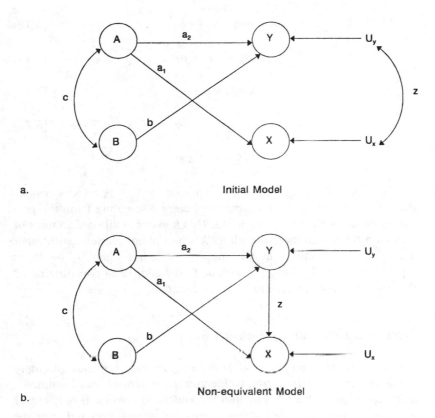

a.   Initial Model

b.   Non-equivalent Model

Figure 3.3. An Example Illustrating the Importance of Retaining the Partial Correlation Constraints for the Generation of Equivalent Models

$$\text{Corr}_{X,Y} = z + a_1 a_2 .$$ [3.16]

The relationship between X and Y is represented by the residual correlation z. If variables A and B form a preceding block and variables X and Y a focal block, then the residual correlation between X and Y may be replaced by $X \rightarrow Y$ without altering the structure of the partial correlations implied by the initial model. However, the substitution of z by $X \leftarrow Y$ alters the structure of the implied partial correlations:

$$\text{Corr}_{A,B} = c .$$ [3.17]

$$\text{Corr}_{A,Y} = a_2 + bc \,. \tag{3.18}$$

$$\text{Corr}_{A,X} = a_1 + a_2 z \,. \tag{3.19}$$

$$\text{Corr}_{B,Y} = b + a_2 c \,. \tag{3.20}$$

$$\text{Corr}_{B,X} = a_1 c + bz \,. \tag{3.21}$$

$$\text{Corr}_{X,Y} = z + a_1 a_2 \,. \tag{3.22}$$

When the residual correlation is replaced by $X \leftarrow Y$, no longer does the effect variable have the same predictors originating from the preceding block as the source variable. This induces additional sources of variation for X, and therefore alters X's partial correlations with other variables. In the initial model $\text{Corr}_{(B,X).A} = 0$, but when $U_X \leftrightarrow U_Y$ is replaced by $X \leftarrow Y$, $\text{Corr}_{(B,X).A} \neq 0$ due to the additional contribution of the path bz to the correlation between B and X.

Tetrad Equalities and Equivalent Models

In order for two or more models to be equivalent, they must all imply the same correlational constraints. Identical partial correlation constraints, a necessary and sufficient condition for model equivalence, is only one of a number of different types of constraints that may be imposed upon the correlational pattern. The product of correlations is another type of constraint, the best known example of which are *tetrad equalities*.

Let $X_1, X_2, X_3,$ and X_4 be a set of four standardized variables, although tetrad equalities are applicable to nonstandardized variables as well. Six correlations may be computed from four variables. In order to form tetrads, the correlations are taken, two at a time, and multiplied, in order to form three inequivalent products:

$$\text{Corr}_{X_1,X_2} \times \text{Corr}_{X_3,X_4} \tag{3.23}$$

$$\text{Corr}_{X_1,X_3} \times \text{Corr}_{X_2,X_4} \tag{3.24}$$

$$\text{Corr}_{X_2,X_3} \times \text{Corr}_{X_1,X_4} \tag{3.25}$$

From these correlation products, three independent tetrad equalities can be formed:

$$\text{Corr}_{X_1,X_2} \times \text{Corr}_{X_3,X_4} = \text{Corr}_{X_1,X_3} \times \text{Corr}_{X_2,X_4} \qquad [3.26]$$

$$\text{Corr}_{X_1,X_2} \times \text{Corr}_{X_3,X_4} = \text{Corr}_{X_2,X_3} \times \text{Corr}_{X_1,X_4} \qquad [3.27]$$

$$\text{Corr}_{X_1,X_3} \times \text{Corr}_{X_2,X_4} = \text{Corr}_{X_2,X_3} \times \text{Corr}_{X_1,X_4} \qquad [3.28]$$

Within a model, any or all of the tetrad equalities may be implied.

A relationship exists between the tetrad equalities and partial correlations implied by a model: The pattern of partial correlations among a set of four variables implies the equality of certain tetrads (Glymour, Scheines, Spirtes, & Kelly, 1987). Specifically, for the partial correlations to imply a tetrad equality, each of the four correlations involved in the tetrad equality must be equal to zero when the same third variable is partialled from each correlation. The best known example of this situation is Spearman's g factor theory of intelligence, wherein the correlations among a set of cognitive measures are due to the influence of a single intellective factor. Partialling out the influence of g removes the correlations among the cognitive measures.

Figure 3.4 provides an example of the tetrad equalities implied by partial correlation constraints. There is one tetrad equality implied by the model:

$$\text{Corr}_{X_1,X_3} \times \text{Corr}_{X_2,X_4} = \text{Corr}_{X_1,X_4} \times \text{Corr}_{X_2,X_3} , \qquad [3.29]$$

$$(ab)(d + bc) = (ad + abc)(b) . \qquad [3.30]$$

The path model in Figure 3.4a implies the following two partial correlations:

$$\text{Corr}_{(X_1,X_4).X_2} = 0 , \qquad [3.31]$$

$$\text{Corr}_{(X_1,X_3).X_2} = 0 . \qquad [3.32]$$

In addition, the following two partial correlations are true by definition:

$$\text{Corr}_{(X_2,X_4).X_2} = 0 , \qquad [3.33]$$

$$\text{Corr}_{(X_2,X_3).X_2} = 0 . \qquad [3.34]$$

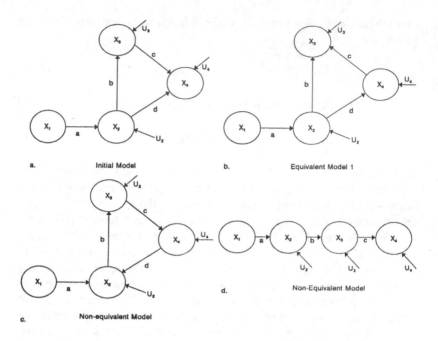

a.   **Initial Model**   b.   **Equivalent Model 1**

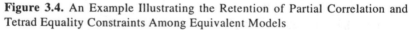

c.   **Non-equivalent Model**   d.   **Non-Equivalent Model**

Figure 3.4. An Example Illustrating the Retention of Partial Correlation and Tetrad Equality Constraints Among Equivalent Models

Note that the tetrad equality of Equation 3.29 consists of four correlations that vanish when the same third variable (X_2) is partialled from them. Conversely, neither of the other two tetrad equalities are implied by the model, because except for the "true by definition" partial correlations (e.g., $Corr_{(X_2,X_3).X_2} = 0$), not all of the correlations involved in the two tetrad equalities vanish when conditioned upon the same third variable.

The model shown in Figure 3.4b is equivalent to the model of Figure 3.4a. According to the replacing rule, $X_3 \rightarrow X_4$ may be replaced by $X_3 \leftarrow X_4$ (a symmetric focal block). Both models imply the same partial correlation and tetrad equality constraints. On the other hand, the model of Figure 3.4c, by substituting $X_2 \rightarrow X_4$ by $X_2 \leftarrow X_4$, violates the focal block symmetry requirement, and is therefore not equivalent to Figures 3.4a and 3.4b, destroying both the required partial correlation and tetrad constraints.

Although equivalent models imply the same constraints on the pattern of tetrad equalities, the converse does not necessarily hold: The identical patterns of tetrad equalities do not necessarily imply equivalent models. A simple demonstration of this is shown by the model of Figure 3.4d. Although Figures 3.4a, 3.4b, and 3.4d all imply the same tetrad equality, the partial correlation constraints have been altered. The model of Figure 3.4d is not equivalent to either Figures 3.4a, 3.4b, or 3.4c. Identical tetrad equalities are a necessary but not sufficient condition for model equivalence. Note too that the degrees of freedom of Figure 3.4d differs from that of the other models.

Equivalent models imply identical constraints upon the pattern of correlations, whether these constraints be first- or higher order partial correlations, or tetrad or higher order correlation products (e.g., pentads). Because the retention of the partial correlation constraints is a necessary and sufficient condition for model equivalence, the discovery of equivalent models should be guided generally by the structure of the partial correlations, and not, for example, by tetrad equalities or other types of correlation products. Correlation products will almost always be more difficult to specify than partial correlations, and only provide a necessary condition for model equivalence.

The Reversed Indicator Rule and Measurement Models

Measurement models within structural equation modeling are factor analytic models, but with an important difference from traditional (exploratory) factor analysis models. As is well known, the traditional factor analysis model is underidentified, with the resulting factor pattern subject to an infinite number of rotational solutions. Therefore, an infinite number of equivalent solutions exist. On the other hand, the specific (confirmatory) pattern of factor loadings obtained within structural equation modeling is at least just-identified (or should be) and is unique up to and including rotation. For a given set of variables, and a hypothesized factor structure, the problem of equivalent measurement models would appear not to be problematic. However, model equivalence is still very much an issue for two reasons.

First, the pattern of intercorrelations among a set of observed variables may indicate both the existence of a factor common to all the variables and the existence of two or more distinct factors nested within the general common factor. For example, the basic measurement model

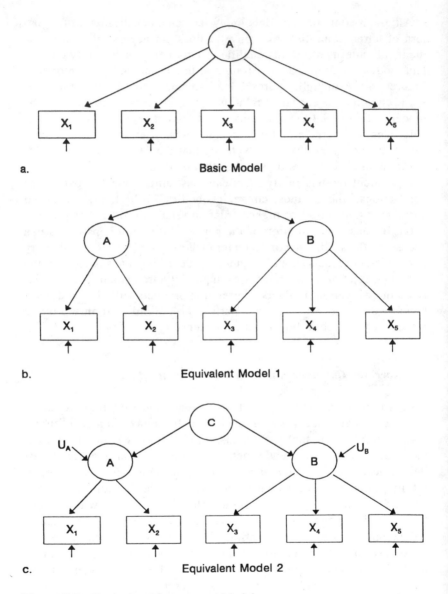

a.   Basic Model

b.   Equivalent Model 1

c.   Equivalent Model 2

Figure 3.5a. Equivalent Measurement Models

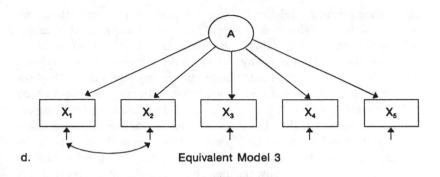

d.   Equivalent Model 3

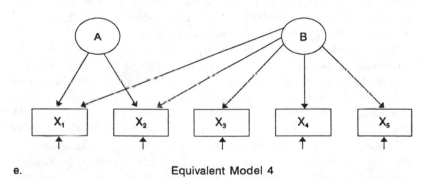

e.   Equivalent Model 4

Figure 3.5b. Equivalent Measurement Models

in Figure 3.5 depicts a single common factor indicated by five observed variables. Assume that this model was tested on a set of data and rejected, the rejection apparently stemming from a high correlation between X_1 and X_2, a correlation high relative to X_1 and X_2's correlation with the other three variables. In order to represent the relatively high correlation between X_1 and X_2, the researcher may specify any one of four equivalent measurement models. These four equivalent models are shown in Figure 3.5b through 3.5e. If tested against a set of data, identical fit statistics would be obtained for each model. Each equivalent measurement model also implies the same partial correlations and tetrad equalities. Whenever a significant but unanalyzed correlation occurs between two variables, the potential for model equivalence increases due to the many ways in which the source of the unanalyzed correlation may be represented. Another factor may be specified (Figures 3.5b, 3.5c, and 3.5e), or the correlation between the two variables may be left as a residual covariance (Figure 3.5d). If the additional factor representation is selected, the choice then becomes whether the association between the two factors will be represented by an unanalyzed correlation (Figure 3.5b), a higher order factor (Figure 3.5c), or shared indicators (Figure 3.5e). Obviously, how the unanalyzed correlation is represented is based upon substantive theory and not statistical fit. Indeed, an analogy can be drawn (although the circumstances under which the two situations occur differs) between the interchangeability of a directed path and a residual covariance, and the interchangeability of a newly specified, correlated factor and a residual covariance. Dillon and Kumar (1985) considered the equivalence of similar measurement models arising from the statistical interchangeability of correlated factors and residual covariances in the context of attitude-behavior relations.

The second reason why model equivalence will be a problem for measurement models is described by the *reversed indicator rule.* According to the reversed indicator rule, the direction of a path between a latent variable and an observed variable is arbitrary for one and only one latent-observed variable path in an exogenous measurement model, and therefore, this path may be reversed. In addition, a single recursive path may also be replaced by equated nonrecursive paths. Reversing the direction of the path, or replacing the recursive path with equated nonrecursive paths, results in an equivalent model. Two requirements exist, in addition to the reversal of only one indicator, for application of the reversed indicator rule. One, the measurement model should be completely exogenous or affected by only one indicator before and after the rule's application, and two, the exogenous latent variable must be uncorrelated with other exogenous latent variables before and after the rule's application.

In Figure 3.6, three equivalent measurement models are presented. These three models, statistically equivalent by the reverse indicator rule, imply very different conceptualizations. In Figure 3.6a, in the initial model, a latent variable exerts a common effect on a set of observed indicators: individual differences on the latent variable are reflected by individual differences on all four indicators. For example,

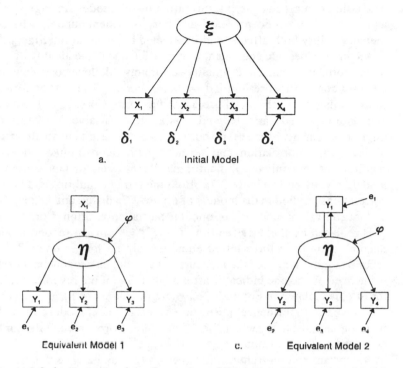

a.   Initial Model

h   Equivalent Model 1   c.   Equivalent Model 2

Figure 3.6. An Example of the Generation of Equivalent Measurement Models Using the Reversed Indicator Rule

if the latent variable were general intelligence, and the observed indicators memory, verbal, quantitative, and logical reasoning tests, variation in general intelligence should cause variation in all four cognitive measures. In contrast, in Figure 3.6b, variation in a latent variable is caused by variation in a observed indicator. The latent variable itself, as in Figure 3.6a, causes variation in its three observed indicators. Thus, if observed indicator X_1 was the memory test, the model of Figure 3.6b implies that memory affects general intelligence, which itself is still an influence on verbal, quantitative, and logical reasoning ability. Note that now memory ability is not affected by general intelligence; rather memory affects cognitive performance. Memory ability is still correlated with the other ability tests through the common association with general intelligence. Bollen and Lennox (1991) provide a detailed discussion contrasting the interpretation of the models in Figure 3.6a and 3.6b. Figure 3.6c presents another equivalent model, whereby memory ability both affects, and is affected by, general intelligence.

All three models are equivalent in Figure 3.6 due to the identity of their partial correlation and tetrad equality constraints. All three possible tetrad equality constraints are implied by these models. The partial correlations implied by each model are all of the form, $\text{Corr}_{(if).F} = 0$, where i and j are observed variables and F is a latent variable. Violating the three requirements of the reversed indicator rule results in an alteration of the partial correlation and tetrad equality constraints. The first requirement, that only one indicator may be reversed for a measurement model, is violated in Figure 3.7a. Both the tetrad equalities and partial correlations implied in the models of Figure 3.7a differ, and hence, they are not equivalent models. For one, the partial correlation, $\text{Corr}_{(x_1,x_2).\xi} = 0$, is replaced by the specification, $\text{Corr}_{x_1,x_2} = 0$, in the second model. Second, two of the three tetrad equalities are no longer implied. The second requirement, that the measurement model be exogenous, or only influenced by the one indicator after application of the reversed indicator rule, is violated in Figure 3.7b, where the indicator Y_2 (now X_3) has been reversed to influence η. Because a measurement model ξ precedes η in the causal chain, when the Y_2 indicator is reversed, Y_2's partial correlation with ξ disappears (η was the original covariate), replaced by a constant zero correlation between Y_2 (X_3) and ξ. The structure of the tetrad equalities has been altered as well. For the third requirement, examination of Figure 3.7c shows why the measurement model to which the reversed indicator is to be applied must be uncorrelated with other exogenous measurement models. Reversing the direction of X_1 produces an effect identical to the reversal of Y_2 in Figure 3.7b: X_1's partial correlation with ξ_2 (i.e., $\text{Corr}_{(x_1,\xi_2).\xi_1} = 0$) is replaced by the nonequivalent specification, $\text{Corr}_{x_1,\xi_2} = 0$. Again, the tetrad equalities differ between the two models.

Identifying equivalent measurement models before the data collection stage of research, most critically when theories are in the process of formation or hypotheses are first advanced, is as important as identifying equivalent structural models. Quite reasonably, the identification of equivalent measurement can be deemed even more important, due to the natural priority of the measurement models over the structural relations among the measurement models. A structural model cannot link legitimately ill-conceived measurement models.

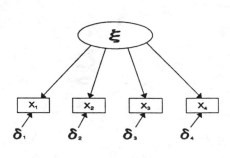
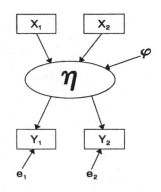

a.

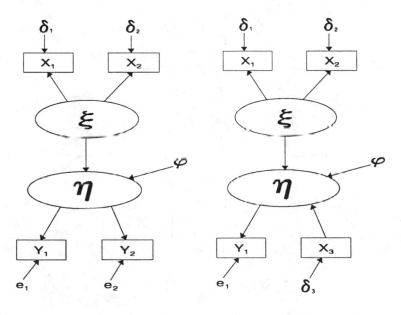

b.

Figure 3.7a, b. Violations of the Requirements of the Reversed Indicator Rule Leading to Nonequivalent Models

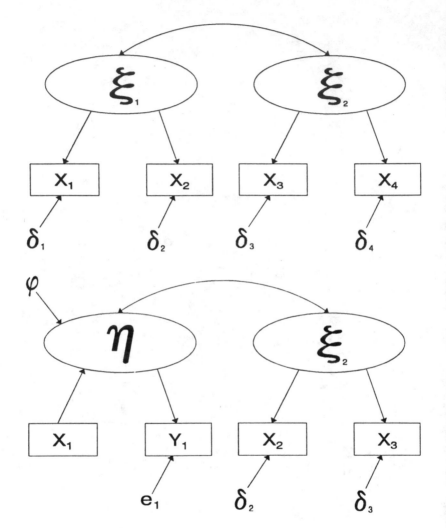

C.

Figure 3.7c. Violations of the Requirements of the Reversed Indicator Rule Leading to Nonequivalent Models

Summary of Rules for Specifying Equivalent Models

Before three empirical examples are discussed showing the importance of identifying equivalent models, a summary of the rules for specifying equivalent models is in order.

Structural Model

The Replacing Rule—General Case. Given a directed path between two variables, $X \rightarrow Y$ in a focal block, the directed path may be replaced by the residual covariance, $U_X \leftrightarrow U_Y$, if:

1. Only recursive paths exist between blocks;
2. Only recursive paths exist within a focal block (condition may be relaxed when the block is a symmetric focal block); and
3. The predictors of the effect variable are the same as or include those for the source variable.

Replacing Rule—Symmetric Focal Blocks. Given a directed path between two variables, $X \rightarrow Y$ in a focal block, the directed path may be replaced by the residual covariance, $U_X \leftrightarrow U_Y$, or $X \leftarrow Y$, or $X \Leftrightarrow Y$, if:

1. Only recursive paths exist between blocks;
2. When the original specification is replaced by a nonrecursive relation, the two paths are equated; and
3. The source and effect variables have the same predictors.

Replacing Rule—Just-Identified Preceding Block. Given a directed path between two variables, $X \rightarrow Y$, in a focal block that is a just-identified preceding block, the directed path may be replaced by the residual covariance, $U_X \leftrightarrow U_Y$, or $X \leftarrow Y$, or $X \Leftrightarrow Y$, if:

1. Only recursive paths exist between the preceding (focal) block and succeeding block; and
2. When the original specification is replaced by a nonrecursive relation, the two paths are equated.

By definition, the variables of a just-identified block are symmetrically determined; a just-identified preceding (focal) block is a symmetric focal block.

Measurement Model

The Reversed Indicator Rule. Given a directed path between a latent variable and an observed indicator, $\eta \to Y$, the directed path may be replaced by $\eta \leftarrow Y$, or $\eta \Leftrightarrow Y$, if:

1. Only the directed path for one indicator for each measurement model is altered;
2. The latent variable is affected by a single indicator, or is completely exogenous, before and after application of the rule;
3. The latent variable is uncorrelated with other exogenous latent variables; and
4. When the original specification is replaced by a nonrecursive relation, the two paths are equated.

For any model consisting of both measurement and structural portions, the model equivalence rules may be applied to both portions, as long as the requirements of the rules for both are met.

Empirical Examples

Structural Model of Social Support and College Graduation

The first example is based upon a study of racial differences in perceived social support in a university environment and its effect on graduation (Hershberger & D'Augelli, 1992). Figure 3.8 shows a variation of a path model presented by the authors of the study. According to this model, racial difference in the probability of graduation is mediated by precollege performance, how close the student's relationship is to family and friends, and the degree of perceived social support and well-being. The standardized values of the path coefficients have been included in the path diagram. For clarity, the measurement models of the latent variables of this path model have not been included; as pointed out earlier, alterations to the structural model will generally not have an effect on the parameter values in the measurement model.

Three potential focal blocks exist in the initial model of Figure 3.8 that will allow the application of the replacing rule. The first focal block is the directed path between race and precollege performance; this focal block can be considered a just-identified, preceding block. Two revi-

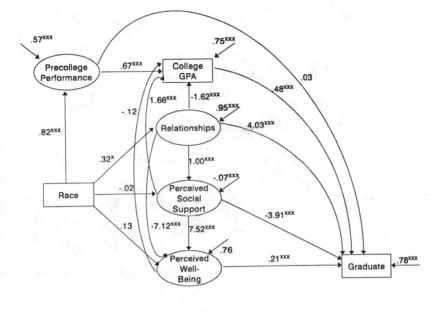

Initial Model

Figure 3.8. Initial Model for Example 1

sions are possible for the relationship between race and precollege performance: The directed path from race to precollege performance may be reversed or a residual correlation may be specified. Only the latter substitution is sensible. The second focal block consists of the directed paths among relationships, perceived social support, and perceived well-being. This focal block is a symmetric focal block, for each of three latent variables has the same predictor from the preceding block, race. Thus any (or all) of the directed paths may be reversed or replaced with correlated residuals. Indeed, 32 equivalent models could be generated from this focal block (7 alterations resulting in the reversal of the directed paths, 7 alterations resulting in correlated residuals, and 18 from their combinations). The extreme problem of model equivalence that this focal block creates could be greatly ameliorated if, for example, the directed (and nonsignificant) path between race and perceived social support were removed. Only 2 equivalent models would remain of the 32: The directed path in the perceived social support →

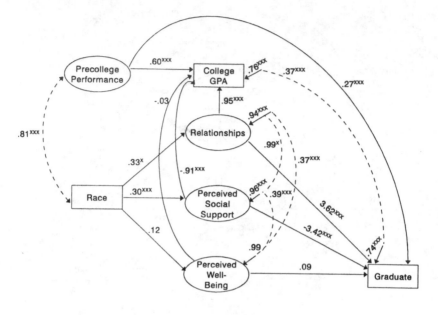

Equivalent Model

Figure 3.9. Equivalent Model for Example 1

perceived well-being focal block could be replaced by a residual covariance, as could the directed path in the relationships → perceived
well-being focal block. The third focal block, which is another example
of a symmetric focal block, is the directed path between college grade
point average (GPA) and graduate. Both college GPA and graduate have
as their source relationships, perceived social support, and perceived
well-being, the latent variables of the preceding block. Of the two
equivalent models possible from this focal block, the specification of
correlated residuals is the only logical choice.

Figure 3.9 presents a model equivalent to the initial model of Figure
3.10, with the new values of the standardized path coefficients. Those
sections of the equivalent model that have undergone revision from the
initial model are represented by dashed lines. This equivalent model
emphasizes the tenuousness of causal statements based simply upon the
discovery of a significant directed path in a structural model. In the
initial model, race had a direct effect upon variation in precollege

performance, yet the undirected correlation between the two variables, arising from unknown sources outside the model, does as well in fitting the data. In addition, the ability of the researcher to unambiguously assert the directionality of the paths among relationships, perceived social support, and perceived well-being is called into question by the now present residual correlations among these latent variables. The directed path between college GPA and graduate in the initial model has been replaced by a residual correlation as well.

Also apparent in the equivalent model are changes in the magnitude, sign, and significance of paths *outside* the revised focal blocks. In the initial model, the directed path between race and perceived social support was $-.02$ and not significant; in the equivalent model this path is $.30, p < .001$. The path between precollege performance and graduate in the initial model had been $.03$ and not significant; in the equivalent model this same path is $.27, p < .001$. A comparable situation exists for the path between perceived well-being and graduate, which initially had been $.21, p < .001$, but upon revision of the model, becomes $.09$, n.s. The two most dramatic path changes occur for relationships $\rightarrow$ college GPA, and perceived social support $\rightarrow$ college GPA, where the paths remain significant but change sign: In the former case, the path changes from 1.66 to -0.91; in the latter, from -1.62 to 0.95. Although equivalent models ultimately imply identical correlations among observed variables, the paths that produce these correlations can be of varying magnitude, sign, and significance.

Structural Model of the Development of Sexual Preference in Males

The next example, an adaptation of a model presented by Bell, Weinberg, and Hammersmith (1981), is concerned with the developmental antecedents of sexual preference in males. Data were obtained from a retrospective interview with adult participants, and all variables in the model were observed. One of the benefits of developmental models, from the perspective of reducing the number of equivalent models, lies in the logical time precedence of age-related events. Thus, for example, in the initial model of Figure 3.10, events occurring in childhood precede events occurring in adolescence, both of which precede adult homosexuality. Even if it were possible to obtain an equivalent model by reversing the directionality between two of these age groups, such a revision would be highly questionable. Within a particular age group, however, the directionality among the variables is less well defined, and as shown in a model

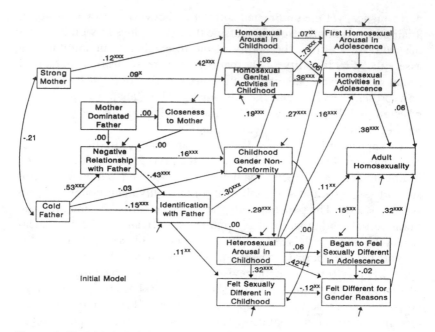

Figure 3.10. Initial Model for Example 2

equivalent to the model of Figure 3.10, nonrecursive specifications frequently fit the data as well as recursive specifications.

Figure 3.11 presents a model equivalent to the initial model of Figure 3.10. Altered structural relationships are again indicated by dashed lines, and standardized path coefficients have been included. Recursive paths have been replaced by nonrecursive paths at four locations in the model where symmetric focal blocks exist. For example, in the initial model it was hypothesized that a strong mother was correlated with a cold father, the source of this correlation remaining outside the model. On the other hand, the nonrecursive paths between these two variables in the equivalent model suggest these respective characteristics of mothers and fathers are promoted by the other spouse. Further, homosexual arousal, in the initial model, was hypothesized to influence homosexual activities, both in childhood and adolescence. The equivalent model substitutes a nonrecursive relationship between arousal and activities, again suggesting the reciprocal promotion of one variable by another. Perhaps the most interesting theoretical change between the two models occurs for the "childhood gender nonconformity—identifi-

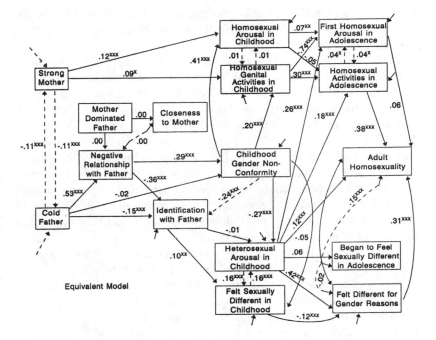

Figure 3.11. Equivalent Model for Example 2

cation with father" relationship. As implied by the initial model, the authors of the study assume that a failure to identify with a father will contribute to gender nonconformity for males. At least for the initial model presented here, this directed path may be reversed to suggest that gender nonconformity itself may lead to a failure to identify, possibly through rejection by the father or through the child's lack of interest in the father as a gender model. The replacement of two directed paths in the initial model with residual correlations emphasizes the uncertainty of causality inherent in nonexperimental data. For example, "began to feel sexually different in adolescence" may well be a causal factor in adult homosexuality, but even more likely, the association between the variables arises through the common effects of other, unspecified variables.

Measurement and Structural Model of Depression

In the third empirical example, the reversed indicator rule is applied to a measurement model of depression; then the depression measurement model is embedded within a structural model for application of the replacing rule. Data for this example were obtained from the Swedish Adoption/Twin Study of Aging (Pedersen, McClearn, Plomin, Nesselroade, Berg, & de Faire, 1991).

Bollen and Lennox (1991), in the context of a paper concerned with the appropriate theoretical and psychometric circumstances for the specification of "effect" versus "causal" indicators for a measurement model, question the purely causal indicator specification implied by the construction of the Center for Epidemiological Studies Depression Scale (CES-D; Radloff, 1977). That is, the construction and analysis of this scale implies that a latent variable of depression is hypothesized to "effect" an individual's response to each of the 20 self-report items of the CES-D, as opposed to the behaviors assessed by the items "causing" an individual's level of depression. For example, one CES-D item, "I felt lonely," may be an effect of depression, but it may also reasonably be thought of as a cause of depression.

Figure 3.12 illustrates an effect indicator measurement model of depression, with the five CES-D depressed mood subscale items. Application of the reversed indicator rule to this initial model of depression results in the transformation of one item, in this case "felt lonely," to the status of a causal indicator, as shown in Figure 3.12 as equivalent model 1. Equivalent model 2 goes one step further and specifies a nonrecursive relationship between loneliness and depression.

Next, the equivalent measurement model 2 of Figure 3.12 is, in Figure 3.13a, embedded within an initial structural model of the effects of depression on the latent variables life satisfaction and job satisfaction, whose effect indicators are not shown for reasons of clarity. Life satisfaction and job satisfaction form a symmetric focal block, thus allowing the replacement of their residual correlation with a directed path from life satisfaction to job satisfaction in equivalent model 1. An interesting statistical change has occurred with the path alteration between the initial and equivalent models: In the initial model, greater depression is significantly associated with lower job satisfaction, but in equivalent model 1, greater depression is significantly associated with greater job satisfaction. On the other hand, in equivalent model 2 in Figure 3.13b, with the reversal of the directed path between job and life satisfaction found in model 1, the results of the initial model are replicated. When, as in equivalent model 3, a nonrecursive specification is given between life and job satisfaction, the relationship between depression and job satisfaction becomes nonsignificant. Therefore, equivalent models not only provide theoretical alternatives to an initial

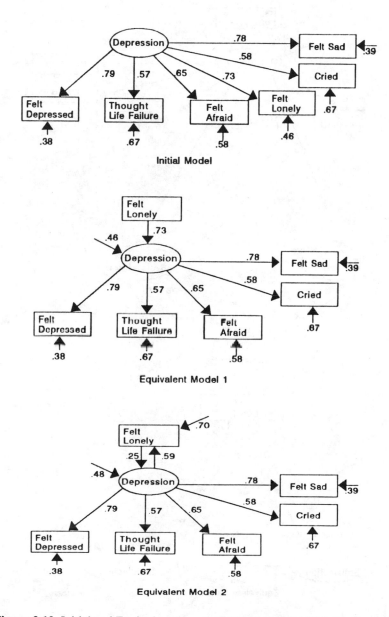

Figure 3.12. Initial and Equivalent Measurement Models for Example 3

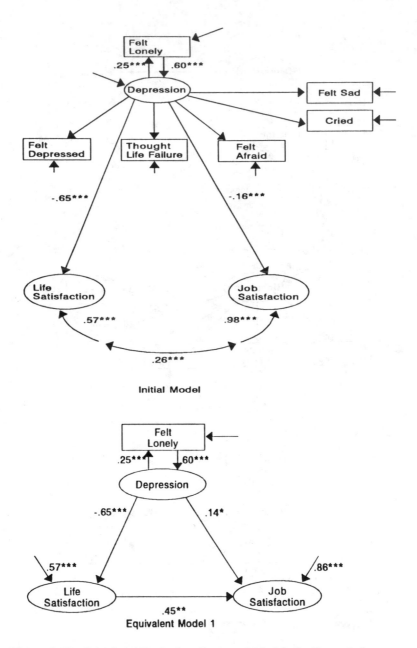

Figure 3.13a. Initial and Equivalent Structural Models for Example 3

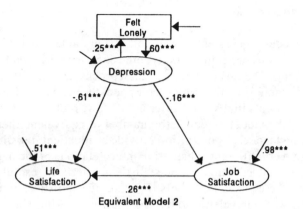

Equivalent Model 2

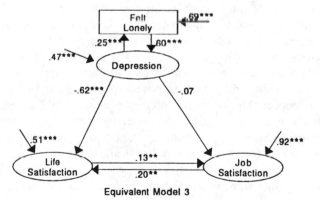

Equivalent Model 3

Figure 3.13b. Equivalent Structural Models for Example 3

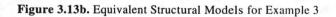

model through deliberate path respecifications, but through statistical changes in nonaltered paths as well.

Concluding Remarks

When models equivalent to a hypothesized model exist, the already difficult task of confirming the hypothesized model is rendered even more difficult. The earlier in the research process equivalent models are identified, therefore, the better equipped the researcher will be to confront this potentially fatal inferential flaw, preferably through the revision of the model to reduce the number of equivalent alternatives.

Equivalent models by definition provide an identical statistical fit but may imply very different substantive interpretations of the data. Nonetheless, there are occasions when statistical criteria are useful in deciding among the equivalent models. For one, the statistical assumptions underlying the equivalent models may differ. Karlin, Cameron, and Chakraborty (1983) point out that the method of reverse paths introduces statistical constraints not present in the initial, unreversed model. Secondly, experience has shown that the number of iterations to reach a final solution can differ dramatically among equivalent models, and more often than not, the most iteratively difficult model is the most theoretically unlikely. But most often the selection of a model from a family of equivalent models will be predicated on the researcher's assumptions and knowledge concerning the phenomena under investigation. Perhaps the greatest benefit of identifying equivalent models lies in the ensuing obligation imposed on the researcher to gather further evidence, external to the preferred model itself, to justify the researcher's selection. For example, referring back to the measurement model of depression, experimental evidence could be collected to test the direction of effects between loneliness and depression. Such experimental evidence would resolve the direction of effects issue and simultaneously enhance our knowledge of the causes and consequences of depression.

References

Anderson, J. C., & Gerbing, D. W. (1988). Structural equation modeling in practice: A review and recommended two-step approach. *Psychological Bulletin, 103,* 411-423.

Bell, A. P., Weinberg, M. S., & Hammersmith, S. K. (1981). *Sexual preference: Its development in men and women.* Bloomington: Indiana University Press.

Bollen, K., & Lennox, R. (1991). Conventional wisdom on measurement: A structural equation perspective. *Psychological Bulletin, 110,* 305-314.

Breckler, S. J. (1990). Applications of covariance structure modeling in psychology: Cause for concern? *Psychological Bulletin, 107,* 260-273.

Brouwer, L.E.J. (1911). Beweis der invarianz der dimensionenzahl [Proof of the invariance of the number of dimensions]. *Mathematische Anaalen, 70,* 161-165.

Carey, G. (1986). A general multivariate approach to linear modeling in human genetics. *American Journal of Human Genetics, 39,* 775-786.

Carroll, J. D., & Chang, J. J. (1972, June). *IDIOSCAL (individual differences in orientation SCALing): A generalization of INDSCAL allowing IDIOsyncratic reference systems as well as analytic approximation to INDSCAL.* Paper presented at the meeting of the Psychometric Society, Princeton, NJ.

Dillon, W. R., & Kumar, A. (1985). Attitude organization and the attitude-behavior relation: A critique of Bagozzi and Burnkrant's reanalysis of Fishbein and Ajzen. *Journal of Personality and Social Psychology, 49,* 33-46.

Duncan, O. D. (1969). Some linear models for two-wave, two-variables panel analysis. *Psychological Bulletin, 72,* 177-182.

Glymour, C. (1980). *Theory and evidence.* Princeton, NJ: Princeton University Press.

Glymour, C., Scheines, R., Spirtes, P., & Kelly, K. (1987). *Discovering causal structure: Artificial intelligence, philosophy of science, and statistical modeling.* New York: Academic Press.

Hershberger, S. L., & D'Augelli, A. R. (1992). The relationship of academic performance and social support to graduation among African American and white university students: A path-analytic model. *Journal of Community Psychology, 20,* 188-199.

Karlin, S., Cameron, E. C., & Chakraborty, R. (1983). Path analysis in genetic epidemiology: A critique. *American Journal of Human Genetics, 35,* 695-732.

Kmenta, J. (1971). *Elements of econometrics.* New York: Macmillan.

Lee, S., & Hershberger, S. (1990). A simple rule for generating equivalent models in covariance structure modeling. *Multivariate Behavioral Research, 25,* 313-334.

Luijben, T.C.W. (1991). Equivalent models in covariance structure modeling. *Psychometrika, 56,* 653-665.

MacCallum, R. C., Wegener, D. T., Uchino, B. N., & Fabrigar, L. R. (1993). The problem of equivalent models in applications of covariance structure analysis. *Psychological Bulletin, 114,* 185-199.

Pedersen, N. L., McClearn, G. E., Plomin, R., Nesselroade, J. R., Berg, S., & de Faire, U. (1991). The Swedish Adoption/Twin Study of Aging: An update. *Acta Geneticae Medicae et Gemellologiae, 33,* 243-250.

Radloff, L. S. (1977). The CES-D Scale: A self-report depression scale for research in the general population. *Applied Psychological Measurement, 1,* 385-401.

Stelzl, I. (1986). Changing a causal hypothesis without changing the fit: Some rules for generating equivalent path models. *Multivariate Behavioral Research, 21,* 309-331.

Tucker, L. R. (1972). Relations between multidimensional scaling and three-mode factor analysis. *Psychometrika, 37,* 3-27.

Wright, S. (1968). *Evolution and the genetics of populations: Vol. 1. Genetic and biometric foundations.* Chicago: University of Chicago Press.

PART 2

Analysis of Latent Variables in Developmental Research: Continuous Variables Approaches

4

The Effect of Unmeasured Variables and Their Interactions on Structural Models

PHILLIP K. WOOD

Failure to include relevant predictor variables in linear models makes interpretation of parameter estimates from such mis-specified models difficult. Freedman (1987), for example, uses examples of such model mis-specification errors as the basis for a general critique of structural equation modeling (although, curiously, not extending this critique to include regression and analysis of variance). In contrast, researchers and methodologists have paid relatively little attention to the possible effects of unmeasured interactions on estimated linear models. Limitations of inference based on mis-specified models in the presence of unmeasured interactions are often dealt with only marginally (Daniel & Wood, 1980) or even left to the reader as exercises (Hanushek & Jackson, 1977). While such unmeasured variables can often lead to uninterpretable parameter estimates, common opinion regarding this problem is that such an effect is not detectable given only the data from the mis-specified model. Common opinion regarding the effects of

AUTHOR'S NOTE: Preparation of this chapter was supported in part by the Fund for the Improvement of Post-Secondary Education Grant #P116B00926 subcontract to Phillip Wood.

Correspondence concerning this chapter should be addressed to Phillip Wood, Department of Psychology, University of Missouri-Columbia MO 65211.

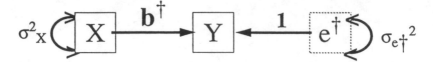

Figure 4.1. Underspecified Regression Model Employing One Criterion

unmeasured interactions is that such relationships do not affect interpretations of parameter estimates of the obtained linear model in any substantial way.

A Path Diagram Example of Model Mis-Specification

This chapter examines the effects of such unmeasured variables and their interactions from a structural equations perspective. For example, for the case of a single predictor variable, researchers familiar with the RAM conventions for structural equation path models (McArdle, 1980) can compare the underspecified model shown in Figure 4.1 (which estimates performance on Y based only on X) with a true model of the phenomenon shown in Figure 4.2, where the endogenous variable Y is a function of three predictors, X, U and an interaction term, UX. Throughout the chapter the superscript, †, is used to indicate a parameter associated with the mis-specified model of Figure 4.1.

Scatterplot Examples of Model Mis-Specification

For the simplest case where the unmeasured variable U is a dichotomous variable, two plausible scatterplots of X, U with Y are shown in Figure 4.3. In the top figure, the regression slope of X with Y is lower for those individuals for which $U = -1$ than for individuals for whom $U = 1$. The dashed line, labeled $b^\dagger$, is used to indicate the regression weight for the mis-specified model.

Under an interaction model, this type of relationship can occur when there is a main effect for U and X as well as a significant contribution of the interaction vector, UX. In unbalanced designs, such as those frequently encountered in regression and other structural equation models, such a graphic relationship could also exist if there is a main effect for U, a main effect for X, and a positive covariance between U and X. Such a graphic relationship is given in the top half of Figure 4.3. The bottom half of this figure shows a second possible relationship between X, U,

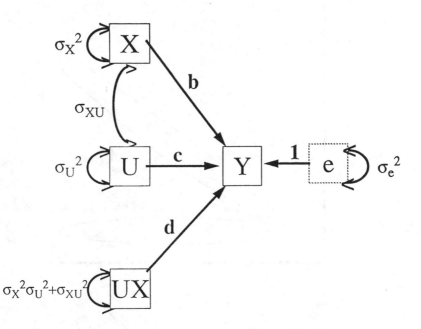

Figure 4.2. True Fully Specified Model Employing an Interaction Effect

and Y. In this figure, the relationship between X and Y is positive or negative, depending on the sign of U. For this situation, there is no main effect due to X, but a significant main effect for U and the interaction vector, UX.

The structural relationships portrayed in Figures 4.1 and 4.2 are not limited to path analytic models with a single dichotomous unmeasured variable such as those shown in Figure 4.3. The unmeasured variable U could also be taken to be an unmeasured continuous variable. In addition, the bias of regression weights associated with X and the diagnostics for testing for an unmeasured interaction can be easily extended to situations where the unmeasured variable U is a multicategory variable, resulting in the U variable being replaced by a design matrix conveying group membership in the figure. In addition, any of the X, U, or Y variables represent latent variables that are indicated by multiple manifest variables in the model, meaning that the traditional "square" used to represent an observed variable would be replaced by a "circle" used to indicate an unmeasured latent variable.

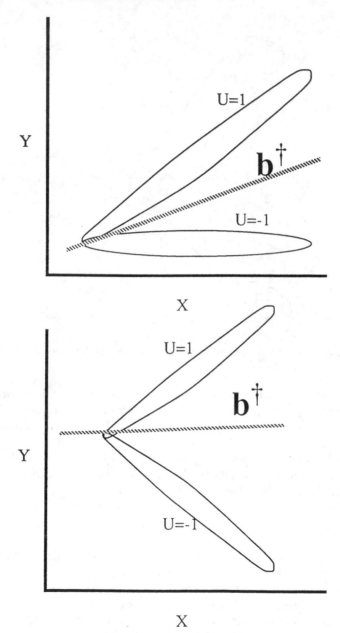

Figure 4.3. Interaction Model Involving One Continuous and One Dichotomous Variable (Model A: $\sigma_{X,U} > 0$ Model B, $\sigma_{X,U} = 0$, ME for U)

Research Contexts in Which Unmeasured Variables and Their Interactions Are Likely to Occur

While research situations in which interaction effects exist in behavioral research are commonplace (e.g., Busemeyer & Jones, 1983; Jaccard, Turrisi, & Wan, 1990), discussions of research situations in which it is reasonable to expect the presence of an unmeasured variable or its interaction are few. Practical research contexts in which it would seem reasonable to expect the presence of an unmeasured variable or its interaction will now be outlined in the areas of differential growth and change, unmeasured treatment populations, gene/environment interactions, and construct validity studies. This discussion is an adaptation of the contexts described in Wood and Games (1991, pp. 296-298).

Research Involving Differential Growth and Change

Methodologists have often pointed out that traditional linear statistical approaches can lead to erroneous conclusions in longitudinal research designs. This criticism is based on the observation that such linear models often assume that all individuals in a sample display equal rates of growth or change over time (Tucker, 1966). Often, the average rate of growth observed at a population level may not typify the growth patterns of any particular individual and may mask distinctly different patterns of development over time. For this reason some have stressed the importance of assessing the behavior of many individuals over time (Cattell, 1989; Nesselroade, 1991). Similarly, educational researchers have noticed that some students in educational settings appear to show steeper rates of growth than others (Bryk & Weisberg, 1977; Campbell, 1967, 1977; Campbell & Boruch, 1975; Kenny, 1975; Levin, 1972; Preece, 1982; Rogosa, Brandy, & Zimoski, 1982). The top of Figure 4.3 may represent two distinctly different trajectories in a population of interest. Here, X represents the time dimension and Y a measure of learning. The unmeasured variable, U, represents two types of developmental trajectories over time. The individual with a developmental trajectory $U = 1$ has a much slower rate of growth than the individual with a trajectory $U = 1$. The phenomenon of unmeasured developmental trajectories in studies of learning has led to a discussion of whether change scores or analysis of covariance are preferable in analyzing such data (e.g., Preece, 1982; Rogosa et al., 1982). Campbell and Boruch (1975) have shown that this phenomenon can lead to a systematic underestimation of the effects of educational interventions.

Differential Treatment Effects Across Unmeasured Subpopulations

A second research area involving unmeasured variables is based on the observation that variance in performance often changes as a result of experimental treatment. One example of this occurs in clinical psychology where the classification of an individual's condition is an agglomeration of many true types of classifications, as is the case in schizophrenia (Hamer & Schwab, 1982). In effect, obtained classifications of schizophrenics are really aggregates of many schizophrenias with many causes but similar manifestations. Experimental treatments for helping a particular type of schizophrenia may only result in positive change for some but not all individuals in a treatment group. This case is again reducible to an underspecified model because the unmeasured predictor variable that interacts with treatment is the individual's true classification. As applied to Figure 4.3, Y may represent improvement in treatment, X may represent levels of a particular drug to treat schizophrenia, and the unmeasured trajectory, U, could represent two different types of schizophrenia. For some types of schizophrenia the treatment has a positive effect ($U = 1$), while for others there is no effect on performance ($U = -1$). Given such a pattern, it is possible to construct many alternative scenarios involving types of schizophrenia for which the treatment is only moderately successful, or even perhaps harmful.

Heterogeneity in Gene/Environment Interactions

A biological analog to the case of unmeasured subpopulations occurs in studies of the genetic heritability of traits and more specifically under the topic of the gene/environment interaction. Some strains of organisms show a high degree of variability in phenotypes across environments relative to others. Some have suggested that some "pure strains" of organisms may in fact be populations with more heterogenous genetic makeup than other strains (Erlenmeyer-Kimling, 1972). Still others have explained this phenomenon as a genetic characteristic of a strain: Some genotypes possess a greater range of adaptability to environmental conditions (Gottesman, 1963). This phenomenon has been shown in several studies of the heritability of traits (e.g., Henderson, 1970, 1981). For example, Parsons (1972) explicitly discusses "heterosis" frequently observed in enriched laboratory conditions that is characterized by both an overall better performance on the task accompanied by a wide variation of performance on the task. Unmeasured variables of either genetic characteristics or differential individual adaptability across trains may interact with other observed independent variables to produce a complete explanation of behavior. To apply this to Figure 4.3, if X represents time and Y represents, for example, body weight, one strain of organisms may be composed only of individuals who have a linear growth curve described by $U = 1$ or that represented by $U = -1$. The general pattern manifest to the researcher who does not have access to U is that of increasing variability in the population as a function of time.

Construct Validity Studies Involving Unmeasured Subskills

In construct validity studies the correlation coefficient (or some other measure of linear association) is taken as an index of the degree to which two measures can be thought to assess the same construct. Some researchers (e.g., Brabeck & Wood, 1987; Cruce-Mast, 1975) have argued that a measure of correlation, taken by itself, is not sufficient grounds for concluding that two measures assess the same skills. They argue that one measure may involve assessment of additional abilities beyond those assessed by the other. As such, the relationship between one construct and another may be "necessary but not sufficient."

As an example of this rationale, Wood (1983) argued that the relationship between the ability to solve well-structured problems is related to the ability to solve ill-structured problems. Additional types of competencies are thought to be required to solve ill-structured problems. Even though individuals who fail to solve well-structured problems will fail to solve ill-structured ones, success in well-structured problem solving does not guarantee success in ill-structured problem solving. This relationship can be explained in terms the top of Figure 4.3 by assuming that X and Y represent ability to solve well-structured and ill-structured problems respectively. The unmeasured variable, U, represents additional skills required to solve ill-structured problems (such as the ability to reason probabilistically; King & Kitchener, in press). Individuals who possess these additional skills are in the group $U = 1$, while those who do not possess these skills are in the group $U = -1$. Since the ability to reason probabilistically is not an all-or-none phenomenon, it seems reasonable in practice to extend the graph of Figure 4.3 to include a variety of levels of U indicating different levels of ill-structured problem solving.

Implications of Unmeasured Interactions on Linear Models: Mathematical Relationships

The bias introduced by, and means for detecting, unmeasured inter-actions is closely related to the effects of unmeasured variables on the endogenous variable(s) of interest. For this reason the commonly known effects of failing to specify a particular variable will first be discussed. After that the role of unspecified interactions will be discussed as well.

Effects of Failure to Specify a Linear Effect

The effect of a failure to completely specify all exogenous variables in a structural model is well known and forms the basis of some critiques of structural equation modeling (e.g., Freedman, 1987). The effect of such an error is easy to estimate by examining the path diagrams of Figures 4.1 and 4.2 and calculating the predicted variance/covariance matrix from these models. These models are given in Table 4.1. The special case of no interaction occurs by assuming that path coefficient, d, is set to zero.

From Table 4.1, it can be seen that the mis-specified model assumes that the covariance between X and Y is represented by $b^{\dagger}$, while for the true model, the covariance between X and Y is given as $b + c\sigma_{XU}$. Thus, whenever the product, $c\sigma_{XU}$, is the same sign as b, $b^{\dagger}$ will be an overestimate (in absolute value) of b. An algebraic derivation of this effect is given in Kmenta (1971, pp. 392-395).

Although a case has been made above for unmeasured interactions in the research contexts above, it seems reasonable that unmeasured main effects are frequently present in linear models of behavior. When growth over time is differential, it seems reasonable that the unmea-sured variables are positively correlated with the observed predictors. For example, if a researcher is interested in examining growth in performance over time, unmeasured variables (such as the long-term beneficial effect of socioeconomic status or nutrition) show their effect more strongly over the course of time. Thus, such unmeasured variables are probably correlated with time.

As is suggested by the scatterplots of Figure 4.3, Wood and Games (1991) showed that when $c\sigma_{X,U}$ is the same sign as b, squared errors of prediction based on the mis-specified model are positively correlated with X. Accordingly, one appropriate statistical test for such mis-specification would be to test whether squared errors of prediction are correlated with

Table 4.1

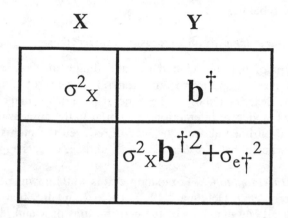

Predicted Variance/Covariance Matrix from Mis-specified Model

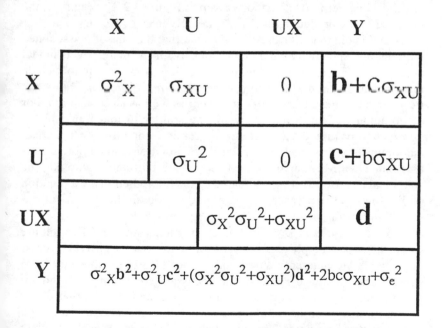

Predicted Variance/Covariance Matrix from True Model

X, indicating a "fan-spread" pattern between X and Y. Such a statistical test is outlined below.

Effects of Failure to Specify an Unmeasured Interaction

The pattern of bias introduced by, and diagnostics for detecting, unmeasured interactions mirror the general patterns of unmeasured linear effects described above. The general pattern for detection of a mis-specified model for interactions is similar to the unmeasured main effects model outlined above. The bias introduced for such situations only occurs when either X or U is skewed and these effects appear to be marginal.

X and U Unrelated to UX. For example, it is well known (Bohrnstedt & Goldberger, 1969; Goodman, 1960, 1962; Kendall, Stuart, & Ord, 1987) that if all odd moments of the distributions of X and U are zero (as is found when X and U are normally distributed) that the covariance of X or U with the product UX is zero. The path coefficients and variance of the product term, UX, are those given in Figure 4.2. For example, the variance of the product term, UX, is then given as $\sigma_X^2\sigma_U^2 + \sigma_{X,U}^2$.

From this diagram, it can be easily seen that the bias of b associated with the mis-specified model is the same as for the main effects model noted above. No particular bias in b is introduced by failure to include the interaction term UX in the model. In some situations, however, $\sigma_{X,U} = 0$, and a main effect of U is present as well as an interaction. For dichotomous U, this situation would be similar to that found in the bottom half of Figure 4.3 where the regression slope for $U = 1$ is equal and opposite in sign to $U = -1$. For these situations, squared residuals associated with the mis-specified model are correlated with X. The statistical test for detecting if squared errors of prediction are a function of X allows the researcher to investigate the possibility of an unmeasured interaction.

X and U Related to UX. The effects of model mis-specification are somewhat more complicated when the odd moments (such as skewness) of U and X are not zero. Wood and Games (1991) explore this more general case for linear models. The necessary conditions reported are easily understood by reference to Figure 4.2 and require that either $\sigma_{X,U}^c$ must be zero or the same sign as b and $\sigma_{XU,X}^d$ must be the same sign as b. The bias associated with $b^\dagger$ is then also a function of the product of $\sigma_{XU,U}^d$. For these situations, squared errors of prediction are also correlated with X. In practice, however, it seems that the covariances associated with the interaction are quite small, even for very skewed data as noted by Aiken and West (1991). To give an example, I conducted a small computer simulation in SAS of 3,000 independent, centered random variates consisting of a normally distributed X and an unmeasured variable distributed as χ_1^2. Correlation coefficients of these variables with the product UX were .014 and .019, respectively. Additional analyses with even more skewed data or even bimodal data yielded similar results.

Cook and Weisberg's Test for Heteroscedasticity

As noted before, whenever $c\sigma_{XU}$ is the same sign as b or whenever a main effect for U is present and $d \neq 0$ a pattern of heteroscedasticity exists which is a function of X. Researchers using structural equation models would be well advised to investigate scatterplots of their exogenous and endogenous variables in order to learn if such patterns are present in their data. Wood and Games (1991) reviewed available statistical tests for such patterns of "moderated" heteroscedasticity. Although no test seems most appropriate for all research situations, Cook and Weisberg's (1983) test appears to demonstrate acceptable statistical power and robustness to nonnormality while being relatively easy to calculate using traditional software and allowing the researcher to consider multiple predictor variables simultaneously.

The test can be easily calculated using statistical programs that allow the researcher to save residual scores from a regression. The first regression to be calculated is analogous to that shown in Figure 4.1 and represents the mis-specified model. Residual scores, e, from this regression are then saved. These residuals are then squared and divided by a scaling factor equal to the sum of squares error divided by the total degrees of freedom in the study (not the usual error df). These scaled e^2 are entered as dependent variables to a second regression, in which the independent variables are those that the researcher believes are associated with an increasing pattern of heteroscedasticity. The sum of squares regression for this second regression is divided by 2 and is asymptotically distributed as χ_d^2 where d is the number of independent variables thought to be associated with the increasing pattern of heteroscedasticity. Examples of computation of this test statistic in situations involving a single predictor and criterion are given in Cook and Weisberg (1983) as well as Wood and Games (1991). It seems appropriate to give an example of a complex research situation involving the presence of categorical variables and/or curvilinear relationships between criteria and predictor.

Given that a statistically significant relationship between X and squared errors of prediction have occurred under Cook and Weisberg's test, it is appropriate to remind the researcher that no definitive proof of an unmeasured variable's existence has been established. As Wood and Games (1991) note, alternate interpretations to the presence of an unmeasured variable and/or its interaction include scaling errors, ceiling or floor effects, or a mis-specified interaction model. Following Shepperd's (1991) comments on "statistically significant" moderator or trend effects, researchers should proceed on the basis of reasonable theory in deciding between such competing models and not on the basis of "fishing expeditions" for statistical significance. In the absence of a conceptual basis, a valid finding under Cook and Weisberg's test can merely serve notice to the researcher that some critical assumption of the existing model has occurred.

Example of Necessary but Not Sufficient Relationship: A Secondary Analysis of Reflective Judgment Ability. The present example involves assessment of a construct taken to be a general outcome of college education, Reflective Judgment. Since more detailed descriptions of the administration and scoring of the Reflective Judgment Interview (RJI) are given elsewhere (e.g., King & Kitchener, in press), a brief description of the construct, the interview itself, and its scoring will be given. Briefly, the Reflective Judgment Interview is designed to assess the adequacy with which students deal with "ill-structured problems" (Wood, 1983); that is, problems that do not allow of a single correct answer (i.e., problem situations in which qualified experts can be reasonably expected to disagree). The instrument consists of a semi-structured interview in which subjects are presented with four ill-structured problems by a trained interviewer. For example, one ill-structured problem asks students to give their opinion about whether food additives (or any given food additive) are safe to consume. Transcripts from these four topics are then rated by judges on a 7-point scale that indicates the general adequacy of the answers the students give. Overall, the RJI has been found to be an extremely reliable measure of ill-structured problem-solving ability in cross-sectional and longitudinal studies in samples ranging from junior high school students to advanced doctoral students (King, Kitchener, & Wood's, in press, meta-analysis of all reported RJI reliabilities by educational level yielded a median coefficient alpha of .85). The upward progression over time and sequentially of the instrument has been examined in several cross-sectional and longitudinal studies. Pascarella and Terenzini (1991), in their review of 20 years of educational research, describe the Reflective Judgment model as "the best known and most extensively studied" model of post-formal operations (p. 123).

Previous research on the RJI has shown that verbal ability (Wood & Games, 1991) and traditional measures of critical thinking (Wood, 1993) show a necessary but not sufficient relationship with the RJI: Low levels of these measures are accompanied by generally poor performance on the RJI; high levels of these measures are accompanied by generally higher performance on the RJI, but also by a greater variability in performance.

The strongest correlate of the RJI across many studies appears to be the educational attainment of the student. This has been found in studies of intact groups (King, Wood, & Mines, 1990) as well as studies that match students on levels of verbal ability across educational levels (e.g., Kitchener & King, 1981). Growth on the RJI is thought to be slow and positive from junior high through advanced graduate study.

In the present study, a secondary analysis was conducted of all available RJI data (described in more detail in Wood, 1993). Of the 14 studies using the RJI, 2 studies did not code information on student gender and so were excluded from the analysis. The remaining 12 studies represent data from 1,016 students with educational levels ranging from eighth grade to advanced doctoral study. An initial examination of the relationship of educational level to RJI revealed a curvilinear relationship between the two constructs, with statistically significant quadratic and cubic terms. As can be seen from the graph in Figure 4.4, RJI performance appears to be rather flat across junior high school samples, with an upward trend across the college years. Overall, the curvilinear relationship of educational level on RJI is moderate ($r^2 = .45$).

In order to examine the question of whether educational level represents a necessary but not sufficient condition for performance on the RJI, it is necessary to incorporate more information than that provided in the curvilinear relationship involving only educational level. Spurious patterns of increasing variability could be due to differences across studies in the educational levels examined. In addition, the relationship between educational level and RJI could be different for different studies. In order to investigate the possible necessary but not sufficient relationship between educational level and the RJI, an initial model involving several independent variables was considered: Study (a categorical

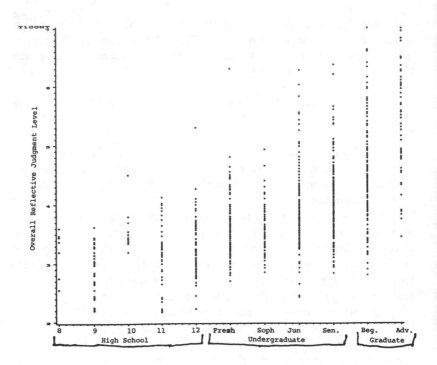

Figure 4.4.

variable), gender, educational level (ranging from eighth grade to advanced doctoral), quadratic and cubic terms of educational level, and an interaction term involving study and educational level. Since only one study examined students from all educational levels from eighth grade to advanced graduate, educational level is, to some extent, confounded with study in this design. All of these effects were statistically significant ($p < .01$) as was the overall model [$F(27,988) = 52.24$; $p < .001$].[1]

In order to explore whether patterns of increasing variability were present that would indicate a necessary but not sufficient relationship, residuals from the general linear model described above were generated. These residuals were then squared and scaled by the sum of squares error divided by total df (407.51/1,015). These scaled residuals were then entered as the dependent variables in a regression with two candidate independent variables thought to be associated with the RJI in a necessary but not sufficient way, educational level and gender. To test

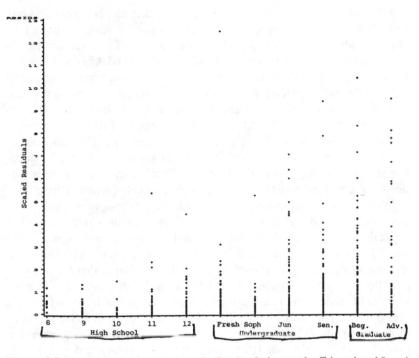

Figure 4.5. Plot of Scaled Residuals of Reflective Judgment by Educational Level

whether a pattern of increasing heteroscedasticity was present, the sum of squares regression from this second model was divided by the number of parameters estimated (3; two predictors and the regression constant). This quantity, $146.89/3 = 48.96$ is, under the null hypothesis of homoscedasticity, distributed as χ^2_3 and is, in this case, statistically significant at any conventional level. Follow-up examinations involving only gender or educational level revealed that each of these variables singly demonstrated a pattern of increasing heteroscedasticity: Greater variability was associated with higher educational levels (as shown in Figure 4.5) χ^2_2 $= 63.19$. Males (in addition to performing slightly higher) showed a greater variability in performance on the RJI $\chi^2_2 = 12.66$.

When these variables are compared, it appears that effects are much stronger for educational level than gender: In terms of SS for the model, educational level accounted for $298.11/407.51 = .73$ of explained variability in RJI while gender accounted for only $30.53/407.51 = .07$. In addition, as noted above, χ^2 statistics for testing for moderating heteroscedasticity were much higher for educational level than gender. An examination of the standard deviations by gender and educational level also reinforces this interpretation: The mean scaled residuals were 0.89 and 0.57 for males and females, respectively. Scaled residuals by educational level ranged from 0.85 for the eighth grade group to 1.77 for the advanced doctoral group.

A pattern of increased variability could occur when increased measurement error is associated with higher educational levels. In order to investigate the possibility of alternate explanations, internal consistency estimates were computed for the RJI separately by each educational level. Contrary to the differential reliability explanation, reliabilities for the RJI increased across educational levels (Wood, 1993).

In summary, these analyses suggest that the relationship between educational level and RJI is a necessary but not sufficient one, even after adjusting for possible curvilinear relationships between educational level and RJI performance; taking into account between-study differences in students of the same educational level and the possibility that the relationship between educational level and RJI may be different for different samples of student, the relationship between educational level and RJI is a necessary but not sufficient one. Surprisingly, it also appears that a pattern of increased variability is associated with gender, with males performing overall more highly on the RJI and with more variability. Taken together, these results suggest that gains in RJI do not occur for all individuals as they advance through educational levels. Rather, differential trajectories of growth may exist in the data, certain educational experiences (which not all student have) may foster Reflective Judgment, or growth in RJI scores may occur for only some types of students.

Finally, some researchers (Kitchener, Lynch, Fischer, & Wood, 1993) who adopt a skill theory model of RJI development (Fischer, 1980) may take the increased level and variability by both educational level and gender to mean that the RJI is a measure of "typical" performance (that can vary greatly as a function of an individual's disposition at the moment) rather than a measure of "optimal" performance (meaning the best performance that a subject is capable of under conditions of high environmental support for a "good" or "correct" answer).

Discussion

The research contexts outlined above have described a common statistical pattern typified by either: (a) the presence of an unmeasured variable that is correlated with an exogenous variable in a study or (b) a statistically significant interaction accompanied by a main effect associated with the unmeasured variable. Both of these research situations manifest a plot of increasing variability as a function of observed predictor variables in the study. Graphical or statistical evidence (such as Cook & Weisberg's test) can be used to reveal such a pattern of increasing variation and so can alert the researcher to such model mis-specification. The discussion in the present chapter has many clear links to investigation of other types of interactions than those considered here (Fisher, 1988), as well as to more general structural variable models that involve similar regressions to those described here, but conducted at the level of unobserved, latent predictor and criterion constructs (discussed below).

If it seems reasonable to believe that the suspected unmeasured variable is related to the observed exogenous variable, the value of the mis-specified regression weights may be inaccurate. In many research situations it seems reasonable to assume that the regression weight of the observed predictor (b) and the product of the regression weight of the unmeasured variable and σ_{XU} are the same sign, implying that obtained regression weights from mis-specified regressions are frequently overestimates in an absolute sense of their true values.

In many ways such arguments form the basis of criticisms of structural equation approaches in general, such as Freedman's (1987) critique. The present chapter examines the role, if any, that unmeasured interactions play in the interpretation of path coefficients of mis-specified models. The bias in regression weights introduced by unmeasured interactions appears small relative to that due to the presence of unmeasured variables that are correlated with observed exogenous variables and also explain the endogenous variables of interest. It is worth noting that the bias and errors of inference found are due not to any special property of structural models but rather to the linear model itself. It seems appropriate, therefore, to extend Freedman's criticism to any analysis of variance or traditional regression based on data in which the researcher cannot assume that random assignment has occurred, thereby allowing an unmeasured variable to have an effect.

If structural equation modelers believe that the presence of an unmeasured variable or interaction has occurred based on an examination of residuals, two strategies seem indicated in future studies of the phenomenon. Obviously one avenue of research would be to investigate candidate constructs that could be the unmeasured variable. In some situations it is quite easy to do this. For example, the structural models discussed here are equivalent to those mentioned in Lubinski and Humphreys's (1990) discussion of moderator effects in regression. Lubinski and Humphreys note that their unmeasured variables, quadratic terms of predictors, are correlated with estimates of interactions (a situation similar to that reported in the top of Figure 4.3). Testing for the presence of such an unmeasured quadratic term becomes a mere matter of computing a polynomial of predictors and recalculating the statistical model. It is worthwhile to note that Aiken and West (1991) recommend computing interaction vectors based on deviation or residualized scores to eliminate correlation between predictor variables. This transformation of the data changes situations similar to the top of Figure 4.3 to that found at the bottom of Figure 4.3 in which no covariance between X and U is present, but a main effect for U and UX is present. In both situations, though, squared errors of prediction are still a function of the observed predictor variable.

While identifying the unmeasured variable by transforming existing variables or including promising new variables in subsequent research is obvious, psychological phenomena may involve several unmeasured variables all of which are correlated, in some way, with the exogenous variables of interest. Another strategy for uncovering functional relationships would involve experiments that hold constant the effects of such unmeasured variables and examine patterns of variation that remain. For example, suppose that researchers in an area employ traditional cross-sectional research (in Cattell's, 1989, terminology, "R-technique") and that unmeasured interindividual differences (or unmeasured subpopulations) make it difficult to interpret the structural relationships between a predictor and a criterion for reasons outlined here. Such researchers could investigate the performance of the predictor and criterion for a sample of individuals over the course of several occasions (Cattell's "T-technique"). Such an approach would allow the analysis of functional relationships between a predictor and criterion that are different for different types of individuals.

Such a plan of attack is, of course, a familiar one to students of differential intraindividual change (e.g., Tucker, 1966). The presence of other types of unmeasured variables may also be used to prompt researchers to investigate other slices of the data box (such as P-technique or Q-technique approaches) in an effort to control for the effects of such unmeasured variables, if they cannot be experimentally manipulated or even completely identified.

The prospect of testing for the presence of moderating heteroscedasticity would seem extendable to more general structural models and other models of moderator effects than those considered here. Fisher (1988) discusses the "linear" interaction models discussed in this chapter as well as nonlinear interaction models in which a moderator variable is related in an exponential way with a given predictor variable to produce a full explanation of behavior. While not taken up here, the patterns of bias and means for detecting moderating heteroscedasticity can be calculated from a specification of such a regression under the nonlinear constraints that such alternative models require. Choice of metric for these exponential interaction models is of more concern, since choice of scales that fall in the interval −1 to 1 will yield substantially different results for such regressions than models with values outside of these ranges.

Extensions of the Cook and Weisberg (1983) technique to more general latent variable models would seem straightforward as well. The researcher would proceed by first specifying the dependent and independent latent variables of interest, and could then employ Cook and Weisberg's technique using the estimated factor scores from these latent variables.

Note

1. It should be noted that additional analyses to those described here were conducted adding (statistically nonsignificant) higher order terms of educational level (up to a power of 6) and additional interaction vectors of study with these polynomial terms. The necessary but not sufficient pattern found in this analysis was still present. For both models, all F tests based on Type I and Type III were statistically significant.

References

Aiken, L., & West, S. (1991). *Multiple regression: Testing and interpreting interactions.* Newbury Park, CA: Sage.

Bohrnstedt, G. W., & Goldberger, A. S. (1969). On the exact covariance of products of random variables. *Journal of the American Statistical Association, 52,* 1439-1442.

Brabeck, M. M., & Wood, P. K. (1987). Cross-sectional and longitudinal evidence for differences between well-structured and ill-structured problem solving abilities. In M. Commons, F. Richards, & C. Armon (Eds.), *Beyond formal operations II.* New York: Praeger.

Bryk, A. S., & Weisberg, H. I. (1977). Use of the nonequivalent control group design when subjects are growing. *Psychological Bulletin, 84*(5), 950-962.

Busemeyer, J. R., & Jones, L. E. (1983). Analysis of multiplicative combination rules when the causal variables are measured with error. *Psychological Bulletin, 93,* 549-562.

Campbell, D. T. (1967). *The effects of colleges on students: Proposing a quasi-experimental approach.* Unpublished manuscript.

Campbell, D. T. (1977). *Musings on problems and needed developments in factorially similar or parallel pretests in moving average and autoregressive models.* Unpublished manuscript.

Campbell, D. T., & Boruch, R. F. (1975). Making the case for randomized assignment to treatments by considering the alternatives. Six ways in which quasi-experimental evaluations in compensatory education tend to underestimate effects. In C. A. Bennett & A. A. Lumsdaine (Eds.), *Evaluation and experiment: Some critical issues in assessing social changes* (pp. 195-296). New York: Academic Press.

Cattell, R. B. (1989). The data box. In J. R. Nesselroade & R. B. Cattell (Eds.), *Handbook of multivariate experimental psychology* (pp. 69-130). New York: Plenum.

Cook, R. D., & Weisberg, S. (1983). Diagnostics for heteroscedasticity in regression. *Biometrika, 70,* 1-10.

Cruce-Mast, A. L. (1975). The interrelationship of critical thinking, empathy, and social interest with moral judgment. *Dissertation Abstracts International, 36,* 7945A. (University Microfilms No. 76-13, 229)

Daniel, C., & Wood, F. S. (1980). *Fitting equations to data.* New York: Wiley Interscience.

Erlenmeyer-Kimling, L. (1972). Gene-environment interactions and the variability of behavior. In L. Ehrman, G. S. Omenn, & E. Caspari (Eds.), *Genetics, environment, and behavior* (pp. 181-214). New York: Academic Press.

Fischer, K. W. (1980). A theory of cognitive development: The control and construction of hierarchies of skills. *Psychological Review, 87,* 477-531.

Fisher, G. A. (1988). Problems in the use and interpretation of product variables. In J. S. Long (Ed.), *Common problems/proper solutions* (pp. 84-107). Newbury Park, CA: Sage.

Freedman, D. A. (1987). As others see us: A case study in path analysis. *Journal of Educational Statistics, 12,* 101-128.

Goodman, L. A. (1960). On the exact variance of products. *Journal of the American Statistical Association, 55,* 708-713.

Goodman, L. A. (1962). The variance of the product of *K* random variables. *Journal of the American Statistical Association, 57,* 54-60.

Gottesman, I. I. (1963). Genetic aspects of intelligent behavior. In N. Ellis (Ed.), *Handbook of mental deficiency: Psychological theory and research* (pp. 253-296). New York: McGraw-Hill.

Hamer, R. M., & Schwab, B. H. (1982). Analysis of effects on variances using GLM. *Proceedings of the Seventh Annual SAS Users Group International Conference* (pp. 528-532).

Hanushek, E. A., & Jackson, J. E. (1977). *Statistical methods for social scientists.* New York: Academic Press.

Henderson, N. D. (1970). Genetic influences on the behavior of mice can be obscured by laboratory rearing. *Journal of Comparative and Physiological Psychology, 72,* 505-511.

Henderson, N. D. (1981). Genetic influences on locomotor activity in 11-day-old housemice. *Behavior Genetics, 11*(3), 209-255.

Jaccard, J., Turrisi, R., & Wan, C. K. (1990). *Interaction effects in multiple regression*. Sage University Paper series on Quantitative Applications in the Social Sciences, series no. 07-072. Newbury Park, CA: Sage.

Kendall, M., Stuart, A., & Ord, J. K. (1987). *Kendall's advanced theory of statistics* (5th ed., Vol. 1). London: Charles Griffin.

Kenny, D. A. (1975). A quasi-experimental approach to assessing treatment effects in the nonequivalent control group design. *Psychological Bulletin, 82*(3), 345-362.

King, P. M., & Kitchener, K. S. (in press). *The development of reflective judgment: Theory, research and educational applications*. San Francisco: Jossey-Bass.

King, P. M., Kitchener, K. S., & Wood, P. K. (in press). Research on the development of reflective judgment: How students reason about ill-structured problems. In P. M. King & K. S. Kitchener (Eds.), *The development of reflective judgment: Theory, research and educational applications*. San Francisco: Jossey-Bass.

King, P. M., Wood, P. K., & Mines, R. (1990). Critical thinking among college and graduate students. *The Review of Higher Education, 13*, 167-186.

Kitchener, K. S., & King, P. M. (1981). Reflective judgment: Concepts of justification and their relationship to age and education. *Journal of Applied Developmental Psychology, 2*, 89-116.

Kitchener, K. S., Lynch, C., Fischer, K., & Wood, P. K. (1993). Developmental range of reflective judgment: The effect of contextual support and practice on developmental stage. *Developmental Psychology, 29*, 893-906.

Kmenta, J. (1971). *Elements of econometrics*. New York: Macmillan.

Levin, J. R. (1972). *Treatment by age interactions: The problem and a solution* (Theoretical Paper #41). Madison: University of Wisconsin, Wisconsin Research and Development Center for Cognitive Learning.

Lubinski, D., & Humphreys, L. G. (1990). Assessing spurious "moderator effects": Illustrated substantively with the hypothesized ("synergistic") relation between spatial and mathematical ability. *Psychological Bulletin, 107*(3), 385-393.

McArdle, J. J. (1980). Causal modeling applied to psychonomic systems simulation. *Behavior Research Methods and Instrumentation, 12*, 193-209.

Nesselroade, J. R. (1991). Interindividual differences in intraindividual change. In L. M. Collins & J. L. Horn (Eds.), *Best methods for the analysis of change: Recent advances, unanswered questions, future directions* (pp. 92-105). Washington, DC: American Psychological Association.

Pascarella, E., & Terenzini, P. (1991). *How college affects students: Findings and insights from twenty years of research*. San Francisco: Jossey-Bass.

Parsons, P. A. (1972). Genetic determination of behavior (mice and men). In L. Ehrman, G. S. Omenn, & E. Caspari (Eds.), *Genetics, environment and behavior* (pp. 75-98). New York: Academic Press.

Preece, P.F.W. (1982). The fan-spread hypothesis and the adjustment for initial differences between groups in uncontrolled studies. *Educational and Psychological Measurement, 42*, 759-762.

Rogosa, D., Brandy, D., & Zimoski, M. (1982). A growth curve approach to the measurement of change. *Psychological Bulletin, 92*(3), 726-748.

Shepperd, J. A. (1991). Cautions in assessing spurious "moderator effects." *Psychological Bulletin, 110*, 315-317.

Tucker, L. (1966). Learning theory and multivariate experiment: Illustration of determination of generalized learning curves. In R. B. Cattell (Ed.), *Handbook of multivariate experimental psychology* (pp. 476-501). New York: Rand McNally.

Wood, P. K. (1983). Inquiring systems and problem structure: Implications for cognitive development. *Human Development, 26*(5), 249-265.

Wood, P. K. (1993). *Context and development of reflective thinking: A secondary analysis of the structure of individual differences.* Unpublished manuscript. University of Missouri–Columbia.

Wood, P. K., & Games, P. (1991). Rationale, detection and implications of interactions between independent variables and unmeasured variables in linear models. *Multivariate Behavioral Research, 25,* 295-311.

5

Exploratory Factor Analysis
With Latent Variables and
the Study of Processes of
Development and Change

JOHN R. NESSELROADE

Introduction

Recently, in my local newspaper, there was an article titled "Team Claims New Planets Orbiting Star" (*The Daily Progress*, p. 1) which reported some work by astronomers looking for evidence of planet-like systems outside our own solar system. A research team had detected a pattern of wobbling in a pulsar, for which they then tried to account. The wobbling was consistent with what would be expected if two planets were orbiting the pulsar at distances of about 45 million miles. The pulsar is about 1,300 light years from our solar system. The article went on to say that, "*If confirmed* [emphasis mine], the planets from . . . [this and one other investigation] . . . would be the first known outside the solar system."

The contents of the article were ironic to me in several respects. One component I found intriguing was the clearly exploratory aspects of the

AUTHOR'S NOTE: The support of the MacArthur Foundation Research Network on Successful Aging and the Max Planck Institute for Human Development and Education, Berlin, is gratefully acknowledged. The helpful comments of Paul Baltes, Jack McArdle, and Rolf Steyer on an earlier version of this chapter are deeply appreciated.

discovery. The erratic behavior was discovered because of close and systematic observation of the pulsar's movements rather than because two planets were known (or hypothesized) to be orbiting it and should therefore cause it to wobble. A plausible reason for the wobbling is provided by the two planets but these were hypothesized after the wobbling was observed. The comments reported by other investigators about the findings had a definite cast. They included, "It's a credible story they're telling. Time will tell if it holds up," and "very persuasive-looking. . . . I think they've really got something interesting here." The emphasis was on the need for confirmation of the existence of the hypothesized planets by appropriate analytic techniques.

A second aspect of the article held an even greater irony. The situation described in the newspaper involved two unseen, one might say unmeasured, entities that, at least in two-dimensional space, are generally represented as circles. These unmeasured entities were presumed to influence a number of manifest variables (meter and dial readings), the workings of which are usually housed in boxes. Thus, implied were causal arrows directed from the circles to the boxes. How appropriate, I mused, for representing critical relationships in a situation that precludes experimental manipulation of key variables.

A Perspective on Exploratory Factor Analysis

The case for modeling with latent variables will not be examined in this chapter. I find a number of discussions of the matter quite persuasive (e.g., Bentler, 1980; Cattell, 1957; Horn & McArdle, 1980; Loehlin, 1987; McArdle, 1988; McDonald, 1985). Rather I will emphasize the *exploratory factor analysis* aspect of the title of this chapter. That is what I understand to be my principal charge set by the editors of this volume. In an historical era when most of "the action" seems to be in the confirmatory analysis arena, several of the stalwarts of which are contributors to this volume, this is a somewhat daunting task. Nevertheless, I acknowledge my charge while consoling myself in the belief that, in any case, it is a mistake to take the dichotomy too seriously. For example, Paul Baltes and I (Nesselroade & Baltes, 1984), in an examination of the application of structural-causal modeling to developmental issues, argued for a distinction between an exploratory hypothesis testing orientation in *analytic procedures* as opposed to *theoretical purposes*. One of our central points in that discussion was that the criteria for determining whether a particular instance is exploratory or confirmatory are complex and often ill-considered. Notions of simple structure, bi-factorial representations, and two-factor theories of intellectual performance, for example, represent strong beliefs about the nature of nature but they may well be involved, sometimes only tacitly, in exploratory applications of analytic method. In the remainder of this chapter, I will use the terms *exploratory* and *confirmatory* in what I believe is their generally intended meaning but will, in the final section, remind the reader of the complexity that the two terms may tend to hide (see also Gorsuch, 1988).

The lines between *exploratory* and *confirmatory* factor analysis have been drawn by various authors, including Gorsuch (1988) and Mulaik (1988) in adjacent chapters in the second edition of the *Handbook of Multivariate Experimental Psychology* (Nesselroade & Cattell, 1988). Mulaik (1988) argued that the two approaches reflect no less than two different approaches to the philosophy of science. He linked exploratory factor analysis to inductivism and confirmatory factor analysis to hypotheticism. Mulaik recognized the potential usefulness of exploratory factor analysis for hypothesis generation but not for hypothesis testing and argued that it may not be optimal for hypothesis generation. Gorsuch (1988) identified four general situations in which *exploratory* factor analysis can be used to assist the investigator. These are: (1) orthogonalizing a set of variables; (2) reducing variable sets; (3) scale analysis by factoring items; and (4) dimensional analysis. These situations may or may not involve some notion of hypothesis testing, depending on the user's a priori information concerning the domain of variables under investigation.

The controversial nature of exploratory factor analysis is well known. In addition to its supporters, and an enthusiastic lot they have been, there is also a lengthy list of vocal detractors. Since the 1930s, it has not been uncommon for the techniques to be ill-used, overused, and abused, and some of the antagonists were responding to such excesses. The negative reactions of others seemed to arise from a more "alimentary" level. It was Gordon Allport, I believe, who once wrote that factors were like sausage that had failed to pass the pure food and drug laws. Twenty years ago, in a review of the comparative use of factor analysis to study developmental phenomena, Reinert (1970) noted published opinions spanning only 7 years that ranged, on the one hand, from "factorial study is not in its infancy" to "factor analysis is dead," on the other. Reinert went on to note that "a review of the literature in developmental psychology might lead to the impression that factor analysis has never been alive" (p. 468). In the developmental literature of some 20 years later this has changed remarkably. One now finds numerous examples of the use of the most advanced applications of factor analysis and closely related modeling procedures to attack developmental issues. Indeed, to paraphrase Mark Twain, the reports of the demise of factor analysis seem to have been greatly exaggerated.

The Question

But what of exploratory factor analysis today? Is it a primitive, ill-adapted, weakened species on the verge of extinction that has been kept alive only in protected, out-of-the-way gullies as the ever more prolific confirmatory methods thunder across the plains of social and behavioral research? Or, to change the metaphor, is exploratory factor analysis an old jalopy about to be "blown off the road" by the big, fast, and shiny software of mathematico-statistical model fitting now roaring down the freeways of inquiry? Or does exploratory factor analysis continue to have some utility; some merit that is recognized by a sufficient number of researchers that it continues to be applied and even occasionally taught to the next generation of researchers? I believe that it has considerable value and take this opportunity to try to support that belief by identifying a couple of arenas in which pointedly exploratory factor analysis can be usefully applied. In so doing, I will focus primarily on the study of processes of development and other kinds of changes.

The Interplay Between Exploratory and Confirmatory Approaches

The matter of interplay between exploratory and confirmatory approaches in the development of a scientific discipline has been noted at quite different levels. Sometimes this is a lofty activity guided by abstract notions of the interdependence of general approaches in the progress of a scientific discipline. Other times, the interplay is more insidious. For example, various writers have cautioned the field concerning the fuzzy interface between confirmatory and exploratory modeling procedures at the practical level (e.g., Cliff, 1983; Nesselroade & Baltes, 1984). When models are fitted to data by means of a confirmatory factor analysis procedure there are several ways that this activity can "slide" toward exploratory analysis. If the initially hypothesized model does not fit the data acceptably, who can resist the urge to tinker with the parameters of the model until it does? Of course, it is far better to tinker with one's model than with one's data, but the fact is that the fit of a model to a given set of data can often be significantly improved by the addition of a few pathways that were not originally contemplated. "Loosening" one's hypothesized model is not necessarily wrong, but it is less than "pure" from a strict confirmatory point of view.

Consider another example of the interplay between confirmatory and exploratory analyses. When a factor model is not fully specified, for example, the factor loadings are constrained but the factor covariance matrix is not, fitting the model to data involves a degree of "exploration." One person's confirmatory analysis with free factor intercorrelations might just as easily be construed as another person's exploratory analysis with some constraints on the loadings.

In discussions of the "natural progression" of scientific disciplines, an early, descriptive, concept-hunting phase that relies heavily on exploration and induction is recognized. West (1985, p. 10), for example, identified five stages of model building in the maturation of a discipline. These included:

1. Detailed verbal descriptions culminating in general concepts that synthesize observations into a few fundamental principles.

2. The quantification of Stage 1 concepts and their subsequent rendering into static linear (mathematical) relationships.

3. The generalization of the relationships in Stage 2 into a linear dynamic description from which the relaxation of the process toward the Stage 2 relations can be determined.

4. A fundamental shift in perspective to re-examine the representation of Stage 1 idea [sic] to include the concept of dynamical steady states. Such states require a nonlinear representation and may have little or no direct relation to Stage 3 concepts.

5. The faithful mathematical transcription of Stage 1 understanding into a fully dynamical nonlinear theory whose "solutions" approach the dynamical steady states in Stage 4 with increasing time.

In a different context, Cattell (1966b) described the course of scientific progress as an inductive-hypothetico-deductive spiral in which science leans on inductive, exploratory work to identify concepts to be explored further within a more deductive, confirmatory mode. The outcome of those efforts then shapes further inductive and deductive interaction as description and explanation both contribute to the evolution of more complete representations of phenomena.

The 1940s, 1950s, 1960s, and early 1970s represented a high point in the application and use of exploratory factor analysis. Despite the relatively primitive computational equipment available to researchers during that era, the largely exploratory analyses then conducted led to the identification and further elaboration of some of the more longevous concepts and measures of interindividual differences in ability performance and temperament (see, e.g., Goldberg, 1993). So, one may ask, is there still a need for exploratory factor analysis? The "natural history" of disciplinary development argues for its retention as a tool to be used in conjunction with more confirmatory ones. Both the reciprocations referenced in West's (1985) Stage 4, for example, and the nature of the inductive-hypothetico-deductive spiral described by Cattell (1966b) highlight continuing roles for both inductive, exploratory and deductive, confirmatory approaches in the development of more comprehensive representations of phenomena.

It is my impression, however, that over the past couple of decades, the inductive-hypothetico-deductive spiral has become a little lopsided. Despite strong articulation of the case for exploratory factor analysis by contemporary writers such as Gorsuch (1988) and Tisak and Meredith (1988), its perceived worth has declined and the decline is in proportion to the ascendancy of confirmatory factor analysis. To a large extent, this most recent offensive against exploratory factor analysis has been mounted primarily from within the factor analysis camp (e.g., Mulaik, 1988).

There is another indicator of what seems to be a much more general trend away from exploratory research. During service on research proposal review groups for a significant portion of my professional life, I have witnessed a swing, very noticeable in the past few years, toward an insistence that research proposals feature explicit hypotheses to be tested if they are to receive a positive recommendation from the review group. Clearly, it would be cause for great rejoicing if this development were emblematic of social and behavioral science having indeed passed dramatically and successfully through a descriptive, exploratory phase of its development. Unfortunately, there is little compelling evidence that this is the case. On the one hand, theory development is an essential activity and some progress has been made, as was noted earlier, in the identification of apparently robust and worthy concepts around which to build theories. On the other hand, for many behavioral and social scientists, the available set of fundamental concepts is not yet convincing as an array of elements from which broad and useful theories can be evolved. When one contemplates the amount of progress in representing change processes and dynamics there is even less cause for celebration.

The current literature shows that sound research involving important questions and the serious, enlightened use of confirmatory factor analyses is being conducted in a variety of areas (e.g., Hertzog & Schaie, 1986; McArdle & Goldsmith, 1990; McArdle & Prescott, 1992; Steyer, Ferring, & Schmitt, 1992; Tanaka & Huba, 1984). But, given strong environmental press for explicit hypotheses to drive empirical research and the fact that it does not take much ingenuity to create a plausible conceptual framework and set of hypotheses related to one's area of inquiry, research of a relatively trivial nature from the standpoint of its contribution to theory building can ease in on the coat tails of powerful, confirmatory methodologies. As an aside, note that this is what was being said about exploratory factor analysis a few decades ago.

Even cross-validation of models, as valuable and central as it is to good science, is not particularly impressive from a hypothetico-deductive perspective. Models that have been "discovered" in earlier exploratory analysis (or on half of a randomly divided sample) need to be cross-validated, but cross-validation can be accomplished with very little grounding in substantive theory. Many readers will recall that there was an enormous amount of conceptual and empirical work done in the 1950s and 1960s on cross-validation in regression analyses. Most of those same readers would agree that, 30 to 40 years later, our theories concerning the behavior of regression weights are far more precise and complete than are our theories concerning the behavior of people.

I hasten to add that I am not pleading that we return to the "thrilling days of yesteryear." Social and behavioral science has gained a great deal, substantively as well as methodologically, from the confirmatory modeling techniques of the past two decades. That said, I want to examine some additional gains that I believe we are in a position to make by the further use of exploratory factor analysis.

Exploration of Development and Other Kinds of Change

Whether or not one believes that psychology has found its lasting, principal concepts of interindividual differences, it is my contention that there remain many promising applications for exploratory factor analysis. These include the further exploitation of extant data through secondary data analysis, examining alternatives to "failed" measurement models, and estimating the number and nature of dimensions spanning various domains of content. The application on which I want to focus the remainder of this discussion is the study of processes of development and other kinds of changes. Despite several creditable attempts to fit confirmatory models to developmental data (e.g., Hertzog & Schaie, 1986; Horn & McArdle, 1980; McArdle, 1988), it seems hardly the case that we have left an inductive phase of research far enough behind that all that remains to be done is to extend existing theories and models by means of confirmatory analyses. Rather, I believe that there remains a clear need for exploratory strategies, tactics, and methods in the study of process. This contention rests on two premises: (a) typically, good theories about structures emphasizing static relationships and primitive notions of change come before good theories of dynamics; and (b) as yet, we don't have (m)any good theories of either static or dynamic relationships. What services can exploratory factor analysis render to the study of processes of development and change or, in West's (1985) terms, to help move us in the direction of steady state, dynamic representations?

To move from static to dynamic representations of phenomena seems to require at least two different lines of activity. One involves augmenting and extending the findings from prior research. As stated by Cattell in the final section of this chapter, it is important to try to determine, for example, the developmental course of well-established concepts such as ability and personality traits that have been isolated through prior exploratory and confirmatory work. Such objectives are an important extension of research programs that have identified and described individual differences.

But there is a second line of activity, one that derives from the notion that the articulation and elaboration of newer concepts arising directly out of focusing on growth, development, and other kinds of changes might necessitate the abandonment of, or at least radical departures from, those generated from the study of static phenomena. Given the history of other sciences, for example, the gains in physics from augmenting classical mechanics with quantum mechanics, I see no reason to suppose that full apprehension of the nature of dynamics will come from concentrating further research solely on what originated as static concepts. For instance, to what extent should developmentalists focus only on established interindividual differences attributes (e.g., the pri-

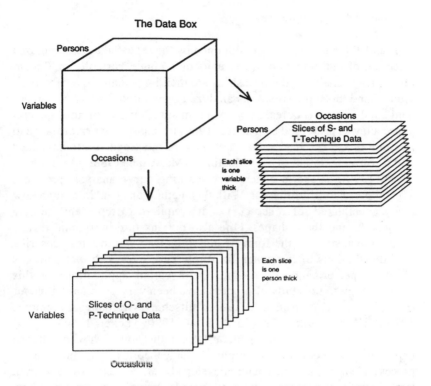

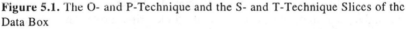

Figure 5.1. The O- and P-Technique and the S- and T-Technique Slices of the Data Box

mary mental abilities or fluid and crystallized intelligence) and study how they grow, develop, and change, in lieu of exploring attributes that are identified directly within the context of dynamics and change?

In examining a continuing role for exploratory factor analysis in studying changes, I would like to draw attention to two kinds of data defined within the familiar data box (Cattell, 1952, 1966a). As specified in the version of the data box shown in Figure 5.1, the two are what Cattell called S- and T-technique data and O- and P-technique data. The dimension of the data box that they have in common is the occasions of measurement dimension. Both kinds of data involve repeated measurements and thus supply empirical information concerning the nature of both change and stability.

Analysis of T-Technique Data

S- and T-technique data are obtained by the repeated assessment of a selection of individuals or other units on a single variable. In T-technique factor analysis, the occasions are then interrelated over the individuals and those interrelations analyzed by common factor or component analysis procedures. A very promising variant of this general approach was presented by Tucker (1966) for analyzing performance in learning tasks. The basic ideas have now been extended into advanced latent variable modeling applications (McArdle, 1988; Meredith & Tisak, 1990). Tucker's generalized learning curve analysis produces several pieces of information. With this method one can determine how many generalized reference curves are required to represent the data adequately and their shapes. One also obtains interindividual differences information in the form of individualized weights that describe the contributions of the generalized reference curves to that person's observed performance over time. Quite varied applications of this methodology to the study of process have been very promising thus far (Cate, Huston, & Nesselroade, 1986; Hultsch, Nesselroade, & Plemons, 1976; McArdle, 1988; Meredith & Tisak, 1990; Tucker, 1966).

Clearly, one can apply this general T-technique approach with either an exploratory or a confirmatory emphasis. Some theories about the nature of processual change are sufficiently developed that their extensions warrant a more confirmatory stance. For example, in Tucker's description of how to analyze learning data, he articulated a three-criteria rotation scheme that involved the (a) signs of loadings, (b) direction of slopes, and (c) existence of asymptotes, of the reference curves. These prescriptions clearly signify a strong theory and a confirmatory stance concerning the *shapes* of the learning functions. In contrast to the matter of specifying the shapes of learning curves, however, determining the *number* of such curves required to fit a given set of data may well be a matter of exploratory analysis.

For developmentalists interested in interindividual differences in intraindividual change patterns this general approach has a strong appeal as an alternative to simply plotting an average change function. There is scant reason to assume, a priori, that an average curve will give a useful representation of processual information. Even though an observable phenomenon (e.g., performance in a paired associates learning task or a physiological response to stress) has been studied for some time, and researchers are convinced that they know the shape of the average function, there may be dissatisfaction with the average. At the same time, however, there may be no guiding theory regarding alternative representations, including multiple functions. Thus, even in an "established" domain, determining the number of reference curves that are required to characterize adequately a set of T-technique data may well be an exploratory matter. Application of exploratory analysis offers a way to check for whether or not multiple functions are needed to characterize such process data and, if so, gives an indication not only of how many but also of their shapes.

I want to illustrate these ideas with some data that were collected in the laboratories of Marilyn Albert at Massachusetts General Hospital and Teresa Seeman at Yale University in connection with work of the MacArthur Foundation Research Network on Successful Aging.[1] We have examined these data using the exploratory methodology just described and have found the results to be quite informative. In both laboratories, the data were collected in a standard experimental protocol that involved obtaining a base-level cortisol assay, giving an injection of corticotropic releasing hormone, and then assaying cortisol levels for several hours (see, e.g., Albert, Greenspan, Nesselroade, & Rowe, 1992). The subjects in both studies were older adults in sound health. Thus, there are two distinct sets of T-technique data consisting of cortisol assays on nine successive occasions of measurement.

The data from each laboratory were analyzed separately by exploratory methods. Based on the eigenvalues of the mean cross-products matrices, two components were extracted to represent the data. Because there was no reason to suppose that the rotational criteria applied to learning data would be useful in modeling the cortisol response, the two components were rotated not according to Tucker's three criteria but by a smoothing procedure developed by Arbuckle and Friendly (1977). The two curves resulting from the analyses are presented in Figures 9.2 and 9.3. What is striking is the general similarity of the curves obtained using these relatively simple exploratory methods on the two data sets. There is the "expected" cortisol function for this experimental protocol (Figure 5.2). In addition, there is a second curve (Figure 5.3) that also appears to be very similar across the two sets of data. That there are two curves, both of which replicate across laboratories, is a potentially valuable outcome of exploratory analysis in a field where the focal phenomenon is usually represented as an average curve. Admittedly, there is much to be done to understand the significance of these exploratory findings but they strongly suggest that there are two aspects of the cortisol response, rather than only one, for which there is a need to account.

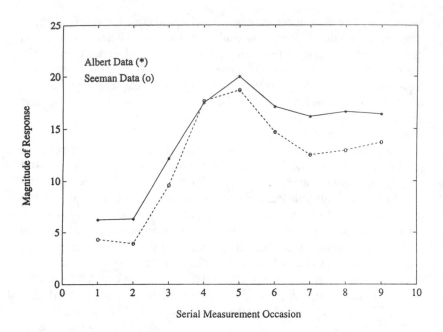

Figure 5.2. First Cortisol Response Component Curve

P-Technique Factor Analysis

I now turn to P-technique exploratory factor analysis. The data for P-technique factor analysis are scores for one individual or other entity measured on a selection of variables repeatedly over a selection of occasions. The data are analyzed by intercorrelating variables over occasions and performing factor or component analysis on the resulting correlations. By virtue of the design, what is reflected in those correlations are intraindividual variability patterns. This approach to identifying such patterns of intraindividual variability was introduced almost 50 years ago (Cattell, Cattell, & Rhymer, 1947).

A number of writers have pointed out the dangers of simply applying the usual common factor model to P-technique data (e.g., Molenaar, 1985; Wohlwill, 1973). The autocorrelation structure found in many kinds of repeated measures data can dramatically influence factor analytic results. Thus, caution needs to be used in analyzing such data and refinements and improvements in the analytical techniques are ever

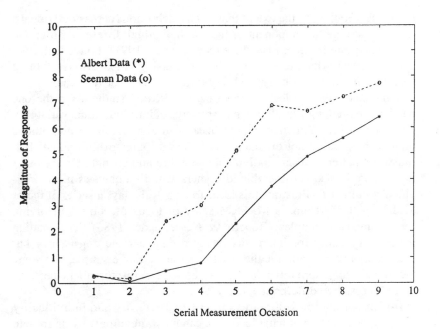

Figure 5.3. Second Cortisol Response Component Curve

more desirable. To date, refinements of the basic approach have involved both design and analysis aspects. The former include simultaneous replications of multiple persons or other units in what we have called Multivariate, Replicated, Single-subject, Repeated Measurements (MRSRM) designs (Corneal & Nesselroade, in press; Jones & Nesselroade, 1990) and the latter include sophisticated developments such as *dynamic factor analysis* (Molenaar, 1985; see also McArdle, 1982) that more appropriately take into account the character of frequently repeated measurements data than does simple P-technique factor analysis.

A survey of MRSRM studies (Jones & Nesselroade, 1990) indicated that there is now a considerable body of information regarding the nature of short-term intraindividual variability on a variety of behavioral and psychological measures. It seems fair to say that such intraindividual variability in a wide variety of measures, including those we tend to regard as measuring highly stable attributes, has a structure and a coherence and should not be uncritically relegated to the role of error or "noise." Rather, to the extent that it is asynchronous across individuals, it can be a notable component of the interindividual differences found at any given point in time. Elsewhere (Nesselroade, 1991), I have identified and discussed what seem to be some promising implications of these findings on intraindividual variability for the study of development.

What else have we learned from these MRSRM studies? On the one hand, there is enough similarity in the patterns of intraindividual variability from one person to another to push ahead with the search for nomothetic relationships based not on stable, trait-like attributes of individuals but, rather, on patterns of intraindividual variability and change. On the other hand, there is also considerable idiosyncrasy and uniqueness in the individual patterns. To illustrate this idea, Table 5.1 displays a series of factor loading patterns from an MRSRM study of locus of control involving several married couples (Roberts & Nesselroade, 1986). The loading pattern, especially for internality, showed considerable consistency but there was also an individuality to the patterns. For example, for some individuals, the Internality items load on a single factor; for others the items divide across two different factors.

It is important to explore this mixture of similarity and individuality in order to ascertain at what level one can most meaningfully aggregate information across individuals. For example, in self-reports people do use language somewhat idiosyncratically. In debriefing participants from one of our studies (Mitteness & Nesselroade, 1987), one subject who described herself as anxious meant that she was anxious; another who described herself as anxious meant that she was eager. We are convinced, and judging from the interest among substantive researchers so are others, that there is much mileage to be made from further careful exploration of intraindividual variability patterns but at this point such work requires a flexibility and a freedom to explore relationships because of the idiosyncratic nature of the patterns at some levels but, presumably, not at all levels. For example, in another set of P-technique factor analysis outcomes (Lebo & Nesselroade, 1978), a similarity of correlational patterns was found at the level of factors (factor intercorrelations) that was not apparent at the level of variables. This outcome is displayed in Table 5.2. Thus, somewhat idiosyncratic, but still identifiable, factor loading patterns at the first order seemed to "absorb" a large amount of the individual measurement idiosyncrasies and offered the possibility of meaningful aggregation at the next order of abstraction. Such possibilities remain to be pursued further but the existing data indicate that the payoff could be substantial.

Table 5.1 Loading Patterns of Internal Factors By Participant[a]

| | | Participant | | | | | | | | | | | | |
| Item | Dimension[b] | Husband A | | Wife A | | Hus-band B | Wife B | | Husband C | | Wife C | | Hus-band D | Wife D |
		I	II	I	II	B	I	II	I	II	I	II	D	D
Competent	I	.71				.61	.72			.48		.50	.95	.56
In control	I	.54		.53		.73	.81		.55	.30	.58		.92	.78
Accomplished	I	.39		.87		.74	.67		.72	.46			.33	.69
Plans being completed	I	.31	.91	.35		.57	.68		.86	.89			.32	.80
I can get what I want	I	.60			.93	—	—	—	.57		.47	.57	.52	.79
Decisive	I				.36	.53	.64	.31	.31				.85	.47
Lucky	CF			.75		—	—	—		.55	.75			.59
Fortunate	CF			.63			.46		.31	.44	.84		.32	.53
Driven	CF					−.30	.43	.57		−.33	.49	.54		
Destined	CF	—	—	—	—	—	—	—			.45			−.69
Controlled by others	PO	−.33						.63						
Like a follower	PO									−.63	.84			
Need to please	PO								.35					
Fit in with others	PO									−.46	.42			
Take care of others	PO													

NOTES: a. After Roberts and Nesselroade (1986). Used with permission of the *Journal of Research in Personality*.
b. Items are from the scale presented by Levenson (1972). I = Internality dimension items; CF = Chance/Fate dimension items; PO = Powerful Others dimension items. Factor loadings of .30 or greater are given. Dashes (—) signify that item was not used in the analysis of that couple's data.

How Confirmatory Factor Analysis Can Help

Before concluding, I want to return briefly to the role of confirmatory factor analysis. Certainly, the intent of my comments has not been to downgrade the importance of being able to specify and test models using confirmatory methods. As a student of development, I use these methods and I appreciate their importance. My concern is that investigators not reject out of hand the contributions of exploratory analysis, especially when the focus is on the knotty problems of process and change.

Table 5.2 Pattern of Intraindividual Variability Factor
Intercorrelations Across 5 P-Technique Participants
(Apparent inconsistencies are noted in boldface)

| | | Factor | | |
	Energy	Well Being	Social Affection	Fatigue
Energy	—			
Well Being	+.35, +.60	—		
	+.76, −.35			
	+.66			
Social Affection	+.48, −.04	+.65, +.25	—	
	+.32, —	+.46, —		
	—	—		
Fatigue	−.50, −.68	−.18, −.31	−.08, +.15	—
	—, −.58	—, +.37	—	
	−.56	−.42		

NOTE: There was no Social Affection factor for Participants 4 and 5 and no Fatigue factor for Subject 3.

Exploratory analyses in the study of change and development can benefit immensely from lessons learned from two decades or so of applying confirmatory factor analysis procedures. For example, we have been forced to think harder about what we are doing when we embark on a factor analytic investigation; about which measures we choose, how we design our data collection, and so forth. Because of the experience with confirmatory modeling, we may be more inclined to emulate the kind of careful measurement development argued for by Thurstone (1938), for instance, in his explorations of the primary mental abilities.

The assessment of change requires a stable reference frame. As discussed elsewhere (e.g., Nesselroade, 1990; Nesselroade & Boker, 1994), this can involve some form of factorial invariance (e.g., over time) or some form of stability of individuals' endowments. The search for invariant relationships has been strongly emphasized in the exploratory factor analysis literature (Ahmavaara, 1954; Cattell, 1944; Meredith, 1964; Thurstone, 1957). Cattell's confactor rotation (see, e.g., McArdle & Cattell, 1994), for example, represents an attempt to resolve the ambiguity of rotational positions in exploratory factor analysis by capitalizing on the concept of factorial invariance. There remains a close linkage between the concept of invariance and exploratory factor analysis, but it is also clear that one of the strengths of confirmatory techniques is that they permit rather rigorous tests of the extent to which invariant features of the factor model hold across different subpopulations, across different occasions of measurement, and so forth. Thus, through its capacity to bring multiple data matrices into a common analytical framework and, for example, allow the specification of invariant loadings across multiple occasions, confirmatory methods have provided an important way to structure change.

Concluding Remarks

The invitation to write a chapter on exploratory factor analysis was one to which I responded quite positively. Of special significance to me is the fact that the year of this writing is the silver anniversary of my receipt of the Ph.D. degree, the apprenticeship for which was served in Raymond B. Cattell's laboratory at the University of Illinois. Cattell is a distinguished scholar whose investigation of personality, broadly defined, represents a program of research work as closely identified with the use of exploratory factor analysis as anyone's of which I am aware. Now in the ninth decade of his life, but still continuing to publish his ideas, Cattell has worn the methods and techniques of exploratory factor analysis as a mantle, has waved them as a flag, and when the occasion requires, has wielded them as a broadsword. It was principally in Cattell's laboratory that I learned to use these methods, but my experience was enriched through class work with Lloyd Humphreys, Henry Kaiser, and Ledyard Tucker, and association with more senior graduate students such as Richard Gorsuch, John Horn, and Peter Schoenemann. By no means does this group represent a monolithic perspective on exploratory factor analysis; thus my reference to "enriched" experiences.

When I began assembling ideas for this chapter, it occurred to me that it would be interesting to many readers to hear from someone with Cattell's credentials regarding his perceptions of the role of exploratory factor analysis in a major research program. I sent Cattell a letter with 10 questions and asked him to respond if he were so inclined. He responded with a very short latency; evidence I chose to construe as continuing high regard for the value of exploratory factor analysis and his eagerness to mount the podium yet one more time, if only vicariously, and pound out his message to the unconverted. Here are his perspectives.

A Conversation With Raymond B. Cattell

Q. As one of the premiere developers and users of exploratory factor analysis in the 1940s, 1950s, 1960s, and 1970s, you saw many changes in the method. What are your general thoughts about the role exploratory factor analysis has played in the development of psychological science?

A. Exploratory factor analysis has been a very busy horse the whole time. Or to change the metaphor it has been busy bailing the storm-encircled boat, while the bivariate conservatives have been raking the water out with teaspoons. Psychology has been reduced to advancing only as fast as a few overworked bailers could clear up the problem of unitary sources, where bivariate methods have been in vain.

Q. You first published the results of a factor analysis over a half-century ago. What would you have done differently then, had you known what you know now about the strengths and weaknesses of the method?

A. The only real problem and source of confusion in factor analysis has been that of finding the unique rotation position in component hyperspace. Thurstone's simple structure was rather crudely conceived, and its dependence on choice of variables and the difficulty of knowing when it was significantly reached and when not, led to despairing disagreements. A real test of significance rested on a demonstration that an unimprovable plateau had been reached in the hyperplane count. Human lack of conscientious persistence stood in the way of this, aided by push-button rotation programs no one of which, except *maxplane,* maximized what actually needed to be maximized. Confactor rotation, with a slight adaptation to oblique structure, offers a logical answer to the problem of locating the real influences.

What I would have done differently at the beginning, is what we actually did: tighten up the sources of weakness. These were: a test for the number of factors, estimation of the communalities, admission of differences of factor size in the behavioral equation (true

zero factor analysis), trial and error discovery of nonlinear relations, recognition of error factors and method factors from super
matrix true factors, and so on. Kaiser, Guttman, and others played
with all sorts of variants in expressing factors, but these did really
nothing for the main advances.

Q. Which of your own methodological contributions to exploratory
factor analysis do you feel has had the most impact on psychology?

A. The insistence that rotation could be aided by Rotoplot, and given
significance by hyperplane count.

   The value of factor analysis has been recognized because of the
ultimate agreements of researchers on trait structure in ability,
personality, and dynamics, across many researchers and in different countries. The structures discovered agreed with clinical, educational, developmental, and physiological observations.

Q. Confirmatory factor analysis methods have been available for a
long time (e.g., Procrustes rotation, multiple group factor analysis).
Currently available confirmatory methods are elegant and quite
sophisticated. Are psychologists using these methods well?

A. Since it is extremely difficult to define hypotheses to test by confirmatory factor analysis, I regard it as a useful appendage to exploratory factor analysis. The actual findings "from scratch" are diminutive
and its use in checking exploratory factor analysis has so far been
quite insufficiently applied. I would say psychologists are using
confirmatory well when they go over the whole furniture from the
exploratory factor analysis systematically.

Q. Does exploratory factor analysis have an important role to play in
contemporary psychological research?

A. Of course! The mainstream has gone off into "bitty" cognitive psychology using imaginary concepts represented by a single variable.
This will get them nowhere. Unless the concepts used are first discovered and *measured* as unitary factors nothing final can be proved. For
example, measuring speed in relation to anxiety is a waste of time if
you represent anxiety by an electrical skin resistance variable.

Q. Don't conceptions of cultural change and dynamics imply that we
may always need to keep exploratory techniques available, at least
until we have good theories of the nature of dynamics and change?

A. I must wholly agree. The "theories of the nature of dynamics and change" are what you discover *as a base* by exploratory factor analysis. I can already refer to this in the list of ergs and sems discovered to replace Murray and Freud. The resultant theories regarding conflict, decision, evolution of personality, and so forth, have been spelled out now for 20 years, awaiting the "mainstream" dabblers to work upon.

Q. From the perspective of one who has been observing the field for 60 years, do the debates about orthogonal versus oblique rotation seem as important now as they did earlier?

A. Quite irrelevant. There *are* no orthogonal factors in Nature. Once this is grasped, by substantive experience, the debate is dead.

Q. What do you see as the most lasting contribution of exploratory factor analysis to psychology?

A. The real structure of personality and ability, in traits and states. These are the dominoes by which *process* and *developmental* [issues] can begin to be studied.

    Without the past 50 years of continuous, programmatic research, we should still be in complete chaos, or retreating into philosophy and physiology. The Wundtian abstract research on process can get nowhere without what enters into the process.

Q. Do you see anything particularly frightening or ominous in the predominant ways factor analysis is being used today?

A. The enthusiasm for confirmatory factor analysis, though justified by its elegance, puts it out of proportion as an economical working tool. The history of research needs to be perceived as a functional, two-handed use of exploratory factor analysis and confirmatory factor analysis used intelligently in sequence.

    A more vulgar danger is the use of either method by those who think only a computer and a program are necessary. We need a complete change in the training of psychologists and the staffing of psychology departments. There is no "elementary" experimental psychology. McDougall said it long ago, "Psychology is too difficult for psychologists." Advanced research centers must lead the way. Ph.D. theses are for testing the student.

Q. What is the most important piece of methodological advice you would give to today's young psychological researchers?

A. Give equal importance to ANOVA and CORAN [correlational analysis]. Many Ph.D.s are qualified only in ANOVA. In factor analysis itself, I revert to my emphases on finding true simple structure, and improving confactor. Don't do factor analyses in a vacuum; always include markers for the factors already known in the area, when you enter with new variables. Otherwise, you finish in the air.

The development and proliferation of confirmatory factor analysis methods has brought new interest and enthusiasm into the research enterprise and has forced a sharpening of the arguments offered in defense of both exploratory and confirmatory factor analyses. I am persuaded by Cattell's description of advancement in science as an inductive-hypothetico-deductive spiral and I believe that exploratory factor analysis will continue to play a valuable role in several important arenas of behavioral and social research. Given a belief that what are generally thought of as competing approaches (exploratory vs. confirmatory) are more accurately portrayed as representing differences in explicitness concerning what is imposed a priori in analyzing data, I believe there is a better way to express the sentiment of the preceding sentence. To the extent that building a knowledge base involves both inductive and deductive activities, exploration will remain an integral part of scientific activity. From this perspective, a useful index of how far we have progressed in a discipline is not how little we use exploratory techniques but rather how extensive and solid is the base on which further exploration rests.

With particular regard for the study of development and other kinds of change processes, I am inclined to the belief that critically important gains will come from the further exploration of intraindividual variability data in which interindividual differences in change have not first been "averaged out" or otherwise adulterated through the restrictions and manipulations of group designs. From a scientific perspective, it is obviously necessary to demonstrate that relationships hold across individuals, but alternative routes to these discoveries must be considered. One that I believe deserves a fairer test involves seeking generalities among the higher order abstractions developed by using exploratory factor analysis to study individuals intensively over time. Given our current lack of knowledge about specifics, the need to model the individual's changes and stabilities first, prior to seeking generalities in those models of individuals, seems to me to beg for delaying the abandonment of exploratory factor analysis.

Note

1. I wish to thank Marilyn Albert and Teresa Seeman for allowing me to analyze and present cortisol response data from their laboratories.

References

Ahmavaara, Y. (1954). The mathematical theory of factorial invariance under selection. *Psychometrika, 19,* 27-38.

Albert, M. S., Greenspan, S., Nesselroade, J. R., & Rowe, J. W. (1992). *Responsiveness of the HPA axis to pharmacologic and non-pharmacologic stimulation in healthy elderly.* Unpublished manuscript. Department of Psychiatry, Massachusetts General Hospital, Harvard Medical School.

Arbuckle, J., & Friendly, M. L. (1977). On rotating to smooth functions. *Psychometrika, 42,* 127-140.

Bentler, P. M. (1980). Multivariate analysis with latent variables: Causal modeling. In M. R. Rosenzweig & L. W. Porter (Eds.), *Annual review of psychology.* Palo Alto, CA: Annual Reviews.

Cate, R. M., Huston, T. L., & Nesselroade, J. R. (1986). Premarital relationships: Toward the identification of alternative pathways to marriage. *Journal of Social and Clinical Psychology, 4,* 3-22.

Cattell, R. B. (1944). "Parallel proportional profiles" and other principles for determining the choice of factors by rotation. *Psychometrika, 9,* 267-283.

Cattell, R. B. (1952). The three basic factor analytic research designs—Their interrelations and derivatives. *Psychological Bulletin, 49,* 267-283.

Cattell, R. B. (1957). *Personality and motivation structure and measurement.* New York: World Book.

Cattell, R. B. (1966a). The data box: Its ordering of total resources in terms of possible relational systems. In R. B. Cattell (Ed.), *Handbook of multivariate experimental psychology* (pp. 67-128). Chicago: Rand McNally.

Cattell, R. B. (1966b). Psychological theory and scientific method. In R. B. Cattell (Ed.), *Handbook of multivariate experimental psychology* (pp. 1-18). Chicago: Rand McNally.

Cattell, R. B., Cattell, A.K.S., & Rhymer, R. M. (1947). P-technique demonstrated in determining psycho-physical source traits in a normal individual. *Psychometrika, 12,* 267-288.

Cliff, N. (1983). Some cautions concerning the application of causal modeling methods. *Multivariate Behavioral Research, 18,* 115-126.

Corneal, C., & Nesselroade, J. R. (in press). A stepchild's experience across two households: An investigation of emotional response patterns by P-technique factor analysis. *Multivariate Experimental and Clinical Psychology.*

Goldberg, L. R. (1993). What the hell took so long? Donald Fiske and the big-five factor structure. In P. E. Shrout & S. T. Fiske (Eds.), *Advances in personality research, methods and theory: A festschrift honoring Donald W. Fiske.* Hillsdale, NJ: Lawrence Erlbaum.

Gorsuch, R. L. (1988). Exploratory factor analysis. In J. R. Nesselroade & R. B. Cattell (Eds.), *Handbook of multivariate experimental psychology* (2nd ed.) (pp. 231-258). New York: Plenum.

Hertzog, C., & Schaie, K. W. (1986). Stability and change in adult intellectual development: 1. Analysis of longitudinal covariance structures. *Psychology and Aging, 1,* 159-171.

Horn, J. L., & McArdle, J. J. (1980). Perspectives on mathematical/statistical model building (MASMOB) in research on aging. In L. W. Poon (Ed.), *Aging in the 1980s: Selected contemporary issues in the psychology of aging.* Washington, DC: American Psychological Association.

Hultsch, D. F., Nesselroade, J. R., & Plemons, J. K. (1976). Learning-ability relations in adulthood. *Human Development, 19,* 234-247.

Jones, C. J., & Nesselroade, J. R. (1990). Multivariate, replicated, single-subject designs and P-technique factor analysis: A selective review of intraindividual change studies. *Experimental Aging Research, 16,* 171-183.

Lebo, M. A., & Nesselroade, J. R. (1978). Intraindividual differences dimensions of mood change during pregnancy identified in five P-technique factor analyses. *Journal of Research in Personality, 12,* 205-224.

Levenson, H. (1972). Distinctions within the concept of internal-external control: Development of a new scale. *Proceedings of the 80th Annual Convention of the American Psychological Association, 7,* 259-260.

Loehlin, J. C. (1987). *Latent variable models: An introduction to factor, path, and structural analysis.* Hillsdale, NJ: Lawrence Erlbaum.

McArdle, J. J. (1982). Structural equation modeling of a dynamic system. *Report to the National Institute on Alcohol Abuse and Alcoholism* (NIAAA AA-05743).

McArdle, J. J. (1988). Dynamic but structural equation modeling of repeated measures data. In J. R. Nesselroade & R. B. Cattell (Eds.), *Handbook of multivariate experimental psychology* (2nd ed.) (pp. 561-614). New York: Plenum.

McArdle, J. J., & Cattell, R. B. (1994). Structural equation models of factorial invariance in parallel proportional profiles and oblique confactor problems. *Multivariate Behavioral Research, 29,* 63-113.

McArdle, J. J., & Goldsmith, H. H. (1990). Alternative common factor models for multivariate biometric analyses. *Behavior Genetics, 20,* 569-608.

McArdle, J. J., & Prescott, C. A. (1992). Age-based construct validation using structural equation modeling. *Experimental Aging Research, 18,* 87-115.

McDonald, R. P. (1985). *Factor analysis and related methods.* Hillsdale, NJ: Lawrence Erlbaum.

Meredith, W. (1964). Notes on factorial invariance. *Psychometrika, 29,* 177-185.

Meredith, W., & Tisak, J. (1990). Latent curve analysis. *Psychometrika, 55,* 107-122.

Mitteness, L. S., & Nesselroade, J. R. (1987). Attachment in adulthood: Longitudinal investigation of mother-daughter affective interdependencies by P-technique factor analysis. *The Southern Psychologist, 3,* 37-44.

Molenaar, P.C.M. (1985). A dynamic factor model for the analysis of multivariate time series. *Psychometrika, 50,* 181-202.

Mulaik, S. (1988). Confirmatory factor analysis. In J. R. Nesselroade & R. B. Cattell (Eds.), *Handbook of multivariate experimental psychology* (2nd ed.) (pp. 259-288). New York: Plenum.

Nesselroade, J. R. (1990). Adult personality development: Issues in assessing constancy and change. In A. I. Rabin, R. A. Zucker, R. A. Emmons, & S. Frank (Eds.), *Studying persons and lives.* New York: Springer.

Nesselroade, J. R. (1991). The warp and the woof of the developmental fabric. In R. Downs, L. Liben, & D. Palermo (Eds.), *Visions of aesthetics, the environment, and development: The legacy of Joachim F. Wohlwill.* Hillsdale, NJ: Lawrence Erlbaum.

Nesselroade, J. R., & Baltes, P. B. (1984). From traditional factor analysis to structural-causal modeling in developmental research. In V. Sarris & A. Parducci (Eds.), *Experimental psychology in the future* (pp. 267-287). Hillsdale, NJ: Lawrence Erlbaum.

Nesselroade, J. R., & Boker, S. M. (1994). Assessing constancy and change. In T. Brotherton & J. Weinberger (Eds.), *Can personality change?* Washington, DC: American Psychological Association.

Nesselroade, J. R., & Cattell, R. B. (Eds). (1988). *Handbook of multivariate experimental psychology* (2nd ed.). New York: Plenum.

Reinert, G. (1970). Comparative factor analytic studies of intelligence throughout the human life-span. In L. R. Goulet & P. B. Baltes (Eds.), *Life-span developmental psychology: Research and theory* (pp. 467-484). New York: Academic Press.

Roberts, M. L., & Nesselroade, J. R. (1986). Intraindividual variability in perceived locus of control in adults: P-technique factor analyses of short-term change. *Journal of Research in Personality, 20,* 529-545.

Steyer, R., Ferring, D., & Schmitt, M. (1992). States and traits in psychological assessment. *European Journal of Psychological Assessment, 8,* 79-98.

Tanaka, J. S., & Huba, G. J. (1984). Confirmatory hierarchical factor analyses of psychological distress measures. *Journal of Personality and Social Psychology, 46,* 621-635.

Thurstone, L. L. (1938). *Primary mental abilities.* Chicago: University of Chicago Press.

Thurstone, L. L. (1957). *Multiple factor analysis.* Chicago: University of Chicago Press.

Tisak, J., & Meredith, W. (1988). Exploratory longitudinal factor analysis in multiple populations. *Psychometrika, 53,* 261-281.

Tucker, L. R. (1966). Learning theory and multivariate experiment: Determination of generalized learning curves. In R. B. Cattell (Ed.), *Handbook of multivariate experimental psychology* (pp. 476-501). Chicago: Rand McNally.

West, B. J. (1985). *An essay on the importance of being nonlinear.* Berlin: Springer-Verlag.

Wohlwill, J. F. (1973). *The study of behavioral development.* New York: Academic Press.

6

Dynamic Latent Variable Models in Developmental Psychology

PETER C. M. MOLENAAR

1. Introduction

Empirical study of developmental processes requires the availability of pertinent statistical methods that, among other things, capture the dynamics underlying age-related changes. For instance, Wohlwill (1991) concludes his discussion of the relationship between methods and theory in developmental research by a request for

> methodologies that allow one to model the interpatterning between two sets of processes each of which is undergoing change, in part as function of the other. The closest approach to the kind of modeling that is indicated for this purpose are probably some of the models from the field of ecology, and similar systems-analytical work. (p. 139)

AUTHOR'S NOTE: The author wishes to thank the Methodology Center, Department of Human Development and Family Studies, and The Pennsylvania State University, for providing the opportunity to write this chapter during a working visit. The author also wants to thank Professor John R. Nesselroade for his continuing interest in, and stimulation of, the work presented in this chapter.

Mathematical system theory indeed provides an excellent framework for the derivation of process-oriented methods that meet Wohlwill's criteria. Linear system theory, based on linear algebra and complex variable theory, has proven to be very successful in the analysis, design, and control of arbitrarily complex linear systems. More recently, differential geometry has proven to be an almost equally powerful means of analysis and design of nonlinear systems (cf. Isidori, 1989). It therefore is almost self-evident that concepts and techniques of mathematical system theory will predominate in our discussion of dynamic latent variable models in developmental psychology.

In what follows we will be mainly concerned with the accommodation of the normal linear factor model to multivariate time series data. Hence we consider the so-called dynamic factor model, involving a one-to-many mapping of latent metrical factor series to manifest metrical series. The dynamic factor model will be represented as a particular instance of the state-space model that underlies much of mathematical system theory. In this way the stage is set for the introduction of system-theoretical concepts, like observability and reachability, that have an important bearing on dynamic factor analysis. Moreover, the state-space representation enables a concise specification of several restrictive versions of the dynamic factor model that have appeared in the published literature. But most importantly, this representation naturally lends itself to the definition of a new, generalized dynamic factor model that may be especially pertinent to the analysis of developmental processes.

Up until now, applications of the dynamic factor model always have proceeded under the restrictive assumption that the basic model parameters stay invariant in time. That is, the dynamic factor model was required to be a time-homogeneous model (cf. Gardiner, 1990, p. 60). For the first time, at least to the best of our knowledge, a completely inhomogeneous dynamic factor model is presented in which an arbitrary subset of parameters can be time-varying. Moreover, the way in which the latter parameters vary with time can be determined in an empirical way. Hence, this generalized dynamic factor analysis opens up the possibility of tracing the continual reorganizations that characterize many developmental processes.

In the second part of this chapter we will discuss parameter estimation in the inhomogeneous dynamic factor model by means of the expectation-maximization algorithm and present some illustrative results obtained in a simulation study. The first part of this chapter is devoted to general, mainly system-theoretical, issues related to dynamic factor analysis. Here we also present a concise discussion of ergodicity, a central concept in delineating the relationship between time series analysis and standard psychometrics.

2. Aspects of State-Space Models

Consider a p-variate manifest time series $y(t) = [y_1(t), \ldots, y_p(t)]'$ in discrete time $t = 0, 1, 2, \ldots$, where the superscript $'$ denotes transposition (we will represent vectors by bold lowercase letters and matrices by bold uppercase letters). A schematic state-space model of $y(t)$ is given by:

$$s(t + 1) = A_t s(t) + B_t u(t) + w(t)$$

$$y(t) = H_t s(t) + v(t) \qquad [6.1]$$

The model can be conceived of as an abstract system, the manifest output of which is $y(t)$. The latent n-variate state of this system is $s(t)$, $u(t)$ denotes the system's manifest m-variate input, $w(t)$ its latent n-variate input, and the p-variate series $v(t)$ can be interpreted as measurement error. The subscript t of A_t $(n \times n)$, B_t $(n \times m)$, and H_t $(p \times n)$ indicates that the entries of these system matrices can be functions of time.

Major fields of application of models like (6.1) are

Prediction. Determine for $k > 0$ an optimal estimate of

$$E[s(t + k) \mid y(t), y(t - 1), \ldots] , \qquad [6.1.1]$$

that is, the expected state at time $t + k$ given observations up to time t. For $k = 0$ or $k < 0$ this is called filtering or interpolation, respectively.

Analysis of Time Series Designs. Determine an optimal estimate of b in

$$s(t + 1) = A_t s(t) + D_t b + w(t) , \qquad [6.1.2]$$

where D_t is a design matrix.

Optimal Control. Determine the value $u^*(t)$ of the manifest input that minimizes the discrepancy between $s(t + 1)$ and its desired value $s^*(t + 1)$:

$$u^*(t) = F_t[y(t), Q_s, Q_u] , \qquad [6.1.3]$$

where $F_t[.]$ denotes the feedback function from output $y(t)$ to input $u(t)$, Q_s is a positive-definite weight matrix in the quadratic form penalizing the discrepancy $[s(t + 1) - s^*(t + 1)]$, and Q_u is an analogous matrix in the quadratic form penalizing the costs involved in applying $u^*(t)$.

Structural Modeling. This includes dynamic factor analysis and will be the main subject in what follows.

Please notice that this brief overview of major applications of state-space models leaves out a host of details and qualifications. These can be found in textbooks on prediction (e.g., Goodwin & Sin, 1984), time series designs (e.g., Kashyap & Rao, 1976), and optimal control (Whittle, 1982, 1990). We will proceed with definitions of some general aspects of Model 6.1. First, certain variants of stationarity are considered.

Stationarity

As $w(t)$ and $v(t)$ in (6.1) denote random processes, $y(t)$ also is a random process. Consequently, $y(t)$ is characterized by an ensemble of finite-dimensional probability distributions

$$P(y;t) = \text{Prob}[y(t) < y] \,,$$

$$P(y_1, y_2; t_1, t_2) = \text{Prob}[y(t_1) < y_1; y(t_2) < y_2] \,, \text{ etc.} \qquad [6.1.4]$$

Accordingly, $y(t)$ can be regarded as a random time-dependent function and we can talk about its first-order moment (mean) function, second-order moment (covariance) function, etc. In general these moment function can be time-varying. If, however, the first-order moment function is a constant,

$$E[y(t)] = c_y \,, \qquad [6.2]$$

then $y(t)$ is called first-order stationary. In a similar vein $y(t)$ is called second-order stationary if its covariance function only depends upon the interval (lag) between t_1 and t_2:

$$E[y(t_1), y(t_2)'] = C_y(t_2 - t_1) = C_y(k) \,, \quad k = t_2 - t_1 \,. \qquad [6.3]$$

If $y(t)$ is both first- and second-order stationary, it is called weakly stationary. If in addition all its higher-order moment functions are stationary, $y(t)$ is called strictly stationary. A related important concept is asymptotic second-order stationarity:

$$\lim T^{-1}\sum_{t=1}^{T} y(t)y(t+k)' = C_y(k) .$$ [6.4]

Together these variants of stationarity will suffice for our purposes. In fact, they also are sufficient for most applied time series analysis. In particular, weak stationarity is all that is needed for spectral analysis of time series. If $y(t)$ is weakly stationary then the frequency domain representation of (6.1), in which all system matrices now are time-homogeneous, is

$$(e^{if}I - A)s(f) = Bu(f) + w(f)$$

$$y(f) = Hs(f) + v(f) ,$$ [6.5]

where $I(n \times n)$ denotes the unity matrix, i is the imaginary unit, and f the frequency.

Structural Identifiability

To ease the introduction of structural identifiability, it will be assumed that $y(t)$ is weakly stationary and the state-space model is time-homogeneous. Yet, the model now contains unknown parameters which are collected in q:

$$s(t + 1) = A(q)s(t) + B(q)u(t) + w(t)$$

$$y(t) = H(q)s(t) + v(t)$$

$$E[w(t), w(t+k)'] = C_w(q)d(k) , \quad E[v(t), v(t+k)'] = C_v(q)d(k) ,   [6.6]$$

where $d(k)$ denotes Kronecker's delta (which equals 1 if $k = 0$, and 0 otherwise). Notice that $w(t)$ and $v(t)$ are taken to be white noise series, the covariance functions of which are zero for nonzero lags k. Loosely speaking, then, structural identifiability concerns the existence of a unique estimate of q in (6.6) after having resolved structural issues associated with the background Model (6.1). Hence we first have to deal with these structural issues.

State-space models like (6.1) are in general not unique. What we actually observe are the manifest series $y(t)$ and $u(t)$, as well as their functional relationship

$$y(t) = \sum_u B(u)u(t-u) + \sum_u K(u)e(t-u) , \qquad [6.7]$$

where $e(t)$ is a p-variate residual white noise process. The functional relationship between $y(t)$ and $u(t)$ is characterized by the set of matrices $\{B(u), K(u); u = 0, 1, \ldots\}$, which is called the transfer function. The relationship between (6.7) and (6.1) is one-to-many in that there exists an infinite number of state-space models that can reproduce a given transfer function. These so-called transfer function equivalent models may have state-spaces of different dimension. Furthermore, transfer function equivalent models with the same state-space dimension are, in the notation of (6.1), related by

$$A^* = TAT^{-1} , \quad H^* = HT^{-1} , \quad B^* = TB , \qquad [6.8]$$

where T is an arbitrary positive-definite matrix. In order to bring this multitude of equivalent state-space representations under control, we will outline a procedure described in Hannan and Deistler (1988).

Firstly, the subset of models reproducing (6.7) and having minimal state-space dimension is determined. Following Hannan and Deistler (1988, pp. 17-20), we therefore reformulate (6.1) as a so-called innovations model

$$s(t+1) = As(t) + Bu(t) + Ke(t)$$

$$y(t) = Hs(t) + e(t) , \qquad [6.9]$$

where $e(t)$ is given by (6.7) and is referred to as the innovations series. Next we define for (6.9) two important characteristics of mathematical systems, namely observability and reachability. The system (6.9) is observable if in the absence of $u(t)$ and $e(t)$ the state $s(t)$ can be determined uniquely at time $t + n - 1$, where n is the dimension of the state. More specifically, (6.9) is observable if

$$O' = (H', A'H', \ldots, A'^{m-1}H') \qquad [6.9.1]$$

is of full rank n. The system (6.9) is reachable if we can maneuver $s(t)$ into any state given any initial state $s(t - n + 1)$ and with $u(t - 1)$, $e(t - 1)$, ..., $u(t - n + 1)$, $e(t - n + 1)$ under our control. Specifically, (6.9) is reachable if R is of full rank n, where

$$R = [(B, K), A(B, K), \ldots, A^{n-1}(B, K)] \qquad [6.9.2]$$

We now are ready to state the main result concerning minimality of state-space dimension. A state-space system is minimal if and only if it is observable and reachable (Hannan & Deistler, 1988, theorem 2.3.3). Hence by ascertaining minimality, the number of equivalent state-space models associated with a given transfer function is reduced substantially. Effective algorithms transforming (6.1) to minimal form can be found in Aplevitch (1991). The requirement that (6.1) be minimal solves the structural issues alluded to earlier and paves the way to determine the identifiability of the parameter vector q in (6.6). Notice that there actually is an infinite number of equivalent minimal systems which are related to each other by (6.8) (K in (6.9) is transformed like $B: K^* = TK$). Glover and Williams (1974; also Hannan & Deistler, 1988, pp. 80-81) show that structural identifiability for a minimal system like (6.6) can be determined by checking the rank of a matrix of contrasts between equivalent forms defined by (6.8). Unfortunately, an application of this structural identifiability criterion to dynamic factor models involves quite complex alpha-numerical computations for which no suitable computer program seems to be available. An alternative frequency domain approach, making use of existing algorithms, was proposed in Molenaar (1989) and has been applied to dynamic factor models in Molenaar, de Gooijer, and Schmitz (1992).

For the moment this concludes the discussion of structural identifiability. In the second part of this chapter we will briefly return to it in the context of inhomogeneous systems. Determination of structural identifiability is a necessary step in the application of any parametric model and it was our intention to indicate how for a state-space model like (6.6) it is linked up with central system-theoretical concepts like observability and reachability. We now turn to a concept of different origin, ergodicity, that will be interpreted in a somewhat unusual way.

Ergodicity

What can be said about the possible relationships between structural models for single-subject time series and analogous models defined over a population of subjects? More specifically, how are dynamic factor models related to traditional (longitudinal or cross-sectional) factor models? This is an important question not only in the modeling of developmental process (see Jones & Nesselroade, 1990) but for psychometrics in general. For instance, in their textbook on statistical theories of mental test scores, Lord and Novick (1968) initially define true and error scores for the case in which a given test is repeatedly administered to a single subject, but then proceed with a consideration of only models for a population of subjects. Yet the precise relationship between single- versus multiple-subject test theory is left unexplained. For instance, what is the relevance of a classical reliability coefficient for single-subject time series data?

If we take the covariance function (6.3) of a zero-mean weakly stationary time series as an example, and fix the lag k at $k = 1$ to ease the discussion, then an important question is under what conditions $C_y(1)$ for single-subject time series data equals $C_y(1)$ for multiple-subject longitudinal data. Notice that the obvious time series estimator for $C_y(1)$ is

$$C_y^{\wedge}(1) = T^{-1} \sum_{t=1}^{T-1} y(t)y(t+1)', \qquad [6.9.3]$$

where T is the length of the series and where for convenience the mean correction has been neglected. In contrast, the longitudinal estimator for two consecutive waves at t_0 and t_1 is

$$C_y^{\sim}(1) = N^{-1} \sum_{n=1}^{N} y_i(t_0)y_i(t_1)', \qquad [6.9.4]$$

where N is the number of subjects in the sample and where again mean correction has been neglected. Now $y(t)$ is called ergodic if, letting T and N approach infinity, $C_y^{\wedge}(1)$ equals $C_y^{\sim}(1)$. Stated more generally, a random process is ergodic if asymptotic averages over a single realization of the process equal asymptotic averages over multiple realizations of this process.

The concept of ergodicity arose in equilibrium statistical mechanics, where it can be given a nice interpretation: If a system is ergodic then it will in the long run visit every region of its state-space infinitely often.

Hence following a single trajectory during a long time will yield the same results as instantaneous sampling of many points or small regions in the state-space. This will be elaborated somewhat further in the closing section. At present, we would like to stress that processes are ergodic only if they obey strict regularity conditions. The reader is referred to Hannan (1970, chap. 4) for a detailed discussion of these conditions. Suffice it to say that many psychological and developmental processes may fail to obey these requirements and therefore be nonergodic. For these nonergodic processes it is an open question how analyses of single trajectories relate to analyses of pooled multicase data, even if the processes concerned are stationary.

3. Overview of Dynamic Factor Models

Until now, dynamic factor analyses always seem to have been based on time-homogeneous models. That is, in order for these analyses to apply a particular subset of the moment functions of the manifest random process, $y(t)$ has to be stationary. Dynamic factor models differ in the number and type of stationarity assumptions about $y(t)$. We will present a concise description of two types of such models, where the second type includes the first one. Furthermore, analysis of each of these models can be carried out in the time domain or in the frequency domain, thus yielding a list of four dynamic factor analyses techniques. The models concerned will be presented in their original representation; their equivalent state-space representation then will be immediately apparent.

A Hierarchy of Dynamic Factor Models

If it is assumed that both the mean and covariance function of $y(t)$ are stationary, then the following time-domain dynamic factor models obtain

$$f(t) = z(t)$$

$$y(t) = \sum_{u=0}^{s} L(u)f(t-u) + e(t) \qquad [6.10]$$

In this model $f(t)$ is a q-dimensional latent factor series and $L(u)$, $u = 0$, $1, \ldots, s$ denotes a sequence of lagged $p \times q$ factor loading matrices. Usually (but not necessarily) the covariance function of the p-variate residual series $e(t)$ is taken to be diagonal, which implies that univariate component series of $e(t)$ may be auto-correlated but are not cross-correlated between each other. It was proved in Molenaar (1985) that if no restrictions are placed on the lagged factor loadings in $L(u)$, the covariance function of $f(t)$ has to be fixed in order to obtain a structurally identified model. A convenient choice then is to define $f(t)$ as a standardized white noise series $z(t)$, although any other choice is acceptable [e.g., $f(t)$ might be defined as a given autoregressive-moving average process]. Notice that (6.10) is a causal or physically realizable model in that $y(t)$ only depends on the input $f(t)$ up to time t. Notice also that (6.10) can be reformulated as a time-homogeneous instance of the state-space model (6.1) by introducing the extended state $s(t)' = [f(t)', \ldots, f(t - s)']$ (see Molenaar, 1985, for a detailed description of this reformulation).

The frequency domain analogue of (6.10) is

$$f(f) = z(f)$$

$$y(f) = L(f)f(f) + e(f) \qquad [6.11]$$

where all variables now are complex-valued but otherwise have the same interpretations as in (6.10). Both from a mathematical-statistical and a computational point of view, (6.11) is much better conditioned than (6.10). Yet (6.11) inheres a major flaw: Transforming it back to the time domain does not yield a causal or physically realizable model in that $y(t)$ may depend on future input $f(t + u)$ for positive lags u. This lack of physical realizability has been a persistent problem with frequency domain models like (6.11). It arises because each distinct column of $L(f)$ is only identified up to multiplication by $\exp[ig]$, where g is an arbitrary real-valued phase variable (e.g., Brillinger, 1975, p. 354). A principled solution to this problem, involving separate unitary rotations to minimum phase of each column in $L(f)$, has been given in Molenaar (1987).

We next consider a type of dynamic factor model in which the first-order moment function of the latent factor series is allowed to be nonstationary. More specifically, it is assumed that $E[f(t)]$, and hence $E[y(t)]$, is linear in t:

$$f(t) = gt + z(t)$$

$$y(t) = \sum_{u=0}^{s} L(u)f(t - u) + e(t) \qquad [6.12]$$

where g is a q-dimensional vector of trend coefficients. Notice that (6.12) implies that $E[f(0)] = \boldsymbol{0}$. In fact it is shown in Molenaar et al. (1992) that by judiciously scaling the linear mean function of the latent factor series in (6.12), the raw second-order moment function of $y(t)$ is asymptotically stationary. Proceeding in the same way as with (6.10), they also show that (6.12) can be reformulated as a state-space model.

A frequency domain analogue of (6.12) is

$$f(f) = g(f) + z(f)$$

$$y(f) = L(f)f(f) + e(f) \qquad [6.13]$$

In (6.13) $g(f)$ is conceived of as the Fourier transform of a transient $g(t)$, that is, $g(t)$ only is nonstationary within a time interval of limited extent. For a more detailed argumentation that (6.13) indeed is well defined in the frequency domain, the reader is referred to Molenaar (1989).

Models (6.10)-(6.13) cover almost all variants of dynamic factor analysis that appear in the published literature. In a recent paper, Aoki (1991) introduced a state-space model that resembles (6.12) but can accommodate a more general class of nonstationary first-order moment functions. Like the models considered in this section, however, Aoki's model also is time-homogeneous. In contrast, one would like to have available an inhomogeneous model that resembles the general state-space model (6.1) as closely as possible. That is, a dynamic factor model in which an arbitrary subset of the unknown parameters is allowed to vary with time. Such a model will be presented shortly.

Estimation in Dynamic Factor Models

A variety of statistical methods has been employed in applied dynamic factor analyses. Here, however, we will restrict ourselves to a brief presentation of those estimation techniques that actually have been used in our own work. For alternative approaches the reader is referred to, for example, Brualdi and Schneider (1989) and Hannan and Deistler (1988, chap. 6).

Let the p-variate series $y(t)$ be weakly stationary, with vanishing mean function, and consider the stacked vector $y_r{}' = [y(t)', y(t-1)', \ldots, y(t-r+1)']$. Then $E[y_r, y_r']$ consists of ($p \times p$) blocks $C(k) = E[y(t), y(t+k)']$, $k = r+1, \ldots, 0, \ldots, r-1$, which are arranged according to a Toeplitz structure. In Molenaar (1985) it has been shown how models like (6.10) can be fitted to the observed block-Toeplitz matrix by means of commonly available software for covariance-structure modeling. In this approach the standard maximum likelihood (ML) fitting function is almost always optimized, even though the requirement of independent observations cannot be met. Yet, this so-called pseudo-ML approach appears to outperform less restrictive methods in comparative simulation studies. Furthermore, in a preliminary comparative study between pseudo-ML estimates and those obtained by Browne's (1984) asymptotically distribution-free method (involving in this case the asymptotic covariance matrix associated with the observed block-Toeplitz matrix), it was found that parameter estimates and their standard errors were almost identical for both methods. It would seem then, that the ML method is quite robust against deviations from the requirement of independent observations. Of course, this observation needs further theoretical underpinning (see Satorra & Bentler, Chapter 12, this volume).

Perhaps the basic message of Brillinger's (1975) beautiful treatise is that there exists a complete correspondence between ordinary multivariate statistical analysis techniques and those of weakly stationary time series in the frequency domain. Hence for each ordinary technique such as analysis of variance, regression analysis, discriminant analysis, canonical correlation analysis, and so forth, there is a frequency domain analogue. It therefore will come as no great surprise that factor analysis in the frequency domain is a well-defined subject (see Engle & Watson, 1981). In fact, complex-valued models like (6.11) can be rewritten as real-valued ones by making use of a convenient transformation (see Brillinger, 1975, p. 71), thus making it possible to apply standard factor analysis software to fit the model at each frequency. That is, if $C = \text{Re } C + i\text{Im } C$ then the transformation concerned yields C^r, where

$$C^r = \begin{pmatrix} \text{Re} C & -\text{Im} C \\ \text{Im} C & \text{Re} C \end{pmatrix} \qquad [6.13.1]$$

Evidently, estimation is more complicated in dynamic factor models of multivariate time series that are only asymptotically stationary. The generalization of (6.10) to (6.12) implies that one now has to consider the block-Toeplitz augmented moment structure associated with the stacked vector $y_r' = [y(t)', 1, y(t-1)', 1, \ldots, y(t-r+1)', 1]$. Model (6.12) could again be fitted to this augmented moment structure by means of the pseudo-ML approach alluded to above. It then appears, however, that the inclusion of the mean function has a strong deteriorating effect on the condition of the observed block-Toeplitz matrix as well as on the condition of a matrix of latent lagged cross-products obtained from (6.12). In Molenaar et al. (1992) an alternative, better conditioned, approach is followed that is based on the observation that the linear mean function in (6.12) constitutes a modest form of first-order nonstationarity that yields fast convergence to weak stationarity if the length of the observed series increases. More specifically, after substituting the asymptotic form of the matrix of latent cross-products associated with the linear mean function of the latent factor series in (6.12), they arrive at a reformulation of the structural model for the augmented block-Toeplitz matrix that no longer is in immediate danger of being (nearly) singular. This approach readily lends itself to several interesting extensions, like the accommodation to cyclic mean functions, but these have yet to be explored.

A frequency domain analyses of models like (6.13), in which the mean function of the latent factor series is a transient, builds upon the mathematical-statistical groundwork underlying spectral analysis of weakly stationary time series, but also has to transcend it in at least two ways. First, as has been explained in the seminal paper by Cameron and Hannan (1979), the handling of the transient mean function $g(f)$ in (6.13) differs considerably from the way in which the remaining random terms are dealt with. Secondly, at each frequency (6.13) defines a constrained complex-valued structural model that could be tediously fitted to the data by means of commonly available software (Jöreskog & Sörbom, 1981). A much more efficient approach, however, is to use special purpose software (cf. Dolan, 1992), which makes the fit of (6.13) to the data a comparatively easy, though still computationally involved, exercise. To the best of our knowledge, a successful application of (6.13) was for the first time reported in Molenaar (1989). In contrast to a remark made by Granger and Engle (1983, p. 104) it therefore appears that one does not have to fall back on the much more intricate time domain methods in dealing with constrained complex-valued structural models like (6.13). Incidentally, our frequency domain approach can be regarded as a direct generalization of current spectral estimation techniques in radar imaging (O'Sullivan & Snyder, 1990). All approaches to estimation in dynamic factor models considered so far belong to the so-called batch type in which a given realization $\{y(t), t = 0, 1, \ldots, T - 1\}$ can be analyzed off-line. That is, the complete set of observations is available before the analysis is carried out. In contrast, a recursive approach can be applied on-line (i.e., simultaneously with the measurement of the ongoing process) and involves estimates that are sequentially updated each time a new observation $y(t)$ becomes available. Notice that the basic distinction between these two types of estimators is whether or not they are sequential; the possibility of applying them on-line or off-line is only subsidiary. In fact, batch estimators in combination with a finite buffer have been used on-line, while we will shortly employ recursive estimation in an off-line setting. Taking the time-homogeneous state-space model with unknown parameters (6.6) as our starting point, a recursive estimator is obtained by first introducing the extended state

$$s^e(t)' = [s(t)', q']$$ [6.13.2]

and then invoking a filter (see Section 2) to estimate this extended state. Schematically, such a filter can be represented as

$$s^e(t \mid t) = F_1[s^e(t \mid t - 1), y(t), u(t)]$$

$$s^e(t + 1 \mid t) = F_2[s^e(t \mid t)]$$ [6.14]

where $s^e(t_2 \mid t_1)$ denotes the estimated extended state at t_2 given observations up to time t_1.

As a preliminary to the next section, it may be helpful to elaborate the implications of (6.14) somewhat further. First, given the linear state-space model (6.1) in which there are no unknown parameters, the filter equations (6.14) reduce to the well-known Kalman filter (see Goodwin & Sin, 1984, p. 248ff, for a complete specification and further discussion of the Kalman filter). Second, we note that even if the background model (6.1) is linear, the substitution of the extended state implies that the associated state-space model becomes nonlinear. A convenient recursive filter now can be obtained by invoking a Taylor expansion about $s^c(t|t)$, keeping only terms up to first order, and then apply the Kalman filter to this linearized model (cf. Sage & Melsa, 1971, chap. 9, for an excellent discussion of various alternative approaches, such as keeping terms up to second order in the Taylor expansion concerned). The result is called the extended Kalman filter (cf. Goodwin & Sin, 1984, p. 293ff). Third, it is remarkably easy and straightforward to construct recursive estimators for time-varying and/or random parameters in the state-space model (cf. Molenaar, 1987, for an application to psychotherapeutic process analysis). Fourth, it has to be acknowledged that recursive parameter estimation by means of (variants of) the extended Kalman filter generally requires that the length of the observed series (in off-line applications) or the stopping time (in on-line applications) is considerable (Saridis, 1977, p. 221, presents the results of a relatively simple simulation study requiring several hundreds of recursions for the extended Kalman filter to converge). Fifth, it is possible to formulate a recursive spectral estimator (cf. Ahmed & Rao, 1975, p. 44ff), although this interesting frequency domain analogue still awaits further exploration. Sixth and finally, it is evident that the precision of a recursive filter will be less than that of its batch-type analogue. This is because in a filter only a forward sweep through the data occurs in which the information in the initial observations is used sub-optimally. Hence, so-called recursive smoothers have been constructed that involve a forward as well as a backward sweep and therefore have the same precision as their batch-type analogues (cf. Sage & Melsa, 1971, p. 479ff, for many further details).

Mixed Designs

Multivariate time series as observed in developmental psychology usually are relatively short, at least much too short to warrant application of the extended Kalman filter. But what could be accomplished with, for instance, a five-variate time series observed at $T = 15$ time points? Actually, such a time series also is much too short for the purpose of carrying out a batch-type dynamic factor analysis, even though the dimension of the observed series is rather small. One way to proceed with short time series is to consider an ensemble of these series obtained with a homogeneous group of multiple cases (subjects, systems, etc.). Our data set then consists of multiple realizations of what presumably is the same process. For this mixed design a reasonable estimator for the covariance function of a weakly stationary process is

$$C_y^{\#}(k) = (TN)^{-1}\sum_i\sum_t \, [\,y_i(t) - c_{yi}\,][\,y_i(t+k) - c_{yi}\,] \, , \qquad [6.15]$$

where N is the number of cases, T is the number of time points, and c_{yi} denotes the estimated mean function of the ith realization. Notice that pooling across realizations as well as time points relates to the assumption that the process under consideration is ergodic (see Section 2).

4. Estimation in Time-Inhomogeneous Dynamic Factor Models

In the foregoing we already alluded to the desirability of having available an inhomogeneous dynamic factor model with unknown parameters that approaches the generality of the state-space model (6.1) as closely as possible. Developmental processes can be expected to be nonstationary in many possible ways, which is why we need the full generality of model (6.1) for their analysis. Of course the application of such a model to a single realization of a multivariate process is only feasible if the inhomogeneity is restricted to a subset of the unknown parameters. Moreover, the time-variation of this inhomogeneous subset of parameters has to be smooth in some sense. Both requirements have deliberately been stated in vague terms because at present no formal characterization is available of the boundaries of structural identifiability for inhomogeneous dynamic factor models. A general approach to determine structural identifiability for time-varying systems is outlined in Walter (1988) but still needs to be worked out in the present context. In view of this we will only present results of a simulation study based on simple inhomogeneous dynamic factor models. Apart from issues related to structural identifiability, these results have to be considered preliminary in at least two other ways. First, the algorithm to be described below was implemented only recently. It employs rather crude optimization procedures and still lacks a procedure for the estimation of standard errors. Much more work remains to be done in order to arrive at a complete and flexible implementation. Second, only a few simulations were carried out; a much larger number of simulations under various conditions is required to corroborate the validity of our approach in a more definite way.

Outline of the General Model

In what follows only state-space representations of dynamic factor models will be considered. That is, it is understood that the dynamic factor models concerned have been rewritten as state-space models according to the rules presented in Molenaar (1985). The general inhomogeneous model we have in mind then is given by

$$s(t+1) = A(q_t)s(t) + B(q_t)u(t) + w(t)$$

$$y(t) = H(q_t)s(t) + v(t)$$

$$E[w(t), w(t+k)'] = C_w(q_t)d(k) ; \quad E[v(t), v(t+k)'] = C_v(q_t)d(k)$$

$$q_t = q_0 + q_1 t + q_2 t^2 + \ldots \qquad [6.16]$$

Notice that (6.16) is the inhomogeneous analogue of (6.6) in which the vector of unknown parameters now is a polynomial function of time. Both the degree of this polynomial (which can be different for each entry in q_t, i.e., each unknown parameter in the state-space model) as well as its coefficients $q_0, q_1, \ldots$, have to be estimated. Notice also that by constraining the maximum degree of the polynomials characterizing the entries of q_t, the smoothness of the time-dependent variation of the inhomogeneous parameters can be controlled. In particular if this maximum degree is constrained to be zero, the time-homogeneous model (6.6) is obtained. The parameterization of the time-variation of parameters in terms of polynomials of low degree ensures that the inhomogeneities concerned are smooth (i.e., have only low-frequency variation at a scale that is much smaller than for the random variables.

Likelihood Maximization

If both $w(t)$ and $v(t)$ are zero mean Gaussian white noise series, then minus two times the logarithm of the likelihood is

$$-2 \ln L(y, q) = \ln | C_q(t) | + e_q(t)' C_q(t)^{-1} e_q(t)$$

$$C_q(t) = H(q_t)P_q(t \mid t-1)H(q_t)' + C_v(q_t)$$

$$e_q(t) = y(t) - H(q_t)s_q(t \mid t - 1)$$

$$P_q(t \mid t - 1) = E\{[s(t) - s_q(t \mid t - 1)], [s(t) - s_q(t \mid t - 1)]'\} \quad [6.17]$$

Here $e_q(t)$ is the innovations series, like in (6.7) and (6.9). Notice that the likelihood depends upon two types of variables: on the one hand the unknown parameter vector q_t and on the other hand the estimated state $s_q(t \mid t - 1)$ and its covariance $P_q(t \mid t - 1)$. Following Shumway (1988, pp. 178ff), an iterative expectation-maximization (EM) algorithm is used to deal with this situation. Heuristically speaking, in the E-step q_t is considered to be fixed (at its estimated value obtained in the previous iteration) and terms associated with $s_q(t \mid t - 1)$ are determined by invoking a recursive smoothing algorithm. In the M-step the terms associated with $s_q(t \mid t - 1)$ are considered to be fixed (at their smoothed values obtained in the previous iteration) and q_t is estimated by maximizing the likelihood. On request, a complete description of the algorithm as well as the source code of its current Fortran implementation can be obtained from the author.

The Basic Simulation Model

For the reasons given above, variants of a simple dynamic one-factor model were used in all simulations. In this model $u(t)$ was taken to be zero, hence the mean function of the observed series always was stationary:

$$s(t + 1) = .7s(t) + w(t)$$

$$y(t) = Hs(t) + v(t)$$

$$E[w(t), w(t + k)] = C_w d(k) ; \quad E[v(t), v(t + k)'] = C_v(k)d(k)$$

$$H' = (.9, .8, .7, .6, .5)$$

$$C_w(0) = 1; \quad C_v(0) = \text{diag}[1, 1, 1, 1, 1] \quad [6.18a]$$

This model generated a realization of $y(t)$ for $T = 50$ time points. Alternatively, an ensemble of $N = 5$ realizations for $T = 15$ time points was generated.

To investigate the performance of the algorithm with models involving a limited subset of inhomogeneous parameters, two variants were employed:

$$h_{t1} = .9 - 1.8t \qquad\qquad\qquad [6.18b]$$

$$a_t = .7 - .7t \qquad\qquad\qquad [6.18c]$$

where $t = t/T$. In (6.18b) the first loading in H is inhomogeneous, while in (6.18c) the parameter in the autoregressive model of the factor series is inhomogeneous. Both models generated realizations of $y(t)$ according to the same design as used for (6.18a).

For (6.18a) the vector q contains 11 unknown parameters [the variance of $C_w(0)$ of $w(t)$ is not identifiable]. For (6.18b) and (6.18c) the vector q_t contains 12 unknown parameters. The results presented below were obtained by fitting the true model structures to the data. Of course this implies a severe restriction of their generalizability to real data where the true model is unknown, but our first concern was to study the performance of the new algorithm and not the issue of model selection (the latter issue will be considered in a forthcoming simulation study).

Results

With each variant of the simulation model two data sets have been generated: a single realization at $T = 50$ time points and an ensemble of $N = 5$ realizations at $T = 15$ time points. The results obtained with the former data set are labeled "single," while those obtained with the latter are labeled "multi." Each data set has been analyzed twice, by means of the new EM algorithm and again by means of the covariance structure modeling (LISREL) approach described in Molenaar (1985). Results obtained by the first method are labeled "em," while those obtained with the second method are labeled "lisrel." Accordingly, the results obtained by applying the EM algorithm to a single realization generated according to (6.18a) are labeled "single-em-a," and so forth. No special notation will be used for parameter estimates. Moreover, the label "diag" for C_v will be dropped in this section.

single-em-a:
$a = .72$, $H' = (1.12, .82, .96, .68, .48)$, $C_v = (.84, 1.35, .93, .75, 1.10)$

single-lisrel-a:
$a = .58$, $H' = (1.21, .85, .97, .52, .56)$, $C_v = (.85, 1.35, .92, .83, 1.04)$

multi-em-a:
$a = .83$, $H' = (1.03, .81, .74, .64, .60)$, $C_v = (.80, .89, .83, 1.28, .84)$

multi-lisrel-a:
$a = .73$, $H' = (1.06, .81, .78, .67, .59)$, $C_v = (.82, .97, .87, 1.19, .98)$

It can be seen that for the data generated by the homogeneous model (6.18a) the results obtained with the EM algorithm closely correspond to those obtained by the LISREL method. The distance between the latter estimates and their true values is always less than two standard errors. Notice that the mixed data give rise to the same pattern of results as obtained with the single realization (here also the distance between the parameter estimates obtained with the LISREL method and their respective true values is always less than two standard errors).

single-em-b:
$a = .78$, $H_t' = (.91 - 1.72t, .78, .86, .66, .42)$, $C_v = (.95, 1.35, 1.12, .71, 1.17)$

single-lisrel-b:
$a = .68$, $H' = (.28, .80, .81, .49, .47)$, $C_v = (1.71, 1.26, 1.12, .78, 1.09)$

multi-em-b:
$a = .79$, $H_t' = (1.06 - 2.25t, .90, .85, .75, .70)$, $C_v = (.93, .96, .82, 1.25, .82)$

multi-lisrel-b:
$a = .74$, $H' = (-.39, .78, .73, .67, .61)$, $C_v = (1.67, 1.02, .98, 1.14, .90)$

The inhomogeneous loading h_{t1} is faithfully recovered by the EM algorithm. In contrast, the estimates of this loading and the first entry of C_v obtained by means of the LISREL method are severely biased because this method cannot accommodate the inhomogeneity concerned. Yet, as will be discussed below, the usual indices for screening the fit of the LISREL model, like the standard errors of the first entry of H and C_v or the standardized differences between the observed and fitted block-Toeplitz matrix, do not at all indicate this deterioration.

single-em-c:

$a_t = .74 - .72t$, $H' = (1.22, .82, .92, .63, .56)$, $C_v = (.74, 1.32, 1.02, .78, 1.08)$

single-lisrel-c:

$a = .35$, $H' = (1.35, .81, .91, .45, .64)$, $C_v = (.69, 1.36, .98, .83, 1.03)$

Again it appears that the EM algorithm correctly tracks the inhomogeneous autoregressive parameter associated with the factor series, whereas the analogous LISREL estimate is severely biased. And again the usual indices for screening the fit of the LISREL model concerned do not indicate this lack of fit. Similar results have been obtained in the "multi" condition.

Model Validation

The inhomogeneous parameters in (6.18b) and (6.18c) vary considerably in time: h_{t1} changes linearly from .9 to $-.9$, and a_t from .7 to 0, each within an observation interval comprising 50 (single condition) or 15 (multi condition) time points. Given these rather severe inhomogeneities one might expect that application of the LISREL method, which is tied up with a homogeneous model, will show clear signs of lack of fit. However, we have already indicated that such is not the case. The reason for this is straightforward: The LISREL method is based on the covariance function $C_y(k)$ of $y(t)$, not the realization of $y(t)$ itself, and the estimator (6.15) for $C_y(k)$ freezes the nonstationary aspects of $y(t)$ in that it simply takes the average over all time points. Hence we will have to return to the observed series $y(t)$ itself in order to detect nonstationarities.

Now consider the condition single-lisrel-b. The model that has been fitted to these data can be used in combination with the Kalman filter to estimate the innovations series $e(t)$, $t = 0, \ldots, T - 1$. If the fitted model holds, then this innovations series should conform to a weakly stationary white noise series. This can be diagnosed in various ways (see Tong, 1990, pp. 322ff, for a convenient overview of such tests); for instance, by testing whether the covariance function of $e(t)$ conforms to $C_e(k) = \text{diag } C_e \, d(k)$ and scrutinizing the plot of the standardized realization of $e(t)$. All this does not yield convincing results with the present data set, however, which appears to be due to the relatively large measurement error $v(t)$. Therefore, another simulation was carried out with the variant

$$h_{t1} = .9 - 1.8t, \quad C_v = (.1, .1, .1, .1, .1) \qquad [6.18d]$$

The results now are

single-em-d:
$a = .78, H_t' = (.94 - 1.87t, .85, .80, .64, .52), C_v = (.09, .13, .12, .07, .11)$

single-lisrel-d:
$a = .67, H' = (.15, .84, .77, .58, .52), C_v = (.78, .11, .12, .08, .10)$

multi-em-d:
$a = .85, H_t' = (1.06 - 2.11t, .89, .80, .69, .59), C_v = (.09, .10, .08, .12, .09)$

multi-lisrel-d:
$a = .73, H' = (-.41, .90, .80, .70, .59), C_v = (.72, .10, .10, .11, .10)$

The present results are similar to those obtained with (6.18b). The standardized residuals still are not indicative of the true state of affairs. But as the proportion of variance explained by the latent factor series now is much larger than for (6.18b), diagnosing the Kalman filtered innovations series yields clear results. For instance, the autocorrelation of $e(t)$ at lag $k = 1$ does not deviate more than two standard errors from zero in the single-em-d and multi-em-d conditions. In contrast, this autocorrelation for the first component series $e_1(t)$ is .60 in the single-lisrel-d condition (which is more than four standard errors removed from zero). Figure 6.1 shows the standardized $e_1(t)$ series obtained in the single-em-d and the single-lisrel-d conditions; it is seen that the latter has a definite negative slope.

5. Discussion and Conclusion

Almost by definition, developmental processes are nonstationary. It appears that for the first time we now have available a method with which arbitrary inhomogeneous dynamic factor models can be fitted to relatively short nonstationary time series. To wit, there exists a promising frequency domain approach to nonstationary time series (see Priestley, 1988, pp. 145ff), but in our experience with this so-called evolutionary spectral analysis it appears that it always requires

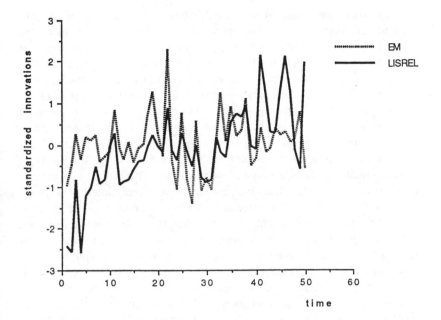

Figure 6.1. Kalman Filtered Standardized Innovations in the Single-em-*d* and the Single-Lisrel-*d* Conditions

the availability of very long time series. Incidentally, the accommodation of evolutionary spectral analysis to dynamic factor modeling still has to be worked out.

Of course the results presented in the preceding section are limited in many ways and therefore can only suggest the feasibility of the new method. Much more work remains to be done; in particular, power studies and the algorithmic determination of structural identifiability are important desiderata. Yet it seems that the EM algorithm is capable of faithfully tracking substantially inhomogeneous parameters. Following the guidelines put forward by Baltes, Reese, and Nesselroade (1977), these inhomogeneous parameters can be regarded as being associated with qualitative change in developmental systems. Hence the new method could provide an appropriate tool for studying quantitative and qualitative development from a systems theoretical point of view (cf. Ford & Lerner, 1992).

We also touched upon the relationship between analyses of single and multiple realizations of a given process. In our view this is an underrated issue in psychometrics, where the focus always has been on multi-case analyses. At an abstract level, however, generalization over a population of time points and generalization over a population of subjects/systems are conformable operations and therefore the question arises, notably in developmental system analysis, in which ways these two perspectives can relate to each other. In the first part of this chapter it was argued that in resolving this question the concept of ergodicity will figure prominently. Furthermore, its relevance for the study of developmental processes may be even broader. This can be appreciated by returning to the statistical mechanical characterization of an ergodic process given earlier: The trajectories of such a process in the long run cover the entire Euclidian space. In contrast, the state-space of a chaotic process is non-ergodic in that such a process only covers a space with fractal dimension. A consideration of chaotic processes, and nonlinear processes in general, is necessary to understand emergent properties of developmental systems (see Molenaar, in press). Yet, the non-ergodicity of these chaotic processes then may have fundamental consequences for the applicability of many traditional statistical analysis techniques.

In closing, it is indicated that the EM algorithm in combination with a recursive smoother can be readily generalized to accommodate nonlinear dynamic factor models. One then has to replace the recursive Kalman smoother by an extended Kalman smoother that is based on a locally linearized factor model. Work along this line now is in progress. All in all, the new approach to dynamic factor analysis outlined in this chapter appears able to become a versatile tool in the applied analysis of complex developmental systems.

References

Ahmed, N., & Rao, K. R. (1975). *Orthogonal transforms for digital signal processing.* New York: Springer-Verlag.

Aplevitch, J. D. (1991). *Implicit linear systems.* Lecture Notes in Control and Information Sciences, Vol. 152. Berlin: Springer-Verlag.

Baltes, P. B., Reese, H. W., & Nesselroade, J. R. (1977). *Life-span developmental psychology: Introduction to research methods.* Monterey, CA: Brooks/Cole.

Brillinger, D. R. (1975). *Time series: Data analysis and theory.* New York: Holt, Rinehart & Winston.

Browne, M. W. (1984). Asymptotically distribution-free methods for the analysis of covariance structures. *British Journal of Mathematical and Statistical Psychology, 37,* 1-21.

Brualdi, R. A., & Schneider, H. (Eds.). (1989). Linear systems and control. Special issue of *Linear Algebra and Its Applications,* 122-124.

Cameron, M. A., & Hannan, E. J. (1979). Transient signals. *Biometrika, 66,* 243-258.

Engle, R. F., & Watson, M. (1981). A one-factor multivariate time series model of metropolitan wage rates. *Journal of the American Statistical Association, 76,* 774-781.

Ford, D. H., & Lerner, R. M. (1992). *Developmental systems theory: An integrative approach.* Newbury Park, CA: Sage.

Gardiner, C. W. (1990). *Handbook of stochastic methods for physics, chemistry and the natural sciences.* Berlin: Springer-Verlag.

Glover, K., & Williams, J. C. (1974). Parameterizations of linear dynamical systems: Canonical identifiability. *IEEE Transactions on Automatic Control, AC-19,* 640-645.

Goodwin, G. C., & Sin, K. S. (1984). *Adaptive filtering, prediction and control.* Englewood Cliffs, NJ: Prentice-Hall.

Granger, C.W.J., & Engle, R. (1983). Applications of spectral analysis in econometrics. In D. R. Brillinger & P. R. Krishnaiah (Eds.), *Handbook of statistics 3: Time series in the frequency domain* (pp. 93-109). Amsterdam: North-Holland.

Hannan, E. J. (1970). *Multiple time series.* New York: John Wiley.

Hannan, E. J., & Deistler, M. (1988). *The statistical theory of linear systems.* New York: John Wiley.

Isidori, A. (1989). *Nonlinear control systems: An introduction.* Berlin: Springer-Verlag.

Jones, C. J., & Nesselroade, J. R. (1990). Multivariate, replicated, single-subject designs and P-technique factor analysis: A selective review of intraindividual change studies. *Experimental Aging Research, 16,* 171-183.

Jöreskog, K., & Sörbom, D. (1981). *LISREL V users guide,* Uppsala: University of Uppsala.

Kashyap, R. L., & Rao, A. R. (1976). *Dynamic stochastic models from empirical data.* New York: Academic Press.

Lord, F., & Novick, M. R. (1968). *Statistical theories of mental test scores.* Reading, MA: Addison-Wesley

Molenaar, P.C.M. (1985). A dynamic factor model for the analysis of multivariate time series. *Psychometrika, 50,* 181-202.

Molenaar, P.C.M. (1987). Dynamic factor analysis in the frequency domain: Causal modeling of multivariate psychophysiological time series. *Multivariate Behavioral Research, 22,* 329-353.

Molenaar, P.C.M. (1989). Aspects of dynamic factor analysis. In *Annals of statistical information* (pp. 183-199). Tokyo: The Institute of Statistical Mathematics.

Molenaar, P.C.M., de Gooijer, J. G., & Schmitz, B. (1992). Dynamic factor analysis of nonstationary multivariate time series. *Psychometrika, 57,* 333-349.

Molenaar, P.C.M. (in press). Some innovatory methodological aspects of longitudinal studies of health and aging. In J.J.F. Schroots (Ed.), *Aging, health and competence.* Amsterdam: Elsevier.

O'Sullivan, J. A., & Snyder, D. L. (1990). High resolution radar imaging using spectrum estimation methods. In F. A. Grunbaum, J. W. Helton, & P. Khargonekar (Eds.), *Signal processing, Part II: Control theory and applications* (pp. 335-346). New York: Springer-Verlag.

Priestley, M. B. (1988). *Non-linear and non-stationary time series analysis.* London: Academic Press.

Sage, A. P., & Melsa, J. L. (1971). *Estimation theory with applications to communications and control.* New York: Academic Press.

Saridis, G. N. (1977). *Self-organizing control of stochastic systems.* New York: Marcel Dekker.

Shumway, R. H. (1988). *Applied statistical time series analysis.* Englewood Cliffs, NJ: Prentice-Hall.

Tong, H. (1990). *Non-linear time series: A dynamical system approach.* Oxford: Clarendon Press.

Walter, E. (Ed.). (1988). *Identifiability of parametric models.* Oxford: Pergamon.

Whittle, P. (1982). *Optimization over time.* (Vol. 1). Chichester, John Wiley.

Whittle, P. (1990). *Risk-sensitive optimal control.* Chichester: John Wiley.

Wohlwill, J. F. (1991). Relations between method and theory in developmental research: A partial-isomorphism view. In P. van Geert & L. P. Mos (Eds.), *Annals of theoretical psychology* (Vol. 7, pp. 91-138). New York: Plenum.

7

Latent Variables Models and Missing Data Analysis

MICHAEL J. ROVINE

1. Introduction

Missing data estimation remains one of the knottiest problems in data analysis. A number of reviews have described methods for estimating missing data in observed data problems (Affifi & Elashoff, 1966; Kim & Curry, 1977; Little & Rubin, 1987; Rovine & Delaney, 1990). At least one generally available package, BMDP, contains a missing data estimation procedure (BMDPAM; Dixon, 1990). A number of methods have been considered that extend the missing data problem to models that include latent variables. These methods either (a) use sufficient statistics to estimate a complete data matrix that is then used as input to estimate the parameters of the latent variable model as if the data were complete or (b) consider the missing data patterns as multiple groups and by constraining certain parameter values across the groups estimate the parameters of the model. In this chapter we will consider missing data estimation for models using latent variables by concentrating on these two basic strategies.

AUTHOR'S NOTE: I would like to thank Alexander von Eye, Peter C. M. Molenaar, and Peter Bentler for comments on a previous draft. This work was supported in part by NIA Grant No. 5 R01 AG09984-02.

181

To estimate complete data matrices, we will consider (a) using a differentiable likelihood function to solve directly for the parameter estimates and standard errors (Little & Rubin, 1987), (b) factoring a likelihood function when certain optimal patterns of missing data exist (Marini, Olsen, & Rubin, 1980), and (c) using EM-type algorithms for general patterns of missing data (Dempster, Laird, & Rubin, 1977). A data example will be used to demonstrate the use of a sweep operator for the factored case. A sample program is included to help users to estimate means and covariance matrices for similar problems. As many latent variable problems are essentially patterned covariance matrix problems, we will indicate how to take the pattern imposed on the matrix into account for the case when factor analysis is used to describe a measurement model.

For direct parameter estimation, we will consider multiple group models that use additional parameters to model the missing data (Allison, 1987). These "phantom variables" will result in a computational model that can be used to estimate parameters under multiple group constraints. Once again a sample program is included.

2. Imputing Values to Create Complete Data Moments, Covariance, or Correlation Matrix

The input of a matrix of correlations, covariances, or moments (along with a vector of means) is sufficient for estimating the parameters of latent variable models. Although programs estimating these models are sophisticated in just about all aspects, they tend to be relatively simplistic in the way they handle missing data. In PRELIS, for example, the options available are for the estimation of either a list-wise or pair-wise matrix.

Problems with these two methods have been documented (see Rovine & Delaney, 1990). List-wise deletion provides consistent estimates if the data are missing completely at random (Little & Rubin, 1987), but the method is generally inefficient. Pair-wise deletion similarly provides consistent estimates and may be somewhat more efficient for certain data structures (Brown, 1983; Donner & Rosner, 1982), but tends to produce inconsistent estimates of the true standard errors (Allison, 1987).

Other methods exist that try to maximize the likelihood of observing both the complete data and some parameter-based estimation of the missing data (Little & Rubin, 1987). These methods, in general, have some very nice statistical properties, which I will mention below.

3. Methods Based on the Likelihood Function

In general, the density function for any complete data problem can be written as

$$f(Y \mid \theta) = f(Y \mid \theta_1, \theta_2, \ldots, \theta_d) \qquad [7.1]$$

For example, a variable that is normally distributed would have the density function of

$$f(Y \mid \mu, \sigma^2) = (2\pi\sigma^2)^{-n/2} \exp\left[-\frac{1}{2}\sum_{i=1}^{n} \frac{(y-\mu)^2}{\sigma^2}\right] \qquad [7.2]$$

where for particular values of μ and λ, f gives the height of the density function for that value of y. While the density is a function of the y values conditioned on the parameters, the likelihood,

$$L(\theta \mid Y_{obs}) = L(\theta_1, \theta_2, \ldots, \theta_d \mid Y_{obs}) \qquad [7.3]$$

reexpresses the density as a function of the parameters conditioned on a set of observations here called Y_{obs}. Maximizing the likelihood looks for values of the parameters that make the observed values most probable. For the univariate normal distribution, one would select the mean of the observed data as one of the parameter estimates since that would maximize the joint probability of observing the data where the probability of observing each data point would be the height of the density function at that point multiplied by a small but arbitrary constant.

The likelihood is a function of the set of parameters, θ, for fixed Y. Since the likelihood expresses the joint probability of observing each of the n data points, and the joint probability is the product of the n terms representing the probability of observing each, the likelihood is usually transformed by taking its log. The terms are then summed.

The scoring function,

$$S(\theta \mid Y) \equiv \frac{\partial l(\theta \mid Y)}{\partial \theta} = 0 \qquad [7.4]$$

is defined by taking the partial derivative of the log-likelihood with respect to each of the d parameters represented by θ. Setting the result for each of the d equations equal to 0 and solving them simultaneously can yield the ML estimates of θ when the estimates are unique and the likelihood is differentiable and bounded.

Inferences regarding the parameters are made by considering the parameters to be distributed as

$$\sqrt{n}(\theta - \hat{\theta}) \sim N(0, C) \qquad [7.5]$$

where C is a square matrix with dimensions equal to the number of parameters (Little & Rubin, 1987). By Taylor's theorem, an estimate of the scoring function can be written as

$$0 = S(\hat{\theta} \mid Y) = S(\theta \mid Y) - I(\theta \mid Y)(\hat{\theta} - \theta) + r(\hat{\theta} \mid Y) \qquad [7.6]$$

where I is the information matrix defined as

$$I(\theta \mid Y) = \frac{\partial^2 l}{\partial \theta \partial \theta^{\mathrm{T}}} \qquad [7.7]$$

If the remainder can be ignored, then the scoring function becomes

$$S(\theta \mid Y) \simeq I(\theta \mid Y)(\hat{\theta} - \theta) \qquad [7.8]$$

If J is defined as the expected value of the information given θ,

$$J(\theta) = E[I(\theta \mid Y) \mid \theta] = \int I(\theta \mid Y) f(Y \mid \theta) dY \qquad [7.9]$$

then C is defined as

$$J(\theta) \simeq J(\hat{\theta}) \simeq I(\hat{\theta} \mid Y) \quad C = J^{-1}(\hat{\theta}) \qquad [7.10]$$

and the confidence interval around the parameters is given as

$$n(\theta - \hat{\theta})^T C^{-1}(\theta - \hat{\theta}) \leq \chi_d^2 \qquad [7.11]$$

4. The Likelihood for Incomplete Data

If some of the data are missing, the "observed" data vector, Y, is actually composed of both observed data, Y_{obs}, and missing data, Y_{mis}. The density for the data can be expressed as

$$f(Y \mid \theta) \equiv f(Y_{obs}, Y_{mis} \mid \theta) \qquad [7.12]$$

Integrating over the missing data yields the marginal density for the observed data

$$f(Y_{obs} \mid \theta) = \int f(Y_{obs}, Y_{mis} \mid \theta) dY_{obs} \qquad [7.13]$$

Consider a missing marker variable, R, defined as

$$r_{ij} = \begin{cases} 1 & y_{ij} \text{ observed} \\ 0 & y_{ij} \text{ missing} \end{cases} \qquad [7.14]$$

As Little and Rubin (1987) point out, R can be treated as a random variable, and if the mechanism generating the missing data is called Ψ, the following equation gives the density for the observed data given the θ parameters and the missing data mechanism:

$$f(Y, R \mid \theta, \Psi) = f(Y \mid \theta) f(R \mid Y, \Psi) \qquad [7.15]$$

This density is the product of the distribution of Y and the distribution of the marker variable. The density of the observed data is obtained by integrating the missing data out of the equation. If the distribution of the missing data, R, does not depend on the missing values, the second term of the marginal density

$$f(Y_{obs}, R \mid \theta, \Psi) = \int f(Y_{obs}, Y_{mis} \mid \theta) f(R \mid Y_{obs}, Y_{mis}, \Psi) dY_{mis} \qquad [7.16]$$

becomes

$$f(R \mid Y_{\text{obs}}, Y_{\text{mis}}, \Psi) = f(R \mid Y_{\text{obs}}, \Psi) , \qquad [7.17]$$

which is no longer conditioned on the values that are missing, and the second term comes out of the integral. The resultant equation is

$$f(Y_{\text{obs}}, R \mid \theta, \Psi) = f(R \mid Y_{\text{obs}}, \Psi) \int f(Y_{\text{obs}}, Y_{\text{mis}} \mid \theta) dY_{\text{mis}} \qquad [7.18]$$

When Equation 7.17 holds, the data are said to be missing at random (MAR). This is the pattern of missingness that is required for the likelihood-based estimation that we will consider. Little and Rubin (1987) present methods for dealing with more complex patterns of missingness.

Patterns of missing data can be described easily by considering each data set as consisting of variables that are complete for all cases and variables that have some values missing. Consider one set of variables, X, which are complete, and another set, Y, which have some values missing. If the reason why the data are missing is dependent on the Y (and maybe the X), the data are neither observed nor missing at random. If the missing data are dependent on the X but not on the Y, the data are missing at random (MAR). If the missing data mechanism is dependent on neither Y nor X, the data are both missing at random (MAR) and observed at random (OAR). Data that are both MAR and OAR are considered missing completely at random (MCAR).

5. Methods Based on Factoring the Likelihood

Given that the likelihood function for complete data can be complex (even more so when based on complete and incomplete data), closed form solutions such as solving the scoring function are often very difficult if not impossible. However, there are certain patterns of missing data for which the likelihood can be reexpressed in terms of an equivalent set of parameters that allows the problem to be solved. In particular, given the likelihood function for observed data, $L(\theta, Y_{\text{obs}})$, that is, a function of a set of parameters, θ, there may exist an alternative set of parameters, $\phi = \phi(\theta)$, that allows the likelihood to be expressed as a product of separate terms where each of the terms is a complete data problem. Maximizing the likelihood (or the log-likelihood) then becomes a problem of maximizing the separate terms as in the following equation:

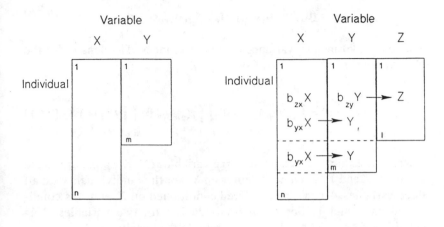

Figure 7.1. Monotone Data Patterns

$$l(\phi \mid Y_{obs}) = l_1(\phi_1 \mid Y_{obs}) + l_2(\phi_2 \mid Y_{obs}) + \ldots + l_j(\phi_j \mid Y_{obs}) \quad [7.19]$$

When the data are monotone (Marini et al., 1980), this becomes a particularly useful strategy.

Consider a sample that can be broken down so that each member of a particular subsample has complete data on one block of variables and missing data on the remainder of the variables. The characteristic of monotone patterns of missing data is that there exists a sequence of subsets of data for which each sequence contains complete data on fewer variables than the prior subset. Figure 7.1 presents this pattern for two and three variables. To generalize somewhat, each block could be a set of variables—not just a single variable—and the pattern (not to mention the techniques to be described) would still hold.

A particular monotone pattern of missing data occurs often in longitudinal studies. This nested pattern simply requires that individuals who drop out of a study do not reenter the study.

5.1. Factoring the Likelihood

The vector of parameters for the three-variable problem is

$$\theta = (\mu_x, \mu_y, \mu_z, \sigma_{xx}, \sigma_{yy}, \sigma_{zz}, \sigma_{xy}, \sigma_{xz}, \sigma_{yz}) \qquad [7.20]$$

and consists of means, variances, and covariances. The density for the observations is

$$f(Y_{\mathrm{obs}} \mid \theta) = \prod_{i=1}^{l} f(x_i, y_i, z_i \mid \theta) \prod_{l+1}^{m} f(x_i, y_i \mid \theta) \prod_{m+1}^{n} f(x_i \mid \theta) \qquad [7.21]$$

where l cases have scores on all three variables (X, Y, Z), m cases have scores on X and Y, and n have scores on X. For the l individuals with all three variables, Y can be considered conditioned on X, and Z is conditioned on X and Y. For the m individuals with two variables, Y is conditioned on X. This allows us to rewrite the density as

$$f(Y_{\mathrm{obs}} \mid \theta) = \left[\prod_{i=1}^{l} f(x_i \mid \theta) f(y_i \mid x_i, \theta) f(z_i \mid x_i, y_i, \theta) \right] \times$$
$$\left[\prod_{\substack{i= \\ l+1}}^{m} f(x_i \mid \theta) f(y_i \mid x_i, \theta) \right] \left[\prod_{\substack{i= \\ m+1}}^{n} f(x_i \mid \theta) \right] \qquad [7.22]$$

With terms gathered, the density takes on the monotone pattern:

$$f(Y_{\mathrm{obs}} \mid \theta) = \prod_{i=1}^{n} f(x_i \mid \theta) \prod_{i=1}^{m} f(y_i \mid x_i, \theta) \prod_{i=1}^{l} f(z_i \mid x_i, y_i, \theta) \qquad [7.23]$$

Since we express certain variables as conditioned on other variables, we can summarize the directional nature of the conditional relationship with the regression relationships among the different sets of variables. As a result, the reparameterization of Equation 7.23 makes a lot of sense. We do this by specifying

$$\theta = (\mu_x, \mu_y, \mu_z, \sigma_{xx}, \beta_{y0}, \beta_{yx}, \beta_{z0}, \beta_{zx}, \beta_{zy}, \sigma_{yy.x}, \sigma_{zz.x.y}) \qquad [7.24]$$

The likelihood based on the reparameterized density becomes

$$L(\varphi \mid Y_{obs}) = \left[\prod_{i=1}^{n} f(x_i \mid \mu_x, \sigma_{xx}) \right]\left[\prod_{i=1}^{m} f(y_i \mid x_i, \beta_{y0}, \beta_{yx}, \sigma_{yy.x}) \right] \times$$

$$\left[\prod_{i=1}^{l} f(z_i \mid y_i, x_i, \beta_{z0}, \beta_{zx}, \sigma_{zz.x.y}) \right] \qquad [7.25]$$

This equation represents the goal of expressing the likelihood as the product of separate terms, each of which represents a complete data problem. Maximizing the likelihood, then, involves maximizing the factors of the likelihood serially. The first bracket requires simply calculating the mean and variance for the n complete values of X. The second bracket requires calculating the regression of Y onto X for the m complete cases of X and Y. The third bracket requires the calculation of the regression of Z onto X and Y. These parameter estimates can then be used to determine estimates of the original parameter vector. They can also be used to construct the complete data covariance (or moments) matrix.

For the three-variable case, this latter step is relatively simple. When X, Y, and Z represent blocks of variables, however, a more efficient method may be desired. The sweep operator provides the computational power to handle these more complex problems. We will now look at the sweep operator for three blocks of variables.

5.2. The Sweep Operator

The sweep operator (Beaton, 1964; Dempster, 1969) operates on some type of moments or augmented moments matrix and produces regression estimates. The sweep operator SWP(k) is defined as follows:

A $p \times p$ matrix, M, will be said to have been swept on row k and column k of M is replaced by another $p \times p$ matrix, N, whose (i,j) element, n_{ij}, is related to the (i,j) element m_{ij} of M as follows:

$$n_{kk} = -1/m_{kk}$$

$$n_{ik} = m_{ik}/m_{kk}$$

$$n_{kj} = m_{kj}/m_{kk}$$

$$n_{ij} = m_{ij} - m_{ik}m_{kj}/m_{kk} \quad \text{for } i = k \text{ and } j = k \qquad [7.25.1]$$

In the simplest sense, sweeping on a variable turns that variable from a dependent variable to an independent variable. The results of a sweep of an M matrix place the regression results into the corresponding N matrix. Following Little and Rubin (1987), consider a $(p \times 1)(p \times 1)$ matrix of scaled crossproducts augmented by a vector of means:

$$M = \begin{pmatrix} m_{11} & m_{12} & m_{13} & m_{14} \\ m_{21} & m_{22} & m_{23} & m_{24} \\ m_{31} & m_{32} & m_{33} & m_{34} \\ m_{41} & m_{42} & m_{43} & m_{44} \end{pmatrix} \qquad [7.26]$$

where m_{ll} is defined as l, the m_{lj} and m_{il} elements are means, and the remaining elements are scaled crossproducts. Sweeping on the first row and column (the means row and column are usually designated row 0) yields the augmented covariance matrix and a -1 in the $(1,1)$ position of the matrix. The N matrix becomes

$$N = \text{SWP}(0)M = \begin{pmatrix} \dfrac{1}{m_{11}} & \dfrac{m_{12}}{m_{11}} & \dfrac{m_{13}}{m_{11}} & \dfrac{m_{14}}{m_{11}} \\[2ex] \dfrac{m_{21}}{m_{11}} & m_{22} - \dfrac{m_{21}^2}{m_{11}} & m_{23} - \dfrac{m_{21}m_{13}}{m_{11}} & m_{24} - \dfrac{m_{21}m_{14}}{m_{11}} \\[2ex] \dfrac{m_{31}}{m_{11}} & m_{32} - \dfrac{m_{31}m_{12}}{m_{11}} & m_{33} - \dfrac{m_{31}^2}{m_{11}} & m_{34} - \dfrac{m_{31}m_{14}}{m_{11}} \\[2ex] \dfrac{m_{41}}{m_{11}} & m_{42} - \dfrac{m_{41}m_{12}}{m_{11}} & m_{43} - \dfrac{m_{41}m_{13}}{m_{11}} & m_{44} - \dfrac{m_{41}^2}{m_{11}} \end{pmatrix}$$

$$[7.27]$$

which is of the form

$$\text{SWP}(0) = \begin{pmatrix} -1 & \overline{x_1} & \overline{x_2} & \overline{x_3} \\ \overline{x_1} & s_{11} & s_{12} & s_{13} \\ \overline{x_2} & s_{12} & s_{22} & s_{23} \\ \overline{x_3} & s_{13} & s_{23} & s_{33} \end{pmatrix} \qquad [7.28]$$

The terms are sometimes easier to understand when compared with the following computational formula for a crossproduct:

$$\sum (x - \bar{x})(y - \bar{y})/N = \sum xy/N - \bar{x}\bar{y} \qquad [7.28.1]$$

Sweeping on row and columns 0 and 1 yields the following matrix:

$$\text{SWP}(0, 1) = \begin{pmatrix} -1 - \dfrac{\bar{x}_1^2}{s_{11}} & \dfrac{\bar{x}_1}{s_{11}} & \bar{x}_2 - \dfrac{s_{12}\bar{x}_1}{s_{11}} & \bar{x}_3 - \dfrac{s_{13}\bar{x}_1}{s_{11}} \\[2ex] \dfrac{\bar{x}_1}{s_{11}} & \dfrac{-1}{s_{11}} & \dfrac{s_{12}}{s_{11}} & \dfrac{s_{13}}{s_{11}} \\[2ex] \bar{x}_2 - \dfrac{s_{12}\bar{x}_1}{s_{11}} & \dfrac{s_{12}}{s_{11}} & s_{22} - \dfrac{s_{12}^2}{s_{11}} & s_{23} - \dfrac{s_{12}s_{13}}{s_{22}} \\[2ex] \bar{x}_3 - \dfrac{s_{13}\bar{x}_1}{s_{11}} & \dfrac{s_{13}}{s_{11}} & s_{23} - \dfrac{s_{12}s_{13}}{s_{22}} & s_{33} - \dfrac{s_{13}^2}{s_{22}} \end{pmatrix} \qquad [7.29]$$

This effectively partitions the matrix, N, into four parts,

$$\begin{array}{cc} -A & B \\ B^{\text{T}} & C \end{array} \qquad [7.28.2]$$

in which B contains the regression coefficients of the remaining variables on variable l and C is the residual covariance matrix of the dependent variables. A can be used to get the covariance matrix of the estimated regression coefficients.

A reverse sweep operator, REVSWP(k), exists that correspondingly turns independent variables back into dependent variables. This operator is defined as

$$m_{kk} = -1/n_{kk}$$

$$m_{ik} = -n_{ik}/n_{kk}$$

$$m_{kj} = n_{kj}/n_{kk}$$

$$m_{ij} = n_{ij} - n_{ik}n_{kj}/n_{kk} \quad \text{for } j = i \text{ and } k = i \qquad [7.29.1]$$

In the case of blocks of variables that follow the monotone pattern, the use of the sweep operator is a direct result of the factorization of the likelihood function.

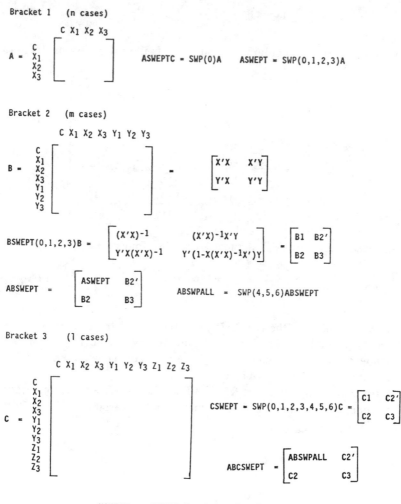

Bracket 1   (n cases)

$$A = \begin{matrix} C \\ X_1 \\ X_2 \\ X_3 \end{matrix} \begin{bmatrix} & \\ & \\ & \\ & \end{bmatrix} \begin{matrix} C\ X_1\ X_2\ X_3 \end{matrix}$$

ASWEPTC = SWP(0)A   ASWEPT = SWP(0,1,2,3)A

Bracket 2   (m cases)

$$B = \begin{matrix} C \\ X_1 \\ X_2 \\ X_3 \\ Y_1 \\ Y_2 \\ Y_3 \end{matrix} \begin{bmatrix} & \\ & \\ & \\ & \\ & \\ & \\ & \end{bmatrix} = \begin{bmatrix} X'X & X'Y \\ Y'X & Y'Y \end{bmatrix}$$

$$BSWEPT(0,1,2,3)B = \begin{bmatrix} (X'X)^{-1} & (X'X)^{-1}X'Y \\ Y'X(X'X)^{-1} & Y'(1-X(X'X)^{-1}X')Y \end{bmatrix} = \begin{bmatrix} B1 & B2' \\ B2 & B3 \end{bmatrix}$$

$$ABSWEPT = \begin{bmatrix} ASWEPT & B2' \\ B2 & B3 \end{bmatrix}$$

ABSWPALL = SWP(4,5,6)ABSWEPT

Bracket 3   (l cases)

$$C = \begin{matrix} C \\ X_1 \\ X_2 \\ X_3 \\ Y_1 \\ Y_2 \\ Y_3 \\ Z_1 \\ Z_2 \\ Z_3 \end{matrix} \begin{bmatrix} & \\ & \\ & \\ & \\ & \\ & \\ & \\ & \\ & \\ & \end{bmatrix}$$

CSWEPT = SWP(0,1,2,3,4,5,6)C = $\begin{bmatrix} C1 & C2' \\ C2 & C3 \end{bmatrix}$

ABCSWEPT = $\begin{bmatrix} ABSWPALL & C2' \\ C2 & C3 \end{bmatrix}$

MAXEST = RSWP(0,1,2,3,4,5,6)ABCSWEPT

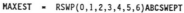

Figure 7.2. Sweeping the Blocked Data Matrix

5.3. Sweeping a Blocked Data Matrix

Consider again the factored and reparameterized likelihood function represented by Equation 7.25. The matrix representing this bracket is pictured in Figure 7.2. The first bracket represents complete data for all subjects on the block 1 variables. With an augmented scaled cross-products matrix as input, we could sweep the matrix of complete block variables on the constant and generate the likelihood estimates of the covariance matrix. We could also start with an augmented covariance matrix and place a -1 in the $(1,1)$ position. This is the matrix ASWEPTC. Now consider the second bracket. If we have targeted the X variables as the regression predictors, we have partitioned the matrix. To get the likelihood estimates for the m cases with block 1 and block 2 variables, we sweep the augmented scaled crossproducts matrix on the constant and the X variables. The swept matrix is partitioned as in Figure 7.2. The B_2 submatrix contains the regression coefficients of block 2 onto block 1. The B_3 submatrix contains the covariance of the regression residuals. We have, however, more information than is available in the matrix. In particular, the B_1 portion of the matrix is swept only for m cases. By sweeping the n-case matrix on the block 1 variables, we get a matrix that we can substitute for the B_1 portion of the m-case matrix. This will include all of the information from the first two steps of the analysis in a single matrix. ASWEPT has been swept on the constant and the block 1 variables. The resulting matrix is called ABSWEPT. Its composition appears in Figure 7.2. This matrix will be swept on the block 2 variables to prepare it to be passed along to the next step.

For the third bracket, the l cases with all three blocks are used to create an augmented scaled crossproducts matrix. This matrix is swept on the constant, block 1 and block 2 variables. The resultant matrix includes the parameter estimates and the regression residual variances and covariances. The A-part of this matrix can be replaced by the m-case matrix swept for block 1 and block 2 variables. This creates a matrix that includes the maximum likelihood information generated by all three likelihoods. To reparameterize the regression estimates into the estimates of the means, variances, and covariances, it remains only to reverse sweep this final matrix on the block 1 and block 2 variables.

5.4. An Example

We selected some data from the Child-Family Development Project (Belsky & Rovine, 1990). Since some individuals returned to the study after missing a data point, we deleted all data that did not conform to the nested pattern. Four subscales from the Braiker-Kelly Marital Adjustment Inventory were used. An augmented covariance matrix was calculated for the three occasions of measurement using pair-wise

Table 7.1   Estimated Moments and Covariance Matrices Braiker-Kelly Scales

Moments Matrix
Maximum Likelihood Estimates
Pair-wise Deletion
List-wise Deletion

	LOVE3	CONF3	AMB3	LOVE9	CONF9	AMB9	LOVEX	CONFX	AMBX
LOVE3	6250.6								
	6225.8								
	6214.0								
CONF3	1577.3	456.1							
	1583.0	461.5							
	1605.5	467.7							
AMB3	771.7	227.3	133.3						
	777.8	233.2	137.0						
	774.6	229.7	130.9						
LOVE9	6037.0	1531.1	751.2	5883.3					
	6043.6	1531.2	736.1	5905.5					
	5987.6	1551.4	749.8	5823.4					
CONF9	1693.1	469.9	236.8	1633.4	512.5				
	1691.7	470.9	236.3	1631.7	510.7				
	1709.2	479.7	236.4	1642.7	519.8				
AMB9	920.4	258.4	142.1	869.5	282.0	182.7			
	922.4	259.7	141.6	864.6	280.4	180.6			
	940.3	268.7	144.9	882.4	290.0	190.7			
LOVEX	5904.1	1496.1	739.2	5725.2	1604.1	867.7	5722.8		
	5857.1	1528.6	750.9	5707.1	1616.1	878.9	5695.1		
	5866.0	1519.3	738.9	5675.8	1614.6	882.6	5681.6		
CONFX	1725.5	478.0	237.8	1665.7	507.1	278.6	1606.8	535.1	
	1740.4	498.2	245.9	1666.7	511.3	284.1	1629.0	550.1	
	1743.3	488.9	239.1	1676.2	515.6	287.9	1604.3	544.4	
AMBX	970.3	273.0	146.6	927.9	292.2	176.4	863.4	308.6	214.0
	975.9	288.4	152.5	922.1	292.5	178.7	881.3	318.1	218.1
	983.6	280.7	147.7	935.5	297.8	182.9	873.1	315.2	218.6
MEANS	78.55	20.41	10.25	76.01	21.81	11.98	74.53	22.13	12.59
	78.37	20.54	10.37	76.18	21.79	11.94	74.42	22.46	12.80
	78.41	20.76	10.23	75.67	21.99	12.23	74.29	22.37	12.75
	LOVE3	CONF3	AMB3	LOVE9	CONF9	AMB9	LOVEX	CONFX	AMBX

continued

deletion, list-wise deletion, and the ML procedure. The results appear in Table 7.1. Some of the estimates were relatively discrepant. For the most discrepant cases, the ML estimates usually fell somewhere be-

Table 7.1   Continued

Covariance Matrix
Maximum Likelihood Estimates
Pair-wise Deletion
List-wise Deletion

	LOVE3	CONF3	AMB3	LOVE9	CONF9	AMB9	LOVEX	CONFX	AMBX
LOVE3	80.48								
	83.38								
	66.03								
CONF3	−21.11	39.74							
	−27.42	39.51							
	−23.34	36.65							
AMB3	−33.94	17.91	28.09						
	−35.79	19.33	29.50						
	−28.37	17.21	26.31						
LOVE9	65.70	−20.58	−28.47	104.40					
	65.18	−20.58	−28.32	103.47					
	54.22	−20.45	−25.12	97.53					
CONF9	−20.23	24.68	13.06	−24.77					
	−19.99	24.54	13.18	−24.97	36.09				
	−14.67	23.13	11.37	−21.70	36.45				
AMB9	−21.23	13.67	19.11	−41.75	20.50	38.98			
	−20.65	13.63	19.06	−40.99	20.25	38.19			
	−19.42	14.67	19.80	−44.01	21.04	41.28			
LOVEX	49.42	−25.35	−25.22	59.13	−21.71	−25.82	167.40		
	42.79	−24.57	−24.16	54.96	−19.41	−25.86	157.74		
	41.15	−23.91	−22.61	54.15	−19.03	−26.75	163.93		
CONFX	−13.50	26.13	10.73	−17.29	24.14	13.16	−43.31	44.93	
	−13.76	24.72	12.21	−17.55	24.02	14.57	−43.10	45.86	
	−11.10	24.42	10.21	−16.97	23.81	14.25	−42.29	44.25	
AMBX	−18.86	15.92	17.40	−29.35	17.53	25.41	−75.19	29.79	55.47
	−18.57	16.44	18.35	−29.93	17.29	26.56	−71.74	30.86	54.66
	−16.54	15.95	17.34	−29.87	17.48	27.05	−75.01	30.11	56.41
MEANS	78.55	20.41	10.25	76.01	21.81	11.98	74.53	22.13	12.59
	78.37	20.54	10.37	76.18	21.79	11.94	74.42	22.46	12.80
	78.41	20.76	10.23	75.67	21.99	12.23	74.29	22.37	12.75
N	—	—	—	—	—	—	—	—	—
	172	172	172	165	165	165	140	140	140
	126	126	126	126	126	126	126	126	126

tween the pair-wise and list-wise estimates and tended to be somewhat closer to the pair-wise estimates. The program used to estimate the matrix appears in the chapter's Appendix.

Since the estimation does not require that data be missing completely at random, this procedure tends to reduce bias in the estimates compared to non-ML methods. The procedure, however, produces no standard errors.

The complete estimated matrix can be used as input to regression procedures. The standard errors of the regression will tend not to be consistent estimates of the true standard errors. Used as input for overidentified models, the results of this method may not yield efficient estimates of the parameters.

6. The EM Algorithm

For MAR data, iterative algorithms exist that make it relatively easy to estimate missing data solutions. If the likelihood is differentiable and unimodal, ML estimates can be found by solving the simultaneous equations represented by the scoring function (Little & Rubin, 1987).

Iteratively, this can be accomplished using, for example, the Newton-Raphson algorithm of the type

$$\theta^{(t+1)} = \theta^{(t)} + I^{-1}(\theta^{(t)} \mid Y_{\text{obs}}) S(\theta^{(t)} \mid Y_{\text{obs}}) \qquad [7.30]$$

where I is the observed information. It is often the case, however, that a closed form solution is impossible. For this situation, EM algorithms (Dempster et al., 1977) that do not require the differentiation of the likelihood function are generally preferable.

The EM (or Expectation-Maximization) algorithm consists of the M-step, which estimates the θ vector of parameters as if the data were complete, and the E-step, which finds the conditional expectation of the sufficient statistics. The expectations are used to get the new estimates of the missing data values that are then fed into the M-step, which yields ML estimates of θ which in turn allows the new expectations to be determined. These steps alternate until the solution converges.

Methods based on the EM algorithm are less restrictive in the patterns they can handle than methods described previously. Consider three variables collected on a sample. Assume that the data are both multivariate normal and MAR.

There are seven possible patterns of missing data, as shown in Figure 7.3 (eight if you include all three missing). For each separate pattern, the means and covariances can either be computed (if present in the sample)

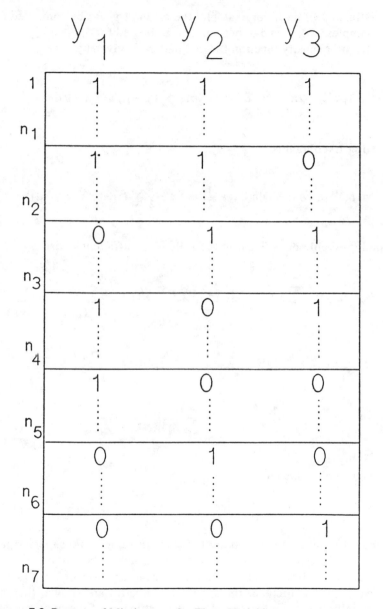

Figure 7.3. Patterns of Missingness for Three Variables

or estimated (if not). For example, the mean of y_1 can be computed for subsamples 1, 2, 4, and 5, but must be estimated for 3, 6, and 7.

The joint density function for this pattern is given by

$$f(Y_{\text{obs}} \mid \mu, \Sigma) = 2\pi^{(-nk/2)} \mid \Sigma \mid^{-n/2} \exp\left[-\sum_{i=1}^{n} (y_i - \mu)\Sigma^{-1}(y_i - \mu)^{T\!/2} \right] \quad [7.31]$$

The log-likelihood is

$$L(Y \mid \mu, \Sigma) = -\frac{3}{2} n \ln(2\pi) - \frac{n}{2} \ln \mid \Sigma \mid - \frac{1}{2} \sum_{i=1}^{n} (y_i - \mu)\Sigma^{-1}(y_i - \mu)^{T} \quad [7.32]$$

The log-likelihood is linear in the following sufficient statistics

$$s_1 = \sum_{i=1}^{n} y_{i1} \quad s_2 = \sum_{i=1}^{n} y_{i2} \quad s_3 = \sum_{i=1}^{n} y_{i3} \quad s_{11} = \sum_{i=1}^{n} y_{i1}^2 \quad s_{22} = \sum_{i=1}^{n} y_{i2}^2 \quad s_{33} = \sum_{i=1}^{n} y_{i3}^2$$

$$s_1 = \sum_{i=1}^{n} y_{i1} \quad s_2 = \sum_{i=1}^{n} y_{i2} \quad s_3 = \sum_{i=1}^{n} y_{i3} \quad s_{11} = \sum_{i=1}^{n} y_{i1}^2 \quad s_{22} = \sum_{i=1}^{n} y_{i2}^2 \quad s_{33} = \sum_{i=1}^{n} y_{i3}^2$$

$$s_{12} = \sum_{i=1}^{n} y_{i1} y_{i2} \quad s_{13} = \sum_{i=1}^{n} y_{i1} y_{i3} \quad s_{23} = \sum_{i=1}^{n} y_{i2} y_{i3} \quad [7.33]$$

The current parameter estimates,

$$\theta^{(t)} = (\mu^{(t)}, \Sigma^{(t)}) \quad [7.34]$$

(which for the first iteration are the starting values), are superscripted by t. The E-step can be broken down by whether the parameter to be estimated is a first or second moment (mean or variance/covariance). Once the expectations of the sufficient statistics are known, they are essentially being used to calculate new estimates of the missing data, which are then included along with the observed data to estimate the new parameter values. The general form for the expectations is

$$E\left(\sum_{i=1}^{n} y_{ij} \mid Y_{\text{obs}}, \theta^{(t)}\right) = \sum_{i=1}^{n} y_{ij}^{(t)} \quad \text{for } j = 1, \ldots, J \qquad [7.35]$$

and

$$E\left(\sum_{i=1}^{n} y_{ij} y_{ik} \mid Y_{\text{obs}}, \theta^{(t)}\right) = \sum_{i=1}^{n} y_{ij}^{(t)} y_{ik}^{(t)} + C_{ijk}^{(t)} \quad \text{for } j = 1, \ldots, J; \ k = 1, \ldots, K$$
$$[7.35.1]$$

respectively, where $y_{ij}^{(t)} = y_{ij}$ when observed, $y_{ij}^{(t)} = E(y_{ij} | Y_{\text{obs}}, \theta^{(t)})$ when missing, $c_{ijk} = 0$ if either is observed, and $c_{ijk} = \text{cov}(y_{ij} y_{ik} | Y_{\text{obs}}, \theta^{(t)})$ if both are missing.

The E-step for variable y_1 is given in Figure 7.4. The expectation for y_1 sums the values over the seven subsamples. Values are summed for 1, 2, 4, and 5. Subsample 3 has both y_2 and y_3. Regression weights from the prior M-step are used to "fill in" the missing values. Subsamples 6 and 7 each have a single measured variable. Regression weights are similarly used to fill in those values. A similar procedure holds for the expectation of the sums of squares and crossproducts. With the expectations of the sufficient statistics, the new estimates of the means, variances, and covariances can be used to get the new estimates of the regression coefficients necessary for the next step. The M-step appears in Figure 7.5.

7. Patterned Covariance Matrices

The three-variable problem might have limited interest for those dealing with latent variable models. The use of an EM algorithm for estimating a factor analysis, however, is probably more interesting.

Those estimating latent variable models often employ covariance matrices upon which a structure has been imposed. The hypothesis of either a confirmatory factor structure or a set of regression relationships among observed or latent variables imposes the expectation that a particular covariational pattern will appear in the observed data. When requiring a particular pattern, one can include that restriction in the estimation of the parameters of a model. Using an EM algorithm provides a powerful way both to impose a structure upon a covariance

For Y, the expectations are

$$E\left(\sum_{i=1}^{n} Y_{i1} | Y_{\text{obs}}, \mu, \Sigma\right) = \sum_{i=1}^{n_1} y_{i1} + \sum_{i=n_1+1}^{n_2} y_{i1} + \sum_{i=n_2+1}^{n_3} (\beta_{230} + \beta_{21}y_{i2} + \beta_{31}y_{i3})$$

$$\sum_{i=n_3+1}^{n_4} y_i + \sum_{i=n_4+1}^{n_5} y_{i1} + \sum_{i=n_5+1}^{n_6} (\beta_{20} + \beta_{21}y_{i2}) + \sum_{i=n_6+1}^{n_7} (\beta_{30} + \beta_{31}y_{i3})$$

$$E\left(\sum_{i=1}^{n} Y_{i2}^2 | Y_{\text{obs}}, \mu, \Sigma\right) = \sum_{i=1}^{n_1} y_{i1}^2 + \sum_{i=n_1+1}^{n_2} y_{i1}^2 + \sum_{i=n_2+1}^{n_3} (\beta_{230} + \beta_{12}y_{i2} + \beta_{13}y_{i3})^2 + \sigma_{11.23}$$

$$\sum_{i=n_3+1}^{n_4} y_{i1}^2 + \sum_{i=n_4+1}^{n_5} y_{i1}^2 + \sum_{i=n_5+1}^{n_6} (\beta_{20} + \beta_{12}y_{i2})^2 + \sigma_{11.2} + \sum_{i=n_6+1}^{n_7} (\beta_{30} + \beta_{13}y_{i3})^2 + \sigma_{11.3}$$

and

$$E\left(\sum_{i=1}^{n} y_{i1}y_{i2} | Y_{\text{obs}}, \mu, \Sigma\right) = \sum_{i=1}^{n_1} y_{i1}y_{i2} + \sum_{i=n_1+1}^{n_2} y_{i1}y_{i2}$$

$$\sum_{i=n_2+1}^{n_3} (\beta_{230} + \beta_{12}y_{i2} + \beta_{13}y_{i3})y_{i2} + \sum_{i=n_3+1}^{n_4} y_{i1}(\beta_{130} + \beta_{21}y_{i1} + \beta_{23}y_{i3})$$

$$\sum_{i=n_4+1}^{n_5} y_{i1}(\beta_{10} + \beta_{21}y_{i1}) + \sum_{i=n_5+1}^{n_6} (\beta_{20} + \beta_{12}y_{i2})y_{i2} + \sum_{i=n_6+1}^{n_7} \text{cov}(y_{i1}y_{i2} | Y_{\text{obs}})$$

and so on for y_2, y_3.

Figure 7.4. The E-Step

$$\mu_1^{(t+1)} = E(\sum_{i=1}^{n} y_{i1} | \theta^{(t)}, Y_{obs}) / n$$

$$\mu_2^{(t+1)} = E(\sum_{i=1}^{n} y_{i2} | \theta^{(t)}, Y_{obs}) / n$$

$$\mu_3^{(t+1)} = E(\sum_{i=1}^{n} y_{i3} | \theta^{(t)}, Y_{obs}) / n$$

$$\sigma_{11}^{2(t+1)} = E(\sum_{i=1}^{n} y_{i1}^2 | \theta^{(t)}, Y_{obs}) / n - (\mu_1^{(t+1)})^2$$

$$\sigma_{22}^{2(t+1)} = E(\sum_{i=1}^{n} y_{i2}^2 | \theta^{(t)}, Y_{obs}) / n - (\mu_2^{(t+1)})^2$$

$$\sigma_{33}^{2(t+1)} = E(\sum_{i=1}^{n} y_{i3}^2 | \theta^{(t)}, Y_{obs}) / n - (\mu_3^{(t+1)})^2$$

$$\sigma_{12}^{(t+1)} = E(\sum_{i=1}^{n} y_{i1} y_{i2} | \theta^{(t)}, Y_{obs}) / n - \mu_1^{(t+1)} \mu_2^{(t+1)}$$

$$\sigma_{13}^{(t+1)} = E(\sum_{i=1}^{n} y_{i1} y_{i3} | \theta^{(t)}, Y_{obs}) / n - \mu_1^{(t+1)} \mu_3^{(t+1)}$$

$$\sigma_{23}^{(t+1)} = E(\sum_{i=1}^{n} y_{i2} y_{i3} | \theta^{(t)}, Y_{obs}) / n - \mu_2^{(t+1)} \mu_3^{(t+1)}$$

Figure 7.5. The M-Step

matrix (Rubin & Thayer, 1982) and estimate parameters in the presence of that structure and missing data (Little & Rubin, 1987).

Rubin and Thayer (1982) demonstrate how the EM algorithm can be used to estimate a factor solution by assuming a particular pattern to a covariance matrix.

To estimate the factor mode they consider two types of variables. Y-variables are observed and Z-variables are unobserved latent variables. The latent variables are simply treated as missing.

The logic of factor analysis always considers a set of regression relationships in which latent variables are functioning as predictors of their indicators. Sweeping the matrix on all of the latent variables generates the factor pattern. The sweep operator places the regression estimates, the factor loadings, in the off-diagonal block. The block corresponding to the observed variables contains the covariance matrix of the residuals, which in this case are the uniquenesses. This is the M-step of the EM algorithm. This generates maximum likelihood estimates as if the data were complete. The only problem at this point is that the individuals' values on the latent variables (the factor scores) do not exist. This is taken care of in the E-step, which predicts the Z-variables from the Y-variables using sufficient statistics. Figure 7.6 is a schematic representation of this process.

The patterned covariance matrix, Σ, is partitioned as

$$\Sigma^{(t)} = \begin{pmatrix} \Sigma_{11}^{(t)} & \Sigma_{12}^{(t)} \\ \Sigma_{21}^{(t)} & \Sigma_{22}^{(t)} \end{pmatrix} \qquad [7.37]$$

The sufficient statistics for Σ are s_{11}, the scaled crossproducts of the observed variables, s_{22}, the scaled crossproducts of the latent variables, and s_{12}, the scaled crossproducts between Y and Z. Given a set of starting values for the latent variables, one can find the expectation of the quadrants of Σ. The expectation of s_{11} is the observed scaled crossproducts matrix for the complete observed data. The expectation of s_{12} is generated from knowledge of the regression relationship between observed and latent variables. Sweeping the Σ matrix including current values of the factor scores yields the regression estimates of Z onto Y. These are not to be confused with the factor loadings. The sufficient statistics can be rewritten as shown in Figure 7.7. The expectation of s_{12} then becomes the s_{11} times the matrix of regression coefficients that we have just calculated, using the sweep operator. The expectation of

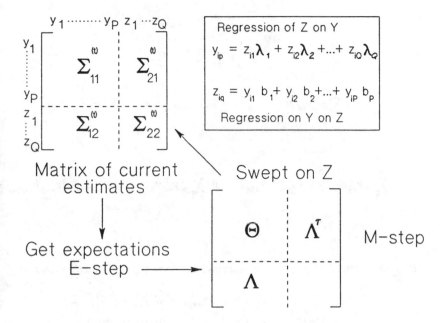

Figure 7.6. Patterned Covariance Matrix (factor analysis)

s_{22} is composed of the part of the latent variable covariance matrix that is predicted by the observed variables and the part that is residual. These terms are also available from the sweep operator. These sufficient statistics are then used by the M-step to calculate the next set of estimates.

Some controversy exists over the effectiveness of the EM algorithm as compared to other ML estimation procedures (Arminger & Sobel, 1990; Bentler & Tanaka, 1983; Brown, 1983; Rubin & Thayer, 1983). However, in the presence of missing data the EM algorithm provides a way of combining ML estimation with missing data estimation under the constraints of an imposed pattern, one example of which can be an assumed measurement model.

For confirmatory factor analysis, the M-step is a little more compli-cated. Whereas for the exploratory factor analysis, we swept on all factors, with a confirmatory structure we must first determine how many sets of observed variables there are with distinct patterns of loadings on

$$\Sigma^{(t)} = \begin{bmatrix} \Sigma_{11}^{(t)} & \vdots & \Sigma_{12}^{(t)} \\ -- & -- & -- \\ \Sigma_{21}^{(t)} & \vdots & \Sigma_{22}^{(t)} \end{bmatrix}$$

$$S_{11} = \sum y_j y_k / N \qquad S_{22} = \sum z_j z_k / N \qquad S_{21} = \sum y_p z_q / N$$

$$E(\sum_{i=1}^{N} (y_{ij} y_{ik}/N) \mid Y_{obs}) = S_{11}$$

$$E[\sum_{i=1}^{N} (y_{ip}^T z_{iq})/N \mid Y_{obs}, z_{est}] = E[\sum_{i=1}^{N} (y_{ip}^T y_{ip} * b_p)/N \mid Y_{obs}, z_{est}]$$

$$S_{11} E[\sum_{i=1}^{N} b_p \mid Y_{obs}, z_{est}] = S_{11} \Sigma_{21}^{(t)} \Sigma_{11}^{(t)^{-1}}$$

$$E[\sum_{i=1}^{N} z_j z_k / N \mid Y_{obs}, z_{est}] = [regression\ part] + [residual part]$$

$$E[\sum_{i=1}^{N} (b_p^T y_{ip}^T)(y_{ip} b_p)/N\ Y_{obs}, z_{est}] + \Sigma_{22}^{(t)} - \Sigma_{21}^{(t)} \Sigma_{11}^{(t)^{-1}} \Sigma_{12}^{(t)}$$

$$= \Sigma_{21}^{(t)} \Sigma_{11}^{(t)^{-1}} S_{11} \Sigma_{11}^{(t)^{-1}} \Sigma_{12}^{(t)} = \Sigma_{22}^{(t)} - \Sigma_{21}^{(t)} \Sigma_{11}^{(t)^{-1}} \Sigma_{12}^{(t)}$$

Figure 7.7. Sufficient Statistics for the Patterned Covariance Matrix

the latent variables. Each set must then be swept only on those latent variables with nonzero loadings.

7.1. Measurement Models With Missing Data

When some of the values of observed variables are missing, the same general procedure can be used. As in the prior EM example, however, the data set must be broken down into however many distinct patterns of missing data exist and sufficient statistics must be calculated for each pattern to determine the overall expectation.

8. Direct Parameter Estimation

Although all missing data problems can be handled by imputation or at least the use of sufficient statistics as shown above, many of the same problems can be modeled directly. A number of authors (Allison, 1987; Lee, 1986; Muthen, Kaplan, & Hollis, 1987; Werts, Rock, & Grandy, 1979) suggest using multiple group structural models with constraints across groups.

Werts et al. (1979) estimated parameters for a complete data group and used those values where appropriate on the missing data groups. Groups as a result had different numbers of variables; apparently no single model was estimated. Finkbeiner (1979) derived an ML estimator based on Wilks (1932) and used the estimator to estimate a factor model. Lee (1986) used a generalized least squares estimator that apparently was summed over multiple patterns of missing data.

The strategy that I would like to consider was described by Allison (1987) and uses "phantom variables" for those subgroups for which a particular variable is missing. This strategy divides the sample into groups, each of which represents a missing data pattern. For each group, some variables will be missing. These phantom variables will be assigned distributional characteristics which will allow us to estimate the model.

Consider the model in Figure 7.8. This is an observed variable regression. Assuming the data are missing at random (MAR), one can model the relationships with the following three equations:

$$y_3 = \beta_{31} y_1 + \zeta_3 \qquad [7.38]$$

$$y_4 = \beta_{42} y_2 + \beta_{41} y_1 + \zeta_4 \qquad [7.39]$$

$$y_5 = \beta_{53} y_3 + \zeta_5 \qquad [7.40]$$

Assume that the data can be divided into two groups. The first group has complete data on all five variables, the second has some missing data on y_3. The sample means and covariance matrix for the two groups would have the following pattern indicated by the matrices, S_1 and S_2:

$$S_1 = \begin{bmatrix} - & - & - & - & - \\ - & - & - & - & - \\ - & - & - & - & - \\ - & - & - & - & - \\ - & - & - & - & - \end{bmatrix} \qquad [7.41]$$

$$M_1 = [- \; - \; - \; - \; -] \qquad [7.42]$$

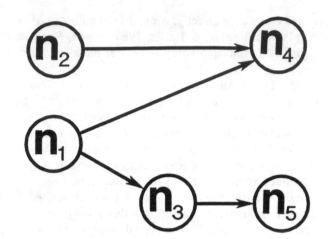

Figure 7.8. Complete Data Model

$$S_2 = \begin{bmatrix} - & - & 0 & - & - \\ - & - & 0 & - & - \\ 0 & 0 & 1 & 0 & 0 \\ - & - & 0 & - & - \\ - & - & 0 & - & - \end{bmatrix}$$ [7.43]

$$M_2 = [- \; - \; 0 \; - \; -]$$ [7.44]

where a "—" represents a nonmissing value. The variance of the missing variable for group 2 is set to 1, the covariances that include variable y_3 and the mean for that variable are set to 0. These pseudovalues allow one to estimate the two-group model. An appropriate computational model for estimating the parameters is not the one that would be directly derived from the previous figure, but appears in Figure 7.9. The modifications suggested by Allison and represented by that model are designed to estimate the correct regressions, while at the same time reproduce the pseudovalues for group 2.

The "measurement model" to be estimated has an additional latent variable that will be used to model the means of an augmented moments matrix. The measurement model is

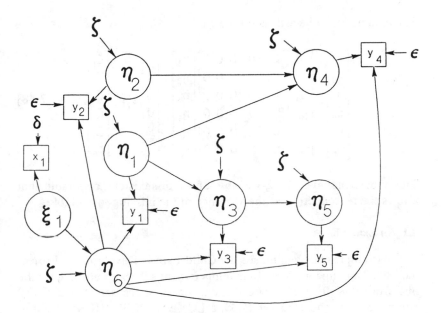

Figure 7.9. Computational Model

$$y = \Lambda_y \eta + \varepsilon \qquad [7.45]$$

The parameters to be considered in this estimation are

$$\begin{bmatrix} y_1 \\ y_2 \\ y_3 \\ y_4 \\ y_5 \end{bmatrix} = \begin{bmatrix} 1 & 0 & 0 & 0 & 0 & \lambda_{16} \\ 0 & 1 & 0 & 0 & 0 & \lambda_{26} \\ 0 & 0 & \lambda_{33} & 0 & 0 & \lambda_{36} \\ 0 & 0 & 0 & 1 & 0 & \lambda_{46} \\ 0 & 0 & 0 & 0 & 0 & \lambda_{56} \end{bmatrix} \begin{bmatrix} \eta_1 \\ \eta_2 \\ \eta_3 \\ \eta_4 \\ \eta_5 \\ \eta_6 \end{bmatrix} + \begin{bmatrix} \varepsilon_1 \\ \varepsilon_2 \\ \varepsilon_3 \\ \varepsilon_4 \\ \varepsilon_5 \end{bmatrix} \qquad [7.46]$$

For group 1, $\lambda_{33} = 1$. For group 2, λ_{33} and $\lambda_{36} = 0$, and the variance of $\varepsilon_3 = 1$. The functions of the λs associated with η_6 are to reproduce the means of the y-variables. The structural model is

$$\eta = B\eta + \Gamma\xi + \zeta \qquad [7.47]$$

The parameters to be estimated are

$$
\begin{bmatrix} \eta_1 \\ \eta_2 \\ \eta_3 \\ \eta_4 \\ \eta_5 \\ \eta_6 \end{bmatrix} = \begin{bmatrix} 0 & 0 & 0 & 0 & 0 & 0 \\ 0 & 0 & 0 & 0 & 0 & 0 \\ \beta_{31} & 0 & 0 & 0 & 0 & 0 \\ \beta_{41} & \beta_{42} & 0 & 0 & 0 & 0 \\ 0 & 0 & \beta_{53} & 0 & 0 & 0 \\ 0 & 0 & 0 & 0 & 0 & 0 \end{bmatrix} \begin{bmatrix} \eta_1 \\ \eta_2 \\ \eta_3 \\ \eta_4 \\ \eta_5 \\ \eta_6 \end{bmatrix} + \begin{bmatrix} 0 \\ 0 \\ 0 \\ 0 \\ 0 \\ 1 \end{bmatrix} [\xi_1] + \begin{bmatrix} \zeta_1 \\ \zeta_2 \\ \zeta_3 \\ \zeta_4 \\ \zeta_5 \\ \zeta_6 \end{bmatrix} \qquad [7.48]
$$

This model includes the ξ-variable and a nonexistent x-variable that allows the reproduction of the variance of the missing y_3-variable.

8.1. An Example

The example once again uses the Child-Family Development Project data set. This time we have four temperament subscales along with the one Braiker-Kelly scale. The missing data pattern selected has 158 complete cases and 15 cases lacking LOVE. LISREL VII was used to estimate the computational model. The results of the model appear in Table 7.2. The degrees of freedom for the chi-square are wrong by the number of pseudovalues included in the input matrices.

Bentler provides a simplified procedure for computing the same model (EQS Manual; Bentler, 1989) that requires neither phantom variables nor adjustments in degrees of freedom. Bentler (1990) also has suggested a way to use all cases that would be thrown out in the approach described here; in particular, those subgroups whose patterns of missing data occur rarely.

9. A More General Solution

Arminger and Sobel (1990) suggest problems with the direct parameter approaches. First, the normality is often not reasonable. Second, because of the requirements of maximum-likelihood estimation, each subgroup input matrix representing a different missing data pattern must be positive definite. One necessary condition for each matrix is, then, that the number of variables cannot exceed the number of cases with that pattern. For samples with many different missing data patterns, this requirement could cause the exclusion of a large number of cases. They

Table 7.2   Results of the Direct Parameter Estimation Model

MOMENT MATRIX (Group 1—Complete Data Group)

	FUSSY	DULL	LOVE	UN-ADAPT	UN-PREDICT	CONST.
FUSSY	562.682					
DULL	105.605	34.316				
LOVE	1429.450	434.926	6185.000			
UNADAPT	164.013	48.430	672.214	85.831		
UNPREDICT	172.050	51.127	711.280	79.950	91.771	
CONST.	18.370	5.580	78.120	8.640	9.150	1.000

MOMENT MATRIX (Group 2—Missing Data Group)

	FUSSY	DULL	LOVE	UN-ADAPT	UN-PREDICT	CONST.
FUSSY	296.217					
DULL	98.177	36.566				
LOVE	0.000	0.000	1.000			
UNADAPT	117.717	38.077	0.000	51.481		
UNPREDICT	157.043	52.214	0.000	62.274	88.472	
CONST.	16.730	5.870	0.000	6.730	8.930	1.000

LISREL ESTIMATES (STANDARD ERRORS) (Group 1—Complete Data Group)

LAMBDA Y

	ETA1	ETA2	ETA3	ETA4	ETA5	ETA6
FUSSY	1.000	0.000	0.000	0.000	0.000	18.235
						(1.097)
DULL	0.000	1.000	0.000	0.000	0.000	5.604
						(0.134)
LOVE	0.000	0.000	1.000	0.000	0.000	78.131
						(0.719)
UNADAPT	0.000	0.000	0.000	1.000	0.000	8.484
						(0.248)
UNPREDICT	0.000	0.000	0.000	0.000	1.000	9.132
						(0.216)

LAMBDA X

	KSI1
CONST	1.000

continued

suggest an alternative covariance-structure model that includes as special cases the more common models (e.g., LISREL). Their model, however, removes the normality restrictions and generates estimates

Table 7.2   Continued

BETA

	ETA1	ETA2	ETA3	ETA4	ETA5	ETA6
ETA1	0.000	0.000	0.000	0.000	0.000	0.000
ETA2	0.000	0.000	0.000	0.000	0.000	0.000
ETA3	−0.026	0.000	0.000	0.000	0.000	0.000
	(0.050)					
ETA4	0.027	−0.011	0.000	0.000	0.000	0.000
	(0.017)	(0.140)				
ETA5	0.000	0.000	−0.043	0.000	0.000	0.000
			(0.025)			
ETA6	0.000	0.000	0.000	0.000	0.000	0.000

GAMMA		PHI	
	KSI1		KSI1
ETA1	0.000	KSI1	1.000
ETA2	0.000		
ETA3	0.000		
ETA4	0.000		
ETA5	0.000		
ETA6	1.000		

PSI

	ETA1	ETA2	ETA3	ETA4	ETA5	ETA6
ETA1	208.325					
	(22.339)					
ETA2	0.000	3.098				
		(0.333)				
ETA3	0.000	0.000	82.138			
			(9.217)			
ETA4	0.000	0.000	0.000	10.487		
				(1.128)		
ETA5	0.000	0.000	0.000	0.000	7.954	
					(0.857)	
ETA6	0.000	0.000	0.000	0.000	0.000	0.000

continued

based on pseudo-maximum likelihood theory (Arminger & Schoenberg, 1989). In addition, the model gives a consistent estimate of the asymptotic covariance matrix when the normality assumption does not hold.

Table 7.2   Continued

LISREL ESTIMATES (STANDARD ERRORS) (Group 2—Missing Data Group)
LAMBDA Y

	ETA1	ETA2	ETA3	ETA4	ETA5	ETA6
FUSSY	1.000	0.000	0.000	0.000	0.000	18.235 (1.097)
DULL	0.000	1.000	0.000	0.000	0.000	5.604 (0.134)
LOVE	0.000	0.000	0.000	0.000	0.000	0.000 (0.000)
UNADAPT	0.000	0.000	0.000	1.000	0.000	8.484 (0.248)
UNPREDICT	0.000	0.000	0.000	0.000	1.000	9.132 (0.216)

LAMBDA X

	KSI1
CONST	1.000

BETA

	ETA1	ETA2	ETA3	ETA4	ETA5	ETA6
ETA1	0.000	0.000	0.000	0.000	0.000	0.000
ETA2	0.000	0.000	0.000	0.000	0.000	0.000
ETA3	−0.026 (0.050)	0.000	0.000	0.000	0.000	0.000
ETA4	0.027 (0.017)	−0.011 (0.140)	0.000	0.000	0.000	0.000
ETA5	0.000	0.000	−0.043 (0.025)	0.000	0.000	0.000
ETA6	0.000	0.000	0.000	0.000	0.000	0.000

GAMMA		*PHI*	
	KSI1		KSI1
ETA1	0.000	KSI1	1.000
ETA2	0.000		
ETA3	0.000		
ETA4	0.000		
ETA5	0.000		
ETA6	1.000		

continued

Table 7.2   Continued

PSI	ETA1	ETA2	ETA3	ETA4	ETA5	ETA6
ETA1	208.325					
	(22.339)					
ETA2	0.000	3.098				
		(0.333)				
ETA3	0.000	0.000	82.138			
			(9.217)			
ETA4	0.000	0.000	0.000	10.487		
				(1.128)		
ETA5	0.000	0.000	0.000	0.000	7.954	
					(0.857)	
ETA6	0.000	0.000	0.000	0.000	0.000	0.000

Chi-square with 28 degrees of freedom is 51.54
(Prob. level = 0.004)
Goodness of fit index is 0.606
Root mean square residual 54.805

10. Discussion

Other models have been estimated using missing latent variables. McArdle and Aber (1990) used latent variables as place savers in a short time series autoregressive model. Abbey and Rovine (1992) analyzed a stress/support model, in which stress was unfortunately not measured. In both cases the latent variable appeared as both predicted and predicting. The pattern of constraints allowed paths to and from that latent variable to be estimated. These models represent strong hypotheses that one must be careful that they are informative and not merely computational exercises.

These data all assume that mechanism causing the missing data can be ignored. As this is not always the case, methods that allow estimation when the mechanism is non-ignorable are necessary. Such methods are considered in Little and Rubin (1987). In addition, there exist a number of models in the literature that deal with specific missing data problems. Laird and Ware (1982) consider random effects models that have implications for, among other things, the estimation of growth curves. Muthén and Jöreskog (1983) discuss models that deal with the problem of selectivity in nonrandom samples.

Up to this point the number of methods almost seems to outstrip the number of simulations done to compare them. Since missing data is such a universal problem and the selection of a technique may be critical to the outcome of a study, we are under some obligation to try to determine what methods work best under which conditions.

References

Abbey, A., & Rovine, M. (1992). *The effects of positive and negative aspects of social relations on well-being.* Unpublished manuscript, The Pennsylvania State University, University Park.

Affifi, A. A., & Elashoff, R. M. (1966). Missing observations in multivariate research: I. Review of the literature. *Journal of the American Statistical Association, 61,* 595-604.

Allison, P. D. (1987). Estimation of linear models with incomplete data. In C. C. Clogg (Ed.), *Sociological methodology 1987* (pp. 71-103). Washington, DC: American Sociological Association.

Arminger, G., & Schoenberg, R. (1989). Pseudo maximum likelihood estimation and a test for misspecification in mean and covariance structure models. *Psychometrika, 54,* 400-426.

Arminger, G., & Sobel, M. E. (1990). Pseudo maximum likelihood estimation of mean and covariance structures with missing data. *Journal of the American Statistical Association, 85,* 195-203.

Beaton, A. E. (1964). The use of special matrix operation in statistical calculus. *Educational Testing Service Research Bulletin,* RB-64-51.

Belsky, J., & Rovine, M. (1990). Patterns of marital change across the transition to parenthood. *Journal of Marriage and the Family, 52* (February), 5-19.

Bentler, P. M. (1989). *EQS structural equations program manual.* Los Angeles: BMDP Statistical Software.

Bentler, P. M. (1990). EQS structural models with missing data. *BMDP Communications, 22,* 9-10.

Bentler, P. M., & Tanaka, J. S. (1983). Problems with the EM for ML factor analysis. *Psychometrika, 48,* 247-253.

Brown, C. H. (1983). Asymptotic comparison of missing data procedures for estimating factor loadings. *Psychometrika, 48,* 269-291.

Dempster, A. P. (1969). *Elements of continuous multivariate analysis.* Reading, MA: Addison-Wesley.

Dempster, A. P., Laird, N. H., & Rubin, D. B. (1977). Maximum likelihood from incomplete data via the EM algorithm. *Journal of the Royal Statistical Society, B39,* 1-38.

Dixon, W. J. (1990). *BMDP statistical software* (rev. printing). Berkeley: University of California Press.

Donner, A., & Rosner, B. (1982). Missing values in multiple linear regression with two independent variables. *Communications in Statistics-Theory and Methods, 11,* 127-140.

Finkbeiner, C. (1979). Estimation for the multiple group factor model when data are missing. *Psychometrika, 44,* 409-420.

Kim, J. O., & Curry, J. (1977). The treatment of missing data in multivariate analysis. *Sociological Methods and Research, 6,* 215-240.

Laird, N. M., & Ware, J. H. (1982). Random-effects models for longitudinal data. *Biometrics, 38,* 963-974.

Lee, S. Y. (1986). Estimation for structural equation models with missing data. *Psychometrika, 45,* 309-324.

Little, R.J.A., & Rubin, D. B. (1987). *Statistical analysis with missing data.* New York: John Wiley.

Marini, M. M., Olsen, A. R., & Rubin, D. B. (1980). Maximum likelihood estimation in panel studies with missing data. In K. F. Shuessler (Ed.), *Sociological methodology 1980* (pp. 314-357). San Francisco: Jossey-Bass.

McArdle, J. J., & Aber, M. (1990). Patterns of change within latent variable structural equation models. In A. von Eye (Ed.), *Statistical methods in longitudinal research* (Vol. 1, chap. 5). Boston: Academic Press.

Muthén, B., & Jöreskog, K. (1983). Selectivity problems In quasi-experimental studies. *Evaluation Review, 7,* 139-174.

Muthén, B., Kaplan, D., & Hollis, M. (1987). On structural equation modeling with data that are not missing completely at random. *Psychometrika, 52,* 431-462.

Rovine, M., & Delaney, M. (1990). Missing data estimation in developmental research. In A. von Eye (Ed.), *Statistical methods in longitudinal research* (Vol. 1, chap. 2). Boston: Academic Press.

Rubin, D. B., & Thayer, D. T. (1982). EM algorithms for factor analysis. *Psychometrika, 47,* 69-76.

Rubin, D. B., & Thayer, D. T. (1983). More on EM for ML factor analysis. *Psychometrika, 48,* 253-257.

Werts, C. E., Rock, D. A., & Grandy, J. (1979). Confirmatory factor analysis applications: Missing data problems and comparisons of path models between populations. *Multivariate Behavioral Research, 14,* 199-213.

Wilks, S. S. (1932). Moments and distributions of estimates of population parameters from fragmentary samples. *Annals of Mathematical Statistics, 3,* 163-195.

Appendix

DIRECT PARAMETER ESTIMATION USING A TWO-GROUP LISREL MODEL

```
ALLISON ESTIMATION (GROUP 1 COMPLETE DATA GROUP)
DA NG = 2 NI = 5 NOBS = 158 MA = AM
LABELS
*
'FUSSY' 'DULL' 'LOVE' 'UNADAP' 'UNPRED'
CM FU
*
```

```
226.66      3.12     -5.65      5.33      3.99
  3.12      3.20     -0.99      0.22      0.07
 -5.65     -0.99     82.79     -2.76     -3.54
  5.33      0.22     -2.76     10.80      0.90
  3.99      0.07     -3.54      0.90      8.10
ME
*
 18.37      5.58     78.12      8.64      9.15
SE
'FUSSY' 'DULL' 'LOVE' 'UNADAP' 'UNPRED' 'CONST'/
MO NY = 5 NE = 6 NX = 1 NK = 1 LY = FU,FI BE = FU,FI PS = SY,FI TE = DI,FI C
         LX = FU,FI PH = FU,FI TD = DI,FI GA = FU,FI
PA LY
*
0 0 0 0 0 1
0 0 0 0 0 1
0 0 0 0 0 1
0 0 0 0 0 1
0 0 0 0 0 1
PA TE
*
0 0 0 0 0
PA BE
*
0 0 0 0 0 0
0 0 0 0 0 0
1 0 0 0 0 0
1 1 0 0 0 0
0 0 1 0 0 0
0 0 0 0 0 0
PA PS
*
1
0 1
0 0 1
0 0 0 1
0 0 0 0 1
0 0 0 0 0 0
PA LX
*
0
PA TD
*
```

```
0
PA PH
*
0
PA GA
*
0
0
0
0
0
0
MA LY
*
1 0 0 0 0 18.37
0 1 0 0 0 5.58
0 0 1 0 0 78.12
0 0 0 1 0 8.64
0 0 0 0 1 9.15
MA TE
*
0 0 0 0 0
MA BE
*
0 0 0 0 0 0
0 0 0 0 0 0
.1 0 0 0 0 0
.1 .1 0 0 0 0
0 0 .1 0 0 0
0 0 0 0 0 0
MA PS
*
17
0 1
0 0 20
0 0 0 6
0 0 0 0 5
0 0 0 0 0 0
MA LX
*
1
MA TD
*
```

```
0
MA PH
*
1
MA GA
*
0
0
0
0
0
1
OU PT SE TV NS MI SS RS TM = 40
TITLE ALLISON ESTIMATION (GROUP 2 MISSING DATA GROUP)
DA NOBS = 15
LABELS
*
'FUSSY' 'DULL' 'LOVE' 'UNADAP' 'UNPRED'
CM FU
*
   17.49     -0.03      0        5.49      8.19
   -0.03      2.26      0       -1.53     -0.22
    0         0         1        0         0
    5.49     -1.53      0        6.63      2.33
    8.19     -0.22      0        2.33      9.35
ME
*
   16.73      5.87      0        6.73      8.93
SE
'FUSSY' 'DULL' 'LOVE' 'UNADAP' 'UNPRED' 'CONST'/
MO LY = FU,FI TE = DI,FI BE = IN PS = IN LX = IN C
        PH = IN TD = IN GA = IN
PA LY
*
0 0 0 0 0 1
0 0 0 0 0 1
0 0 0 0 0 0
0 0 0 0 0 1
0 0 0 0 0 1
PA TE
*
0 0 0 0 0
MA LY
```

```
*
1 0 0 0 0 16.73
0 1 0 0 0 5.87
0 0 0 0 0 0
0 0 0 1 0 6.73
0 0 0 0 1 8.93
MA TE
*
0 0 1 0 0
EQ LY 1 1 6 LY 2 1 6
EQ LY 1 2 6 LY 2 2 6
EQ LY 1 4 6 LY 2 4 6
EQ LY 1 5 6 LY 2 5 6
OU
END USER
```

SAS IML PROGRAM FOR COMPUTING THE COMPLETE DATA MATRIX BASED ON FACTORING THE LIKELIHOOD

```
OPTIONS NOCENTER LINESIZE = 72 NODATE NONUMBER;
PROC IML;
START;
CONSTANT = -1;
***                                          ;
*** WAVE 1 MEANS AND VARIANCE/COVARIANCE MATRIX;
***                                          ;
*** COVARIANCE MATRIX (WAVE 1 COMPLETE N = 172);
COV1 =  {84.16    -27.583   -36.311,
          27.583    39.7458   19.3379,
         -36.311    19.3379   29.7292};
MEANS1={78.35465
        20.55233
        10.41279);
*** CORRELATION MATRIX;
*COV1 =  {1.00000  -0.47692  -0.72593,
         -0.47692   1.00000   0.56257,
         -0.72593   0.56257   1.00000};
*MEANS1 = {0.0 0.0 0.0};
***                                          ;
*** CONCATENATE WAVE 1 MATRIX ;
```

```
***                                    ;
A1 = CONSTANT||MEANS1;
A2 = MEANS1'||COV1;
A = A1//A2;
PRINT A;
ACAT = A;
***                                    ;
*** SWEEP WAVE 1 MATRIX;
***                                    ;
ASWEPT =      {0 0 0 0,
               0 0 0 0,
               0 0 0 0,
               0 0 0 0};
ASWEEPST = 2;
ASWEEPEN = 4;
ROWS = 4;
COLUMNS = 4;
DO K = ASWEEPST TO ASWEEPEN;
  ASWEPT(|K,K|) = -1/ACAT(|K,K|);
DO I = 1 TO ROWS;
  IF I = K THEN GOTO CONTIN2;
  ASWEPT(|I,K|) = ACAT(|I,K|)/ACAT(|K,K|);
  CONTIN2: COMMENT;
DO J = 1 TO COLUMNS;
  IF J = K THEN GOTO CONTIN3;
  ASWEPT(|K,J|) = ACAT(|K,J|)/ACAT(|K,K|);
  CONTIN3: COMMENT;
  IF I = K THEN GOTO CONTIN1;
  IF J = K THEN GOTO CONTIN1;
  ASWEPT(|I,J|) = ACAT(|I,J|)-ACAT(|I,K|)#ACAT(|K,J|)/ACAT(|K,K|);
  CONTIN1: COMMENT;
END;
END;
PRINT ASWEPT K "RUN";
ACAT = ASWEPT;
END;
PRINT ASWEPT;
ACAT = ASWEPT;
PRINT ACAT;
***                                              ;
*** WAVE 2 MEANS AND VARIANCE/COVARIANCE MATRIX;
***                                              ;
*** COVARIANCE MATRIX (1 AND 2 N = 160);
```

```
COV2 =    {80.4881  -26.1151  -33.9469   65.7066  -20.2736  -21.2321,
          -26.1151   39.7407   17.9188  -20.5864   24.6879   13.6781,
          -33.9469   17.9188   28.0912  -28.4765   13.0672   19.1101,
           65.7066  -20.5864  -28.4765  104.421   -24.77    -41.7545,
          -20.2736   24.6879   13.0672  -24.77     36.7193   20.5071,
          -21.2321   13.6781   19.1101  -41.7545   20.5071   38.981};
MEANS2={78.55000
        20.41250
        10.25625
        76.01875
        21.81250
        11.98750};
*** CORRELATION MATRIX (N = 160);
*COV2 =    {1.00000  -0.46175  -0.71392   0.71672  -0.37292  -0.37905
           -0.46175   1.00000   0.53630  -0.31957   0.64628   0.34752
           -0.71392   0.53630   1.00000  -0.52579   0.40687   0.57750
            0.71672  -0.31957  -0.52579   1.00000  -0.40002  -0.65446
           -0.37292   0.64628   0.40687  -0.40002   1.00000   0.54204
           -0.37905   0.34752   0.57750  -0.65446   0.54204   1.00000
*MEANS2=(0.0 0.0 0.0 0.0 0.0 0.0};
***                                     ;
*** CCONCATENATE WAVE 2 MATRIX;
***                                     ;
B1 = CONSTANT||MEANS2;
B2 = MEANS2'||COV2;
B = B1//B2;
PRINT B;
BCAT = B
***                         ;
*** SWEEP WAVE 2 MATRIX;
***                         ;
BSWEPT =          {0 0 0 0 0 0 0,
                   0 0 0 0 0 0 0,
                   0 0 0 0 0 0 0,
                   0 0 0 0 0 0 0,
                   0 0 0 0 0 0 0,
                   0 0 0 0 0 0 0,
                   0 0 0 0 0 0 0};
BSWEEPST = 2;
BSWEEPEN = 7;
ROWS = 7;
COLUMNS = 7;
DO K = BSWEEPST TO BSWEEPEN;
```

```
  BSWEPT(IK,KI) = –1/BCAT(IK,KI);
DO I = 1 TO ROWS;
  IF I = K THEN GOTO CONTIN4;
  BSWEPT(II,KI) = BCAT(II,KI)/BCAT(IK,KI);
  CONTIN4: COMMENT;
DO J = 1 TO COLUMNS;
  IF J = K THEN GOTO CONTIN5;
  BSWEPT(IK,JI) = BCAT(IK,JI)/BCAT(IK,KI);
  CONTIN5: COMMENT;
  IF I = K THEN GOTO CONTIN6;
  IF J = K THEN GOTO CONTIN6;
  BSWEPT(II,JI) = BCAT(II,JI)–BCAT(II,KI)#BCAT(IK,JI)/BCAT(IK,KI);
  CONTIN6: COMMENT;
END;
END;
BCAT = BSWEPT;
END;
PRINT BSWEPT "RUN";
BCAT = BSWEPT;
PRINT BCAT;
BCAT21 = BSWEPT(I{5 6 7},{1 2 3 4}I);
BCAT12 = BCAT21`;
BCAT22 = BSWEPT(I{5 6 7},{5 6 7}I);
BCAT1 = ASWEPTIIBCAT12;
BCAT2 = BCAT21IIBCAT22;
BCAT = BCAT1//BCAT2;
PRINT BCAT21;
PRINT BCAT12;
PRINT BCAT22;
PRINT BCAT;
***                                    ;
*** WAVE 3 MEANS AND VARIANCE/COVARIANCE MATRIX;
***                                    ;
*** COVARIANCE MATRIX (1,2, AND 3) N = 126;
COV3 =   {66.0363 –23.2403 –28.379    54.2234 –14.6447 –19.427    41.1578
         –11.1072 –16.5457,
         –23.2403   36.6586   17.2152 –20.4595   23.1342   14.6712 –23.9159
          24.4225   15.9509,
         –28.379    17.2152   26.3109 –25.1219   11.3779   19.8069 –22.6145
          10.2145   17.347,
          54.2234 –20.4595 –25.1219   97.5333 –21.7066 –44.0179   54.1523
         –16.9737 –29.8727,
         –14.6447   23.1342   11.3779 –21.7066   36.4559   21.0499 –19.0377
```

```
            23.811    17.478,
           -19.427    14.6712   19.8069  -44.0179   21.0499   41.2869  -26.7505
            14.2545   27.051,
            41.1578  -23.9159  -22.6145   54.1523  -19.0377  -26.7505  163.393
           -42.2944  -75.0152,
           -11.1072   24.4225   10.2145  -16.9737   23.811    14.2545  -42.2944
            44.2517   30.1165,
           -16.5457   15.9509   17.347   -29.8727   17.478    27.051   -75.0152
            30.1165   56.411};
MEANS3={78.41270
        20.76984
        10.23810
        75.67460
        21.99206
        12.23810
        74.29365
        22.37302
        12.75397};
*** CORRELATION COEFFICIENTS N = 126;
*COV3 =  {1.00000  -0.47235  -0.68083   0.67565  -0.29847  -0.37206   0.39623
         -0.20547  -0.27109
         -0.47235   1.00000   0.55432  -0.34216   0.63282   0.37711  -0.30902
          0.60637   0.35076
         -0.68083   0.55432   1.00000  -0.49592   0.36738   0.60096  -0.34491
          0.29935   0.45027
          0.67565  -0.34216  -0.49592   1.00000  -0.36403  -0.69366   0.42897
         -0.25836  -0.40273
         -0.29847   0.63282   0.36738  -0.36403   1.00000   0.54258  -0.24667
          0.59283   0.38541,
         -0.37206   0.37711   0.60096  -0.69366   0.54258   1.00000  -0.32569
          0.33349   0.56053,
          0.39623  -0.30902  -0.34491   0.42897  -0.24667  -0.32569   1.00000
         -0.49739  -0.78136,
         -0.20547   0.60637   0.29935  -0.25836   0.59283   0.33349  -0.49739
          1.00000   0.60278,
         -0.27109   0.35076   0.45027  -0.40273   0.38541   0.56053  -0.78136
          0.60278   1.00000};
*MEANS3 = {0.0 0.0 0.0 0.0 0.0 0.0 0.0 0.0 0.0};
***                                       ;
*** CONCATENATE WAVE 3 MATRIX;
***                                       ;
C1 = CONSTANT||MEANS3;
C2 = MEANS3'||COV3;
```

```
C = C1//C2;
CCAT = C;
PRINT C;
***                              ;
*** SWEEP WAVE 3 MATRIX;
***                              ;
CSWEPT =    {0 0 0 0 0 0 0 0 0 0,
             0 0 0 0 0 0 0 0 0 0,
             0 0 0 0 0 0 0 0 0 0,
             0 0 0 0 0 0 0 0 0 0,
             0 0 0 0 0 0 0 0 0 0,
             0 0 0 0 0 0 0 0 0 0,
             0 0 0 0 0 0 0 0 0 0,
             0 0 0 0 0 0 0 0 0 0,
             0 0 0 0 0 0 0 0 0 0,
             0 0 0 0 0 0 0 0 0 0}
CSWEEPST = 2;
CSWEEPEN = 7;
ROWS = 10;
COLUMNS = 10;
DO K = CSWEEPST TO CSWEEPEN;
  CSWEPT(IK,KI) = -1/CCAT(IK,KI);
DO I = 1 TO ROWS;
  IF I = K THEN GOTO CONTIN7;
  CSWEPT(II,KI) = CCAT(II,KI)/CCAT(IK,KI);
  CONTIN7: COMMENT;
DO J = 1 TO COLUMNS;
  IF J = K THEN GOTO CONTIN8;
  CSWEPT(IK,JI) = CCAT(IK,JI)/CCAT(IK,KI);
  CONTIN8: COMMENT;
  IF I = K THEN GOTO CONTIN9;
  IF J = K THEN GOTO CONTIN9;
  CSWEPT(II,JI) = CCAT(II,JI)-CCAT(II,KI)#CCAT(IK,JI)/CCAT(IK,KI);
  CONTIN9: COMMENT;
END;
END;
CCAT = CSWEPT;
END;
PRINT CSWEPT;
CCAT = CSWEPT;
CCAT21 = CSWEPT(I{8 9 10},{1 2 3 4 5 6 7}I);
CCAT12 = CCAT21';
CCAT22 = CSWEPT(I{8 9 10},{8 9 10}I);
```

```
CCAT11 = BSWEPT;
PRINT CCAT11;
PRINT CCAT12;
PRINT CCAT21;
PRINT CCAT22;
CCAT1 = CCAT11||CCAT12;
CCAT2 = CCAT21||CCAT22;
CCAT = CCAT1//CCAT2;
PRINT CCAT;
***                              ;
*** REVERSE SWEEP FINAL MATRIX;
***                              ;
REVSWP =    {0 0 0 0 0 0 0 0 0 0,
             0 0 0 0 0 0 0 0 0 0,
             0 0 0 0 0 0 0 0 0 0,
             0 0 0 0 0 0 0 0 0 0,
             0 0 0 0 0 0 0 0 0 0,
             0 0 0 0 0 0 0 0 0 0,
             0 0 0 0 0 0 0 0 0 0,
             0 0 0 0 0 0 0 0 0 0,
             0 0 0 0 0 0 0 0 0 0,
             0 0 0 0 0 0 0 0 0 0};
REVSWPST = 2;
REVSWPEN = 7;
ROWS = 10;
COLUMNS = 10;
DO K = REVSWPST TO REVSWPEN;
REVSWP(|K,K|) = 1/CCAT(|K,K|);
REVSWP(|K,K|) = -REVSWP(|K,K|);
DO I = 1 TO ROWS;
IF I = K THEN GOTO CONTIN10;
REVSWP(|I,K|) = -CCAT(|I,K|)/CCAT(|K,K|);
CONTIN10: COMMENT;
DO J = 1 TO COLUMNS;
IF J = K THEN GOTO CONTIN11;
REVSWP(|K,J|) = -CCAT(|K,J|)/CCAT(|K,K|);
CONTIN11: COMMENT;
IF I = K THEN GOTO CONTIN12;
IF J = K THEN GOTO CONTIN12;
REVSWP(|I,J|) = CCAT(|I,J|)-CCAT(|I,K|)#CCAT(|K,J|)/CCAT(|K,K|);
CONTIN12: COMMENT;
END;
END;
```

```
CCAT = REVSWP;
END;
PRINT REVSWP;
***                                          ;
*** PRINT MAXIMUM-LIKELIHOOD ESTIMATES;
***                                          ;
MAXEST = REVSWP;
PRINT MAXEST;
FINISH;
RUN;
```

8

On the Arbitrary Nature
of Latent Variables

PETER C. M. MOLENAAR
ALEXANDER VON EYE

Introduction

This chapter elaborates on the relationship between a variant of latent class models and common factor models. More specifically, Bartholomew (1987) showed that the covariance structure associated with a latent profile model involving metrical manifest variables and categorical latent variables can be represented by a common factor model involving metrical manifest and metrical latent variables. Thus, at the level of latent variables an intriguing relationship is established between models that underlie a typological and a dimensional approach to the study of individual differences.

In this chapter we elaborate Bartholomew's result in a number of ways. First, the covariance structure associated with a latent profile model will be presented in terms of a nonlinearly constrained common factor model. Using this model, the parameters characterizing the categorical latent variables can be recovered. With the exception of a special case, these parameters cannot be obtained using Bartholomew's (1987) original approach.

AUTHORS' NOTE: Alexander von Eye's work on this chapter was supported in part by NIA grant #5T32 AG00110-07.

Second, both the mean and the covariance structure associated with a latent profile model will be represented by another nonlinearly constrained common factor model. Using this model, almost all the parameters of the latent profile model can be recovered. Third, results of a simulation experiment will be reported that indicate that the reverse relationship also obtains: The covariance structure associated with an arbitrary common factor model can be represented by a latent profile model. Hence, at the level of second-order moments the two latent variable models are completely equivalent.

Fourth, we show that the factor rotation problem associated with common factor models carries over to the realm of latent profile models. Specifically, at the level of second-order moments latent profile models are only identified up to orthogonal rotation. A special algorithm for carrying out rotation in latent profile models is presented.

To establish a frame reference, we present an outline of Bartholomew's (1987) original work. We cover latent profile analysis, common factor models, and their relationships.

1. Specifications of Basic Models and Their Relationships

Following Bartholomew (1987), variables are classified as *metrical* or *categorical*. Metrical variables are real-valued. Thus, they can be discrete or continuous. Categorical variables assign each individual to one and only one category. Both manifest and latent—that is, unobserved—variables can be either metrical or categorical. Crossing these dichotomies yields the fourfold classification given in Table 8.1 (from Bartholomew, 1987, Table 1).

This chapter is mainly concerned with a comparison of factor analysis or, more specifically, the *normal linear factor model,* and latent profile analysis. Table 8.1 shows that these two methods share in common that they involve metrical manifest variables. They differ in their concepts of latent variables. The normal linear factor model uses metrical latent variables. In contrast, the latent profile analysis uses categorical latent variables.

In either case, methods are based on the following statements on the mutual dependency of variables x and y. The p-variate density function $f(x)$ of manifest variables x and the q-variate density function $h(y)$ of latent variables y are related by

Table 8.1 Classification of Latent Variable Methods

| | Manifest Variables | |
Latent Variables	Metrical	Categorical
Metrical	Factor analysis	Latent trait analysis
Categorical	Latent profile analysis	Latent class analysis of mixtures

$$f(x) = \int_{R_y} h(y)g(x \mid y)dy \qquad [8.1]$$

where R_y is the range space of the latent variable y, and g is the conditional density of x given y. Inversely, the conditional density of y, given x, is

$$h(y \mid x) = \frac{h(y)g(x \mid y)}{f(x)} \qquad [8.2]$$

Under the *Axiom of Local Independence* $f(x)$ admits the following representation:

$$f(x) = \int_{R_y} h(y) \prod_{i=1}^{p} g(x_i \mid y)dy \qquad [8.3]$$

for some set $\{g_i\}$ of univariate conditional densities. The Axiom of Local Independence implies that the q-variate latent variable y is sufficient to explain the dependencies among the entries of x. If we have y, the unexplained part of x does not contain any dependencies among its entries. In practice one searches for models in which q is much smaller than p. (For a discussion of this axiom in the context of latent class models for measuring see Clogg, 1988.)

1.1. Latent Profile Models

Suppose researchers assume that k latent classes explain the dependencies between their observed metrical variables. Then, the expected density function of x can be described by a *latent profile model* of the following form

$$f(x) = \sum_{j=0}^{k-1} \eta_j \prod_{i=1}^{p} g_i(x_i \,|\, j) \,. \qquad [8.4]$$

where $g_i(x_i \,|\, j)$ describes the univariate conditional distribution of x_i if individuals belong to class j, and $h(y = j) = \eta_j$ is the latent probability of class j, for $j = 0, 1, 2, \ldots, k - 1$.

For the following considerations we take

$$g_i(x_i \,|\, j) = g[x_i \,|\, \mu_i(j), \sigma_i^2(j)] \qquad [8.5]$$

where $g[x_i \,|\, \mu_i(j), \sigma_i^2(j)]$ is normal with mean $\mu_i(j)$ and variance $\sigma_i^2(j)$. Thus, the expected marginal distribution of each x_i is a mixture of k normal densities with arbitrary means and variances.

1.2. The Normal Linear Factor Model

Suppose that the conditional distribution of the manifest p-variate variable x given the latent q-variate variable y depends on y only through its mean. Furthermore, suppose that the conditional distribution concerned is normal. Then we can define a model based on normal distributions as follows:

$$x \,|\, y \approx N_p(\mu + \Lambda y, \Psi) \qquad [8.6]$$

where Λ is a $p \times q$ matrix of coefficients (loadings) and Ψ is a diagonal matrix of variances that does not depend on y. Finally, suppose that

$$y = N_q(0, I) \,. \qquad [8.7]$$

It then follows that x is distributed as

$$x \approx N_p(\mu, \Lambda\Lambda' + \Psi) \qquad [8.8]$$

and obeys the *Normal Linear Factor model*

$$x = \mu + \Lambda y + e \,, \qquad [8.9]$$

where e has a p-variate normal distribution with zero mean and covariance matrix Ψ.

1.3. The Original Relationship Between
the Latent Profile and Factor Models

We now outline the correspondence between a latent profile model with k latent classes, or LPM(k), and a linear factor model with $k-1$ factors, or FM($k-1$), as presented by Bartholomew (1987, pp. 34-38). To establish correspondence, the covariance structure associated with an LPM(k) is rewritten as the covariance structure of an FM(k). Consideration of these moment structures is compatible with the method of moments originally proposed by Lazarsfeld and Henry (1968) for parameter estimation in latent profile models. Typically, current estimation programs use the method of maximum likelihood.

Bartholomew (1987) shows that the dispersion matrix for an LPM(k) can be represented as

$$D(x) = LL' + \Psi \qquad [8.10]$$

where Ψ is a diagonal matrix whose ith diagonal element is

$$\Psi_{i,i} = \sum_{j=0}^{k-1} \eta_j \sigma_i^2(j) \qquad [8.11]$$

and the element l_{ij} of L is

$$l_{ij} = \sqrt{\eta_j} [\mu_i(j) - \overline{\mu}_i] \qquad [8.12]$$

with

$$\overline{\mu}_i = \sum_{j=0}^{k-1} \eta_j \mu_i(j) \qquad [8.13]$$

Thus, the dispersion matrix $D(x)$ of an LPM(k) given by (8.10) has exactly the same structure as the dispersion matrix for an FM(k).

However, a problem arises because the matrix of loadings given by (8.10), L, is not of full column rank. This is because (8.13) implies that

$$\sum_{j=0}^{k-1} \sqrt{\eta_j}\, l_{ij} = 0 \qquad [8.14]$$

for $i = 1, 2, \ldots, p$. This problem can be resolved by using a $p \times (k - 1)$ matrix Λ with linearly independent columns for which

$$LL' = \Lambda\Lambda' \qquad [8.15]$$

holds. Substitution of (8.15) in (8.10) yields

$$D(x) = \Lambda\Lambda' + \Psi. \qquad [8.16]$$

As a result, the covariance structure associated with an LPM(k) is the same as the covariance structure of an FM($k - 1$). This is the basic correspondence originally established by Bartholomew (1987).

1.4. Evaluation and Preview

Given that the covariance structure of an LPM(k) can be mapped onto the covariance structure of an FM($k - 1$), it is important to determine whether the inverse mapping also exists. That is, can the covariance structure of an arbitrary FM($k - 1$) always be mapped onto the covariance structure of an LPM(k)? An affirmative answer to this question would imply the complete formal equivalence of both models at the level of covariance structures. However, to be able to provide a nontrivial answer, we first have to remove an inherent weakness in Bartholomew's (1987) approach.

If (8.16) is fitted to the dispersion matrix generated by an LPM(k), it is impossible to recover distinct parameters in the LPM(k). Specifically, it is impossible to recover the probability density h over the latent classes and the means and variances of the conditional densities (8.5). In our first attempt to correct this weakness the covariance structure of an LPM(k) is mapped onto that of an FM(k) with p nonlinear constraints on the factor loadings. Each constraint fixes the mean of a row of factor loadings with respect to h at zero. This way, the probability density h over the latent classes can be recovered, but not the means and variances of the conditional densities (8.5).

In our next attempt the mean and covariance structure of an LPM(k) is mapped onto the mean and covariance structure of an FM(k) with p nonlinear constraints on the loadings. Each of these constraints now fixes the mean of the ith row of loadings with respect to h at $E[x_i]$. This enables one to recover both h and the means of the conditional densities (8.5) but not their variances.

2. Constraint Factor Models and Latent Profile Models

In the next sections we introduce our constrained factor models. Because of their increased resolution at the parameter level, they provide a stronger approach to studying the formal equivalence of LPMs and FMs at the level of first- and second-order moments. This will enable one to detect a new and intriguing qualification for the identifiability of LPMs.

2.1. A Constrained FM(k) for the Covariance Structure of an LPM(k)

In this section we specify a nonlinearly constrained k-factor model, FMC(k), for the covariance structure associated with an LPM(k). For the dispersion matrix of the latent profile model we state

$$D(x) = \Lambda^* \Phi \Lambda^{*\prime} + \Psi \qquad [8.17]$$

where

$$\Phi = \text{diag}[\eta_0, \ldots, \eta_{k-1}] . \qquad [8.18]$$

and where the ijth element of Λ^* is given by

$$\lambda_{ij}^* = [\mu_i(j) - \overline{\mu}_i] . \qquad [8.19]$$

Parameters $\overline{\mu}_i$ are defined by (8.13). To ensure that (8.17) is identifiable, the ith row of Λ^* is constrained as follows:

$$\sum_{j=0}^{k-1} \eta_j \lambda_{ij}^* = 0 \quad \text{for } i = 1, \ldots, p . \qquad [8.20]$$

The density h over the k latent classes is recovered by (8.18): The probabilities associated with these classes constitute the diagonal elements of Φ. However, (8.19) shows that the means $\mu_i(j)$ of the conditional densities (8.5) cannot be recovered from (8.17). In addition, the diagonal matrix Ψ, defined by (8.11), does not enable the recovery of the variances associated with (8.5).

2.2. An FM(k) for the Raw
Second-Order Structure of an LPM(k)

In this section we specify a nonlinearly constrained k-factor model, FMC*(k), for the raw second-order moment structure associated with an LPM(k). The raw second-order moment matrix $M(x)$ of a p-variate variable x is defined as

$$M(x) = \begin{pmatrix} E(x_1^2) & \cdots & & \cdot \\ E(x_1, x_2) & \cdots & & \cdot \\ \cdot & \cdots & & \cdot \\ \cdot & \cdots & & \cdot \\ \cdot & \cdots & & \cdot \\ E(x_1, x_p) & \cdots & & E(x_p^2) \end{pmatrix} \qquad [8.21]$$

For the raw second-order moment matrix associated with an LPM(k) we consider

$$M(x) = \Lambda^0 \Phi \Lambda^{0\prime} + \Psi, \qquad [8.22]$$

where Φ is defined by (8.18), Ψ is defined by (8.11), and

$$\Lambda^0 = \left\{ \lambda_{ij}^0 = \mu_i(j) \right\}. \qquad [8.23]$$

To ensure identifiability of (8.22), the ith row of Λ^0 is constrained as follows:

$$\sum_{j=0}^{k-1} \eta_j \mu_i(j) = \sum_{j=0}^{k-1} \eta_j \lambda_{ij}^0 = E[x_i], \qquad [8.24]$$

for $i = 1, \ldots, p$.

Again, the density over the k latent classes is obtained from the diagonal elements of Φ. Moreover, the means of the conditional densities (8.5) are obtained as the elements of Λ^0 as given by (8.23). Only the variances of (8.5) can still not be recovered from Ψ.

2.3. Numerical Examples: Simulation Studies

Simulations were performed to illustrate numerically the correspondence between the latent profile and factor models. Simulations were run for two cases. For the first case, the *true (population) covariance matrix* associated with an LPM(k) was generated, and an FM($k-1$) as well as an FMC(k) were fitted to this matrix. For the second case, the *true (population) raw (or central) second-order moment matrix* (moment matrix, for short) associated with an LPM(k) was generated, and an FMC*(k) was fitted to this matrix.

2.3.1. Simulations With Covariance Matrices

For the simulations of the true covariance matrices associated with an LPM(k), we set for the variances

$$\text{var}(x_i) = \sum_{j=0}^{k-1} \eta_j \sigma_i^2(j) + \sum_{j=0}^{k-1} \eta_j [\mu_i(j) - \bar{\mu}_i]^2 , \qquad [8.25]$$

for $i = 1, 2, \ldots, p$. For the covariances we set

$$\text{cov}(x_i, x_m) = \sum_{j=0}^{k-1} \eta_j [\mu_i(j) - \bar{\mu}_i][\mu_m(j) - \bar{\mu}_m] . \qquad [8.26]$$

for $i, m = 1, 2, \ldots, p$ and $i \neq m$.

According to (8.25) and (8.26) we generated covariance matrices differing in size and parameter values. For example, we generated 5×5 and 9×9 covariance matrices associated with LPMs having $k = 2$ or $k = 3$ latent variables and fitted to these matrices FMs having $k = 1$ or $k = 2$ or constrained factor models having $k = 2$ or $k = 3$ factors. In a fashion analogous to this procedure, true covariance matrices were generated from orthogonal k-factor models and latent profile models, each specified as an FMC($k + 1$), were fitted to these matrices.

Results of these simulations indicate that

1. both an FM($k - 1$) and an FMC(k) yield exact fits to a true covariance matrix generated from an LPM(k);
2. an LPM($k + 1$), specified as an FMC($k + 1$), yields an exact fit to a covariance matrix generated from an FM(k).

Thus, we conclude that, *at the level of central moments, there is a complete formal correspondence between latent profile models and factor models.* However, we obtained another, surprising result.

Notice that if an unrestricted FM($k - 1$) is fitted to a covariance matrix, and that regardless of whether or not this covariance matrix was generated from an LPM(k), then the communal part of the unrestricted FM($k - 1$) is identified up to orthogonal rotation. Now, an FMC(k) constitutes a more detailed mapping of the parametric structure of an LPM(k) and, consequently, one might expect that FMCs are uniquely identified. However, this expectation does not appear to be correct. The same rotation problem that affects an unrestricted FM($k - 1$) also affects an FMC(k). Thus, for a given covariance matrix, regardless how it is generated, there exists an infinite set of latent profile models, each specified as a rotated FMC.

2.3.2. Simulations With Moment Matrices

The true moment matrix (8.24) associated with an LPM(k) was generated as follows:

$$E(x_i^2) = \sum_{j=0}^{k-1} \eta_j [\sigma_i^2(j) + \mu_i^2(j)], \qquad [8.27]$$

and

$$E(x_i, x_m) = \sum_{j=0}^{k-1} \eta_j \mu_i(j)\mu_m(j), \qquad [8.28]$$

for $i, m = 1, 2, \ldots, p$, and $i \neq m$. To each true moment matrix thus generated an FMC$^*(k)$ was fitted.

Results of these simulations suggest that

1. an FMC$^*(k)$ yields an exact fit to the true moment matrix of an LPM(k);
2. an FMC$^*(k)$ is affected by the same problem of rotational indeterminacy as FMs and FMCs.

2.4. Evaluation

These results show that the formal equivalence still obtains if the factor models preserve increasingly more of the parametric details of latent profile models. Yet, all factor models concerned are only identified up to orthogonal rotation. Even the FMC*, which preserves most of the parametric structure of an LPM, suffers from rotational indeterminacy. Consequently, to complete this study about the correspondence between the two types of latent variable models, we have to specify orthogonal rotation in LPMs. More specifically, in the next section we present an algorithm for orthogonal rotation in a nonlinearly constrained FMC*.

3. Rotation in the FMC* Representation of LPMs

An effective algorithm for rotation in an FCM* can be described as follows. First, rotation is defined for the standard orthonormal k-factor model defined by (8.9). Because of the orthonormality of the k factors, rotation is a very simple operation. After rotation, the covariance matrix of the factors is still the identity matrix. In contrast, the constrained factor model, FMC(k), for the covariance matrix of an LPM(k) has k orthogonal but not orthonormal factors. In different words, Φ in (8.17) is not equal to the identity matrix. Hence, to keep the simplicity of rotation in orthonormal factor models, the constrained FMC(k) given by (8.17) is reformulated as an equivalent orthonormal FMC(k) by absorbing the square roots of the diagonal elements of Φ in Λ^*. Thus, second, rotation is defined for the orthonormal FMC(k).

Third, we consider the parameters in an LPM(k) that can be recovered from an FMC* (the constrained factor model for the raw moment structure associated with the latent profile model), and notice that these parameters completely determine the communal part of all factor models under consideration. In particular, the probabilities associated with the latent classes and the means of the conditional densities (8.5) completely determine the communal part of the orthonormal FMC(k) obtained in the second step of our strategy. Consequently, these parameters of the LPM(k) recovered by the FMC* enable one to devise a rotation algorithm for the nonlinearly constrained orthonormal FMC(k), and, thus, for the FMC*.

3.1. A Rotation Algorithm for FMC*

Orthogonal rotation in the orthonormal k-factor model (8.9) is defined by post-multiplication of Λ by T, where T is a $k \times k$ matrix such that $TT' = I$. Notice that the rotated factor model still is orthonormal. Next, rewrite the orthogonal FMC(k) given by (8.17) as an orthonormal model in which Φ is the identity matrix. Notice that the general expression is repeated here with a slight change in notation:

$$l_{ij} = \sqrt{\eta_j}\,\mu_i(j) - \sqrt{\eta_j}\,\mu_i\,. \qquad [8.29]$$

Again, orthogonal rotation in the orthonormal FMC(k) is defined by post-multiplication of the matrix L, which is composed of the elements given in (8.29), by T. The loadings in the rotated model can be schematically represented as follows:

$$l_{ij}^* = \sqrt{\eta_j^*}\,\mu_i^*(j) - \sqrt{\eta_j^*}\,\mu_i\,, \qquad [8.30]$$

where the asterisks denote rotated variables.

Now, consider the parameters of an LPM(k) that are recovered by an FCM*(k). These parameters include the probabilities η_j of the latent classes and the conditional means $\mu_i(j)$. Given these recovered parameters, the marginal means μ_i are obtained from (8.13). Notice that, in (8.30), the μ_i are unaffected by rotation. This is because μ_i equals the expected value of the manifest variable x_i, which should not change under rotation. Given this invariance of μ_i under factor rotation, and because rotation is a linear operation, it follows that the second component of the right-hand side of (8.29) is rotated in a simple way. Let h denote the k-vector composed of the square root of the probabilities η_j, for $j = 0, \ldots, k - 1$. Then, h' is rotated by postmultiplication by T. Given the square root of each rotated η_j, it is a straightforward exercise to show that the rotated conditional means $\mu_j^*(j)$ are obtained by division by the square root of the rotated η_j.

As the proper implementation of the above rotation operation in an FMC* is a delicate matter, we will only present a schematic outline of the algorithm. The source code for this algorithm appears in the Appendix.

3.2. An Application

To illustrate the rotation algorithm given in the Appendix, an FCM*(3) was fitted to the true 9×9 raw moment structure associated with an LPM(3). The true probabilities for the latent classes in the LPM(3) were 0.5, 0.3, and 0.2. The analogous probabilities recovered from the FMC*(3) were considerably different from the true probabilities. In addition, the

Table 8.2   Actual and Estimated Conditional Means, Generated From
a Latent Class Model and Fitted With a Constrained
Factor Model

			Actual Values					
Conditional Means								
5	6	7	8	9	8	7	6	5
–4	–3	–2	–1	0	1	2	3	4
3	5	3	5	3	5	3	5	3
Latent Probabilities								
	0.5			0.3			0.2	
			Estimated Values					
Conditional Means								
–5.73	–5.72	–5.74	–5.74	–5.76	–4.47	–3.20	–1.19	–0.65
2.71	2.75	2.62	2.67	2.54	2.05	1.38	0.89	0.23
–4.97	–10.10	5.29	0.16	15.54	3.54	12.05	0.05	8.75
Latent Probabilities								
	0.3156			0.6783			0.0060	

recovered conditional means differed from the true ones. Table 8.2 presents additional details. Yet, the FMC*(3) yielded an exact fit to the raw moment structure.

To explore the pattern of equivalent solutions obtained by orthogonal rotation of the fitted FMC*(3), a total of $25 \times 25 \times 25 = 15,625$ rotations was performed by applying the above algorithm. On each dimension of the FMC*(3) the rotation angle iterated in 25 steps from 0 to 180 degrees. A subset of the rotated densities over the latent classes is depicted in Figure 8.1 (Wilkinson, 1988).

Each of the rotated FMC*(3)s yields an exact fit to the raw moment structure of the same LPM(3). One of the rotated FMC*(3) solutions exactly recovers the true parameter values of this LPM(3) used for generating the moment structure. Figure 8.1 presents only a subset of 3,360 rotated solutions because in our initial implementation of the rotation algorithm not all outcomes were acceptable. The figure only depicts the acceptable rotated solutions. Despite its apparent simplicity, the construction of a completely satisfactory rotation algorithm proved to be a process of trial and error. When the final algorithm is specified as outlined in the last section the entire set of 15,625 solutions will be acceptable.

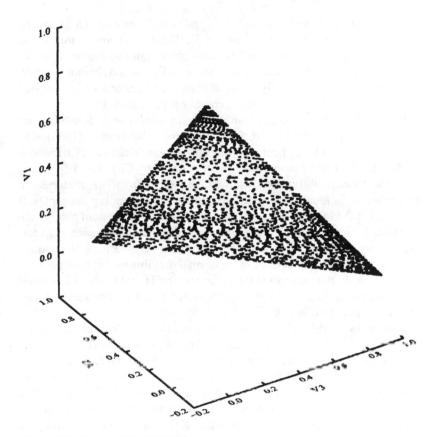

Figure 8.1. Rotated FMC*(3) Vectors

4. Discussion

We start this section by stating what exactly are the main conclusions that can be drawn from the results presented in this chapter. First, results suggest that if attention is restricted to first- and second-order moments of metrical manifest variables, factor and latent profile models yield identical fits to the data. Of course this result already was implicit in Bartholomew's (1987) discussion of the correspondence between both types of models. Second, results suggest that the parameters in a latent profile model can only be partly recovered from first- and second-order manifest moments. Specifically, the probability density h over the latent classes and the means of the conditional densities (8.5) can be recovered, but not the variances of (8.5). Third, we showed that latent profile models fitted to first- and second-order manifest moments suffer from rotational indeterminacy, and we specified a convenient rotation algorithm. We will initially discuss some implications of the second result, and then close with a few general considerations.

Prakasa Rao (1992) presents an interesting overview of identifiability for mixtures of distributions. Referring to a paper by Teicher (1960), Rao shows that the family of finite mixtures of univariate normal distributions is identifiable. Furthermore, referring to a paper by Chandra (1977), Rao shows that identifiability relative to a family of multivariate mixtures can be studied from identifiability relative to the corresponding marginals. It follows that the latent profile models considered in the present chapter are identifiable because the implied marginal distribution of each manifest variable is a finite mixture of univariate normal distributions. In contrast, we found that the variances of these normal distributions cannot be identified. Clearly, the reason for the latter finding is that first- and second-order moments do not completely characterize a finite mixture of univariate normal distributions.

Maximum likelihood estimation in latent profile models is not restricted to the information inherent in first- and second-order moments and therefore would seem capable to also yield estimates of the conditional variances in (8.5). Yet, our preliminary simulation studies of maximum likelihood estimation in normal mixture models suggest that a rather large number of observations is required in order to obtain sufficiently precise parameter estimates. If this result is upheld in further simulation studies, one could consider using a hybrid estimation procedure if only a limited number of observations is available. That is, whereas our constrained factor model for raw moments could be used to obtain parameter estimates of h and the means of (8.5), a conditional likelihood estimator could be used to estimate the variances of (8.5). Perhaps the precision of parameter estimates obtained with our constrained factor model is better than for the analogous estimates obtained in maximum likelihood estimation of the complete set of parameters in latent profile models.

The fact that manifest covariance structures can equally well be described by factor or latent profile models may have far-reaching implications for differential psychological theories. These theories elaborate on the distinction between the so-called typological and dimensional approaches. Our results show, however, that the factor models associated with a dimensional approach can always be replaced, without affecting the goodness of fit, by latent profile models associated with a typological approach. At the level of second-order moments, the reverse also holds. Actually, a similar conclusion already was made more than half a century ago by Hempel and Oppenheim (1936). In their monograph on the concept of types evaluated from the point of view of Fregean logic, it was concluded that types are dimensions in disguise. It would seem that history has repeated itself with respect to this issue.

References

Bartholomew, D. J. (1987). *Latent variable models and factor analysis*. London: Griffin.
Chandra, S. (1977). On mixtures of probability distributions. *Scandinavian Journal of Statistics, 4*, 105-112.
Clogg, C. C. (1988). Latent class models for measuring. In R. Langeheine & D. Rost (Eds.), *Latent trait and latent class models* (pp. 173-205). New York: Plenum.
Hempel, C. G., & Oppenheim, P. (1936). *Der Typusbegriff im Lichte der neuen Logik*. Leiden: Sijthoff.
Lazarsfeld, P. F., & Henry, N. W. (1968). *Latent structure analysis*. New York: Houghton Mifflin.
Rao, P.B.L.S. (1992). *Identifiability in stochastic models. Characterization of probability distributions*. Boston: Academic Press.
Teicher, H. (1960). On the mixture of distributions. *Annals of Mathematical Statistics, 31*, 55-73.
Wilkinson, L. (1988). *SYGRAPH*. Evanston, IL: Systat Inc.

Appendix A: Schematic Outline for Algorithm for Rotation in FMC[*]

Let n be the number of manifest variables and k the number of latent classes. In addition, let A be the $n \times k$ matrix composed of conditional means $\mu_i(j)$ in (8.29), and let ETA be the k-vector composed of the probabilities η_j in (8.29). Both A and ETA are obtained from the FMC(k) fit and given on input. Also given on input is the $k \times k$ orthogonal rotation matrix T. The n-vector U contains on input the marginal means μ_i in (8.29) which had been obtained from (8.13). On output, the matrix B contains the rotated conditional means in (8.30) and vector E contains the rotated probabilities of the latent classes.

```
DIMENSION A(N,K), ETA(K), T(K,K), U(N)
DIMENSION B(N,K), E(K)
DO 10 I= 1,K
E(I) = 0.0
```

```
         DO 10 J= 1,K
  10     E(I) = E(I) + SQRT(ETA(J))*T(J,I)
         DO 20 I=1,N
         DO 20 J=1,K
         B(I,J) =0.0
         DO 30 M= 1,K
  30     B(I,J)=B(I,J)+T(M,J)*SQRT(ETA(M))*A(I,M)
  20     B(I,J) = B(I,J)/E(J)
         DO 40 I=1,K
  40     E(I) = E(I)**2
```

An application of this algorithm is given in Section 3.2.

PART 3

Analysis of Latent Variables in Developmental Research: Categorical Variables Approaches

9

Latent Class Models for Longitudinal Assessment of Trait Acquisition

GEORGE B. MACREADY
C. MITCHELL DAYTON

1. Introduction

Latent class analysis (LCA) was developed to explain observed dependencies among polytomous manifest variables. A basic assumption of LCA is that there exist two or more mutually exclusive types of respondents such that, for each type of respondent, the manifest variables are independent. However, the types of respondents or latent classes are unobserved. Conceptually, LCA is related to factor analysis (FA) models for which observed correlations among variables are assumed to arise from unobserved, or latent, factors that are themselves uncorrelated. For both LCA and FA the apparent dependency among manifest variables is an artifact attributable to ignorance concerning the "true" latent structure of the data.

The focus of this chapter is on models for repeated measurements data that, in a general sense, may be termed developmental. Such models have been described by, for example, Wiggins (1973), Dayton and Macready (1983), Rindskopf (1987), and Hagenaars (1990). Furthermore, Langeheine and Rost (1988) provide a framework for so-called "sequential categorical data" that take on the following types: (1) one variable measured at two or more points in time but with distinct samples of respondents at each time (e.g., mobility data for fathers and sons); (2) one variable

245

measured at two or more points in time with the same sample of respondents (e.g., panel data for one attitude); (3) one variable measured for distinct samples of respondents at two or more points in time (e.g., panel data for husbands' and wives' attitudes); (4) two variables measured at two or more points in time for the same sample of respondents (e.g., multivariate panel data). This final type of data, which may be described as "doubly multivariate data," occurs relatively frequently in applied settings, but poses substantial analytical problems for two major reasons. First, except for the simplest cases, the total number of measured variables becomes quite large and exceeds the analytical capacities of available computer software. And, second, even if special-purpose software were available or specially developed, the number of cases required for stable estimation is often prohibitive. Consider, for example, just three dichotomous variables measured at three different times. This results in $2^9 = 512$ potential response patterns, most of which would show no frequency of response unless an exceptionally large sample were available. A major purpose of this chapter is to explore practical approaches to the analysis of data of this type.

Maximum likelihood estimation procedures for LCA models have been described by Goodman (1974) and Haberman (1977), among others. The MLLSA computer program (Clogg, 1977) for LCA based on frequencies for the various possible response patterns of the manifest variables has been utilized in many applications of LCA. LCA has been applied to a number of areas of research within the behavioral and social sciences. For example, constrained latent class models for psychometric scaling have been presented by Proctor (1970), Goodman (1974, 1975), Dayton and Macready (1976, 1980), and Clogg and Goodman (1984). Assessment of mastery in an educational context has been modeled by Macready and Dayton (1977, 1980) and Bergan, Cancelli, and Luiten (1980), among others. For a general overview of applications to educational research, see Bergan (1983).

2. Latent Class Theory

We consider a relatively complex situation in which observed test items representing response variables are measured for a set of different domains across several occasions and for two or more manifestly different groups of respondents. Depending upon context, occasions might also be referred to as panels or waves. The respondent groups may represent levels of a blocking variable, such as sex or socioeconomic status, or they may represent experimental treatment groups formed for purposes of comparison. More generally, the groups may be based on combinations of blocking and/or treatment variables. For the example considered in Section 3, below, students had been randomly divided among three experimental conditions, each of which was measured on three occasions across four content domains represented, respectively, by two response variables (i.e., test items).

The general approach to LCM adopted here involves two distinct stages of modeling. In the first stage of modeling, referred to as Within Occasion Modeling, the LCM is specified at the item level for a given occasion and domain. The focus during this stage is on modeling the latent structure sufficient to explain responses to items from a specific domain on a given occasion for the manifest respondent groups. Also, consistency among models across occasions can be assessed at this stage. During the second stage of modeling, referred to as Migration Modeling, the LCM is specified across occasions and items for a given domain. For this stage, the focus is on representing change in latent class membership, or so-called migration, by students over occasions.[1]

Although we present notation for general LCMs incorporating response variables, domains, occasions, and groups, for purposes of concreteness reference is made to the specific specifications of the exemplary analysis presented in Section 3, below. Adapting notation from Macready and Dayton (1992), the outcome data are assumed to be comprised of a set of observed response vectors, $r_{igmt} = \{r_{kigmt}\}$ representing the following facets:

Occasion:	$t = 1, \ldots, T$	[$T = 3$ occasions for the example]
Domain:	$m = 1, \ldots, M$	[$M = 4$ domains for the example]
Group:	$g = 1, \ldots, G$	[$G = 3$ treatment groups for the example]
Pattern:	$i = 1, \ldots, I_{mt}$	[Within Occasion: $I_{mt} = 3 \cdot 2^2 = 12$ item response patterns for each domain on each occasion for the example]

or

Pattern:	$j = 1, \ldots, J_m$	[Migration: $J_m = 3 \cdot 2^{3 \cdot 2} = 192$ acquisition-state patterns over occasions for each domain for the example]
Item:	$k = 1, \ldots, K_{mt}$	[$K_{mt} = 2$ items for each domain and occasion for the example]

While, in general, the responses, r_{kigmt}, may take on values $a = 1, \ldots,$ A_{km}, the items for the exemplary analysis were scored either $a = 1$ if correct or $a = 0$ if incorrect with the result that $r_{kigmt} = \{1, 0\}$. To avoid notational complexities, the ensuing models assume dichotomous response variables of this type.

(a) Within-Occasion Models

Consider K_{mt} dichotomous variables, taking on values $\{1, 0\}$, measured for the mth content domain on the tth occasion. For G manifest groups of respondents, the responses may be summarized by $G \cdot 2^{K_{mt}} \equiv I_{mt}$ response vectors, $r'_{igmt} \equiv [r_{i1gmt}, r_{i2gmt}, \ldots, r_{iK_m gmt}, g]$. These response vectors can be arranged in lexicographic order: $r'_{1gmt} = [0, 0, \ldots, 0, g]$, $r'_{2gmt} = [1, 0, \ldots, 0, g], r'_{3gmt} = [1, 1, \ldots, 0, g], \ldots, r'_{I_m gmt} = [1, 1, \ldots, 1, g]$. Note that the first $2^{K_{mt}}$ elements in each response vector represent one of the possible, different patterns of 1,0 responses, whereas the final element represents known membership in a manifest group. For the tth occasion, mth domain, and ith response vector, an LCM based on C_{mt} latent classes per group[2] can be written as:

$$P(r_{igmt} \mid m, t) = \sum_{c=1}^{C_{mt}} \theta_{gmtc} \left[\prod_{k=1}^{K_{mt}} \alpha_{1 1 k gmtc}^{r_{ikgmt}} \cdot (1 - \alpha_{1 1 kgmtc})^{1 - r_{ikgmt}} \right] \quad [9.1]$$

where θ_{gmtc} is the latent class proportion for the gth group and cth latent class, at the tth occasion for the mth domain with the restrictions:

$$\sum_{c=1}^{C_{mt}} \theta_{gmtc} = 1 \quad \text{for all } g, m, t. \quad [9.1a]$$

The term $\alpha_{11kgmtc} = P(r_{ikgmt} = 1 \mid g, m, t, c)$ represents the conditional probability for a response of "1" (i.e., yes, positive, agree, etc.) in the gth group on the kth item in the mth domain at the tth occasion for the cth latent class. In formulating the LCM in Equation 9.1, an assumption of "local independence" is made in the sense that the responses within each latent class are assumed to be independent. Also, it should be noted that the model in Equation 9.1 is a conventional LCM, conditional on manifest group, occasion, and domain in which membership in the manifest groups is known without error. Thus, this LCM is analogous to models for simultaneous latent structure analysis proposed by Clogg and Goodman (1984, 1985).

For LCMs based on dichotomously scored test items, it is natural to interpret the conditional probabilities associated with items in terms of two types of errors that, in theory, may occur when a respondent answers an item. Specifically, the term *intrusion error* refers to a correct response (i.e., "1") by a member of a "non-acquisition" latent class, whereas the term *omission error* refers to an incorrect response (i.e., "0") by a member of an "acquisition" latent class (Dayton & Macready, 1976; Macready & Dayton, 1980). In the present notation, assume that the latent class denoted by $c = 1$ represents non-acquirers and that the latent class denoted by $c = 2$ represents acquirers of the latent attribute of interest. Then, conditional probabilities of the form $\alpha_{1|kgmt1}$ represent intrusion errors, whereas conditional probabilities of the form $\alpha_{0|kgmt2} = 1 - \alpha_{1|kgmt2}$ represent omission errors.

The model in Equation 9.1 contains $K_{mt} \cdot G \cdot C_{mt} + G \cdot (C_{mt} - 1)$ independent parameters. Assuming a two-class model, for the exemplary analysis, this is a total of $2 \cdot 3 \cdot 2 + 3 = 15$ parameters, whereas there is a total of only 12 observed response vectors for each domain and occasion. In addition, it is ordinarily of interest to fit models that reproduce the known total frequencies for the manifest grouping variable (i.e., the sizes of the treatment groups for the exemplary analysis). Thus the 12 observed cells provide information for estimating only nine independent parameters. While this LCM may be constrained in a variety of ways, it is often of interest to compare latent class proportions across groups. Thus, at the initial level, constraints on the conditional item probabilities may be more desirable than constraints on the latent class proportions. For example, the constraint $\alpha_{1|kgmtc} = \alpha_{1|kmtc'}$, which equates conditional item responses across groups, reduces the total number of independent parameters to $K_{mt} \cdot C_{mt} + G \cdot (C_{mt} - 1)$, or 7, for the exemplary analysis, and this yields 2 degrees of freedom for assessing fit of the model to the data. In essence, this set of constraints equates intrusion errors across the groups and equates omission errors across the groups. Errors can be further constrained across items for some or all of the latent classes and, in the extreme case, a single error rate can be postulated across all facets.

(b) Migration Models

The observed data are represented by extending the notation developed for within-occasions models, above, to include responses from all T occasions. For G manifest groups of respondents, there is a total of $G \cdot 2^{T \cdot K_{mt}} \equiv J_m$ response vectors for the mth content domain and each is of the form:

$$v'_{jgm} = [r_{j1gm1}, r_{j2gm1}, \ldots, r_{jK_{m1}gm1}, \ldots, r_{j1gmT}, r_{j2gmT}, \ldots, r_{jK_{mT}gmT}, g] \quad [9.1b]$$

An LCM for each content domain can be written analogous to that presented in Equation 9.1, except that the probabilistic model is not conditioned on time:

$$P(v_{jgm} \mid m) = \sum_{c=1}^{C_{mt}} \theta_{gmtc} \left[\prod_{t=1}^{T} \prod_{k=1}^{K_{mt}} \alpha_{1 \mid kgmtc}^{r_{jkgmt}} \cdot (1 - \alpha_{1 \mid kgmtc})^{1 - r_{jkgmt}} \right] \quad [9.2]$$

Assumptions and interpretations of conditional probabilities are comparable to those presented in the previous section.

The fundamental approach to modeling across occasions is based on considering the types of changes in latent state that might occur over time. It is necessary that an appropriate model for accounting for within-occasion performance has been identified. In this section, we assume the appropriate within-occasion models are based on two latent classes that are interpretable as representing non-acquirers and acquirers, respectively. While the within-occasion models may be as complex as necessary (e.g., several latent classes with differing conditional probabilities for items), the conceptualization of migration models becomes extraordinarily complex unless the within-occasion modeling is relatively easy to interpret. In general, migration models may be considered to be equivalent to various types of scaling models such as those proposed by Proctor (1970), Goodman (1974, 1975), Dayton and Macready (1976, 1980), or Clogg and Goodman (1984, 1985), among others. As illustration, and since we apply them to the exemplary data, we consider three general types of models.

No Migration: Respondents are assumed either to have acquired or not acquired the skills represented by a given domain such that this latent status is constant over time. That is, respondents are consistently in either an acquisition or non-acquisition latent state for all occasions. Allowing non-acquisition to be represented by 0 and acquisition by 1, the latent classes across occasions can be represented by two idealized response vectors of the form [0 0 . . . 0] and [1 1 . . . 1].

Forward Migration: Respondents may change (i.e., migrate) only from non-acquisition to acquisition of skills represented by a given domain. The permissible patterns of change conform to a linear hierarchy, or Guttman scale, and can be represented by $T + 1$ idealized response vectors of the form [0 0 . . . 0], [0 0 . . . 1], . . . , [0 1 . . . 1] and [1 1 . . . 1].

Unconstrained Migration: Respondents may change (i.e., migrate) freely among non-acquisition and acquisition latent states from occasion to occasion. All 2^T possible, different idealized response vectors may occur.

The specification of migration models at the level of the item responses can be accomplished by combining the idealized response vectors or within-occasion models with the idealized response vectors assumed for a given migration model. Consider, for example, a domain represented by two test items on each of three occasions for three manifest groups of respondents. At the item level, the idealized responses for a no-migration model would be:

Occasion
```
 1    2    3   Gp
[0 0  0 0  0 0  1]
[1 1  1 1  1 1  1]
[0 0  0 0  0 0  2]
[1 1  1 1  1 1  2]
[0 0  0 0  0 0  3]
[1 1  1 1  1 1  3]
```

On the other hand, assuming a forward-migration model, these idealized responses would be:

Occasion
```
 1    2    3   Gp
[0 0  0 0  0 0  1]
[0 0  0 0  1 1  1]
[0 0  1 1  1 1  1]
[1 1  1 1  1 1  1]
```

[0 0 0 0 0 0 2]
[0 0 0 0 1 1 2]
[0 0 1 1 1 1 2]
[1 1 1 1 1 1 2]
[0 0 0 0 0 0 3]
[0 0 0 0 1 1 3]
[0 0 1 1 1 1 3]
[1 1 1 1 1 1 3]

Although unconstrained no-migration models can often be fit to actual data sets, it is typical for more complex models, such as those for forward migration or for unconstrained migration, to pose severe estimation problems. In particular, the number of independent parameters in the model can be excessively large, leading to instability during estimation. For the mth domain, there is a total of, say, $K_m = \Sigma_{t=1}^{T} K_{mt}$ items. Assuming C_m latent classes per group, the total number of parameters for an unconstrained model would be $K_m \cdot G \cdot C_m + G \cdot (C_m - 1)$ with G additional constraints due to fitting the sample sizes of the manifest groups. Thus, for example, with two items on three occasions for three groups the data comprise $3 \cdot 2^6 = 192$ distinct response vectors, while an unconstrained forward migration model would be based on a total of $6 \cdot 3 \cdot 4 + 3 \cdot 3 + 3 = 84$ parameters and implicit constraints. While this model is not clearly unidentified, our experience has been poor in obtaining fit for models of this complexity. On the other hand, an unconstrained two-class (i.e., no-migration) model would involve $6 \cdot 3 \cdot 2 + 3 \cdot 1 + 3 = 42$ parameters and implicit constraints and we have been, in general, successful in fitting models of this type.

In addition to the issue of model complexity, there may be unrecognized, implicit restrictions on the item conditional probabilities that render a model unidentified. Thus, it is useful to consider various types of reasonable constraints that may be incorporated into models. As discussed for within-occasion models, above, item conditional probabilities can be constrained across latent classes and/or across manifest groups. Similarly, latent class proportions can be completely or partially constrained across manifest groups. For models with no constraints across domains or occasions, parameter estimation can be carried out separately by domain and/or occasion with results equivalent to those for simultaneous estimation. A number of these ideas is illustrated in the exemplary analyses reported below.

(c) Assessing Fit of Models

Letting the observed frequency of respondents showing response vector $r_{\mathcal{G}_m}$ for the mth domain be $F_{\mathcal{G}_m}$ (where $\mathcal{G}$ stands for some combination of facets defining a "cell" in the data table), the log-likelihood for the sample of cases is given by

$$\log_e (\mathcal{L}) = \sum_{\mathcal{G}} F_{\mathcal{G}_m} \cdot \log_e P(r_{\mathcal{G}_m} \mid m) \qquad [9.3]$$

Assuming identifiability of the LCM, maximum likelihood estimates for the independent parameters can, in general, be found, although the calculations involve solving a system of nonlinear equations. A computationally efficient approach to estimation, based on the EM algorithm as popularized by Dempster, Laird, and Rubin (1977), is the basis for the widely used LCA program, MLLSA, developed by Clogg (1977). Model identification requires, at a minimum, that there be nonnegative degrees of freedom in the sense that the total number of free parameters and inherent constraints in the LCM be no greater than the total number of observed response vectors. Data sparcity and/or unrecognized implicit restrictions in unconstrained or constrained models may, however, result in lack of identification even when this degrees of freedom requirement is met.

Assuming that maximum likelihood (ML) estimates can be calculated for the parameters in the LCM of interest, an issue arises concerning the assessment of how well a model represents the data being analyzed. For example, latent class models with one, two, three, and more classes can be fitted successively to the data and then compared in some reasonable manner in order to decide upon an appropriate number of latent classes for purposes of interpretation. Conventionally, fit of a specific model, relative to a generalized multinomial model that perfectly fits the observed frequencies, has been assessed by asymptotic chi-squared statistics based on the likelihood ratio principle. Letting $\hat{F}_{\mathcal{G}_m}$ represent the expected frequencies associated with some specific LCM denoted as the hth model, the chi-squared value is given by:

$$G_h^2 = 2 \cdot \sum_{\mathcal{G}} F_{\mathcal{G}_m} \cdot \log_e \left[\frac{F_{\mathcal{G}_m}}{\hat{F}_{\mathcal{G}_m}} \right] \qquad [9.4]$$

with degrees of freedom equal to the number of observed response vectors reduced by the number of independent restrictions on the expected frequencies during estimation (i.e., number of independent parameter estimates and other implicit restrictions such as sample sizes). Assuming G_{h*}^2 is another LCM representing a restricted form of the hth model, then the difference $G_{h*}^2 - G_h^2$ may, under suitable conditions, also be distributed as chi-squared with degrees of freedom equal to the difference in degrees of freedom for the respective G^2 values.

It has been recognized for some time that likelihood-ratio chi-squared statistics are not distributed as theoretical, central chi-squared variates in situations in which parameters are restricted to boundary values (Everitt & Hand, 1981, sec. 5.2.2; Titterington, Smith, & Makov, 1985, sec. 1.2.2 and 5.4). Unfortunately, this is often the situation when comparing hierarchically related LCMs. For example, in comparing a model based on two latent classes with a hierarchically related model based on three latent classes, the value of one latent class proportion is constrained to 0, a boundary value. In this regard, Holt and Macready (1989) present evidence for the inadequacy of the likelihood ratio test in the context of LCA.

An alternate approach to model selection that is based on the likelihood principle has been developed by Akaike and applied to, among other problems, the number-of-factors issue in FA (Akaike, 1987). The model selection method advocated by Akaike utilizes the notion of the expected loss in information for future observations that results from using ML estimates from the current sample instead of using the (unknown) true parametric values. The Akaike information criterion, AIC, for the hth model with likelihood $\mathcal{L}_h$ is defined as:

$$AIC_h = -2 \cdot \log_e(\mathcal{L}_h) + 2 \cdot p_h \qquad [9.5]$$

where p_h is the number of independent parameters that are involved in fitting the hth model by the methods of maximum likelihood estimation. The model selection procedure is to choose the model for which AIC is *minimum* among the competing models under consideration; that is, the so-called minimum AIC estimate, MAICE = min(AIC$_h$). The additive term, $2 \cdot p_h$, is, in effect, a penalty reflecting the complexity of the model. It has been noted that the MAICE procedure is not consistent in the sense that increasing sample size does not directly impact the criterion. However, when comparing alternate models for a specific data set, the sample size, N, is fixed and the issue of consistency is not of central importance. Other related model-selection criteria, however, such as those proposed by Schwarz (1978) and Bozdogan (1987), include the sample size in the penalty term and thus are consistent. Furthermore, these criteria tend to select models with fewer parameters than AIC (i.e., more parsimonious models). At present, there is no evidence indicating which of these criteria is superior in the context of latent class modeling. For the examples presented below, AIC was chosen as the approach to illustrate.

Computationally, it is often convenient to derive AIC measures from G^2 chi-squared statistics rather than from Equation 9.5. A quantity differing from AIC only by a constant that does vary from model to model based on the same data set can be found from $AIC^* = G^2 - 2 \cdot DF$, where DF is the degrees of freedom associated with the chi-squared statistic. In the exemplary analyses reported below, the values reported and compared are actually AIC^* rather than AIC from Equation 9.5.

Since the derivation of AIC is based on properties of likelihood ratio statistics, an objection can be raised to its use in the context of mixture models (of which latent class models are examples) since asymptotic results may not hold. As pointed out by Titterington et al. (1985): "Akaike's AIC criterion has been illustrated in a mixture/clustering context by Sclove, . . . A major problem is that the theoretical justification for these criteria, Akaike's in particular, rely on the same conditions as the usual asymptotic theory of the GLR test" (p. 159).

There is, nevertheless, considerable value in studying the behavior of model selection criterion such as AIC since their performance in real-life situations of interest may still be of practical use. In this vein, Sclove (1987) notes: "In this context, some analyticity conditions required for series expansions yielding the model-selection criteria are not met, and though the criteria can be regarded as heuristic figures of merit, more research is required" (p. 338).

There has been relatively limited practical application of information criteria for the selection of models in social science settings. In the present study, the AIC criterion is utilized as the primary model-comparison statistic, although conventional G^2 chi-squared values are reported as well.

3. Exemplary Analyses

Data were collected from a total of 267 middle-school students in a small, metropolitan community in the northwestern United States by one of the authors. On two occasions of measurement, one student was absent yielding a sample size of 266 for these occasions; across all occasions, complete data were available for 265 students. Participating classrooms of students were randomly assigned among three treatment groups in which different instructional approaches to the topic of arithmetic operations on fractions were implemented. Instruction was conducted over a 3-week period, followed by one week of review for all operations, with occasional review of the material during the 8-week period following instruction. The specific instructional sequences were:

1. Forward Instruction—addition and subtraction of fractions (Week 1), multiplication of fractions (Week 2), division of fractions (Week 3), and review of all operations (Week 4);

2. Backward Instruction—multiplication of fractions (Week 1), division of fractions (Week 2), addition and subtraction of fractions (Week 3), and review of all operations (Week 4);

3. Simultaneous Instruction—addition, subtraction, multiplication, division of fractions on successive days (Week 1); all four operations considered (Weeks 2 and 3), and review of all operations (Week 4).

The number of students in the three treatment groups were 84, 70, and 113, respectively, with one student missing from each of groups 2 and 3 for the across-occasions analyses, as noted above.

Assessment of skill acquisition was based on items drawn from domains related to the four basic operations implemented in the instructional sequences. Descriptions of these domains, along with exemplary items, are presented in Table 9.1. The first item domain includes addition, but not subtraction, of fractions. However, comparable items were administered for subtraction and these additional items were utilized in a portion of the analysis [i.e., research question (b), below]. On three separate occasions, two-item pairs were randomly selected from each of the four content domains. For all three treatment groups, these occasions occurred at the end of the first week of instruction, the end of the third week of instruction, and 8 weeks following the end of the 4-week instruction/review period.

Table 9.1 General Description of the Item Domains

Item Domain	Typical Item	Item Features
1	$\frac{3}{12} + \frac{4}{12}$	Involves the addition of two fractions with a common base.
2	$9\frac{4}{12} - 3\frac{7}{12}$	Involves the subtraction of one mixed number from another where (i) the difference is positive and (ii) the fractional portions of numbers have a common base.
3	$\frac{4}{5} \times \frac{1}{8}$	Involves the multiplication of two non-reducable proper fractions with different bases.
4	$\frac{2}{3} + \frac{1}{2}$	Involves the division of a whole number or proper fraction by a proper fraction with a different base.

SOURCE: Roberts and Nesselroade, 1986, pp. 529-545. Used with permission from Academic Press.

(a) Research Questions and Analysis Plan

In summary, the data collection design involved three occasions of measurement (i.e., panels or waves) for four skills (i.e., domains or traits) for three treatment groups. The focus of the analysis was on modeling the acquisition of skills related to arithmetic operations on fractions both within and among occasions of measurement. The within-occasion analyses utilized models that incorporated the notion of a latent class of "acquirers" who had mastered the skills related to the domain and a latent class of "non-acquirers" who had not mastered these skills. The migration analyses utilized models for change from non-acquirer to acquirer states (or vice versa). The analytical plan was based on the following research questions:

(I) For each domain and each occasion of measurement, what is the most appropriate model to represent skill acquisition? Response data can be summarized by the frequencies of responses associated with the four distinct response patterns across the three treatment groups (i.e., $[0, 0, g]$, $[0, 1, g]$, $[1, 0, g]$, and $[1, 1, g]$ for $g = 1, 2, 3$, where 1 represents a correct response to an item and 0 represents an incorrect response to an item). Thus, for each domain on each occasion, the data comprise 12 response patterns resulting from the four patterns of item responses for each of the three treatment groups. Although unrestricted models incorporating acquirer and non-acquirer classes cannot be fitted to the data because of lack of degrees of freedom, restricted models with, for example, equal intrusion and omission errors across items can be assessed. As a baseline for comparison, a (non-latent-class) model assuming complete independence of responses to the items was fitted for each domain and occasion as a preliminary step.

(II) Is the equal-error assumption for skill acquisition reasonable? In order to provide a sufficient number of unique response patterns for fitting an unrestricted two-class model, the two addition-of-fractions items for Domain 1 were augmented with two comparable subtraction-of-fraction items to form a new domain for which responses were available for four items. While addition and subtraction of fractions may represent distinguishable skills, it was believed that the content and skill demands for these tasks were sufficiently similar that a two-state model was reasonable. For this analysis, there was a total of 48 response patterns resulting from the 16 distinct item responses for each of the three treatment groups.

(III) Assuming suitable within-occasion models have been identified in steps (I) and (II), above, is the proportion of students showing skill acquisition (i.e., acquirers) comparable across the treatment conditions? In essence, this analysis requires fitting equal latent class proportions for acquisition across the three treatment conditions.

(IV) Assuming that reasonable models have been identified for within-occasion skill acquisition in steps (I)—(III), above, what is the most appropriate model for migration of acquirers and non-acquirers across occasions? With respect to the three occasions of measurement, there are eight distinct patterns representing membership in acquisition or non-acquisition conditions that can occur. Since there are two items for each of the three occasions, there is a total of $2^6 = 64$ distinct response patterns that can occur for each treatment group, resulting in a total of 192 distinct response vectors across groups. Three types of models corresponding to those described in Section 2b, above, were considered: no migration between acquisition states across occasions; forward migration between acquisition states across occasions; and unconstrained (i.e., forward and backward) migration between acquisition states across occasions.

(b) Within-Occasion Skill Acquisition

(I) Modeling Skill Acquisition

The data collection design incorporated three treatment conditions that represent a manifest grouping variable with fixed numbers of

Table 9.2 Within-Occasion Trait Acquisition Assessment Across Treatment Groups

		Acquisition Model								
		Eq. Errors acr. Grps (df = 2)			Eq. Errors & LC acr. Grps (df = 4)			Independence Model (df = 3)		
Do-main	Occa-sion	G^2	p value	AIC	G^2	p value	AIC	G^2	p value	AIC
1	1	1.106	.575	-2.894[a]	71.416	.000	63.416	27.384	.000	21.384
	2	0.407	.818	-3.593	23.672	.000	15.627	1.421	.701	-4.579[a]
	3	0.271	.873	-3.729[a]	6.239	.182	-1.761	10.292	.016	4.292
2	1	0.834	.659	-3.166[a]	35.622	.000	27.622	39.613	.000	33.613
	2	3.550	.169	-0.450	6.142	.189	-1.858[a]	73.305	.000	67.305
	3	1.700	.427	-2.300[a]	12.530	.014	4.530	47.818	.000	41.818
3	1	1.680	.432	-2.320[a]	25.198	.000	17.198	55.138	.000	49.138
	2	4.421	.110	0.421[a]	8.709	.069	0.709	88.400	.000	82.400
	3	0.594	.743	-3.406	3.605	.462	-4.395[a]	32.885	.000	26.885
4	1	2.908	.234	-1.092[a]	27.828	.000	19.828	47.794	.000	41.794
	2	2.783	.249	-1.217[a]	8.405	.078	0.405	35.177	.000	29.177
	3	0.998	.607	-3.002[a]	8.855	.065	0.855	67.310	.000	61.310

NOTE: a. When minimum AIC value is used as the criterion, this is the preferred model.

students per condition. Thus, LCMs based on the 12 distinct response vectors per domain and occasion were subject to three implicit restrictions resulting from the requirement that expected frequencies sum to the three appropriate observed frequencies for the treatment conditions. As an initial step, an independence model was fitted to the data for each domain and occasion. The independence model is equivalent to an unconstrained "latent-class" model of the form of Equation 9.1, but based on a single class. The final set of three columns in Table 9.2 shows that, in general, the independence model, evaluated with the degrees of freedom, provides poor fit to these data sets. However, for the first domain on the second occasion of measurement, satisfactory fit is attained. It should be noted that this outcome is for the simplest type of item (i.e., addition of two fractions with a common base) at the measurement occasion following the third week of instruction. Overall, we conclude that a more complex acquisition model than that implied by independence of items is required to explain these data.

Table 9.3 Within-Occasion Trait Acquisition Parameter Estimates

Domain	Occasion	Group:	Proportion Masters			Mean Error Rate	
			1	2	3	Intrusion	Omission
1	1		0.969	0.371	0.937	0.232	0.060
	2		1.000	0.426	0.912	0.712	0.038
	3		1.000	0.917	0.966	0.280	0.053
2	1		0.599	0.086	0.535	0.074	0.300
	2		0.491	0.421	0.552	0.248	0.034
	3		0.787	0.541	0.712	0.118	0.163
3	1		0.281	0.697	0.401	0.120	0.180
	2		0.589	0.434	0.445	0.283	0.000
	3		0.707	0.535	0.655	0.256	0.138
4	1		0.132	0.166	0.436	0.110	0.165
	2		0.729	0.473	0.590	0.354	0.103
	3		0.859	0.727	0.902	0.136	0.058

The second stage of analysis, corresponding to research question (I), above, fitted two-class models to each domain and occasion. Due to degrees-of-freedom restrictions, it was assumed that intrusion and omission error rates were constant across the three treatment groups. As noted in Section 2a, above, such models are based on constraints of the form $\alpha_{1|kgmtc} = \alpha_{1|kmtc}$ for $k = 1, 2$ and $c = 1, 2$. The resulting models, which require estimation of four conditional item probabilities (i.e., two intrusion and two omission error rates) and three latent class proportions, result in 2 degrees of freedom for assessing fit. As shown in the first set of results for acquisition models in Table 9.2, these constrained models provide adequate fit for each of the domains and occasions. For each LCM the estimated proportion of acquirers, along with average estimated intrusion and omission error rates for the two items, are summarized in Table 9.3. We note, in all three treatment groups, a tendency for the estimated proportions in the acquirer latent class to increase across occasions of measurement. This trend suggests that the instructional methods were, in general, successful. Also, the second method, utilizing a "backward" instructional approach, tended to show lower estimated proportions of acquirers than the other two methods. Exceptions to this trend occur, for example, in Domain 3 that dealt with multiplication of fractions at the first occasion of measurement. This is not unexpected since multiplication was the first skill taught in this treatment condition. Average estimated omission error rates are modest and appear to be consistent with interpreting the associated latent class with acquisition of the underlying arithmetic skills. The situation is slightly less clear for the non-acquisition latent class since intrusion errors, as estimated, attain an unacceptably high level for the second occasion of measurement in Domain 1 (i.e., .712). It should be noted, however, that in the first and third treatment groups, the bulk of students are operating at an acquisition level on all three measurement occasions and that, overall, these addition items are quite easy for these students.

(II) Assessment of the Equal-Error Assumption

Prior to additional interpretation of the within-occasions acquisition models, it is appropriate to make some assessment of the reasonableness of the constant-error-rate assumption. As noted in research question (II), above, it was possible to combine two additional items with those in Domain 1 to form an augmented domain assessed by four items. Given the 48 distinct response vectors available for this new domain, unconstrained, as well as equal-error, models could be fit to the data. Table 9.4 provides results for two-class constrained equal-error (denoted "Equal Error Acquisition Model"), unconstrained two-class (denoted "Free Error Acquisition Model"), and three-class constrained equal-error (denoted "Equal Error 3 L.C. Model") latent class models. The three-class model was equivalent to the Dayton and Macready (1980) extension of the Goodman (1975) model that incorporates an intrinsically unscalable class. In this case, response errors were constrained to be equal across groups, although conditional probabilities for the third (i.e., intrinsically unscalable) class were unconstrained. The equal-error, two-class model provided satisfactory fit on the second and third occasions of measurement as evidenced by nonsignificant G^2 values and by the fact that this model yielded the smallest AIC value among those considered. However, utilizing the same type of evidence, this model provided relatively poor fit on the first occasion of measurement. While an unconstrained two-class model results in marginally acceptable fit on the first occasion, the most satisfactory model among those considered was a three-class model with equal error rates. Examining parameter estimates for Domain 1 for the three-class solution suggested fitting a model with equal intrusion and equal omission errors for treatment groups 1 and 3, but allowing these errors to be freely

Table 9.4 Within-Occasion Trait Acquisition Assessment for an Augmented Version of Domain 1

	Occasion		
	1	2	3
Equal Error Acquisition Model (df = 34)			
G^2	64.199	32.360	17.220
p value	0.001	0.548	0.993
AIC	−3.801	−35.640[a]	−50.780[a]
Free Error Acquisition Model (df = 18)			
G^2	30.381	6.229	6.745
p value	0.034	0.995	0.992
AIC	−5.619	−29.771	−29.255
Equal Error 3 L.C. Model (df = 19)			
G^2	27.097	8.934	11.202
p value	0.103	0.975	0.917
AIC	−10.903[a]	−29.066	−26.798

NOTE: a. When minimum AIC value is used as the criterion, this is the preferred model.

estimated for treatment group 2. In fact, this post hoc model yielded a G^2 value of 36.534 with 26 degrees of freedom ($p = .082$). Thus, since the associated AIC value is −15.466, this model is preferred over those presented in Table 9.4.

Overall, models with equal rates for intrusion and omission errors across items may be viewed as satisfactory, although there is evidence that a somewhat more complex latent class structure is required on the first measurement occasion. This measurement occasion took place very early in the instructional sequence (i.e., at the end of the first week) and seems to reflect effects due to the somewhat unusual instructional approach utilized in the second treatment group (i.e., moving from relatively complex to relatively simple content over the course of instruction). We conclude, with some reservations, that a two-class model with equal intrusion and equal omission error rates provides a reasonable basis for interpreting results from this study.

(III) Comparison of Treatment Groups

In this study, the grouping variable represented a manipulated treatment variable. Consistent with the third research question, it was, therefore, of interest to compare these groups with respect to acquisition of the arithmetic skills comprising the four domains that were measured. Assuming that a model with equal intrusion and equal omission error rates was satisfactory, the latent class proportions, θ_{gmtc}, were constrained to equality across the three groups (i.e., for each domain and occasion, $\theta_{gmt1} = \theta_{mt1}$ for $g = 1, \ldots, 3$). As shown in the second set of columns for acquisition models in Table 9.2, while this constrained model provided reasonable fit in terms of chi-squared statistics for 6 of the 12 comparisons, it was the preferred model, among the three being compared using AIC, in only 2 cases. Summarizing these results and those from the independence tests, the following conclusions appear relevant: (1) method 2, based on backward instruction, produced less acquisition than the other methods on the first two occasions for Domains 1 and 2, but greater acquisition for Domain 3; (2) at the end of instruction, which was the second measurement occasion, the backward instruction method resulted in less acquisition for the Domain 1, did not differ for Domain 2, and produced less acquisition than forward instruction for Domains 3 and 4; and (3) for the follow-up period represented by the third measurement occasion, the backward instruction method appears to produce less retention of acquisition for Domains 2 and 4, but actually improved for Domain 1. Although not reported here, it should be noted that specific comparisons among the groups could be carried out by imposing equality constraints on pairs of latent class proportions rather than across all three groups.

(IV) Modeling Migration Across Occasions

From Table 9.3 it is apparent that there were substantial changes across occasions in the estimated proportions of students in the latent class associated with acquirers. The final research question addressed the issue of modeling this movement, or migration, between the acquirer and non-acquirer states. Following the rationale presented in Section 2b, above, three general types of models were considered. Idealized response vectors consistent with unconstrained (i.e., forward and backward) migration, forward migration, and no migration across the three occasions of measurement are summarized in Table 9.5 (note that complete sets of item response vectors for the no-migration and forward-migration models were presented in Section 2b, above). Parameter estimates and associated fit statistics were derived for a total of 10 LCMs. These models may be characterized in terms of the type of migration (if any) involved, restrictions (if any) on the intrusion and omission error terms, and restrictions (if

Table 9.5 Idealized Latent Response Vectors for Trait Acquisition Over Occasions

Model Type	Latent Class	Occasions 1	2	3
Unconstrained Migration	1	0	0	0
	2	0	0	1
	3	0	1	1
	4	1	1	1
	5	0	1	0
	6	1	0	0
	7	1	0	1
	8	1	1	0
Forward Migration	1	0	0	0
	2	0	0	1
	3	0	1	1
	4	1	1	1
No Migration	1	0	0	0
	2	1	1	1

Table 9.6 Constraints Imposed on Migration Models Used to Assess Changes in Acquisition Status Over Three Occasions

Model Restrictions	Migration Model									
Restriction on Error	1	2	3	4	5	6	7	8	9	10
Equal Errors Across Latent Classes	X	X		X		X		X		
Equal Errors Across Treatment Groups			X	X	X	X	X	X		X
Restrictions on Latent Class Proportions										
All Proportions Fixed Based on Within-Occasion Analyses					X	X				
Equal Proportions of "Complete Non-Acquirers" Across Treatment Groups							X	X		
Migration Restrictions										
Unconstrained Migration	X									
Forward Migration		X	X	X	X	X	X	X		
No Migration									X	X

any) on the latent class proportions. The 10 models, as summarized in Table 9.6, represent the following conditions (number of free parameters and degrees of freedom shown in parentheses; note that sample size restrictions for the three treatment groups are counted among the estimated latent class proportions):

Model 1: Unconstrained (forward and backward) migration; equal intrusion and equal omission error rates across latent classes (24 latent class proportions including 3 sample-size restrictions; 36 item conditional probabilities; 132 degrees of freedom);

Model 2: Forward migration; equal intrusion and equal omission error rates across latent classes (12 latent class proportions including 3 sample-size restrictions; 36 item conditional probabilities; 144 degrees of freedom);

Model 3: Forward migration; equal intrusion and equal omission error rates across treatment groups; (12 latent class proportions including 3 sample-size restrictions; 24 item conditional probabilities; 156 degrees of freedom);

Model 4: Forward migration; equal intrusion and equal omission error rates across both latent class and treatment groups (12 latent class proportions including 3 sample-size restrictions; 12 item conditional probabilities; 168 degrees of freedom);

Model 5: Forward migration; latent class proportions constrained to values obtained from within-occasion analyses; equal intrusion and equal omission error rates across treatment groups (3 latent class proportions all of which are sample-size restrictions; 24 item conditional probabilities; 165 degrees of freedom);

Model 6: Forward migration; latent class proportions constrained to values obtained from within-occasion analyses; equal intrusion and equal omission error rates across both latent classes and treatment groups (3 latent class proportions all of which are sample-size restrictions; 12 item conditional probabilities; 177 degrees of freedom);

Model 7: Forward migration; proportion in the non-acquirer class constrained equal to average value from within-occasion analyses and set equal across latent classes (note: proportions in other three types of latent classes were not constrained); equal intrusion and equal omission error rates across treatment groups (9 latent class proportions including 3 sample-size restrictions; 24 item conditional probabilities; 159 degrees of freedom);

Model 8: Forward migration; proportion in the non-acquirer class constrained as in Model 7, above; equal intrusion and equal omission error rates across both latent classes and treatment groups (9 latent class proportions including 3 sample-size restrictions; 12 item conditional probabilities; 171 degrees of freedom);

Table 9.7 Comparisons of Migration Models for Domain 1

Model	G^2	DF	p value	AIC
1	47.123	132	0.999	−216.877
2	64.975	144	0.999	−223.025
3	No Conv.	156		
4	86.417	168	0.999	−249.583
5	No Conv.	165		
6	74.931	177	0.999	−279.069[a]
7	No Conv.	159		
8	94.517	171	0.999	−247.483
9	56.549	150	0.999	−243.451
10	88.221	174	0.999	−259.779

NOTE: a. When minimum AIC value is used as the criterion, this is the preferred model.

Model 9: No migration; equivalent to completely unconstrained two-class-per-treatment-group model (6 latent class proportions including 3 sample-size restrictions; 36 item conditional probabilities; 150 degrees of freedom);

Model 10: No migration as in Model 9, above; equal intrusion and equal omission error rates across treatment groups (6 latent class proportions including 3 sample-size restrictions; 12 item conditional probabilities; 174 degrees of freedom).

Results from fitting these 10 models to each of the four content domains are presented in Tables 9.7-9.10, with associated parameter estimates for models preferred on the basis of the minimum AIC criterion shown in Tables 9.11 (latent class proportions) and 9.12 (average error rates across items). For three cases in Domain 1 and one case in Domain 4, convergence could not be attained using MLLSA and, for these cases, there apparently were unrecognized, implicit restrictions resulting from the particular patterns of observed frequencies. Based on the 36 (out of 40) LCMs for which estimates could be obtained, the following conclusions emerge:

1. The model based on unconstrained (forward and backward) migration (Model 1) provided adequate fit, based on G^2, to all four domains, but was never the preferred model based on the minimum AIC criterion.

Table 9.8 Comparisons of Migration Models for Domain 2

Model	G^2	DF	p value	AIC
1	119.366	132	0.777	−144.634
2	139.070	144	0.600	148.930
3	138.348	156	0.842	−173.652[a]
4	198.971	168	0.051	−137.029
5	224.835	165	0.001	−105.165
6	317.744	177	0.000	−36.256
7	151.994	159	0.641	−166.006
8	219.379	171	0.007	−122.621
9	166.727	150	0.166	−133.273
10	226.409	174	0.005	−121.591

NOTE: a. When minimum AIC value is used as the criterion, this is the preferred model.

Table 9.9 Comparisons of Migration Models for Domain 3

Model	G^2	DF	p value	AIC
1	138.038	132	0.342	−125.962
2	161.287	144	0.154	−126.713[a]
3	190.443	156	0.031	−121.557
4	243.178	168	0.000	−92.822
5	209.484	165	0.011	−120.516
6	307.440	177	0.000	−46.560
7	195.758	159	0.025	−122.242
8	244.863	171	0.000	−97.137
9	198.439	150	0.005	−101.561
10	277.531	174	0.000	−70.469

NOTE: a. When minimum AIC value is used as the criterion, this is the preferred model.

2. The models not incorporating migration (Models 9 and 10) provided adequate fit, based on G^2, to three of the four domains, but were never the preferred models based on the minimum AIC criterion.

3. The preferred models based on the minimum AIC criterion all involved forward migration but displayed varying patterns with respect to optimal constraints on error rates and latent class proportions.

4. Three of the four preferred models based on the minimum AIC criterion (Domains 1, 2, and 4) included equality-of-error constraints across the treatment groups.

Table 9.10 Comparisons of Migration Models for Domain 4

Model	G^2	DF	p value	AIC
1	87.486	132	0.999	−176.514
2	106.282	144	0.992	−181.718
3	122.669	156	0.977	−189.331
4	210.843	168	0.014	−125.157
5	No Conv.	165		
6	301.953	177	0.000	−52.047
7	125.931	159	0.975	−192.069[a]
8	221.791	171	0.005	−120.209
9	149.732	150	0.491	−150.268
10	227.276	174	0.004	−120.724

NOTE: a. When minimum AIC value is used as the criterion, this is the preferred model.

Table 9.11 Estimated Proportion of Students Within Each Latent Class for Each of the Treatment Groups Obtained Under Preferred Models

Idealized Response Vector			Group	Item Domain 1	2	3	4
0	0	0	1	0.000	0.118	0.201	0.159
0	0	1		0.000	0.292	0.063	0.723
0	1	1		0.031	0.262	0.540	0.000
1	1	1		0.969	0.328	0.196	0.128
0	0	0	2	0.086	0.440	0.113	0.159
0	0	1		0.487	0.000	0.101	0.587
0	1	1		0.056	0.501	0.086	0.117
1	1	1		0.371	0.060	0.700	0.137
0	0	0	3	0.034	0.253	0.388	0.159
0	0	1		0.043	0.148	0.165	0.433
0	1	1		0.000	0.181	0.080	0.000
1	1	1		0.923	0.418	0.367	0.408

5. Although fixing latent class proportions to those estimated during the within-occasion analyses provided good fit for Domain 1, neither model based on this condition (Models 5 and 6) was satisfactory for the other three domains.

Table 9.12   Mean Estimated Error Rates Across Treatment Groups, Items, and Latent Classes for Each Occasion Obtained Under the Preferred Model

		Item Domain			
Error Type	*Occasion*	*1*	*2*	*3*	*4*
Intrusion	1	0.266	0.226	0.156	0.278
	2	0.791	0.205	0.061	0.496
	3	0.283	0.171	0.253	0.174
Omission	1	0.060	0.223	0.129	0.169
	2	0.057	0.107	0.255	0.195
	3	0.041	0.270	0.098	0.268

6. For Domain 4, which presumably represents the most advanced skill among those tested, the preferred model based on the minimum AIC criterion had equal proportions of non-acquirers across all three measurement occasions for the three treatment conditions.

7. The average intrusion and omission error rates from the preferred migration models (Table 9.12) compare favorably with those obtained during the within-occasion analyses (Table 9.3). In particular, the exceptionally high intrusion error rate for Domain 1 on the second measurement occasion recurs in both analyses.

8. For Domain 1, the preferred model, Model 6, was the most highly constrained model among the 10 compared. This domain, involving the relatively easy skill of adding fractions with common bases, displayed very high estimated proportions in the acquirer (i.e., 1 1 1) latent class for treatment groups 1 and 3. The negligible latent class proportions for some of these idealized response patterns suggest that simpler migration models might be appropriate.

(V) Assessment of Model Selection Procedures

While many early applications of LCA utilized differences among G^2 or Pearson χ^2 statistics to assess relative fit of competing, nested LCMs, recognition that this practice can, in certain cases, lead to misleading results has posed a major problem for real-world applications of LCA (as well as for mixture modeling, in general). Our own recent practice has been to utilize the Akaike information-theory-based measure, AIC, as discussed in Section 2c, above. For certain of the model comparisons that were reported, however, a difference-chi-squared model comparison approach would be appropriate since the constraints imposed on models did not involve restricting parameters to boundary values such as 0 or 1. In particular, for the within-occasion analyses reported in Table 9.2, comparisons between either of the two-class models with the independence model do violate the boundary-value condition, whereas comparisons between the two acquisition models represent a situation in which the simpler model can be obtained from the more complex model by simply imposing equality constraints across the manifest grouping variable. As is easily verified, differences in G^2 chi-squared values, with 2 degrees of freedom, result in three more cases (i.e., Domain 1, Occasion 3, Domain 3, Occasion 2, and Domain 4, Occasion 2) in which the simpler model (i.e., equal errors and equal latent class proportions across groups) would provide no worse fit than the more complex model (i.e., equal errors across groups only). An alternate approach to model selection, noted by Hagenaars (1990, p. 146), is to choose the model with the largest empirical p value for chi-squared. For the within-occasions models summarized in Table 9.2, this strategy provides decisions similar to those based on the minimum AIC criterion, with the exceptions that the independence model is never preferred and preference for the more complex acquisition model for Domain 3 on Occasion 3.

With respect to the migration models summarized in Tables 9.7-9.10, difference-chi-squared comparisons would be justified only within subsets of models based on the same migration conditions (i.e., the same set of latent classes). Thus, having decided on the basis of other evidence that forward migration models were preferable to no-migration or to unconstrained-migration models, it would be appropriate to utilize differences in G^2 values to assess relative fit among Models 2-8. An objection to this approach in the present context is that there is a total of $\binom{7}{2} = 21$ pair-wise comparisons that can be made among the seven models based on forward migration. Thus, for each domain, one would be required to conduct 21 separate, although correlated, chi-squared tests of significance, or a total of 84 such tests for the set of four domains. Our preference for the minimum AIC approach, even for nested models that do not involve boundary conditions, is partially motivated by an effort to avoid the conceptual difficulties that arise due to compounding Type I error rates when extremely large numbers of hypothesis tests are involved in order to arrive at interpretable results.

Related approaches, such as using modified significance levels based on the Bonferroni inequality, have the effect of heavily favoring more complex models since the required empirical p levels needed for significance become, for large numbers of tests, extremely conservative (e.g., with $\alpha = .05$ and 21 tests, the modified significance level for Bonferroni-type tests would be $.05/21 = .0024$).

If the alternate strategy of selecting the model with the largest empirical p value were applied to the 10 models for migration, the result is equivocal for Domain 1 since all empirical p values differ unsubstantially from 1.0. On the other hand, this strategy does pick the same model (Model 3) as minimum AIC for Domain 3. For Domains 3 and 4, however, where the model based on unconstrained migration is favored (Model 1) by the empirical p value strategy, we observe what we believe is a tendency for this approach to select unnecessarily complex models. This is especially apparent for Domain 4 (Table 9.10) in which several of the calculated G^2 chi-squared values are substantially smaller than their degrees of freedom. Thus, p values, alone, do not seem to provide any useful guidance in choosing among these well-fitting, but different, models.

4. Conclusion

This chapter presents a latent class conceptualization of longitudinal data as they might arise in social science settings. To provide a systematic basis for model building, the modeling has been divided into two stages. During the first stage, referred to as within-occasions, an effort is made to locate one, or a related set of two or more, reasonable latent class models for the acquisition of the skills represented at each occasion. Although the term *acquisition* has been utilized in this context since our primary focus has been on modeling development of skills in academic settings, generalization to other situations is straightforward. In a developmental context, for example, it might be more appropriate to replace "acquisition" by a term descriptive of a maturational stage (e.g., "post-operational").

At the second stage of modeling, the focus is on change over time. In the present context, this was described as migration between acquisition states. The use of idealized latent response vectors to represent time-related change, coupled with the notion of intrusion and omission errors, provides a general framework that encompasses situations involving instruction, development, and a variety of scaling frameworks.

Selecting an appropriate latent class model involves comparisons among competing models. In this regard, we illustrate—and argue for—the potential usefulness of the Akaike minimum AIC procedure. Although the results are not without some interpretive problems, the exemplary analyses based on pairs of test items on three occasions for three treatment groups provide a case study in applying relatively complex latent class models to a substantive problem in mathematics education.

Notes

1. Although the two stages of modeling could be combined to form a more general model, the present approach is adopted for two compelling reasons. First, conceptualizing the design is greatly simplified and, second, available computer programs, such as MLLSA, can be utilized.

2. A constant number of latent classes is assumed for the various levels of the grouping variable; the model can be generalized in an obvious manner.

References

Akaike, H. (1987). Factor analysis and AIC. *Psychometrika, 52,* 317-332.

Bergan, J. R. (1983). Latent-class models in educational research. In E. W. Gordon (Ed.), *Review of research in education, 10* (pp. 305-360). Washington, DC: American Educational Research Association.

Bergan, J. R., Cancelli, A. A., & Luiten, J. W. (1980). Mastery assessment with latent class and quasi-independence models representing homogeneous item domains. *Journal of Educational Statistics, 5,* 65-81.

Bozdogan, H. (1987). Model selection and Akaike's information criterion (AIC): The general theory and its analytical extensions. *Psychometrika, 52,* 345-370.

Clogg, C. C. (1977). *Unrestricted and restricted maximum likelihood latent structure analysis: A manual for users.* The Pennsylvania State University, University Park: Population Issues Research Office.

Clogg, C. C., & Goodman, L. A. (1984). Latent structure analysis of a set of multidimensional contingency tables. *Journal of the American Statistical Association, 79,* 762-771.

Clogg, C. C., & Goodman, L. A. (1985). Simultaneous latent structure analysis in several groups. In N. B. Tuma (Ed.), *Sociological methodology 1985* (pp. 81-110). San Francisco: Jossey-Bass.

Dayton, C. M., & Macready, G. B. (1976). A probabilistic model for validation of behavioral hierarchies. *Psychometrika, 41,* 189-204.

Dayton, C. M., & Macready, G. B. (1980). A scaling model with response errors and intrinsically unscalable respondents. *Psychometrika, 45,* 343-356.

Dayton, C. M., & Macready, G. B. (1983). Latent structure of repeated classifications with dichotomous data. *British Journal of Mathematical and Statistical Psychology, 36,* 189-201.

Dempster, A. P., Laird, N. M, & Rubin, D. B. (1977). Maximum likelihood from incomplete data via the EM algorithm. *Journal of the Royal Statistical Society, Series B, 39,* 1-38.

Everitt, B. S., & Hand, D. J. (1981). *Finite mixture models.* New York: Chapman & Hall.

Goodman, L. A. (1974). Exploratory latent structure analysis using both identifiable and unidentifiable models. *Biometrika, 61,* 215-231.

Goodman, L. A. (1975). A new model for scaling response patterns: An application of the quasi-independence concept. *Journal of the American Statistical Association, 70,* 755-768.

Haberman, S. J. (1977). Product models for frequency tables involving indirect observation. *Annals of Statistics, 5,* 1124-1147.

Hagenaars, J. A. (1990). *Categorical longitudinal data.* Newbury Park, CA: Sage.

Holt, J. A., & Macready, G. B. (1989). A simulation study of the difference chi-square statistic for comparing latent class models under violation of regularity conditions. *Applied Psychological Measurement, 13,* 221-231.

Langeheine, R., & Rost, J. (Eds.). (1988). *Latent trait and latent class models.* New York: Plenum.

Macready, G. B, & Dayton, C. M. (1977). The use of probabilistic models in the assessment of mastery. *Journal of Educational Statistics, 2,* 99-120.

Macready, G. B, & Dayton, C. M. (1980). The nature and use of state mastery models, *Applied Psychological Measurement, 4,* 493-516.

Macready, G. B., & Dayton, C. M. (1992). The application of latent class models in adaptive testing. *Psychometrika, 57,* 71-88.

Proctor, C. H. (1970). A probabilistic formulation and statistical analysis of Guttman scaling. *Psychometrika, 35,* 73-78.

Rindskopf, D. (1987). Using latent class analysis to test developmental models. *Developmental Review, 20,* 66-85.

Schwarz, G. (1978). Estimating the dimension of a model. *Annals of Statistics, 6,* 461-464.

Sclove, S. L. (1987). Application of model-selection criteria to some problems in multivariate analysis. *Psychometrika, 52,* 333-343.

Titterington, D. M., Smith, A.F.M., & Makov, U. E. (1985). *Statistical analysis of finite mixture models.* New York: John Wiley.

Wiggins, L. M. (1973). *Panel analysis: Latent probability models for attitudinal and behavior processes.* Amsterdam, The Netherlands: Elsevier.

10

Latent Trait Models
for Measuring Change

CHRISTIANE SPIEL

1. Introduction

The present chapter deals with latent trait models for assessing change in dichotomous item score matrices (for measuring change in ordinal items see e.g., Rost, 1989). First, concepts of global, item-specific, and subject-specific change are introduced by applying the well-known model for analysis of variance (ANOVA) to item response probabilities (Rost & Spada, 1983). Depending on the type and number of first-order interactions taken into account, eight change models are distinguished. They are formulated as logistic test models for dichotomous items. Problems of parameter estimation and interpretation are discussed.

Second, a special class of these models, the linear logistic model with relaxed assumptions (LLRA; Fischer, 1974) is presented, which does not require unidimensionality of item sets. Both the simplest case of the LLRA and generalizations—hybrid models—are discussed. Third, two different types of applications of hybrid LLRA are illustrated using data. Finally, adaptations of such models for long-term developmental research are outlined.

2. Analysis of Variance Models for Assessing Change in Dichotomous Dependent Variables

To simplify notation, a three-dimensional data matrix is used. The cells vit of the data matrix contain the probabilities of positive reactions p_{vit} for subject v to item i at time point t. The following equation shows the ANOVA model if only the three main effects are assumed:

$$p_{vit} = \pi + \alpha_v + \beta_i + \gamma_t + \varepsilon_{vit} \qquad [10.1]$$

where

π is the grand mean;
α_v is the ability level of subject v;
β_i is the difficulty of item i;
γ_t is the effect of time point t; and
e_{vit} is the residual term.

This restricted model can be expanded by including one or more first order interaction parameters. The following equation shows the complete first order interaction model:

$$p_{vit} = \pi + \alpha_v + \beta_i + \gamma_t + \varphi_{vi} + \chi_{vt} + \psi_{it} + \varepsilon_{vit}, \qquad [10.2]$$

where

χ_{vt} denotes subject-specific change,
ψ_{it} denotes item-specific change, and
φ_{vi} denotes item × subject interaction.

Introduction of the second-order parameter w_{vit} into (10.2) results in the saturated model; this model has no residual term.

3. Latent Trait Models for Assessing Change

In item response-theories the relationship between the observed data and the latent-trait parameters is usually given by the logistic function (e.g., Andersen, 1980; Rasch, 1977):

$$p_{vit} = \frac{\exp(\lambda_{vit})}{1 + \exp(\lambda_{vit})} \qquad [10.3]$$

In Equation (10.3) the relationship between p_{vit} and λ_{vit} is *tautological,* analogously to the ANOVA model that includes the second-order interaction. If restrictions are applied as in ANOVA, eight latent trait models for assessing change can be distinguished. These models differ in type and number of first-order interactions considered (see Rost & Spada, 1983; Scheiblechner, 1971b).

The following section presents a taxonomy of these models; the most restricted model (I) includes the three main effects:

$$p_{vit} = \frac{\exp(\xi_v + \sigma_i + \delta_t)}{1 + \exp(\xi_v + \sigma_i + \delta_t)}, \qquad [10.4]$$

where in latent-trait models

ξ_v is a subject parameter,

σ_i is an item parameter, and

δ_t is a time point parameter.

This model, which is analogous to (10.1), corresponds to the multifactorial Rasch model (e.g. Scheiblechner, 1971a; discussed by Spada, 1973). The temporal change in (10.4) is identical for all subjects and all items.

If, analogously to ANOVA, first-order interactions are included, three models result with one interaction parameter each (Models II, III, IV), three models with two interaction parameters each (Models V, VI, VII), and one model including all three first-order interaction parameters (Model VIII). Figure 10.1 shows the eight latent trait models and relations between them (Rost & Spada, 1983). Model (I) is the most restricted one and models at the lower layer are generalizations of connected models at the upper layer.

Models (II), (III), and (IV) reorganize the three-dimensional data matrix to two-dimensional ones while keeping one type of parameter constant. Model (II) quantifies subject-specific changes while item parameters are constant for all subjects and all time-points, and Model (III) quantifies item-specific changes while subject parameters are constant over time. In both cases homogeneity of items across subjects is assumed. This is not true for Model (IV) which allows subject × item

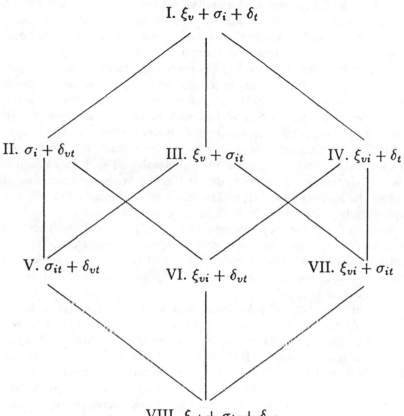

Figure 10.1. Eight Latent Trait Models for Assessing Change and Relations Between Them (see Rost & Spada, 1983, Fig. 2) (The models are derived from the general logistic change model for dichotomous data by applying additive restrictions on λ_{vit}, see Equation (3).)

interaction parameters. Model (IV) quantifies time-specific changes. This model was investigated by Fischer (1974, 1976, 1977a, 1977b, 1983, 1989a). In the following section generalizations of that model and some applications are presented. Models in the lower layer involve two interaction parameters each. Model (VIII) includes all three interaction parameters. In addition, for Models (VI), (VII), and (VIII) the assumption of item homogeneity is dropped.

Andersen (1985) presented a multidimensional Rasch model for the repeated administration of the same items at different time points (conditions) based on Model (II). A model for conditions in which items are not repeated is presented by Embretson (1991).

In principle, for all these models parameters can be estimated that have the same characteristics as parameters in the dichotomous Rasch model (Scheiblechner, 1971b). A controversial question concerns the scale level of the parameters of the Rasch model (e.g., Roskam, 1983). Fischer (1989b) argued in favor of an interval scale. This debate is related to the arguments regarding the topic of "specific objectivity." This term stands for the basic idea of Rasch's (1977) measurement theory. Under the assumption that the model holds, comparisons of subject parameters do not depend on the sample of items and/or subjects under study. This is correct for other model parameters, too. Only the accuracy of estimates depends on the samples. Fischer (1989b) demonstrated that the postulate of specific objective comparisons among subjects and items is necessary and sufficient for the Rasch model (for an overview of recent developments in psychometrics and test theory see Rost & Strauss, 1992).

Rost and Spada (1983) discussed what kinds of parameters actually can be estimated and whether estimates are accurate. To illustrate, they give a numerical example: A test or questionnaire consisting of 20 items is presented to 100 subjects at three points in time. Therefore, depending on what model is applied, various numbers of parameters must be estimated: To assess temporal changes, three parameters must be estimated; to assess item-specific changes, 60 parameters must be estimated; and to assess subject × item interactions, 2,000 parameters must be estimated. Accuracy of parameter estimation depends on the number of responses to items available. This number is inversely related to the number of parameters to be estimated.

4. The Linear Logistic Model With Relaxed Assumptions (LLRA)

The LLRA developed by Fischer (1974) is a generalization of Model (IV). It allows one to quantify changes in experimental and quasi-experimental designs. (For relations between causal inference and experimental designs see Sobel, Chapter 13, and Steyer & Schmitt, Chapter 15, in this volume.) In the simplest case two subject groups are observed at two points in time. Because of different subject groups notation is changed from δ_t to δ_v, see Equation 10.11. In experimental designs, changes across time points are of interest. Therefore, δ_v is set to zero at time point T_1. At time point T_2, δ_v is split up in effects of treatment and trend, see Equations 10.5 to 10.8. For example, subjects can be kindergarten students, assigned to an experimental and a control condition. Responses of all subjects to the same k dichotomous items I_i ($i = 1, \ldots, k$), measuring k different dimensions, for example, verbal competence, logical thinking, and social comprehension, are observed at both time points, T_1 and T_2. (In that case, T is not a random variable.) Subjects in the control group (Group 1) S_v ($v = 1, \ldots, n$) are untreated. For instance, they attend a traditional kindergarten program. Subjects in the experimental group (Group 2) S_v ($v = n + 1, \ldots, N$) undergo a treatment during the time period $[T_1, T_2]$, for example, a training program in social contact behavior. Assuming logistic item characteristic curves (ICCs) for all items I_i, the following equations specify the basic LLRA:

$$\text{Group 1} \qquad p(+ \mid S_v, I_i, T_1) = \frac{\exp(\xi_{vi})}{1 + \exp(\xi_{vi})} \qquad [10.5]$$

$$p(+ \mid S_v, I_i, T_2) = \frac{\exp(\xi_{vi} + \tau)}{1 + \exp(\xi_{vi} + \tau)} \qquad [10.6]$$

$$\text{Group 2} \qquad p(+ \mid S_v, I_i, T_1) = \frac{\exp(\xi_{vi})}{1 + \exp(\xi_{vi})} \qquad [10.7]$$

$$p(+ \mid S_v, I_i, T_2) = \frac{\exp(\xi_{vi} + \tau + \eta)}{1 + \exp(\xi_{vi} + \tau + \eta)} \qquad [10.8]$$

where

(10.5) to (10.8) describe the probabilities of positive responses for subject S_v to item I_i at time points T_1 and T_2; responses are considered realizations of locally independent Bernoulli variables,

ξ_{vi} is the subject × item interaction (see Model (IV)), or, more specifically, the latent ability of subject S_v on the latent dimension D_i. Item I_i is an indicator of D_i, at time point T_1,

η is the effect of treatment given to Group 2, assumed to be the same on each of the latent dimensions D_i within $[T_1, T_2]$,

τ is the "trend" effect comprising all causes of change that are unrelated to the treatment.

As mentioned above, the LLRA assumes subject $\times$ item interactions, that is, item-specific subject parameters. Subjects are not characterized by a parameter but rather by a vector with k parameters, $\xi_{v1}, \ldots, \xi_{vk}$. Each item I_i measures the position of individual P_v on latent dimension D_i. No assumptions are made concerning relationships between the k dimensions; they can be completely independent, or correlated, or functionally dependent, or identical. Thus, the LLRA can be applied in a rather flexible fashion.

The treatment effect η and the trend τ do not depend on the item considered. Given the model holds, the treatment is assumed to induce the same effect η for all subjects in Group 2. In addition, all treatment-unrelated influences are assumed to induce the same change τ in all subjects in both groups. These assumptions must be tested in each empirical application of the LLRA.

The trend and treatment parameter estimates do not depend on the distribution of the subject parameters in the sample since the subject parameters may be factored out of the estimation equation using conditional maximum likelihood (CLM) methods (see Fischer 1989a; Formann & Spiel, 1989). The separability of the parameters can be seen from the log odds ratios (see Formann & Spiel, 1989).

$$\text{Group 1:} \quad l_1 = \tau$$

$$\text{Group 2:} \quad l_2 = \tau + \eta \qquad [10.9]$$

Necessary and sufficient conditions for the existence of unique finite solutions for the LLRA were given (e.g., by Fischer, 1983). Treatment and trend effects are measured on a ratio scale when treatment levels can be placed on a ratio scale, which is trivial when there is only one treatment condition.

Typically, the main purpose of applying the model is to test a variety of hypotheses. Using the likelihood ratio statistic one can test many hypotheses concerning structural parameters in the form of "conditional likelihood ratio tests" (CLR tests) yielding asymptotic χ^2-statistics (Andersen, 1973, 1980). Typical hypotheses are listed below:

a. The effect of the treatment and/or the trend is 0, that is, $\eta = 0$. (Rejection of this hypothesis usually is trivial.)

b. Treatment and trend effects are generalizable over subjects. Rejection of this H_0 is typical in empirical applications. For example, kindergarten girls in the experimental group may benefit more from the training program than boys, η (girls) > η (boys). An analogous result may hold for the trend effect.

c. In analogy to generalizability over subjects, generalizability over items can be evaluated. H_0: All latent dimensions indicated by the items are equally affected by treatment and trend. A reason for rejection of this hypothesis may be that subjects in the treatment condition show a steeper increase in items measuring social competence $(I_i, i = 1, \ldots, l)$ than in the rest of the items $(I_j, j = l + 1, \ldots, k)$, that is, η (items I_i) > η (items I_j).

In general, testing multiple hypotheses requires splitting samples of subjects and/or items into homogeneous subgroups, that is, subgroups of individuals that react similarly to treatments and in subsamples of items that are equally sensitive to change (see Fischer, 1989a).

The standard version of the LLRA described by Equations 10.5 to 10.8 can be generalized to more than two groups with various treatments or treatment combinations. To cover all possible cases, the model is modified as follows:

$$P(+ \mid S_v, I_i, T_1) = \frac{\exp(\xi_{vi})}{1 + \exp(\xi_{vi})} \qquad [10.10]$$

$$P(+ \mid S_v, I_i, T_2) = \frac{\exp(\xi_{vi} + \delta_v)}{1 + \exp(\xi_{vi} + \delta_v)} \qquad [10.11]$$

where δ_v, the amount of change subject S_v exhibits in time period $[T_1, T_2]$, is given as:

$$\delta_v = \sum_{j=1}^{m} q_{vj} \eta_j + \sum_{j=1}^{m-1} \sum_{\substack{h= \\ j+1}}^{m} q_{vj} q_{vh} \gamma_{jh} + \tau \qquad [10.12]$$

where

η_j is the (unknown) effect of one unit of treatment T_j on subjects' position on each of the latent dimensions D_i within $[T_1, T_2]$,

q_{vj} is the (known) amount of treatment T_j applied to subject S_v within $[T_1, T_2]$; for example, hours of training program for kindergarten students,

q_{vh} is the (known) amount of treatment T_h applied to subject S_v within $[T_1, T_2]$,

γ_{jh} is the interaction between treatments T_j and T_h if applied simultaneously; for example, the interaction between training programs in social competence and logical thinking in kindergarten students,

τ is the trend.

(Remember, this model still captures global change. The notation δ_v is used because the amount of change is assumed to be different for subjects getting different treatments or treatment combinations.)

The following constraints limit application of LLRA (for more details see Formann & Spiel, 1989):

a. The assumption that reactions on the same items when presented twice are locally independent excludes potential learning and memory effects (see Krauth, 1983).

b. If changes between T_1 and T_2 are solely in one direction, which can be expected in developmental studies, especially in very young children, point estimates for the corresponding parameter cannot be obtained.

c. If most of the items show no or merely minor changes within $[T_1, T_2]$, parameter estimates only depend on a small portion of the data and become extremely unreliable, because the CML method uses only that part of the items for parameter estimation for which changes have been observed.

5. Hybrid LLRA

To overcome the preceding limitations, the LLRA was generalized by using pairs of items that differ in difficulty level but measure the same latent dimension. This extension was termed "hybrid LLRA" (Fischer, 1977a, 1986, 1989a) because it combines the assumption of multidimensionality across pairs of items with the assumption of unidimensionality within pairs of items. If large changes between T_1 and T_2 are expected—massive treatment effects and/or a massive trend effect—the more difficult item out of each pair is presented at the time point where the probability of a positive reaction is expected to be higher (for parameter estimation see Formann & Spiel, 1989). If only small changes are expected for about half of the item pairs the easier, and for about half of them the more difficult, item is presented at both time points. This rules out possible learning and memory effects and, in addition, artificially increases the number of observable changes.

For the simplest case of the hybrid LLRA with two groups observed at two times, the equations are:

$$\text{Group 1} \quad P(+ \mid S_v, I_i, T_1) = \frac{\exp(\xi_{vi} - \sigma_{i1})}{1 + \exp(\xi_{vi} - \sigma_{i1})} \qquad [10.13]$$

$$P(+ \mid S_v, I_i, T_2) = \frac{\exp(\xi_{vi} + \tau - \sigma_{i2})}{1 + \exp(\xi_{vi} + \tau - \sigma_{i2})} \qquad [10.14]$$

$$\text{Group 2} \quad P(+ \mid S_v, I_i, T_1) = \frac{\exp(\xi_{vi} - \sigma_{i1})}{1 + \exp(\xi_{vi} - \sigma_{i1})} \qquad [10.15]$$

$$P(+ \mid S_v, I_i, T_2) = \frac{\exp(\xi_{vi} + \tau + \eta - \sigma_{i2})}{1 + \exp(\xi_{vi} + \tau + \eta - \sigma_{i2})} \qquad [10.16]$$

where σ_{i1} is the difficulty of item I_{i1} presented at T_1 and σ_{i2} is the difficulty of item I_{i2} presented at T_2 both measuring the same latent dimension D_i. The difference d_i between item difficulties, $d_i = (\sigma_{i2} - \sigma_{i1})$, appears in the log odds ratios as an additional parameter (see Formann & Spiel, 1989).

The problem with this model is that the trend effect is confounded with the differences between item difficulties. Therefore, the trend effect is identified only if the item parameters are known a priori.

The hybrid LLRA can be extended analogously to the standard version. An extension of the model to rating scales was presented by Fischer and Parzer (1991). The hybrid LLRA as well as the standard LLRA can be interpreted as "linear logistic test models" (LLTM) for incomplete data (see Fischer, 1989a; Formann & Spiel, 1989). (For a model description see Fischer, 1983. The LLTM and more general models are discussed by e.g., Embretson, 1989.) The general uniqueness condition for the LLTM was used for deriving a uniqueness condition for the hybrid LLRA (Fischer, 1989a). [For the linear rating scale model, LRSM (Fischer & Parzer, 1991), the exact conditions of the existence and uniqueness of a CML solution could not be shown so far.]

6. Applications of the Hybrid LLRA

In this section, two applications of the hybrid LLRA are presented. In the first example the item difficulties are unknown and in the second the item difficulties are known.

Empirical Example 1

Formann and Spiel (1989; Spiel & Formann, 1988) investigated effects of training text comprehension. 102 students (49 girls and 53 boys) from four classes in one school in Vienna (Austria) participated. In a pretest (time point 1), after reading a story subjects were asked to complete the following four tasks: (1) label the paragraphs, (2) the key passages of the story, (3) write a summary, and (4) identify the message of the story. Then the four classes were randomly assigned to one of four conditions:

> Control Condition: Subjects were not trained in extracting text summaries and were not presented with similar stories.
>
> Experimental Condition 1: Subjects were presented with similar stories but not trained in text comprehension.
>
> Experimental Condition 2: Subjects were trained regarding text structure (Thorndyke, 1977) and forming text summaries (Kintsch & van Dijk, 1978).
>
> Experimental Condition 3: Subjects were trained as under Condition 2. In addition, a similar training was performed using pictures.

In the posttest (time point 2), subjects had to accomplish the same four tasks as in the pretest on a more difficult story (expert ratings) than in pretest. Two raters scored the students' answers as either correct or incorrect. Interrater agreement was greater than 90%.

As mentioned above, difficulties of the tasks were unknown. Thus, the trend τ and the difference of item difficulties, d_i, were confounded, $\tau_i^* = \tau_i - d_i$. Therefore, in the present study interpretation of τ_i is impossible. Even if τ_i^* is constant over subgroups of subjects, one cannot conclude that both τ_i and d_i are constant. Similar problems arise when constancy of trend across items is investigated.

For the "saturated model" changes were assumed to depend on treatment conditions (0, . . . , 3) and on subjects' gender [girls (g), boys (b)] which corresponds to a 4 × 2 design with eight effect parameters. The

Table 10.1 Empirical Example 1: Design Matrices for Different Hypotheses [In the parameters η and τ^*, indices denote: girls (g), boys (b), experimental conditions (0, . . . ,3).]

Hypothesis H_0 (saturated model), design matrix W_0:

		η_{1g}	η_{1b}	η_{2g}	η_{2b}	η_{3g}	η_{3b}	τ_g^*	τ_b^*
Control Condition	girls	0	0	0	0	0	0	1	0
	boys	0	0	0	0	0	0	0	1
Exp. Cond. 1	girls	1	0	0	0	0	0	1	0
	boys	0	1	0	0	0	0	0	1
Exp. Cond. 2	girls	0	0	1	0	0	0	1	0
	boys	0	0	0	1	0	0	0	1
Exp. Cond. 3	girls	0	0	0	0	1	0	1	0
	boys	0	0	0	0	0	1	0	1

Hypothesis H_6, design matrix W_6:

	η_1	η_2	η_3
Control Condition	0	0	0
Exp. Cond. 1	1	0	0
Exp. Cond. 2	0	1	0
Exp. Cond. 3	0	0	1

Hypothesis H_{10}, design matrix W_{10}:

		η_g	η_b
Control Condition		0	0
Exp. Conditions	girls	1	0
	boys	0	1

Hypothesis H_{12}, design matrix W_{12}:

	η
Control Condition	0
Exp. Conditions	1

NOTE: The design matrix W_2 for hypothesis H_2 is identical to W_0 without the last two columns.

design matrix is shown in Table 10.1. Relations to the log odds ratios of the subgroups are given below:

Control Condition	Girls:	$l_{0g} = \tau_g^*$
	Boys:	$l_{0b} = \tau_b^*$

Experimental Condition 1	Girls:	$l_{1g} = \tau_g^* + \eta_{1g}$
	Boys:	$l_{1b} = \tau_b^* + \eta_{1b}$

Table 10.2 Hierarchy of Hypotheses Concerning the Changes
Attributable to the Treatments and to the Trend,
Assumptions for η and τ, Number of Parameters
Estimated, and Results of the Likelihood Ratio Test
(LRT) (see Formann & Spiel, 1989, Table 1)

Hypothesis	η	τ	Parameters	$\ln L$	$\frac{LRT}{H_i\ vs.\ H^*}$	df	χ_0^2
H^*	G×T	G	8	−103.61	−	−	−
H_1	G×T	+	7	−103.85	.48	1	3.84
H_2	G×T	−	6	−104.06	.90	2	5.99
H_3	T	G	5	−108.70	10.18	3	7.82
H_4	T	+	4	−110.00	12.78	4	9.49
H_5	G	G	4	−111.07	14.92	4	
H_6	T	−	3	−110.21	13.20	5	11.07
H_7	+	G	3	−111.11	15.00	5	
H_8	G	+	3	−111.31	15.40	5	
H_9	+	+	2	−111.50	15.78	6	12.59
H_{10}	G	−	2	−111.52	15.82	6	
H_{11}	−	G	2	−111.69	16.16	6	
H_{12}	+	−	1	−111.71	16.20	7	14.07
H_{13}	−	+	1	−112.09	16.96	7	

NOTE: G×T indicates that effect parameters may vary across gender by treatment combinations (interaction).
G and T indicate that parameters are estimated for gender or treatment. "+" indicates that a constant parameter
η is estimated that does not vary across gender categories, or a constant parameter τ is estimated that depends
on neither treatment nor gender. "−" indicates that no parameter is estimated.

Experimental Condition 2   Girls: $l_{2g} = \tau_g^* + \eta_{2g}$

Boys: $l_{2b} = \tau_b^* + \eta_{2b}$

Experimental Condition 3   Girls: $l_{3g} = \tau_g^* + \eta_{3g}$

Boys: $l_{3b} = \tau_b^* + \eta_{3b}$ [10.17]

Each of the restricted hypotheses considered is obtained from the saturated model by fixing parameters, setting parameters equal, or deleting
parameters. Table 10.2 shows all possible hypotheses. However, because
of the confounded trend only H_2 (no trend, but gender-specific effects for
all treatment conditions), H_6 (no trend, treatment-specific effects, no treatment × gender interaction), H_{10} (no trend; identical, but gender-specific
treatment effects), and H_{12} (no trend and identical effects of all treatments),
are of interest. (The design matrices are shown in Table 10.1.)

Table 10.3 Parameter Estimates for the Treatment Effects Under Hypothesis H_2 (see Formann & Spiel, 1989, Table 2)

H_2	Girls	Boys
τ^*	—	—
η_1	.693	.547
η_2	−.405	1.386
η_3	1.041	−.916

These models were contrasted to the saturated model by means of the likelihood ratio statistic

$$-2\ln\lambda = 2(\ln L_0 - \ln L) \qquad [10.18]$$

which is asymptotically distributed as χ^2 with degrees of freedom df $= h_0 - h$. L_0 denotes the likelihood for the saturated model H_0 assuming h_0 parameters are used in the saturated model, and L denotes the likelihood for a restricted model H with h parameters, $h < h_0$.

As Table 10.2 shows, H_{12}, H_{10}, and H_6 are rejected, while H_2 is accepted. Table 10.3 shows parameter estimates for H_2. The trend that is confounded with differences between item difficulties can be neglected. In addition, the likelihood ratio test suggests generalizability of the gender-specific treatment effects across all items.

Empirical Example 2

Barisch (1989) investigated the effects of information about epilepsy on attitudes toward epileptics. The experimental design she used differed in two aspects from the study presented above. First, item difficulties were assessed in a calibration study; second, pretest, treatment, and posttest were presented to subjects at the same occasion in one questionnaire.

Barisch developed a questionnaire that covered six areas of prejudices against epileptics. These are (1) attitudes toward separation of epileptics, (2) attitudes toward epileptic children, (3) attitudes toward marriage and reproduction of epileptics, (4) assumptions concerning employment of epileptics, (5) assumptions concerning epileptics' cognitive competence, and (6) general prejudices against epileptics.

In a calibration study the questionnaire was administered to 196 university students (99 females and 97 males) to establish item homogeneity within the subscales and to assess item difficulties using likelihood ratio tests. After revision the questionnaire consisted of 50 items, which were, separately for each subscale, grouped in pairs of homogeneous items of different item difficulty.

In the main study the easier item out of each pair was presented in the first part of the questionnaire, and the more difficult item was presented in the second part. Subjects were 265 teachers (172 females and 93 males; mean age = 37.2 years, SD = 8.6 years) from 18 schools in Vienna. Teachers were selected because of their influence on attitude formation in children. Subjects were randomly assigned to the treatment or the control group. Treatment group subjects (132 subjects) were presented with two pages of educational material between the two parts of the questionnaire covering types and causes of epilepsies and relations between epilepsies and mental retardation. In the control group (133 subjects) the two questionnaire parts were presented without any interruption.

For the "saturated model," changes were assumed to depend on treatment [Control Condition (1), Experimental Condition (2)], gender [female (f), male (m)] and age [younger/equal 37 years (y) versus older than 37 years (o)] of subjects, and knowledge about epilepsy [good knowledge (g) versus poor knowledge (p)]. This corresponded to a $2 \times 2 \times 2 \times 2$ design with 16 effect parameters. In that study the "true" trend could be estimated because item difficulties were known. Relations to the log odds ratios are given below:

Control Condition

$$l_{1fyg} = \tau_{fyg}$$
$$l_{1fyp} = \tau_{fyp}$$
$$l_{1fog} = \tau_{fog}$$
$$l_{1fop} = \tau_{fop}$$
$$l_{1myg} = \tau_{myg}$$
$$l_{1myp} = \tau_{myp}$$
$$l_{1mog} = \tau_{mog}$$
$$l_{1mop} = \tau_{mop}$$

Experimental Condition

$$l_{2fyg} = \tau_{fyg} + \eta_{fyg}$$
$$l_{2fyp} = \tau_{fyp} + \eta_{fyp}$$

$$l_{2fog} = \tau_{fog} + \eta_{fog}$$
$$l_{2fop} = \tau_{fop} + \eta_{fop}$$
$$l_{2myg} = \tau_{myg} + \eta_{myg}$$
$$l_{2myp} = \tau_{myp} + \eta_{myp}$$
$$l_{2mog} = \tau_{mog} + \eta_{mog}$$
$$l_{2mop} = \tau_{mop} + \eta_{mop} \qquad [10.19]$$

By equating or deleting certain parameters a large number of restricted hypotheses can be tested. Results showed that the restricted model that assumes a general treatment effect and a general trend is acceptable, with $\eta = .27$ and $\tau = .56$. Testing this model against the saturated model yields $\chi^2 = 2(1{,}285.97 - 1{,}276.37) = 19.21$ with df = 14, which is not significant at $\alpha = .05$. Thus, we can conclude that the more constrained model is not significantly inferior to the saturated model.

In a next step it was investigated whether the six areas considered in the questionnaire are influenced in the same way by the treatment and/or the trend. Results showed that only area (5), assumptions concerning epileptics' cognitive competence, was positively changed by treatment but not via trend; areas (1), (2), (4), and (6) were positively changed via trend but not by treatment. Area (4), assumptions concerning marriage and reproduction of epileptics, was not changed at all.

7. Discussion and Outlook

The present chapter encourages application of logistic test models to quantify subject-specific and item-specific changes. Eight change models are presented. One class of these models, the LLRA and the hybrid LLRA, is discussed in more detail. The standard LLRA assumes item-specific subject parameters and thus does not require unidimensionality of item sets. The hybrid LLRA circumvents problems where the standard LLRA may fail, for example, when changes due to memory are present.

Yet, empirical application of the hybrid model can cause problems if item difficulties are not already known. In this case, there are two options: First, item parameters can be determined in an independent calibration study that usually is very extensive; second, the trend effect

Step 1: Presentation of k dichotomous items

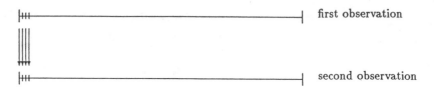

Step 2: Statistical analysis

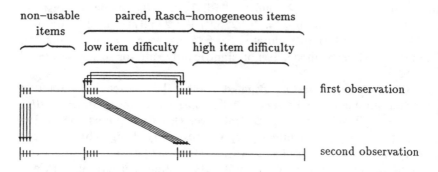

Figure 10.2. Procedure Application of Hybrid LLRA When Item Difficulties and Item Affiliations to Latent Dimensions Are Unknown (The procedure is shown for the case of expected changes between the two time points. To apply hybrid LLRA at time point 1 the "easy" items and at time point 2 the "difficult" items are used.)

is confounded with the item parameters and only treatment effects can be interpreted.

To overcome these problems the following procedure is suggested for which a typical case of item collection is assumed (see Figure 10.2).

A set of k dichotomously scored items with unknown item difficulties and with unknown position on one or more latent dimensions is presented at the two time points, T_1 and T_2, to a sample of n subjects. Within the interval $[T_1, T_2]$ subjects are assigned to different treatment conditions. Items are analyzed to identify pairs of items that both measure the same latent dimension and—if changes within the time period are assumed—differ in difficulty. Such item pairs are used in the hybrid

LLRA; one item out of each pair is represented at time point 1—if increases are expected the easier ones—while the other item of the pair is administered at time point 2. The probability is high that pairs of homogeneous items can be identified. However, items with no "parallel" item cannot be used in applications of hybrid LLRA.

This approach can easily be generalized to more than two time points and provides special advantages for developmental research. In longitudinal studies different instruments must often be applied to adequately assess the same latent dimension according to the current developmental level of the subjects. Thus, it is difficult to identify developmental changes, because differences in results may reflect either changes in latent dimensions, or differences caused by the instruments, or both. This problem is often discussed in the literature, but no definite solution is given. The approach presented above may allow one to circumvent that problem. From the first measurement point on, the original data set is extended by adding more difficult items while the easiest items are deleted. Thus, at each of two subsequent measurement points subjects are presented with a set of paired items. In the longitudinal approach, vectors of homogeneous items with one item per measurement point result. Finally, the hybrid LLRA is applied to these item vectors. This approach allows one to measure latent dimensions in developmental research without changing instruments. However, some problems arise; for example, large data sets are necessary because the number of items that cannot be used for applying hybrid LLRA is unknown before. Nevertheless, for developmental research it may be a useful approach to quantifying change.

References

Andersen, E. B. (1973). A goodness of fit test for the Rasch model. *Psychometrika, 38,* 123-140.

Andersen, E. B. (1980). *Discrete statistical models with social science applications.* Amsterdam: North-Holland.

Andersen, E. B. (1985). Estimating latent correlations between repeated testings. *Psychometrika, 50,* 3-16.

Barisch, S. (1989). *Einstellung zur Epilepsie und Einstellungsänderung durch Information.* [Attitudes toward epilepsy and information as a cause for attitude change.] Unpublished master's thesis, University of Vienna, Vienna. (In German.)

Embretson, S. E. (1989). Latent trait models as an information-processing approach to testing. *International Journal of Educational Research, 13,* 189-203.

Embretson, S. E. (1991). A multidimensional latent trait model for measuring learning and change. *Psychometrika, 56,* 495-515.

Fischer, G. H. (1974). *Einführung in die Theorie psychologischer Tests.* [Introduction to psychometric test theory.] Bern: Huber. (In German.)

Fischer, G. H. (1976). Some probabilistic models for measuring change. In D.N.M. de Gruijter & L. J. Th. van der Kamp (Eds.), *Advances in psychological and educational measurement* (pp. 97-110). New York: John Wiley.

Fischer, G. H. (1977a). Linear logistic latent trait models: Theory and application. In H. Spada & W. F. Kempf (Eds.), *Structural models of thinking and learning* (pp. 203-225). Bern: Huber.

Fischer, G. H. (1977b). Some probabilistic models for the description of attitudinal and behavioral changes under the influence of mass communication. In W. F. Kempf & B. Repp (Eds.), *Mathematical models for social psychology* (pp. 102-151). Bern: Huber.

Fischer, G. H. (1983). Logistic latent trait models with linear constraints. *Psychometrika, 48,* 3-26.

Fischer, G. H. (1986). Ein probabilistischer Ansatz der Veränderungsmessung. [A probabilistic approach for measurement of change.] In H. Pettilon, J.W.L. Wagner, & B. Wolf (Eds.), *Theoretische und empirische Beiträge zur pädagogischen Psychologie* (pp. 159-185). Weinheim: Beltz. (In German.)

Fischer, G. H. (1987). Applying the principles of specific objectivity and generalizability to the measurement of change. *Psychometrika, 52,* 565-587.

Fischer, G. H. (1989a). An IRT-based model for dichotomous longitudinal data. *Psychometrika, 54,* 599-624.

Fischer, G. H. (1989b). Spezifische Objektivität: Eine wissenschaftstheoretische Grundlage des Rasch-Modells. [Specific objectivity: The fundamental principle of the Raschmodel.] In K. D. Kubinger (Ed.), *Moderne Testtheorie* (pp. 87-112). Weinheim: Beltz. (In German.)

Fischer G. H., & Parzer, P. (1991). An extension of the rating scale model with an application to the measurement of change. *Psychometrika, 56,* 637-651.

Formann, A. K., & Spiel, C. (1989). Measuring change by means of a hybrid variant of the linear logistic model with relaxed assumptions. *Applied Psychological Measurement, 13,* 91-103.

Kintsch, W., & van Dijk, T. A. (1978). Toward a model of text comprehension and production. *Psychological Review, 85,* 363-394.

Krauth, J. (1983). Bewertung der Änderungssensitivität von Items. [Assessing item sensitivity to change.] *Zeitschrift für Differentielle und Diagnostische Psychologie, 4,* 7-28. (In German.)

Rasch, G. (1967). An informal report on a theory of objectivity in comparisons. In L. T. Th. van der Kamp & C.A.J. Vlek (Eds.), *Measurement theory* (pp. 1-19). Leyden: University of Leyden. (Proceedings of the NUFFIC International Summer Session in Science in "Het Oude Hof," The Hague, July 14-28, 1966.)

Rasch, G. (1977). On specific objectivity. An attempt at formalizing the request for generality and validity of scientific statements. In M. Blegvad (Ed.), *The Danish yearbook of philosophy* (pp. 58-94). Copenhagen: Munksgaard.

Roskam, E. E. (1983). Allgemeine Datentheorie [General theory about data.] In H. Feger & J. Bredenkamp (Eds.), *Messen und Testen. Enzyklopädie der Psychologie, Themenbereich B: Methodologie und Methoden, Serie I: Forschungsmethoden der Psychologie, Band 3* (pp. 1-124). Göttingen: Hogrefe. (In German.)

Rost, J. (1989). Rasch models and latent class models for measuring change with ordinal variables. In R. Coppi & S. Bolasco (Eds.), *Multiway data analysis* (pp. 473-483). Amsterdam: Elsevier.

Rost, J., & Spada, H. (1983). Die Quantifizierung von Lerneffekten anhand von Testdaten (Quantifying practice effects in test data). *Zeitschrift für Differentielle und Diagnostische Psychologie, 4,* 29-49. (In German.)

Rost, J. & Strauss, B. (1992). Recent developments in psychometrics and test theory. *The German Journal of Psychology, 16,* 91-119.

Scheiblechner, H. (1971a). CML-parameter estimation in a generalized multifactorial version of Rasch's probabilistic measurement model with two categories of answers. *Research Bulletin 4.* Vienna: University of Vienna, Department of Psychology.

Scheiblechner, H. (1971b). The separation of individual- and system influences on behavior in social contexts. *Acta Psychologica, 35,* 442-460.

Spada, H. (1973). Die Analyse kognitiver Lerneffekte mit stichprobenunabhängigen Verfahren. [Analysis of cognitive learning effects using sample independent methods.] *Kognitionspsychologie und naturwissenschaftlicher Unterricht.* Bern: Huber. (In German.)

Spiel, C., & Formann, A. K. (1988). Veränderungsmessung mit paarweise homogenen Items. [The measurement of change based on pairs of homogeneous items.] In K. D. Kubinger (Ed.), *Moderne Testtheorie* (pp. 296-310). Weinheim and Munich: Psychologie Verlags Union. (In German.)

Thorndyke, P. W. (1977). Cognitive structure in comprehension and memory of narrative discourse. *Cognitive Psychology, 9,* 77-110.

11

Measuring Change Using Latent Class Analysis

ANTON K. FORMANN

1. Motivation and Basic Considerations

Measuring change in qualitative data plays an important role in many contexts, especially in the social sciences where typically data of this type are available. Because qualitative data lack a natural metric, the traditional concept of change defined in terms of differences of values measured at different points in time is hard to apply. Therefore, specific models were formulated that allow quantitative statements about change in qualitative data. One of these models is the linear logistic model with relaxed assumptions (LLRA); see Fischer (1972, 1983, 1987, 1989). In the simplest case, there is one group of persons only; for example, an experimental group. The reactions of all persons to the same k dichotomous items $I_1, \ldots, I_k$ (e.g., presence versus absence of certain symptoms) are observed at two points in time, t_1 and t_2. All persons $P_1, \ldots P_n$ receive a treatment (e.g., a therapy) between t_1 and t_2. Then, the LLRA describes this group with respect to its probabilities of positive reactions ("+") at t_1 and at t_2 by the following equations:

$$p(+ \mid P_v, I_i, t_1) = \frac{\exp(\xi_{vi}^*)}{1 + \exp(\xi_{vi}^*)} \qquad [11.1A]$$

and

294

$$p(+\mid P_v, I_i, t_2) = \frac{\exp(\xi_{vi}^* + \delta^*)}{1 + \exp(\xi_{vi}^* + \delta^*)}, \qquad [11.1B]$$

with

ξ_{vi}^* the latent tendency of person P_v for a positive reaction to item I_i at t_1,

and

δ^* the latent change of the persons between t_1 and t_2. (Note that δ^* comprises the effect of the treatment and the trend, i.e., the effect of those uncontrollable influences not attributable to the treatment which are effective between t_1 and t_2.)

In the presence of more than one group having been exposed to different treatments, the structural parameter δ^* can be linearly decomposed into treatment effects, their interactions (if pairs of treatments have been applied to subgroups of the persons), and the trend. In any case, the structural parameters may be separated from the incidental person parameters ξ^*, so that they may be estimated independently of the person parameters by means of the conditional maximum likelihood method. Model controls can be performed by testing the generalizability of the structural parameters over items and over subgroups of the persons which are formed by some further manifest subjects' variables. In practice, the number of such manifest variables is limited and one cannot be sure that the sensitive ones are among them. In other words, generalizability of the structural parameters over the persons is hard to verify. But if one believes that they are constant across persons, and this is not true, this may result in misleading conclusions concerning change as will be shown in the following.

Assume in the sense of latent class analysis (LCA), see Lazarsfeld (1950) and Lazarsfeld and Henry (1968), that the change δ^* is not the same for all persons, but that it depends upon the membership of one of two unobservable types T_1 and T_2. That is, in truth, the population of persons consists of two segments showing different changes. Now as before, for item I_i its latent probability of positive reactions at t_1 is described by (11.1A), but—instead of (11.1B)—at t_2 it is given by

$$p(+ \mid P_v \in \text{type } T_1, I_i, t_2) = \frac{\exp(\xi_{vi}^* + \delta_1^*)}{1 + \exp(\xi_{vi}^* + \delta_1^*)}$$

and   [11.2]

$$p(+ \mid P_v \in \text{type } T_2, I_i, t_2) = \frac{\exp(\xi_{vi}^* + \delta_2^*)}{1 + \exp(\xi_{vi}^* + \delta_2^*)} .$$

Obviously, δ_1^* and δ_2^* are the type-dependent changes between t_1 and t_2 on the logistic scale. Because the probabilities (11.1A) and (11.1B) are person-by-item specific they cannot be estimated, and the corresponding mean probabilities of each type have to be considered. For the sake of simplicity this will be done for a single item only, so that the items' index can be dropped. In this sense, for both types T_h, $h = 1, 2$, and both points in time, t_1 and t_2, result

$$p(+ \mid \text{type } T_h, t_1) = \frac{\exp(\xi_h)}{1 + \exp(\xi_h)}$$

and   [11.3]

$$p(+ \mid \text{type } T_h, t_2) = \frac{\exp(\xi_h + \delta_h)}{1 + \exp(\xi_h + \delta_h)} ,$$

with ξ_h being the latent tendency of type T_h for showing positive reactions at t_1, and δ_h being the type-dependent latent change. Thereby, ξ_h can be conceived as the mean of the person-specific parameters ξ_v^* of those subjects belonging to T_h, or as that parameter that corresponds to the mean of the probabilities (11.1A) of those subjects belonging to T_h; analogously, δ_h can be understood as the "mean" latent change of those persons belonging to T_h. The observed probabilities of positive reactions of the total group of persons being composed of T_1 and T_2 result in weighted means of the type-specific latent probabilities, that is,

$$p(+ \mid t_l) = w\,p(+ \mid \text{type} T_1, t_l) + (1 - w)\,p(+ \mid \text{type} T_2, t_l) , \quad l = 1, 2, \quad [11.4]$$

with the weights w and $(1 - w)$, $0 < w < 1$, being the incidence rates of both latent types.

If the fact is ignored that the population is composed of two types, the observed probabilities of positive reactions will be related to the total-group parameters $\overline{\xi}$ and $\overline{\delta}$ by

$$p(+ \mid t_1) = \frac{\exp(\overline{\xi})}{1 + \exp(\overline{\xi})}$$

and [11.5]

$$p(+ \mid t_2) = \frac{\exp(\overline{\xi} + \overline{\delta})}{1 + \exp(\overline{\xi} + \overline{\delta})},$$

with $\overline{\xi}$ the tendency of the group of persons for showing positive reactions at t_1, and $\overline{\delta}$ the change of that group between t_1 and t_2. (Note that here again, in contrast to the LLRA, the parameter $\overline{\xi}$ does not depend upon the person!) Combining (11.3) with (11.5) gives

$$\frac{\exp(\overline{\xi})}{1 + \exp(\overline{\xi})} = w \frac{\exp(\xi_1)}{1 + \exp(\xi_1)} + (1 - w) \frac{\exp(\xi_2)}{1 + \exp(\xi_2)}$$

and [11.6]

$$\frac{\exp(\overline{\xi} + \overline{\delta})}{1 + \exp(\overline{\xi} + \overline{\delta})} = w \frac{\exp(\xi_1 + \delta_1)}{1 + \exp(\xi_1 + \delta_1)} + (1 - w) \frac{\exp(\xi_2 + \delta_2)}{1 + \exp(\xi_2 + \delta_2)},$$

from which the relation of the parameters $\overline{\xi}$ and $\overline{\delta}$ describing the group to the parameters ξ_1, ξ_2, δ_1, δ_2, and w describing the latent types can be derived. Both $\overline{\xi}$ and $\overline{\delta}$ result as log-odds ratios of weighted means of type-specific latent response probabilities:

$$\overline{\xi} = \log \frac{p(+ \mid t_1)}{p(- \mid t_1)} = \log \left[w \frac{\exp(\xi_1)}{1 + \exp(\xi_1)} + (1 - w) \frac{\exp(\xi_2)}{1 + \exp(\xi_2)} \right]$$

$$- \log \left[w \frac{1}{1 + \exp(\xi_1)} + (1 - w) \frac{1}{1 + \exp(\xi_2)} \right],$$

$$\bar{\delta} = \log \frac{p(+ \mid t_2)/p(- \mid t_2)}{p(+ \mid t_1)/p(- \mid t_1)} \qquad [11.7]$$

$$= \log \left[w \frac{\exp(\xi_1 + \delta_1)}{1 + \exp(\xi_1 + \delta_1)} + (1 - w) \frac{\exp(\xi_2 + \delta_2)}{1 + \exp(\xi_2 + \delta_2)} \right]$$

$$- \log \left[w \frac{1}{1 + \exp(\xi_1 + \delta_1)} + (1 - w) \frac{1}{1 + \exp(\xi_2 + \delta_2)} \right]$$

$$- \log \left[w \frac{\exp(\xi_1)}{1 + \exp(\xi_1)} + (1 - w) \frac{\exp(\xi_2)}{1 + \exp(\xi_2)} \right]$$

$$+ \log \left[w \frac{1}{1 + \exp(\xi_1)} + (1 - w) \frac{1}{1 + \exp(\xi_2)} \right].$$

From the latter relation it follows, for example, that $\bar{\delta} = 0$ if and only if (iff)

$$\frac{p(+ \mid t_2)}{p(- \mid t_2)} = \frac{p(+ \mid t_1)}{p(- \mid t_1)}, \qquad [11.8]$$

or, equivalently, iff

$$w \exp(\xi_1)[\exp(\delta_1) - 1][1 + \exp(2\xi_2 + \delta_2)]$$

$$+ (1 - w) \exp(\xi_2)[\exp(\delta_2) - 1][1 + \exp(2\xi_1 + \delta_1)]$$

$$+ \exp(\xi_1 + \xi_2)\{[2w - 1][\exp(\delta_1) - \exp(\delta_2)] + [\exp(\delta_1 + \delta_2) - 1]\} = 0 \, [11.9]$$

This is the case, for example, when $\xi_1 = \xi_2 = 0$, $w = 1 - w = \frac{1}{2}$, and $\delta_2 = -\delta_1$. From $\bar{\delta} = 0$ one would conclude that there is no change between t_1 and t_2, but in truth both latent types, having the same incidence rate, changed to the same extent, however in opposite directions!

Note as an aside that the relation of the observed to the latent probabilities is a much simpler one if—instead of the linear logistic model—a model is assumed that is additive with respect to the probabilities. Using the shorter notation $\bar{p} = p \, (+ \mid t_1)$, $p_1 = p \, (+ \mid \text{type } T_1, t_1)$, $p_2 = p \, (+ \mid \text{type } T_2, t_1)$, (11.4) can be rewritten in the form

$$\bar{p} = wp_1 + (1 - w)p_2$$

and   [11.10]

$$\bar{p} + \bar{\Delta} = w(p_1 + \Delta_1) + (1 - w)(p_2 + \Delta_2) \, ,$$

with $\bar{\Delta}$, Δ_1, and Δ_2 denoting the changes from t_1 to t_2 in the population and both latent types, respectively. Here, the observed change $\bar{\Delta}$ is simply the weighted mean of the type-specific changes Δ_1 and Δ_2,

$$\bar{\Delta} = w\Delta_1 + (1 - w)\Delta_2 \, .$$ [11.11]

2. Some Possibilities for Measuring Change by Means of LCA

Up to now, only changes of response probabilities were considered that were available from the same persons (panel data) at two points in time. Looking more systematically at the possibilities for measuring change using LCA not only reveals that changes of the incidence rates of latent types may be studied, but that data collected on more than two occasions as well as survey data may also be analyzed.

While changes in the latent response probabilities alone signify an increasing or decreasing tendency for positive reactions without the possibility that the respondent moves from one latent type to another, changes in their incidence rates from one occasion to another reflect the wandering of persons, for example, from one latent type with high probabilities for positive reactions to another latent type having low probabilities for positive reactions. Thereby, the "low" and the "high" probabilities may be constant over time or they may change from one occasion to the next; see Wiggins (1973), and for related mixed Markov models, van de Pol and Langeheine (1990).

As a simple fictitious example assume that the same item was presented to the same persons at three occasions. Assume further that two types of respondents exist, having a high, h, and a low, l, probability of positive reactions, respectively. Between t_1 and t_2 changes from type T_1

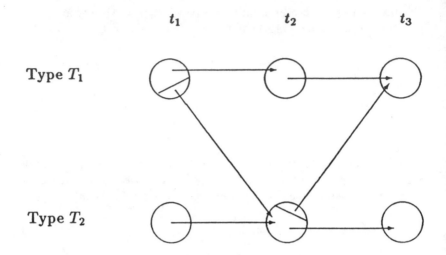

Figure 11.1. Fictitious Example—Changing Latent Types

to type T_2 are allowed, and from t_2 to t_3 switching from type T_2 to type T_1 is possible (see Figure 11.1). So, five classes $C_1, \ldots, C_5$ can be distinguished: C_1 shows the high probability at all three points in time; C_2 shows the high probability at t_1 and changes between t_1 and t_2 from the high to the low probability, where it remains; C_3 shows at t_1 the high probability and changes between t_1 and t_2 from the high to the low probability, but returns to the high probability at t_3; C_4 is at the low probability at t_1 and t_2, but changes before t_3 to the high one; and finally,

Table 11.1 Fictitious Example—Item Latent Probabilities (h = high, l = low) and Class Sizes

Class	$p(+)$			Class Size
	t_1	t_2	t_3	
C_1	h	h	h	w_1
C_2	h	l	l	w_2
C_3	h	l	h	w_3
C_4	l	l	h	w_4
C_5	l	l	l	w_5
Type T_1 (h)	$w_1+w_2+w_3$	w_1	$w_1+w_3+w_4$	$\sum_{j=1}^{5} w_j$
Type T_2 (l)	w_4+w_5	$w_2+w_3+w_4+w_5$	w_2+w_5	$= 1$

C_5 shows the low probability of positive reactions at all three occasions. Denoting the class sizes by $w_1, \ldots, w_5$, according to these assumptions the incidence rates of both types result as shown in Table 11.1

If survey data are available instead of panel data, then the multisample technique of LCA (Clogg & Goodman, 1984) has to be applied. This is also the case if a mixture of panel and survey data should be used to assess changes. Typically, such data arise in applications of the LLRA where the same items are presented at least twice to the same persons, and where the persons are grouped according to different treatment. Remember the introductory example and assume that one experimental group has to be contrasted with the control; then, the control group gives the estimate of the trend, and the experimental group gives the estimate of the treatment effect plus the trend, so that their difference estimates the treatment effect.

All possibilities for measuring change using LCA with equality restrictions (Goodman, 1974) or linear logistic constraints (Formann, 1985, 1992) are summarized in the following few lines.

- Data: panel, survey, or mixed
- Points in time: two or more
- Treatment groups: one or more
- Changes: no / latent response probabilities / incidence rates of latent types / both

3. Examples

Three examples will now be given. The first two refer to panel data and more than two points in time. They differ inasmuch as, in the first example, the changes of the observed response probabilities are attributed to changes of the latent response probabilities, while they are attributed to changes of the incidence rates of latent types as well as to changes of the item latent probabilities in the second example. The third example uses survey data collected at two points in time.

3.1. Example 1: Changes of Fear in Children
During the Preoperative Phase

A sample of 60 children was observed from awakening on the day of operation up to being given anesthesia. This preoperative phase was

Table 11.2 Example 1—Changes of Fear in Children: Response Patterns, a_s, and Their Observed Frequencies, n_s, Resulting for Four Time Intervals $(t_1,...,t_4)$

a_s t_1 t_2 t_3 t_4	n_s	a_s t_1 t_2 t_3 t_4	n_s	a_s t_1 t_2 t_3 t_4	n_s	a_s t_1 t_2 t_3 t_4	n_s
0 0 0 0	5	0 1 0 0	1	1 0 0 0	4	1 1 0 0	2
0 0 0 1	3	0 1 0 1	4	1 0 0 1	4	1 1 0 1	1
0 0 1 0	—	0 1 1 0	—	1 0 1 0	—	1 1 1 0	1
0 0 1 1	4	0 1 1 1	7	1 0 1 1	9	1 1 1 1	15

divided into several time intervals; for each of them, a separate rating for each child on whether it showed fear or not was recorded. Therefore, a single dichotomous symptom (fear vs. no fear), repeatedly observed, is available. Since the sample size was small, the data for four time intervals (see Table 11.2) were selected and then analyzed by means of unrestricted LCA. The two-classes solution fitted the data well; for the goodness-of-fit tests, see Table 11.3. As can be shown by applying linear logistic LCA (cf. Formann, 1989), this unrestricted solution is compatible with the following restricted solution.

Children belonging to one class (C_1) become more fearful the nearer the time of operation comes; for this class, the probability of showing fear increases continuously from the first time interval to the fourth, whereby the linear changes on the logistic scale are governed by a single parameter. Children belonging to the other class (C_2) have a rather stable probability of showing fear with a slight relaxation in the middle of the observation phase; that is, for this class, its probability of showing fear decreases from the first time interval to the second, does not change for the third, and finally increases in the fourth so that it comes back to its starting value.

The corresponding hypothesis was formalized in terms of linear logistic LCA by means of two parameters, ξ_1 and ξ_2, that describe the level of fear for both classes in the first time interval, a single change parameter, δ, and by assuming, with respect to the latent probabilities for showing fear, the following relations:

$$p(+\mid C_1, t_1) = \frac{\exp(\xi_1)}{1 + \exp(\xi_1)}, \qquad p(+\mid C_2, t_1) = \frac{\exp(\xi_2)}{1 + \exp(\xi_2)},$$

$$p(+\mid C_1, t_2) = \frac{\exp(\xi_1 + \delta)}{1 + \exp(\xi_1 + \delta)}, \quad p(+\mid C_2, t_2) = \frac{\exp(\xi_2 - \delta)}{1 + \exp(\xi_2 - \delta)},$$

$$p(+\mid C_1, t_3) = \frac{\exp(\xi_1 + 2\delta)}{1 + \exp(\xi_1 + 2\delta)}, \quad p(+\mid C_2, t_3) = \frac{\exp(\xi_2 - \delta)}{1 + \exp(\xi_2 - \delta)},$$

$$p(+\mid C_1, t_4) = \frac{\exp(\xi_1 + 3\delta)}{1 + \exp(\xi_1 + 3\delta)}, \quad p(+\mid C_2, t_4) = \frac{\exp(\xi_2)}{1 + \exp(\xi_2)}. \quad [11.12]$$

Thus, eight latent probabilities of the unrestricted two-classes solution can be reduced to only three basic parameters of linear logistic LCA; their numerical values ($\xi_1 = 0.37$, $\xi_2 = -0.10$, $\delta = 0.99$), indicate that at t_1 the level of fear is about the same for all children, while its course over time is very discrepant; see also Figure 11.2. That δ differs significantly from zero, so that at least some of the changes are significant, can be deduced from the comparison of this hypothesis (H_1) with that of no change (H_0) assuming

$$p(+\mid C_1, t_1) = \ldots = p(+\mid C_1, t_4) - \frac{\exp(\xi_1)}{1 + \exp(\xi_1)}$$

and   [11.13]

$$p(+\mid C_2, t_1) = \ldots = p(+\mid C_2, t_4) = \frac{\exp(\xi_2)}{1 + \exp(\xi_2)};$$

compare the goodness-of-fit statistics in Table 11.3, also showing those of the corresponding one-class solutions.

3.2. Example 2: Vote Intention in the Elmira Panel

The data of this example are rather old; they were collected in June, August, and October 1948 on the occasion of an election ($N = 562$). The variable is vote intention pro versus contra Republicans. These data (see Table 11.4) can be found in Wiggins (1973, p. 152), who analyzed them by means of some latent class models using determinantal methods of parameter estimation. One of his models was reestimated using the maximum likelihood (ML) method to serve as an example of changing

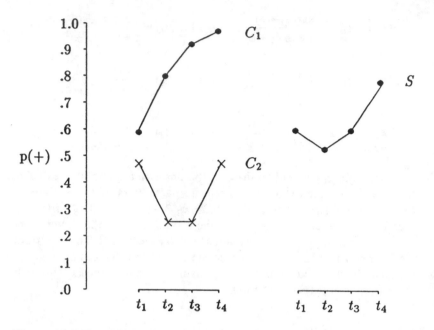

Figure 11.2. Example 1—Changes of Fear in Children: Levels of Fear on Four Occasions According to the Restricted 2 Classes-Solution (C_1, C_2) of LCA (w_1 = .579, w_2 = .421) and in the Sample (S)

Table 11.3 Example 1—Changes of Fear in Children: Goodness-of-Fit Tests

Number of classes	Hypothesis	Number of parameters for classes/items/sum	X^2	Goodness-of-fit tests L^2	df	χ_0^2
1	unrestricted	0/4/4	35.99	33.89	11	19.68
	no change	0/1/1	38.60	44.08	14	23.68
2	unrestricted	1/8/9	4.44	4.77	6	12.59
	H_1	1/3/4	11.97	14.70	11	19.68
	H_0 (no change)	1/2/3	24.54	31.89	12	21.03
	Comparison					
2	unrestricted vs. H_1	—		9.93	5	11.07
2	H_1 vs. H_0	—		17.19	1	3.84

NOTE: X^2 = Pearsons's chi-squared statistic, L^2 = Likelihood ratio statistic.

Table 11.4 Example 2—Vote Intention: Response Patterns, a_s, and Their Observed Frequencies, n_s, Resulting for Three Points in Time (t_1, t_2, t_3)

a_s			n_s	a_s			n_s
t_1	t_2	t_3		t_1	t_2	t_3	
1	1	1	307	0	1	1	46
1	1	0	10	0	1	0	10
1	0	1	13	0	0	1	9
1	0	0	32	0	0	0	135

NOTE: 1 = Republican, 0 = non-Republican.

the type and changes in the latent probabilities. This model assumes two types of voters: latent Republicans and latent non-Republicans; their response probabilities are unrestricted over the three waves, but restricted within each wave for latent Republicans (p) and latent non-Republicans ($1 - p$). Further, it is assumed that between June and August latent change away from Republican is possible. Therefore, three classes exist: C_1's vote intention is Republican at all three occasions; C_2's vote intention is Republican at t_1 and changes between t_1 and t_2 to non-Republican; and C_3's vote intention always is non-Republican.

This model, M_1, fits well; see Table 11.5, where its parameter estimates are also given. They show that for latent Republicans, the probability of having the vote intention Republican increases rather sharply from June to August, with a further slight rise by October. That is, because of the restrictions met for the latent response probabilities, the probability for latent non-Republicans to have the vote intention Republican decreases from wave to wave. Contrary to this, the proportion of latent Republicans decreases from June to October, and, consequently, the proportion of latent non-Republicans increases. The change in the proportion of both latent types is not significant, however, as can be concluded from the application of a further model, M_2. This model, also applied by Wiggins (1973, p. 136ff) but considered to be inadequate, fits the Elmira data without allowing a class of movers; see Table 11.5. That is, in contrast to Wiggins' conclusion, only two classes, corresponding to latent Republicans and latent non-Republicans, describe the vote intention at all three points in time.

Table 11.5 Example 1.2—Vote Intention: Parameter Estimates and Goodness-of-Fit Tests for Two Hypotheses, M_1 and M_2

Model	Class	Class size	t_1	t_2	t_3	Fit tests
				$p(+)$		
M_1	1 (RRR)	.674	.866	.956	.967	$X^2 = 1.86$
	2 $(\overline{R}RR)$	.023	.866	.044	.033	$L^2 = 1.80$
	3 (RRR)	.303	.134	.044	.033	df = 2
						$\chi^2_0 = 5.99$
	$p(\underline{R})$		.697	.674	.674	
	$p(\overline{R})$		.303	.326	.326	
M_2	1 (RRR)	.676	.850	.956	.966	$X^2 = 4.16$
	2 (RRR)	.324	.150	.044	.034	$L^2 = 4.08$
						df = 3
						$\chi^2_0 = 7.81$

NOTE: R = Latent Republican, $\overline{R}$ = Latent non-Republican

3.3. Example 3: Attitude Toward Car-Use and the Environment

In the Netherlands, a series of statements concerning car-use and environment was presented to two samples of 300 persons each at two occasions, the first one before and the second one after a campaign. The dichotomously scored items were suspected to be nonmonotone so that, based on LCA, specific scaling models are applicable. These models are the nonmonotone analogues of Lazarsfeld's (1950) latent distance models for monotone items. For nonmonotone items, the most general variant assumes the item characteristic curves to be step functions, each having two low latent probabilities of agreement for both (extremely) positive and (extremely) negative values on the underlying attitudinal continuum, and one high latent probability of agreement for middle (= neutral) attitudinal positions. Restricted variants arise by equating some of these probabilities within items and/or across items and classes. The latter ones are determined via their latent response probabilities according to the order of the items and that small number of ideal response patterns assumed to exist. A more detailed description can be found in Formann (1988).

For five items concerning car-use and environment, see Table 11.6, the analyses of the first data set (cf. Formann, 1993), that is, before the campaign, showed that four classes corresponding to the ideal response

Table 11.6 Example 1.3—Attitude Toward Car-Use and Environment: Response Patterns, a_S, and Their Observed Frequencies, n_S, Before and After the Campaign

a_S	n_S pre	n_S post	a_S	n_S pre	n_S post	a_S	n_S pre	n_S post	a_S	n_S pre	n_S post
11111	51	71	10111	66	39	01111	9	12	00111	7	4
11110	8	22	10110	7	9	01110	2	2	00110	1	—
11101	21	33	10101	14	5	01101	7	5	00101	4	1
11100	15	15	10100	4	1	01100	4	4	00100	1	1
11011	11	8	10011	3	4	01011	3	3	00011	—	—
11010	7	6	10010	2	—	01010	3	2	00010	—	—
11001	20	23	10001	2	2	01001	2	2	00001	—	1
11000	11	17	10000	1	1	01000	14	7	00000	—	—

Item I_1: Car use cannot be abandoned. Some pressure on the environment has to be accepted.

Item I_2: A cleaner environment demands sacrifices like a decreasing car usage.

Item I_3: It is better to deal with other forms of environmental pollution than car driving.

Item I_4: Technically adapted cars do not constitute an environmental threat.

Item I_5: Considering the environmental problems, everybody should decide for themselves how often to use the car.

patterns $(0,1,0,0,0)$, $(1,1,0,0,0)$, $(1,1,1,1,1)$ and $(1,0,1,1,1)$ suffice to describe the observed frequency distribution of response patterns: Item I_2 starts from the left side of the latent attitudinal continuum with its high latent probability for positive answers, while the other four items start with their low latent probabilities (class C_1); I_1 follows as the second item by jumping from low to high (class C_2), and then the remaining three items I_3, I_4, and I_5, change from their low to their high latent probabilities (class C_3); finally, item I_2 changes from its high to its low latent probability, whereas the other four items remain at their high latent probabilities (class C_4). As can be seen from the solution presented in Table 11.7, in part the response errors (ideally, they are equal to 0) of the low latent probabilities are considerable (items I_1, I_3, and I_5), while they are rather small for the high latent response probabilities. For this solution, the class sizes had to be restricted in order to get an identifiable model: The first three classes have the same size of about 20% of the sample, the fourth class comprises about 40% of the sample.

Table 11.7 Example 3—Attitude Toward Car-Use and Environment: Parameter Estimates and Goodness-of-Fit Tests for Some Hypotheses [Ideal Response Patterns: (0,1,0,0,0), (1,1,0,0,0), (1,1,1,1,1), and (1,0,1,1,1)]

Hypoth-esis	Class	Class size	1	2	$p(+)$ 3	4	5	Goodness-of-fit tests
H_0 t_1	1	.197	.514	.941	.409	.292	.481	$X^2 = 21.40$
	2	.197	.883	.941	.409	.292	.481	$L^2 = 22.72$
	3	.197	.883	.941	.950	.801	.898	df = 17(20) $X^2 = 35.70$
	4	.408	.883	.171	.950	.801	.898	$\chi_0^2 = 27.59$ $L^2 = 39.27$
								(31.41) df = 33(41)
t_2	1	.210	.703	.942	.472	.225	.555	$X^2 = 14.30$ $\chi_0^2 = 47.40$
	2	.210	.893	.942	.472	.225	.555	$L^2 = 16.54$ (56.94)
	3	.210	.893	.942	.946	.884	.822	df = 16(20)
	4	.369	.893	.484	.946	.884	.822	$\chi_0^2 = 26.30$
								(31.41)
H_1	1	.198	.603	.945	.432	.265	.504	$X^2 = 63.82$
	2	.198	.888	.945	.432	.265	.504	$L^2 = 65.92$
	3	.198	.888	.945	.945	.825	.865	df = 44(52)
	4	.406	.888	.340	.945	.825	.865	$\chi_0^2 = 60.48$
								(69.83)
H_2		t_1 t_2						
	1	.198 .257	.619	.942	.473	.299	.527	$X^2 = 57.13$
	2	.198 .257	.892	.942	.473	.299	.527	$L^2 = 55.37$
	3	.198 .257	.892	.942	.955	.845	.876	df = 43(51)
	4	.405 .238	.892	.190	.955	.845	.876	$\chi_0^2 = 59.30$
								(68.67)
H_3		t_1						
	1	.202	.519	.936	.415	.297	.485	
	2	.202	.884	.936	.415	.297	.485	
	3	.202	.884	.936	.954	.805	.901	$X^2 = 35.75$
	4	.392	.884	.151	.954	.805	.901	$L^2 = 39.33$
								df = 34(42)
		t_2						$\chi_0^2 = 48.60$
	1	.202	.701	.945	.461	.217	.549	(58.12)
	2	.202	.892	.945	.461	.217	.549	
	3	.202	.892	.945	.943	.874	.821	
	4	.392	.892	.506	.943	.874	.821	

H_1 vs. H_0	$L^2 = 26.65$	df = 11	$\chi_0^2 = 19.68$
H_2 vs. H_0	$L^2 = 16.10$	df = 10	$\chi_0^2 = 18.31$
H_3 vs. H_0	$L^2 = 0.07$	df = 1	$\chi_0^2 = 3.84$

NOTE: X^2 = Pearson's chi-squared statistic, L^2 = Likelihood ratio statistic. Both the degrees of freedom (df) and the critical χ^2 values are given twice: First, the adjusted values when collapsing those patterns having zero frequencies, cf. Table 1.6, and second, the uncorrected values (in parentheses). The model selection was based on the adjusted values.

If the same model is applied to the second set of data, that is, after the campaign, its fit is also very good; however, it reveals slightly different parameter estimates as compared with those of the first data set; see Table 11.7. To find out which changes must be rated to be relevant, simultaneous analyses of both data sets were performed assuming (a) no changes (H_1), (b) changes of the class sizes alone (H_2), and (c) changes of the item latent probabilities alone (H_3). According to the results of the analyses summarized in Table 11.7 again, the hypothesis of no changes at all (H_1) must be discarded; the other two hypotheses can be maintained.

This can be concluded from the comparison of the three hypotheses with the one that allows both changes of the class sizes and of the item latent probabilities (H_0) being equivalent to the separate analyses of both sets of data. The hypothesis of changes of the item latent probabilities alone (H_3) fits better, but the hypothesis of changes of the class sizes alone (H_2) seems to be more appealing: First, from the conceptual point of view, because H_2 represents a changing attitude in the population that is recorded with a constant instrument of measurement, whereas under H_3 that instrument itself changes, and second, from the statistical point of view, because H_2 is more parsimonious with respect to the number of parameters. It is interesting to note that assuming changes of the class sizes alone, they become rather massive as compared with those resulting from the separate analyses of both sets of data. That is, changes of the item latent probabilities, which are not allowed under this hypothesis, obviously influence the extent to which changes in the class sizes result in the case that solely such changes are allowed.

At first sight, the changes in the class sizes caused by the campaign can hardly be interpreted. But looking at the wording of the five statements led to the insight that item I_2 should be inversely scored. Then, the positive answer at all five items indicates positive attitude toward car-use, and the solution to the scaling problem allows the following simple interpretation: The order of the items is not I_2, I_1, (I_3, I_4, I_5)—the parentheses indicate that I_3, I_4, and I_5 take the same position—but I_1, (I_3, I_4, I_5), and, inversely scored, I_2; the solution based on the assumption of nonmonotone items is equivalent to Lazarsfeld's well-known latent distance model for monotone items; and the effect of the campaign goes toward the intended direction in that those classes showing less positive answers concerning car-use become greater. This solution is graphed in Figure 11.3.

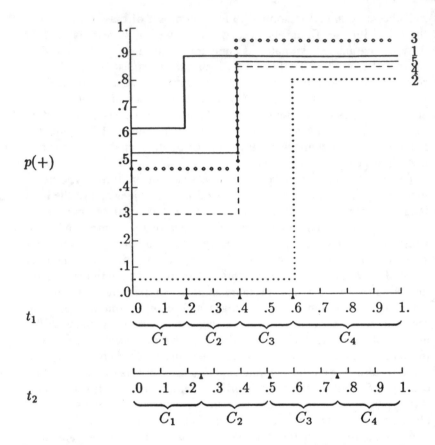

Figure 11.3. Example 3—Attitude Toward Car-Use and Environment: Trace Lines of the 5 Items Under H$_2$ (Item I_2 Inversely Scored)

4. Final Remarks

The considerations of this chapter started from LLRA, for which LCA has been introduced as a means of model control. Even if this claim is correct in principle, in practice LCA offers an approximation to such model controls only due to some discrepancies of both concepts. Note as the first difference that LLRA is applicable to single items having been presented twice, whereas this is not true for LCA, in general. On the other hand, an increasing number of items causes no problems for the LLRA because—concerning change—each additional item is considered to be a replication of the preceding ones, however, possibly being described with respect to the latent tendency for positive reactions by an item-specific parameter per person at t_1; moreover, these incidental parameters are eliminated during parameter estimation by the conditional ML method. Contrary to this, LCA uses the conventional ML method by which no incidental person parameters can be eliminated; as a consequence, in LCA group-specific instead of person-specific parameters describe the latent tendency for positive reactions at t_1. Furthermore, LCA needs the whole response patterns and their frequency distribution, so that an increasing number of items becomes problematical for the goodness-of-fit tests. Therefore, the number of items and/or the number of points in time has to be small if LCA is to be used to measure change and if one is not willing to lose the availability of stringent goodness-of-fit tests. This problem applies especially in cases where polytomous items are analyzed, which is also possible, and for which several generalizations of the LLRA discussed here exist; see, for example, Fischer and Parzer (1991).

However, independent of model controls for the LLRA, LCA gives promising tools for measuring change. Whereas other techniques not relying on the mixture principle want a priori hypotheses concerning differential effects of treatments in observable subgroups of persons, LCA supplies the researcher with a method that allows the identification of unobservable subgroups of persons reacting differently. Because in most cases those latent types becoming identifiable by LCA were not expected on the basis of a priori hypotheses, but merely turn out as an a posteriori result of the application of LCA, the rarely performed confirmation using further data is recommended; first, to safeguard against criticism, and second, to fulfill the requirement of generalizability. The third example (attitude toward car-use and environment) may serve as an illustration of the proceeding: The first data, that is, the data collected before the campaign, were used to find the appropriate scaling model, which was then tested using the second data, that is, the data collected after the campaign. Because the scaling model could be generalized from the first to the second data (both sets of data are composed of the same classes, so that they are structurally identical; moreover, the item latent probabilities can be seen to be the same at t_1 and t_2), the changes of the class sizes can be attributed to the campaign (and the trend). With respect to this example, therefore, both testing generalizability over persons and measuring change were possible at the same time.

References

Clogg, C. C., & Goodman, L. A. (1984). Latent structure analysis of a set of multidimensional contingency tables. *Journal of the American Statistical Association, 79,* 762-771.

Fischer, G. H. (1972). A measurement model for the effect of mass-media. *Acta Psychologica, 36,* 207-220.

Fischer, G. H. (1983). Logistic latent trait models with linear constraints. *Psychometrika, 48,* 3-26.

Fischer, G. H. (1987). Applying the principles of specific objectivity and of generalizability to the measurement of change. *Psychometrika, 52,* 565-587.

Fischer, G. H. (1989). An IRT-based model for dichotomous longitudinal data. *Psychometrika, 54,* 599-624.

Fischer, G. H., & Parzer, P. (1991). An extension of the rating scale model with an application to the measurement of change. *Psychometrika, 56,* 637-651.

Formann, A. K. (1985). Constrained latent class models: Theory and applications. *British Journal of Mathematical and Statistical Psychology, 38,* 87-111.

Formann, A. K. (1988). Latent class models for nonmonotone dichotomous items. *Psychometrika, 53,* 45-62.

Formann, A. K. (1989). Constrained latent class models: Some further applications. *British Journal of Mathematical and Statistical Psychology, 42,* 37-54.

Formann, A. K. (1992). Linear logistic latent class analysis for polytomous data. *Journal of the American Statistical Association, 87,* 476-486.

Formann, A. K. (1993). Latent class models for monotone and nonmonotone dichotomous items. *Kwantitatieve Methoden, 14 (42),* 143-160.

Goodman, L. A. (1974). Exploratory latent structure analysis using both identifiable and unidentifiable models. *Biometrika, 61,* 215-231.

Lazarsfeld, P. F. (1950). The logical and mathematical foundation of latent structure analysis. In S. A. Stouffer, L. Guttman, E. A. Suchman, P. F. Lazarsfeld, S. A. Star, & J. A. Clausen (Eds.), *Studies in social psychology in World War II: Vol. IV. Measurement and prediction* (pp. 362-412). Princeton, NJ: Princeton University Press.

Lazarsfeld, P. F., & Henry, N. W. (1968). *Latent structure analysis.* Boston: Houghton Mifflin.

van de Pol, F., & Langeheine, R. (1990). Mixed Markov latent class models. In C. C. Clogg (Ed.), *Sociological methodology 1990* (pp. 213-247). Oxford: Basil Blackwell.

Wiggins, L. M. (1973). *Panel analysis—Latent probability models for attitude and behavior processes.* Amsterdam: Elsevier.

12

Mixture Decomposition When the Components Are of Unknown Form

HOBEN THOMAS

The notion of latent class models usually conjures up the perspective of cross classification frequency-based data, common in sociology (e.g., McCutcheon, 1987). But there are other perspectives as well, and one alternative perspective is to view the latent class problem as a finite mixture problem, a viewpoint favored by McLachlan and Basford (1988).

While the general mixture model may be defined as a model of the form of

$$f(x) = \int_{\xi} f(x \mid \xi) dG(\xi) ,$$ [12.1]

the most familiar approach to the mixture problem is to view $f(x)$ as a finite mixture distribution with $f(x)$ written as

$$\sum_{r=1}^{k} \pi_r f(x \mid \xi_r)$$ [12.2]

where $g(\xi_r) \equiv \pi_r$ for discrete values of ξ. The components $f(x \mid \xi_r)$ correspond to the model for the recruitment probabilities from the latent class perspective.

313

In general, in order to model data in this way the component distributions must be of some specified functional form. They are almost always of some familiar parametric family. In the case of X continuous, the default option is to regard $f(x \mid \xi_r)$ as a normal density.

Although the theory of mixture distributions is becoming increasingly well developed (e.g., Titterington, Smith, & Makov, 1985), applications of mixtures to real problems can be less than straightforward. For example, there is the practical problem: As far as is known, none of the standard statistical packages have mixture decomposition routines. This difficulty precludes large numbers of end users from exploring mixture approaches to problems. In addition, and more importantly, there are many applications where mixture composition might seem quite sensible but there is little theory to guide the suitable selection of the mixture components. In this case it is not at all obvious how best to proceed.

To illustrate application difficulties, consider the widely studied problem of trying to understand responses to Piaget's water-level task (Piaget & Inhelder, 1967). In the typical task setting, individuals, preschool to old age, are presented with line drawings of rectangular shaped vessels tilted to various angles. They are asked to draw a line representing the water's surface on each of several vessels, with each vessel rotated to a different angular orientation in the frontal plane. Except for very young children, most individuals draw straight lines to represent the water's surface. The correctness of each drawing is usually indexed by the magnitude of the drawing error, measured in degrees about a horizontal axis, the correct response, which is defined as zero degrees. What has held so much intrigue about this task is that there are large individual differences in task performance, both among children and among adults. It is the individual differences among task performers that have the potential of being well captured by a latent class perspective.

The problem is to specify response distributions that seem appropriate as components for a mixture distribution. To illustrate, consider how different response strategies might lead to different response distributions on this task. For individuals who know the principle that still liquid is invariantly horizontal, the line drawings would be expected to be about horizontal. So it would be expected that the error response distribution would probably be approximately symmetrically distributed about zero degrees error, and with small variance. Perhaps a Gaussian distribution would be a reasonable first model. However, it is widely recognized that large numbers of individuals, even at college age and beyond, do not understand the water-level principle of invariant horizontality. Indeed, such individuals have difficulty learning the principle (e.g, Thomas, Jamison, & Hummel, 1973)! What response distribution is to be expected from such individuals? The answer to that question would seem to depend on the response strategy adopted. For example, if individuals are likely to guess, then perhaps a uniform-like response distribution with probably large variance might be expected. Alternatively, suppose some individuals employ a consistent but incorrect rule such as positioning the water line parallel with the vessel's bottom. If so, a third distributional form might be expected. According to Piaget's theory (Piaget & Inhelder, 1967) young children should maintain such beliefs and consequently display such responses.

The trouble is there seems no a priori way of knowing how many latent classes to expect in such data. Worse, if the response strategy determines the distribution of responses expected, it seems likely that mixtures of components from different families might be expected. Problems such as these make clear the potential advantage of being able to proceed nonparametrically without having to specify the functional form of the components.

There has been some recent work on nonparametric approaches, but this work has focused on the estimation of the mixing distribution $G(\xi)$, (e.g., Lesperance & Kalbfleisch, 1992), and this approach does not help here because the components $f(x \mid \xi)$ still need specification. Apparently only Hall (1981) has proposed a general nonparametric approach to the mixture component problem but his solution is not practical. It requires the specification of k, the number of components, and the data must be fully classified in each component. Such data would appear to be rarely if ever obtained. Hall provided no examples and gave no applications. Indeed, the mixture problem appears to lose interest if the data arrive fully classified, because the most interesting inference problems vanish.

The proposed nonparametric approach to the mixture decomposition problem model is based on an elementary fact. Let an individual's response on a task be an observation on a random variable X with an unknown distribution. X can easily be transformed into a new random variable W that has a Bernoulli distribution simply by partitioning the domain of X into two regions, one labeled success, the other failure. With m iid responses available from each respondent, the sum of these m responses is binomial in distribution. In essence, the problem of decomposing a mixture distribution with unspecified component distributions is reduced to the problem of decomposing a mixture of binomial distributions.

The Model

The model is developed somewhat informally here. The precise conditions needed are stated in the appendix.

Let

$$f(x) = \sum_{r=1}^{k} \pi_r f_r(x) \qquad [12.3]$$

be the candidate for modeling X, the (marginal) random variable of interest. It is assumed that the underlying population $\mathcal{P}$ of interest, for example children's responses to a problem-solving task, may be partitioned into k disjoint subpopulations P_r each in proportion π_r. Associated with each subpopulation P_r is a distinct component of $f(x)$, $f_r(x)$.

Consider an observation drawn at random from one of the k components. The probability of the observation X having been sampled from P_r is π_r. Define a new random variable W, and $\mathcal{C}$ a fixed critical region in the domain of X such that

$$W = 1 \quad \text{if } X \in \mathcal{C}$$

$$= 0 \quad \text{if } X \notin \mathcal{C} . \qquad [12.4]$$

Clearly W is a Bernoulli binomial random variable. Consequently,

$$P(X \in \mathcal{C}) = P(W = 1 \mid P_r) = \int_{\mathcal{C}} dF_r(x) \equiv \theta(\mathcal{C}; f_r) . \qquad [12.5]$$

Now consider $j = 1, 2, \ldots, m$ iid independent observations from the same distribution $f_r(x)$. The interpretation is that these m observations represent replicated responses from a single individual. Each observation results in a random variable W. Now define $Y = \sum_{j=1}^{m} W_j$. Clearly Y is binomial in distribution with frequency function denoted by $b[y; \theta(\mathcal{C}; f_r), m]$. Furthermore, the proportion of such individuals in the subpopulation is π_r. Repeating the same reasoning for each of the k subpopulations, latent classes or components, it is clear that $f(x)$ has an associated mixture distribution

$$g(y) = \sum_{r=1}^{k} \pi_r b[y; \theta(\mathscr{C}; f_r), m] .$$ [12.6]

While each distribution $f_r(x)$ has its associated function $b[y; \theta(\mathscr{C}; f_r), m]$ there is no guarantee that each of the associated binomial components will be different. Thus, in order to guarantee that $g(y)$ will have the same number of components as $f(x)$ it is necessary that an additional constraint be placed on the components of $f(x)$, namely, that $\theta(\mathscr{C}; f_r)$ must be distinct for each r. For example, if $k = 2$ it must be that

$$\theta(\mathscr{C}; f_1) = \int_{\mathscr{C}} dF_1(x) \neq \int_{\mathscr{C}} dF_2(x) = \theta(\mathscr{C}; f_2) .$$ [12.7]

Given these conditions the following general result may be given.

A population with an associated mixture distribution $f(x)$ has an associated binomial mixture distribution $g(y)$.

The important and practical fact is that a mixture $f(x)$ of unknown components and unknown weights will have the same number of components and same weights as a mixture of binomials distribution which can be constructed by suitably transforming the original observations. Observe that only very light conditions need to be assumed concerning the components $f_r(x)$. Other than the fact that they must be proper probability distributions, they need not have moments, parameters, nor need they be of any special form.

Estimation

Thus, the approach skirts the problem of trying to decompose $f(x)$ directly, by decomposing the associated binomial mixture $g(y)$. Once the binomial decomposition has been achieved, the decomposition of $f(x)$ can follow as will be illustrated.

The binomial mixture decomposition problem has a simple solution, its EM algorithm (Dempster, Laird, & Rubin, 1977) as given by Everitt and Hand (1981). There are k estimates of θ, and $k - 1$ free estimates of π_r, so there are $2k - 1$ parameters to be estimated. Asymptotic standard errors for the estimates are given by Blischke (1964). The number of components k must be estimated as well, although this problem is usually regarded as a model selection problem rather than a parameter estimation problem. While the problem of which model selection criterion to employ in mixture decomposition procedures remains an open issue, standard criteria such as AIC (Bozdogan, 1987; Sakamoto, Ishiguor & Kitagawa, 1986) or variance accounted for may be used.

Once the parameter estimates of the k component binomial mixture have been obtained, the individuals (or more correctly, their associated responses y) may be grouped into the k components, taking the largest estimated posterior probability of component membership as the parent component, the standard criterion. Classification of responses into the most probable parent component distribution or latent class is a trivial problem because the estimated probability of component membership, given $Y = y$, is an explicit step of the EM algorithm. Once the responses have been allocated to their corresponding components, the associated original responses may be partitioned as well because of the one-to-one correspondence between subpopulations of the binomial components and the corresponding membership in the original components. The estimated mixing weights, the $\hat{\pi}_r$ of the binomial mixture, are the estimated weights of components of $f(x)$. Then depending on the purpose of the study, the conditional distributions (i.e., the distributions associated with each component) may be explored with standard tools.

It is worth emphasizing that there are two distinct identifiability issues. One concerns the requirement that the $\theta(\mathscr{C}; f_r)$ for each $f_r(x)$ be different. This condition was discussed above. The second issue concerns the size of m necessary for a k component binomial mixture to be identifiable. The requirement is that $m \geq (2k - 1)$ (Everitt & Hand, 1981), which means that there must be at least three replications for each individual, should $k = 2$.

Example

The data are from 198 boys, aged 11 to 16, who were given eight water-level task items. Each item was the same two-dimensional drawing of a 6 cm wide by 10 cm tall rectangular bottle with lid. The bottle was tilted to each of the eight clock-hour angular orientations 10, 11, 1, 2, 4, 5, 7, and 8. The clock-hour angles of 12, 3, 6, and 9 are known to be responded to accurately by almost all children by age 8 years or so, consequently items at these angles were not provided. Each item appeared on a separate sheet of paper that displayed the vessel with a corner of the vessel resting on a horizontal surface reference line. Subjects were requested to draw, free handedly with a pencil, a line representing the surface of liquid in the bottle, should the bottle be about half filled with liquid and be tilted to the orientation pictured. The items were included in a booklet. Each boy had the same randomly determined item sequence.

The variable of interest was the angular response error of the subjects. Responses were scored to the nearest degree. A "positively sloping" water surface line was signed positively, a horizontal line was zero, and a line sloping in the other direction was negatively signed. Thus, for each individual there is a response vector length 8 of signed integers and/or zeros. The manner by which such data have been conventionally evaluated has varied. One common procedure has been to take as a summary statistic for each subject the unsigned average response error, for all bottle angles, viewing the corresponding distribution as normal. Differences between groups are then compared within standard shift model frameworks such as the two sample t test, constructing whatever between group comparisons are of focus. Data summarized in this manner, however, are extremely nonnormal in appearance, so this approach can be considered at best very crude. When the present data were summarized in this way and grouped into 5° class intervals the histogram of response frequencies was (with the first the interval of 0 to 5) 91, 33, 22, 21, 7, 5, 4, 4, 4, and 3. This asymmetric response histogram is hardly of normal form.

An alternative procedure is to score the responses as correct or incorrect, depending on the degree of angular error, with a summary score being the number correct for each individual. This procedure was used here, but of course the responses are assumed to have a particular model form.

In the present case several different values of $\mathscr{C}(c) = \{x: -c \leq x \leq c\}$, with c taking values from 5° to 15°, were employed to define a random variable Y with $Y = 0, 1, \ldots, 8$ the number correct for each individual. For example for $\mathscr{C}(10)$ the frequencies in parentheses associated with each outcome were: 0(10), 1(6), 2(11), 3(20), 4(19), 5(19), 6(10), 7(19), and 8(84). This distribution is certainly more revealing than the histogram based on average absolute error and suggests a parent distribution with at least two modes, one at 8 correct, and another with about 3 correct, and perhaps a third mode at 0. The histograms associated with the other $\mathscr{C}(c)$ were very similar, although not all histograms suggested three modes. But each suggested a mode at 8 correct, with a second mode typically around 3.

Table 12.1   Mixture Solutions for Varying k and c

k	$\hat{\pi}_r$	VAF	χ^2	AIC(k)
	$r = 1,2,3$			
$c = 5$				
1	1	25	2457	1,296
2	.54 .46	92	41.01	875
3	.20 .40 .40	99	.91	843
$c = 10$				
1	1	25	10,000	1,189
2	.47 .53	91	66	761
3	.07 .42 .52	99	.84	729
$c = 15$				
1	1	25	30,000	1,081
2	.41 .59	91	69.1	655
3	.04 .38 .58	99	2.74	630

The Y_i, $i = 1, 2, \ldots, 198$, for all subjects was decomposed for each $\mathscr{C}(c)$ into their binomial components, using an EM routine. Table 12.1 shows the solutions for $c = 5$, $c = 10$, and $c = 15$ for $k = 1, 2$, and 3. Three model evaluation criteria are shown: (a) VAF is the ratio of the estimated variance under the fitted model over the sample variance. The variance of a mixture of binomials is $\Sigma_{r=1}^{k} \pi_r \{ m\theta(\mathscr{C}; f_r)[1 - \theta(\mathscr{C}; f_r)] + [m\theta(\mathscr{C}; f_r)]^2 \} - \{ m\Sigma_{r=1}^{k} \pi_r \theta(\mathscr{C}; f_r) \}^2 = \sigma^2$. VAF is $\hat{\sigma}^2/s^2$. Here s^2 is the ordinary sample variance, and $\hat{\sigma}^2$ is σ^2 with estimates replacing the parameters. (b) Pearson's χ^2 goodness-of-fit tests of model to data; such tests were unrestricted (expected cell frequencies were not constrained); (c) Akaike's Information Criterion, or AIC(k) $= -2$loglikelihood $+ 2(2k - 1)$. Estimates of $\theta(\mathscr{C}; f_r)$ represent essentially nuisance parameters and vary with $\mathscr{C}(c)$. Of primary interest is the correspondence between decomposition solutions for different $\mathscr{C}(c)$, and in particular, the associated $\hat{\pi}_r$.

Consider first the mixture solutions shown in Table 12.1. For no c is there evidence that a single component is in agreement with the data. For all three values of c a three-component solution provides an excellent fit to the data, and it is possible three latent classes might have generated the data. However, a two-component solution appears to provide a quite acceptable fit in terms of VAF, and the drop in AIC from a $k = 1$ solution, although the χ^2 indices remain high for $k = 2$. The solutions for $c = 10$ and $c = 15$ for both the two- and three-component solutions are in close agreement. They both differ somewhat, particularly in the $k = 3$ component from the $c = 5$ solutions in the weight estimates $\hat{\pi}$. Both $c = 10$ and $c = 15$, while providing an excellent $k = 3$ fit to the data, show that the second and third components of the $k = 3$ solutions are very similar to the corresponding $k = 2$ solutions. The first of the three components, in both cases, accounts for very few individuals, about 14 in one case and 8 in the other case. Consequently, a two-component solution would appear to provide a reasonably parsimonious model, particularly given the tendency to "over fit" and specify a more complicated model than is necessary. For example, using AIC as the main fit index tends to overestimate the number of components (Windham & Cutler, 1992) and of course there can be other model difficulties that can contribute to poor model fit besides misspecification of the number of mixture components.

The $c = 10$ solution with $k = 2$ was selected for further analysis. The sample of 198 individuals was classified into the two component groups, assigning individuals to the rth components for which their estimated component posterior probabilities, $\hat{P}(r \mid y_i)$, were highest. The procedure resulted in 103 individuals being labeled as Good because they were in the better performing group, while 95 individuals in the poorer performing group were labeled Poor.

With individuals so classified, it is a simple matter to partition the original response distribution: Individuals with Y responses classified in component r have their original X responses similarly classified. The analysis of the response distributions associated with each of the clock-hour orientations was similar. The analysis of one representative distribution, the response distribution for the vessel at the 11 o'clock angle, will be provided for illustration. It provides a contrast for the estimated differences between the components of $f(x)$ when $k = 2$.

An obvious consideration is to compare the two groups' conditional sample moments, estimated in the usual way. It has been suggested, however, that it might be preferable to weight these estimates by their posterior probability estimates thereby taking into account the uncertainty of the component group membership assignment. Taking

$$\hat{E}(X \mid r) = \frac{\sum_i \hat{P}(r \mid x_i) x_i}{\sum_i \hat{P}(r \mid x_i)} \qquad [12.8]$$

Table 12.2 Summary Statistics of Good and Poor Performers

| | Good Performers | | Poor Performers | |
	Weighted	Unweighted	Weighted	Unweighted
$\bar{x}$	.65	.65	.48	.48
s^2	16.01	15.69	232.24	237.55
s	4.00	3.96	15.24	15.41
Range		−15 14		−27 52
n		103		95

as a weighted estimate of the conditional mean and

$$\hat{V}ar(X \mid r) = \frac{\sum_i \hat{P}(r \mid x_i)[x_i - \hat{E}(X \mid r)]^2}{\sum_i \hat{P}(r \mid x_i)} \qquad [12.9]$$

as a weighted estimate of the conditional variance.

One might complain that there is abuse of notion here. There are estimates of $P(r \mid y)$, from the mixed binomial decomposition, but not estimates of $P(r \mid x)$. However, it may not be unreasonable to estimate these unknown posterior probabilities with their associated $\hat{P}(r \mid y)$. A conceptual difficulty arises when doing so, however, because there is not a one-to-one map between the y and their corresponding x, so it is can readily happen, for example, that the same values of $Y = y$ can have different values of X. The problem requires additional study. However, from the standpoint of practical matters, the conditional mean estimates have proven to be very similar in all data which have been checked to date, whether the original observations are weighted or not. The results for the 11 o'clock data are given in Table 12.2. There it may be seen that there are large between group differences in the variances and in the ranges. There appear to be large differences in the parent distributions as well. The empirical distribution functions (cdfs) for the two groups are show in Figure 12.1.

Figure 12.1a shows the cdf for the Good group. It has been graphed in normal probability coordinates, so departures from a straight line reveal departures from normality. The data appear approximately normal. Figure 12.1b shows the cdf for the Poor group. It has been graphed

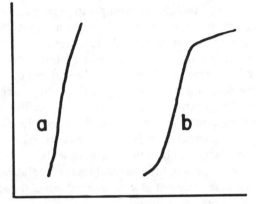

Figure 12.1. Empirical cdfs for $n = 103$ Good subjects (a) and $n = 95$ Poor subjects (b)

in linear coordinates. If the responses were sampled from a uniform distribution the cdf would appear as a straight line. While a reasonable model for this distribution is uncertain, the bulk of the probability mass seems reasonably well modeled by a uniform distribution, as the empirical cdf suggests. There is, of course, nothing to prevent one from estimating the component densities of $f(x)$, constructing a parametric mixture based on the estimates, and then decomposing the mixture distribution $f(x)$ directly.

In fact, an interesting question arises as to what solution is obtained if one does a parametric decomposition of the original data using what would doubtlessly be the default option, normal mixture decomposition. Does a normal decomposition of the origin X data for the 11 o'clock angle agree with the solution described above? That depends: If the estimated conditional moments of the above solution, given in Table 12.2, together with the estimates $\hat{\pi}$, are the starting values, the normal decomposition solution arrives at maximum likelihood estimates (i.e., under normality assumptions), which are similar to these estimates. The normal two-component mixture estimates (in familiar notation) were: $\hat{\mu}_1 = -.099$, $\hat{\mu}_2 = 1.04$; $\hat{\sigma}_1^2 = 2.68$, $\hat{\sigma}_2^2 = 212.66$; and $\hat{\pi}_2 = .45$. The fitted $\chi^2(4) = 54.25$ suggests a marginal fit. However, a histogram of the 198 x observations reveals a distribution skewed right and with two modes: one about zero where most of the data are clustered, and a second much smaller mode at $35°$, which might suggest a second component is located there. If one initialized a decomposition procedure suggested by the data histogram with a second mean located at about 35° the solution converges to a local minimum. And more generally, starting values different from the starting values suggested from the procedures proposed here tend to result in solutions that sometimes did not converge, or if they converged, they did so slowly. This finding suggests parametric normal mixture decomposition may be a useful adjunct to the proposed procedure, but it is not trustworthy as an exploratory method. Normal mixture decomposition is usually only possible if the sample size is moderately large, such as the case here with $n = 198$. In addition, the correspondences between the normal mixture solution and the procedure proposed here were not always evident when the analysis of the other vessel angles was considered.

Discussion

The problem of decomposing a k component mixture distribution without specifying the form of the components appears inherently intractable. But by defining a scoring criterion and transforming the problem into a binomial mixture framework, the problem is approachable. Approaching the problem of mixture decomposition through a binomial framework appears to hold some promise. It may make it possible to understand a variety of tasks that have long been poorly understood, in particular tasks that in the psychological literature are often termed "spatial tasks" and that can reveal, as the water-level example provided here reveals, striking individual differences in task performance. Such differences have in the past been poorly conceptualized. Most generally, individual differences have been viewed as differences expressible within standard shift models (i.e., a model of the form where U and V are random variables and $U + \delta$ has the distribution of V, with δ a constant). The ordinary two-sample t test is of this form. Such approaches have not been fruitful. It is easy to show that mixture models are models of this form only under extremely restrictive circumstances. Consequently, they are generally not shift models.

From a practical perspective, the approach would appear to possess a number of desirable features—even if, for example, it seemed plausible to proceed within more parametric frameworks. Normal mixture decomposition is doubtlessly the default model framework in use. In the two-component normal mixture model there are five parameters to contend with. For most small data sets of 30 or so observations, normal decomposition is likely to be very unreliable, even if the framework seems plausible. Furthermore, as is generally acknowledged, normal mixture decomposition is not always a friendly activity, and as the example provided illustrates, without good starting values normal mixture decomposition can be misleading.

Many of these practical problems disappear in the binomial mixture case. The model is much simpler, it can be applied to smaller data sets (Thomas & Turner, 1991), it has fewer parameters to estimate, and because the parameters are bounded in (0,1) it makes the specification of starting values much less problematic. In addition, because the form of the model is simple, the routine can be easily implemented within almost any standard programming language. A routine can be written within standard computer packages such as Minitab. Decomposition routines are available from the the author. The limitation of the approach is that there must be replicated responses; in practice this means no fewer than three *iid* task replications, from each individual, and desirably more.

There are two assumptions underlying the binomial mixture model approach that need to be investigated more carefully. One assumption is that the responses from each individual are independent of each other from trial to trial, an assumption often called local independence in the latent class literature. The second is that the success probability on successive trials is constant, over individuals within each latent class and within individuals for different task items. It seems unlikely that either of these assumptions will hold exactly in real data, and thus there needs to be systematic investigation of the applicability of the model when these assumptions fail.

While there are as yet no robustness studies that can address concerns regarding assumption failures, it seems likely that the model will perform reasonably well under at least mild departures from assumptions. If so, then the approach could well have much more general applicability for a variety of task domains. Many conventional tests or tasks have multiple items that, while not precisely replicates of one another, may well have, if not identical, then at least similar success probabilities. If distributional problems were of concern in such cases where mixtures might prove useful, the approach proposed here could be attractive.

There are other models that could be considered as alternatives to the binomial mixture model (e.g., Macready & Dayton, 1977; Rost, 1990). But the emphasis here has not been on binomial mixture models or possible alternative models per se; rather the emphasis has been on the applicability of binomial mixtures to the solution of the general mixture problem. The theorem given above applies only to the structure of binomial mixtures and not to somewhat more general models. That analytical fact, plus the fact that the solution of the binomial mixture problem has a relatively simple form, provide two compelling reasons for considering the approach as one approach to the solution of the general mixture problem, or, if you prefer, the general latent class problem.

References

Blischke, W. R. (1964). Estimating the parameters of mixtures of binomial distributions. *Journal of the American Statistical Association, 59,* 510-528.

Bozdogan, H. (1987). Model selection and Akaike's Information Criterion (AIC): The general theory and its analytical extensions. *Psychometrika, 52,* 345-370.

Dempster, A. P., Laird, N. M., & Rubin, D. B. (1977). Maximum likelihood from incomplete data via the algorithm. *Journal of the Royal Statistical Society, Series B, 39,* 1-38.

Everitt, B. S., & Hand, D. J. (1981). *Finite mixture distributions.* New York: Chapman & Hall.

Hall, P. (1981). On the non-parametric estimation of mixing proportions. *Journal of the Royal Statistical Society, Series B, 43,* 147-156.

Lesperance, M. L., & Kalbfleisch, J. D. (1992). An algorithm for computing the nonparametric MLE of a mixing distribution. *Journal of the American Statistical Association, 87,* 120-126.

Macready, G. B., & Dayton, C. M. (1977). The use of probabilistic models in the assessment of mastery. *Journal of Educational Statistics, 2,* 99-120.

McCutcheon, A. L. (1987). *Latent class analysis.* Newbury Park, CA: Sage.

McLachlan, B. J., & Basford, K. E. (1988). *Mixture models: Inference and applications to clustering.* New York: Marcel Dekker.

Piaget, J., & Inhelder, B. (1967). *The child's conception of space.* New York: Norton.

Rost, J. (1990). Rasch models in latent classes: An integration of two approaches to item analysis. *Applied Psychological Measurement, 14,* 271-282.

Sakamoto, Y., Ishiguor, M., & Kitagawa, G. (1986). *Akaike information criterion statistics.* Boston: Reidel.

Thomas, H., Jamison, W., & Hummel, D. D. (1973). Observation is insufficient for discovering that the surface of still water is invariantly horizontal. *Science, 181,* 173-174.

Thomas, H., & Turner, G.F.W. (1991). Individual differences and development in water-level task performance. *Journal of Experimental Child Psychology, 51,* 171-194.

Titterington, D. M., Smith, A. F. M., & Makov, U. E. (1985). *Statistical analysis of finite mixture distributions.* New York: John Wiley.

Windham, M. P., & Cutler, A. (1992). Information ratios for validating mixture analyses. *Journal of the American Statistical Association, 87,* 1188-1192.

Appendix

(A1) Let $\mathcal{F}$ be the set of all density functions (density refers to both density and mass functions in the following); $g(x) \in \mathcal{F}$ if $\int_{-\infty}^{\infty} dG(x) = 1$, $g(x) \geq 0$. Let k be a fixed positive integer and $\pi = (\pi_1, \pi_2, \ldots, \pi_k)$ be a vector of fixed values with $\pi_r > 0$, $r = 1$ to k, and $\sum_{r=1}^{k} \pi_r = 1$.

(A2) If $f_r(x) \in \mathcal{F}$, $r = 1$ to k then $f(x) = \sum_{r=1}^{k} \pi_r f_r(x)$. $f(x)$ is a finite mixture, and $f(x) \in \mathcal{F}$. However, only those mixtures with distinct components are of interest so consider the set of $\mathcal{M} \subset \mathcal{F}$ defined by:

(A3) $\mathcal{M} = \{\sum_{r=1}^{k} \pi_r f_r(x): f_r(x) \in \mathcal{F}, f_1(x), f_2(x), \ldots, f_k(x)$ are densities of different distributions$\}$.

To ensure identifiability of the components through their binomial representation, consider $\mathcal{M}_\pi(\theta) \subset \mathcal{M}$. Mixtures are in $\mathcal{M}_\pi(\theta)$ if, when integrated or summed over a common domain space $\mathcal{C}$, the proportion θ is different for each component.

(A4) $\mathcal{M}_\pi(\theta) = \{f(x) \in \mathcal{M} : 0 < \theta(\mathcal{C}; f_r) = \int_{\mathcal{C}} dF_r(x) < 1, \theta(\mathcal{C}; f_r), r = 1$ to k are distinct$\}$.

(A5) Let $\mathcal{P}$ be a population with mutually disjoint subpopulations. Thus $P_{,,} , t - 1$ to k, $\bigcup_{r=1}^{k} P_r = \mathcal{P}$. Each P_r is in proportion π_r. Associated with each P_r is density $f_r(x)$. Thus, the density associated with $\mathcal{P}$ is the mixture $f(x) = \sum_{r=1}^{k} \pi_r f_r(x)$.

(A6) Take a random sample size 1 from $\mathcal{P}$. The probability of the element being selected from P_r is π_r, and the distribution of the sampled X associated with P_r is $f_r(x)$. Define a new random variable $T(X) = W$ where $T(X)$ is:

$$W = \begin{cases} 1 & \text{if } x \in \mathcal{C} \\ 0 & \text{if } x \notin \mathcal{C} \end{cases} \qquad [12.10]$$

With these conditions we have $P(W = 1 \mid P_r) = \theta(\mathcal{C}; f_r) = \int_{\mathcal{C}} dF_r(x)$. Because $f(x) \in \mathcal{M}_\pi(\theta)$ the $\theta(\mathcal{C}; f_r)$ are all different. Consequently $T(X)$ defines a distinct binomial distribution for each P_r, $b[w; \theta(\mathcal{C}; f_r), 1]$, $r = 1$ to k. Furthermore, if there are m independent observations from subpopulation P_r, then associated with P_r is $Y = \sum_{j=1}^{m} W_j$, which is distributed as $b[y; \theta(\mathcal{C}; f_r), m]$. Thus, P_r has besides an associated $f_r(x)$, an associated $b[y; \theta(\mathcal{C}; f_r), m]$. Therefore $\mathcal{P}$ also has an associated mixed binomial distribution $g(y) = \sum_{r=1}^{k} \pi_r b[y; \theta(\mathcal{C}; f_r), m] \in \mathcal{M}$. To summarize:

Theorem. Given conditions A1 to A6, a population with an associated mixture distribution $f(x) = \sum_{r=1}^{k} \pi_r f_r(x)$ also has an associated binomial mixture distribution $g(y) = \sum_{r=1}^{k} \pi_r b[y; \theta(\mathscr{C}; f_r), m]$.

Corollary. If $f(x) \in \mathscr{F} - \bigcup_{\pi} \mathcal{M}_\pi(\theta)$, $T(X)$ leads to a binomial or mixture of binomials with number of components fewer than k.

13

Latent Variables in Log-Linear
Models of Repeated Observations

JACQUES A. HAGENAARS

1. Introduction

During the 1970s and 1980s, log-linear modeling nearly conquered the world of categorical characteristics and discrete events. And even now, in the early 1990s, the log-linear territory is still expanding (see, among others, Agresti, 1990, and Goodman, 1991). A potentially rich but not totally occupied area is the Latent Variable Sector. Just like its continuous counterpart, the discrete world is infected by measurement error. Therefore, corrections for all kinds of unreliability and invalidity are an essential prerequisite for drawing valid conclusions. This is especially true in longitudinal and developmental research: Measurement unreliability can make for systematical looking, but very misleading, observed patterns of change that do not reflect the true state of affairs. Fortunately, log-linear models with latent variables provide the tools for effectively dealing with measurement error in categorical characteristics (see, among others, Andersen, 1990; Hagenaars, 1990, 1993).

The misleading effects of measurement error as well as the usefulness of latent variable models will be illustrated in the next section by means of a very simple example. In Section 3, measurement models will be presented that may be employed when several related indicators have been measured at several points in time. After a brief discussion of the potentialities of log-linear models with latent variables for the investi-

Table 13.1 Attitude Toward Minority Groups and Watching the Documentary Series on TV

B. Attitude Toward Minorities; Before	C. Attitude Toward Minorities; After	A. Watching the TV Documentary		
		1. Regularly	2. Not Regularly	Total
1. Favorable	1. Favorable	81	326	407
	2. Unfavorable	10	89	99
2. Unfavorable	1. Favorable	10	89	99
	2. Unfavorable	11	484	495
	Total	112	988	1,100

SOURCE: See text.

gation of particular systematic patterns of true change (Section 4), the explanation of processes of change by means of causal (log-linear) models with latent variables will be the topic of Section 5. Section 6 is a brief section on estimation and available computer programs. Concluding and evaluating remarks about present difficulties and future possibilities will be made in the last section.

2. Misleading Effects of Measurement Error: An Example

The number of children coming from families with a non-European background is steadily growing in the Netherlands. It was therefore decided to launch a series of TV documentaries trying to enhance the level of information of white Dutch children about the cultures of relevant minority groups. The documentary was shown once a month during an entire year. An investigation was started to evaluate the effects of the series. At the beginning of the series and a couple of weeks after the last program had been shown, 1,100 white Dutch children were asked, among other things, about their attitudes toward minority groups. The data are presented in Table 13.1.

Even a rather simple table such as Table 13.1 can be used to answer many questions about the nature and the causes of the changes in the characteristics concerned. Table 13.2, for example, a turnover table derived from Table 13.1—restricting the data to just those children that watched the series regularly—shows that the vast majority (89.0%) of the children that had a favorable attitude to begin with kept that

Table 13.2 Turnover in Attitude Toward Minorities Among Those
Watching Regularly

		C. After	
B. Before	1. Favorable (%)	2. Unfavorable (%)	Total (%)
1. Favorable	89.0	11.0	100
2. Unfavorable	47.6	52.4	100
Total	81.3	18.7	100

SOURCE: Table 13.1
NOTE: horizontal percentages

favorable attitude during the whole series, while almost half (47.6%) of
those that started out with an unfavorable attitude changed that attitude
toward a more favorable one.

The difference in Table 13.2 between the transition probabilities 11.0%
and 47.6% for the two groups is indeed dramatic and highly significant:
Pearson-χ^2 = 15.61, df = 1, p = .000. Such findings might be explained
by the fact that among the children who watched the series regularly,
those with an unfavorable attitude form a minority and social pressure
has been exercised toward this "minority" to change their minds or by
the fact that this minority has changed under the influence of the
documentaries.

This latter possibility has to do with the very purpose of this investigation: Did the series influence children's knowledge and attitudes about
minority groups? From the data in Table 13.1 it can be calculated that
among those who watched the series regularly the percentage with a
favorable attitude at the time of the posttest is much higher than among
those who did not watch the series on a regular basis (81.3% vs. 42.0%).
However, as this is not a true experiment, "watchers" and "nonwatchers"
may have had (and actually had) different attitudes from the start. Controlling for these initial differences may be done by means of the log-linear
"covariance" model pictured in Figure 13.1 (Plewis, 1985, chap. 6; Hagenaars, 1990, sec. 5.3; see also Fisher, 1935/1990, sec. 56 & 57).

The covariance model {AB,AC,BC} (using the standard shorthand
notation for hierarchical log-linear models) may be rendered in its
multiplicative form as follows:

$$F_{ijk}^{ABC} = \eta\tau_i^A\tau_j^B\tau_k^C\tau_{ij}^{AB}\tau_{ik}^{AC}\tau_{jk}^{BC},$$ [13.1]

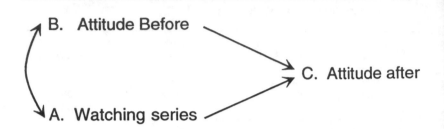

1. Saturated Model {ABC}: $\hat{\lambda}_1^{ABC} = -.101$, s.e. = .072
2. No Effect Model {AB,BC}: $L^2 = 17.11$, df = 2, $p = .00$
3. Covariance Model {AB,AC,BC}: $L^2 = 1.89$, df = 1,

Figure 13.1. Log-Linear Covariance Model

or in log-linear terms:

$$G_{ijk}^{ABC} = \ln F_{ijk}^{ABC} = \theta + \lambda_i^A + \lambda_j^B + \lambda_k^C + \lambda_{ij}^{AB} + \lambda_{ik}^{AC} + \lambda_{jk}^{BC}, \qquad [13.2]$$

where F_{ijk}^{ABC} denotes the expected cell frequency (i,j,k) of the joint variable ABC, where superscripts refer to the variables concerned and subscripts to the categories of these variables and where τ's indicate the multiplicative and λ's the log-linear effects.

As follows from the test statistics mentioned at the bottom of Figure 13.1, model {AB,AC,BC} fits the data in Table 13.1 rather well. It is not necessary to introduce the three-variable effect λ_{ijk}^{ABC}: This effect is very small and not significant, as shown in Figure 13.1, model {ABC}. Deleting the crucial direct effect λ_{ik}^{AC} yields a non-fitting model (model {AB,BC} in Figure 13.1). From the size of the effect parameter $\hat{\lambda}_{11}^{AC}$ in model {AB,AC,BC} (Figure 13.1), it may be concluded that the TV series has exercised a moderately large, statistically significant effect on the attitude toward minorities and that providing information led to a more favorable attitude.

Although in simplified forms, these are types of analyses that are rather characteristic of the ways social and behavioral scientists treat

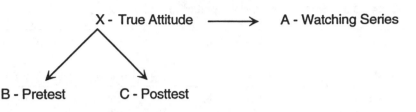

Figure 13.2.

longitudinal data. These data (and the example), however, were made up according to a scheme that had nothing to do with and actually contradicts the conclusions drawn above.

In constructing these artificial data, it was assumed that 10% of the children had watched the series regularly, and 90% had not or had watched irregularly. Among those that regularly watched, 90% were supposed to have a favorable attitude toward minority groups and 10% an unfavorable attitude; for the nonwatchers these percentages were 40% and 60%, respectively. Furthermore, it was assumed that the individual attitudes were stable and did not change during the whole period of investigation. These true (and stable) attitudes were not perfectly observed, however. The probability of getting the correct score at the pretest was .90 for each and every individual (and, accordingly, the probability of a misclassification was .10). The same probabilities were applied to the posttest regardless of the scores obtained at the pretest. Within rounding-off errors, this scheme led to the data in Table 13.1 for $N = 1,100$.

Figure 13.2 presents the "causal" diagram of this scheme: There is a not directly observed, latent (and stable) attitude X that "causes" the children to watch the series and there are two not completely reliable indicators A and B of this true attitude X.

The diagram in Figure 13.2 represents a standard latent class model, or, equivalently, a particular log-linear model with a latent variable. In terms of Lazarsfeld's original parametrization, the latent class model may be rendered as follows (Lazarsfeld & Henry, 1968; Goodman, 1974a, 1974b):

$$F_{ijkt}^{ABCX} = N\pi_{ijkt}^{ABCX} = N\pi_t^X \pi_{it}^{\overline{A}X} \pi_{jt}^{\overline{B}X} \pi_{kt}^{\overline{C}X}, \qquad [13.3]$$

where N is the sample size, π_{ijkt}^{ABCX} denotes the probability of obtaining score (i,j,k,t) on the joint variable $(ABCX)$, $\pi_{it}^{\overline{A}X}$ indicates the conditional

Table 13.3 Latent Class Model Applied to Table 13.1

True Attitude X	$\hat{\pi}_t^X$	A. Watching Series $\hat{\pi}_{it}^{\bar{A}X}$		B. Pretest $\hat{\pi}_{jt}^{\bar{B}X}$		C. Posttest $\hat{\pi}_{kt}^{\bar{C}X}$	
		1. Yes	2. No	1. fav.	2. unfav.	1. fav.	2. unfav.
Latent Class 1	.45	.20	.80	.90	.10	.90	.10
Latent Class 2	.55	.02	.98	.10	.90	.10	.90
		$\hat{\gamma}_{11}^{AX} = 1.86$		$\hat{\gamma}_{11}^{BX} = 3.00$		$\hat{\gamma}_{11}^{CX} = 3.00$	
		$\hat{\lambda}_{11}^{AX} = .623$		$\hat{\lambda}_{11}^{BX} = 1.099$		$\hat{\lambda}_{11}^{CX} = 1.099$	

NOTE: $L^2 = 0$, df $= 0$, $p = 0$.

response probability that someone who belongs to latent class t, $(X = t)$, obtains the score $A = i$, and where the other symbols have analogous meanings.

In log-linear terms, the diagram in Figure 13.2 corresponds with model $\{AX, BX, CX\}$ (Haberman, 1979), that is, with:

$$F_{ijkt}^{ABCX} = \eta \tau_i^A \tau_j^B \tau_k^C \tau_t^X \tau_{it}^{AX} \tau_{jt}^{BX} \tau_{kt}^{CX}. \qquad [13.4]$$

Equation 13.4 represents a special log-linear model in that the variable X is a not directly observed variable. Several algorithms and computer programs have been developed for obtaining the maximum likelihood estimates of the parameters of log-linear models with latent variables, the most important of which are mentioned in Section 6.

The results of applying model $\{AX, BX, CX\}$ with a dichotomous latent variable X to the data in Table 13.1 are presented in Table 13.3.

With three dichotomous indicators, the two-latent-class model is exactly identified and fits the data perfectly, producing as a matter of course the parameter estimates that were used to construct the data in Table 13.1, within the limits of rounding-off errors.

If we had not known how these data came about, it would not have been possible to decide on empirical grounds between the latent class model in Figure 13.2 and the covariance model in Figure 13.1. The implications of the two competing models are, however, very different. According to the latent class model, nobody changes her or his attitude and, as there is no true change, there are also no true "dramatic differences" in transition probabilities between those with a favorable and those with an unfavorable attitude as were observed in Table 13.2. And as far as there are "true" changes in the form of random fluctuations in the characteristics concerned, that is, fluctuations that are registered as unreliability (Hagenaars, 1990, sec. 4.4.1), the unreliability of the measurements as indicated by the probability of a misclassification is the same for each and every child (.10, see Table 13.3) and therefore the same for those with a favorable and an unfavorable attitude.

Furthermore, according to the latent class model, there is no effect from watching the series (A) on the attitude at the posttest (C). In this case, the conclusions drawn from the log-linear covariance model do not reflect the (simulated) true state of affairs; they just mirror the distortions caused by even this small amount of measurement error.

Because unreliability looms everywhere (Hagenaars, 1990, p. 182), latent variable models are useful, at the very least, for drawing the researcher's attention to the possibility that the conclusions directly based on the observed data may be wrong.

Of course, this is not a startling novelty. Decades ago a number of methodologists warned about these kinds of misleading effects of measurement error (Maccoby, 1956; Thorndike, 1942; Wiggins, 1955; and many others since). But researchers keep on ignoring measurement errors (and methodologists fail to inform them adequately). One wonders how much of our present-day "knowledge" about the instability of small groups compared to large groups (e.g., nonvoters vs voters or voters for large vs. small parties —see Barnes, 1990; Hagenaars, 1990, chap. 5) and about the effects of particular "nonexperimental interventions" is based on unreliability of the measurements.

This is a regrettable situation, the more so because the models and algorithms that are now available for estimating the sizes and consequences of unreliability and invalidity are much more powerful than ever before. For continuous variables, Jöreskog's LISREL and Bentler's EQS model are excellent examples. For discrete data, log-linear models with latent variables may be put to much the same uses, as will be partly shown in the remainder of this chapter (see also Hagenaars, 1988b).

3. Measurement Models for Related Characteristics Measured Over Time

It often occurs in panel studies that related characteristics, for example, Preference Political Party and Preference Presidential Candidate,

Table 13.4 Mothers' Mental Health and Loneliness

A. Mental Health time 1		1. Good		2. Poor		
B. Mental Health time 2		1. Good	2. Poor	1. Good	2. Poor	Total
C. Loneli- ness Time 1	D. Loneli- ness Time 2					
1. Absent	1. Absent	72	8	13	11	104
	2. Present	11	2	2	7	22
2. Present	1. Absent	15	2	4	8	29
	2. Present	7	4	11	12	34
	Total	105	16	30	38	189

SOURCE: Plewis (1985, p. 120).

are measured in at least two waves. A common way of analyzing such data is with Lazarsfeld's cross-lagged panel correlation technique. The main purpose of this technique is to determine which characteristic might be regarded as the cause of the other: Does Party Preference determine Candidate Preference or is it the other way around? References regarding origin, extensions, and critiques of this technique are provided by, among others, Hagenaars (1990, pp. 240-248). Along with many other assumptions, application of this technique requires perfectly reliable and valid measurements. Once the possibility of measurement error is allowed, other interesting models arise that may lead to totally different explanations of the data (Goodman, 1974a).

An example is presented in Table 13.4. The data come from a longitudinal study of preschool children and their families and refer to the mother's mental health and feelings of loneliness; the times of measurements were 12 months apart (Moss & Plewis, 1977).

Plewis applies (the well-fitting) "cross-lagged" log-linear model $\{AB, AC,AD,BC,BD,CD\}$ to the data in Table 13.4. From comparing the cross-lagged effects $\hat{\lambda}_{11}^{AC}$ and $\hat{\lambda}_{11}^{BC}$ he then tentatively suggests that Mental Health causes feelings of Loneliness rather than vice versa (Plewis, 1985, pp. 119-122; for a critical review of the appropriateness of this particular log-linear model for determining the causal direction, see Hagenaars, 1990, sec. 5.4).

An alternative look at the variables and data in Table 13.4 follows from the compound hypothesis that perhaps Loneliness and Mental Health are just imperfect indicators of one and the same dichotomous

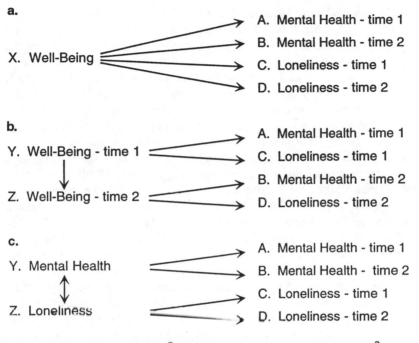

a.

X. Well-Being

A. Mental Health - time 1
B. Mental Health - time 2
C. Loneliness - time 1
D. Loneliness - time 2

b.

Y. Well-Being - time 1

Z. Well-Being - time 2

A. Mental Health - time 1
C. Loneliness - time 1
B. Mental Health - time 2
D. Loneliness - time 2

c.

Y. Mental Health

Z. Loneliness

A. Mental Health - time 1
B. Mental Health - time 2
C. Loneliness - time 1
D. Loneliness - time 2

a. Model $\{AX,BX,CX,DX\}$: $L^2 = 12.56$, df = 6, $p = .05$ (Pearson-$\chi^2 = 12.58$)
b. Model $\{YZ,AY,CY,BZ,DZ\}$: **see text**
c. Model $\{YZ,AY,BY,CZ,DZ\}$: $L^2 = 3.17$, df = 4, $p = .53$ (Pearson-$\chi^2 = 2.98$);
$\hat{\lambda}_{11}^{YZ} = .833$, $\hat{\lambda}_{11}^{AY} = 1.031$, $\hat{\lambda}_{11}^{BY} = .783$, $\hat{\lambda}_{11}^{CZ} = .741$, $\hat{\lambda}_{11}^{DZ} = .775$
NOTE: X,Y,Z are dichotomous latent variables; A through D observed variables

---

Figure 13.3. Measurement Models for Data in Table 4

latent variable Well-Being (X) and that a person's well-being is a rather stable characteristic that does not change easily. This compound hypothesis is represented in Figure 13.3a and corresponds with the standard latent class model, that is, with log-linear model $\{AX,BX,CX,DX\}$. From the test statistics presented in Figure 13.3, model (a), it is not clear whether to accept or reject the model.

Perhaps a better result may be obtained by allowing for true, latent change to occur. If Mental Health and Loneliness are still regarded as indicators of the theoretical construct Well-Being, there will be two dichotomous latent variables Y and Z, where Y refers to Well-Being at Time 1 with indicators A and C, and Z to Well-Being at Time 2 with indicators B and D. The 2×2 latent turnover table YZ then shows the true changes in Well-Being between the two time points. This model is depicted in Figure 13.3b and corresponds with log-linear model $\{YZ,AY, CY,BZ,DZ\}$. Application of this model to Table 13.4 happens to yield, for these particular data, a degenerate solution, in that the two off-diagonal cells $YZ = 1\ 2$ and $YZ = 2\ 1$ are empty: There is no latent change in Well-Being. There are actually just two nonempty latent classes, viz. $YZ = 1\ 1$ and $YZ = 2\ 2$, and, accordingly, for these data, the test statistics and the parameter estimates for the model in Figure 13.3b are identical to those obtained for the standard latent class model of Figure 13.3a.

Another possibility of modifying the standard latent class model in Figure 13.3a is to assume that there is indeed no latent change, but that Mental Health (A, B) and Loneliness (C, D) are not indicators of the same theoretical variable but refer to distinct concepts. Two dichotomous latent variables Y and Z are needed where Y now refers to the (stable) true scores of the characteristic Mental Health, with indicators A and B, and Z to the latent variable Loneliness with indicators C and D (Figure 13.3c). This model $\{YZ,AY,BY,CZ,DZ\}$ fits the data in Table 13.4 excellently, and much better than the standard latent class model (a). [Note, however, that carrying out the standard conditional likelihood ratio test comparing two nested models by subtracting the L^2 (and df) of the less restricted model (c) from the corresponding test statistics of the more restricted model (a) is not allowed here as parameter estimates are involved that lie on the boundary of the permissible parameter space; see Bishop, Fienberg, & Holland (1975, p. 510).]

In model (c), mental health and feelings of loneliness are regarded as distinct concepts rather than aspects of one underlying variable Well-Being. Furthermore, there are no cross-lagged effects to compare; the observed changes result solely from measurement error. The "reliability" of the measurements of these two distinct concepts can be estimated by means of the log-linear parameters concerning the relations between each latent variable and its indicators, that is, by means of $\hat{\lambda}_{11}^{AY}$, $\hat{\lambda}_{11}^{BY}$, $\hat{\lambda}_{11}^{CZ}$, and $\hat{\lambda}_{11}^{DZ}$. These coefficients are presented in Figure 13.3, model (c), and it follows that the scores on the observed variables A, B, C, and D are strongly but not perfectly determined by the true scores on X; indicator A appears to be the most reliable measure.

The true log-linear association between Mental Health and Loneliness, corrected for unreliability of the measurements, is provided by

$\hat{\lambda}_1^{YZ}$ and turns out to be rather strong: [.833—Figure 13.3, model (c)] and in the expected direction. This association between the latent variables is much stronger than the corresponding associations between the manifest variables based on the observed two-dimensional tables (for table AC: .164; for AD: .472; for BC: .188; and for BD: .195), a result that parallels the "correction for attenuation" well known from classical test theory (Nunnally, 1978, p. 237).

If the last model had failed to fit, still other models with latent variables taking measurement error into account would have been possible. For example, it seems theoretically reasonable to assume that Mental Health is a more stable phenomenon than feelings of Loneliness. So, on theoretical grounds, a model with three dichotomous latent variables might have been proposed: W—Mental Health with indicators A and B; Y—Loneliness at Time 1 with indicator C; Z—Loneliness at Time 2 with indicator D, leading to model {WYZ,AW,BW,CY,DZ}.

This model seems to have zero degrees of freedom, because it has as many parameters to be independently estimated as observed cell frequencies. However, it is not identified. (For expositions of identifiability, see De Leeuw, Van der Heijden, & Verboon 1990; Goodman, 1974b; Van der Heijden, Mooijaart, & De Leeuw, 1992.) Extra restrictions are needed to make it identifiable.

First, it is possible to impose in various ways restrictions on the "reliabilities" (resulting in nonhierarchical log-linear models). In terms of conditional response probabilities, this usually amounts to setting the probabilities of giving the "correct" answer in agreement with the latent score equal to each other for particular manifest variables for particular categories of the latent variables (Goodman, 1974b; Mooijaart & Van der Heijden, 1992); for example: $\pi_{11}^{AW} = \pi_{22}^{AW} = \pi_{11}^{CY} = \pi_{22}^{CY}$. Restricting the "reliabilities" in terms of log-linear parameters means setting all or some of the two-variable parameters λ_{iq}^{AW}, λ_{jq}^{BW}, λ_{kr}^{CY}, and λ_{ls}^{DZ}, equal to each other; for example: $\lambda_{11}^{AW} = \lambda_{11}^{CY}$. Computer programs are available to introduce all these kinds of restrictions routinely (see Section 6). When imposing these equality constraints, the user has to be aware that, in general, restrictions on the conditional response probabilities result in different models than imposing restrictions on the log-linear two-variable parameters [although restrictions on the conditional response probabilities can be expressed in terms of (combinations of) restrictions on the log-linear one- and two-variable effects; see Hagenaars, 1990, pp. 111, 185; and especially, Heinen, 1993].

Despite the apparent gain in degrees of freedom, however, restrictions on the "reliabilities" do not necessarily make model {WYZ,AW, BW,CY,DZ} identifiable when applied to Table 13.4 (definitely not for the sets of restrictions that were actually tried out). Additional restrictions, resulting in an identifiable model, may be found by defining a nonsaturated log-linear model for the relations among the latent variables, for example, model {WY,YZ,AW,BW,CY,DZ}. These kinds of restrictions can also be routinely applied, using existing software.

Theoretical considerations are the most important when one tries to obtain well-fitting models. These theoretical notions may be guided by "empirical" means, however, especially by the (adjusted or standardized) residual frequencies of the baseline model (Haberman, 1978, p. 78). With latent variable models, such an inspection often reveals that the strength of the observed association between particular indicators is underestimated by the proposed model. By introducing into the log-linear model direct relations between the indicators concerned (thus violating the basic latent class assumption of local independence) a tremendous improvement of fit is often obtained at the cost of just one or two degrees of freedom (Hagenaars, 1988a, 1993). Such direct effects between manifest variables point to the fact that the observed relations among the indicators concerned are not fully explained by the latent variables in the model. There are other, omitted (unmeasured, "latent") variables that cause association among the manifest variables over and above the association caused by the included latent variables. In other words, there are correlated errors.

Now, it often is a plausible assumption in longitudinal and developmental research that the measurement errors of a particular characteristic are correlated over time. In such cases, improving the fit of the baseline model by introducing direct effects among the indicators may be the sensible thing to do. If, however, there are no clear substantive explanations for the extra direct effects between the indicators, a purely empirical, atheoretical way of achieving a good fit should be avoided.

4. Systematic Patterns of Latent Change

The log-linear model with latent variables has been mainly treated so far as a (modified) latent class model, that is, as a measurement model for investigating the relations between the latent and the manifest variables. However, log-linear models with latent variables can also be used for finding the causes and consequences of the true, latent changes, which will be the topic of the next section, and for exploring the nature of the true, latent change, the latter to be discussed in this section. This exposition will be even more informal than the ones above, the main purpose being to give a first impression of the many possible applications of log-linear modeling with latent variables for the study of patterns of latent change and of the work that has been done in this area.

Still close to the latent class (measurement) model are a set of models that have been developed for the analysis of large turnover tables, where the variables concerned have many (five or more) categories. Clogg (1981a), Marsden (1985), and Luijkx (1988) have proposed ingenious and useful models for such tables in the context of social mobility research; Hagenaars (1990, sec. 4.4.2) reviewed these procedures and applied them to turnover tables on Voting (the Dutch political system produces a lot of political parties); Van der Heijden et al. (1992) extended some of these models into a general approach for "latent time budget models."

The basic idea behind these approaches is that the movements among the many categories in the observed turnover table (e.g., among occupations or political parties) can be explained by the fact that each respondent belongs to one of the few postulated latent classes (e.g., to one of three social classes or one of the three basic political orientations) and that this latent position determines with a certain probability the belonging to particular manifest categories at each point in time. In some models, people may change their latent positions over time, in others not.

If latent change is allowed for, one might be interested in investigating whether the changes follow a particular pattern. In general, whenever a model allowing for latent change—for example, model (b) in Figure 13.3—has been set up, one may want to investigate whether the latent change follows particular systematic patterns.

One might wonder, for example, whether a square latent turnover table YZ is symmetric, that is, whether the entry of cell (r,s) is the same as cell frequency (s,r) for all values of s and r, $s \neq r$. Or perhaps one suspects that the square latent turnover table is quasi-symmetric, that is, symmetric as far as the differences between the (latent) marginals allow it. Symmetry and quasi-symmetry models can be easily defined in terms of restrictions on the log-linear parameters (Bishop et al., 1975, chap. 8; Haberman, 1979, chap. 8; Hagenaars, 1986).

Another interesting angle from which latent turnover tables might be viewed is (quasi)-independence (Goodman, 1968). Perhaps at the latent level, people are inclined to occupy the same latent position over time, that is, to belong to one of the main diagonal cells of the square turnover table YZ, but once they change their latent position they may have no special preferences for particular other positions. The independence model $\{Y,Z\}$ is postulated for the off-diagonal cells of the latent turnover table YZ, while no special restrictions are applied to the main diagonal cells.

Especially in developmental research, other patterns of latent change may be relevant. The latent variables may involve a particular ability that once acquired will not be lost. If the latent variables Y and Z each have three categories referring to increasing levels of ability, a model such as model (b) in Figure 13.3 may be fitted with the additional restriction that in the latent turnover table YZ the cells (2,1), (3,1), and (3,2) are empty. If, moreover, development takes place only through successive stages, then also cell frequency (1,3) implying a jump from level 1 directly to level 3 must be restricted to zero.

Even when at the manifest level these "impossible" cells are not empty in the observed turnover table(s), the proposed developmental model might still hold on the latent level, that is, if measurement errors are accounted for. In this way, a wide variety of latent trajectories can be defined; the parameters of such models can be estimated by means of most programs for carrying out latent class analysis.

Finally, when a particular characteristic is measured at more than two points in time, still other possibilities for modeling latent change arise. For example, when a particular characteristic has been measured in each wave of a four-wave panel study, there are four manifest variables A (Wave 1) through D (Wave 4). Allowing for latent change to occur at each point in time yields four latent variables V (Wave 1), W (Wave 2), Y (Wave 3), and Z (Wave 4). A possible model for such data would be model $\{VW,WY,YZ,AV,BW,CY,DZ\}$, depicted in Figure 13.4.

The model in Figure 13.4 represents a first-order latent Markov chain, in that the latent scores on Time t are only directly influenced by the latent scores on Time $t-1$. A standard (stationary) Markov chain would require the additional restriction that the corresponding transition probabilities of all turnover tables between successive time points—of the marginal turnover tables VW, WY, and YZ—are identical. This particular restriction, however, leads us outside the boundaries of log-linear modeling. Van de Pol and Langeheine (1990) discuss maximum likelihood

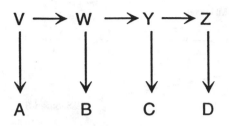

Figure 13.4.

estimation for the parameters of a very general class of Markov models, including (nonstationary) log-linear models like the model in Figure 13.4.

So, although the log-linear model with latent variables does not encompass all possible models of discrete latent change, it is sufficiently powerful to adequately test most of a researcher's ideas about systematic patterns of true change in categorical characteristics (Collins & Wugalter, 1992; Hagenaars, 1990).

5. Causal Modeling With Latent Variables

In this section, log-linear models will be discussed from the viewpoint of carrying out causal analyses. Because the causal log-linear models considered in this section bear a clear resemblance to regular LISREL models, they have been termed "modified LISREL models" (Hagenaars, 1988b). Typical for these modified LISREL models is that, because of the assumed causal order of the variables, their parameters have to be estimated, in principle, in the stepwise fashion indicated by Goodman (1973; see also Section 6). For an illustration of the "modified LISREL approach," the example in Table 13.4 on mothers' well-being has been (fictitiously) extended, yielding the causal model in Figure 13.5 (for real world examples, see Hagenaars, 1990, 1993).

There are three latent variables in Figure 13.5: W—stable Mental Health, measured at the first wave by means of B and at the second wave by means of C; Y—the true feelings of Loneliness at the first wave, with indicator D; and Z—Loneliness at the second wave, measured by means of E. Besides the indicators B, C, D, and E, there are the directly observed variables A—Age and F—Divorced or not one year after Wave 2 was finished. The observed variables A and F are not indicators

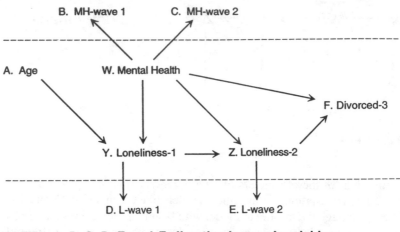

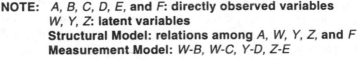

NOTE: *A, B, C, D, E*, and *F*: **directly observed variables**
        W, Y, Z: **latent variables**
        Structural Model: relations among *A, W, Y, Z*, **and** *F*
        Measurement Model: *W-B, W-C, Y-D, Z-E*

Figure 13.5. Causal Models With Latent Variables

of some latent variable but part of the structural model, in which the assumed causal connections among *A, W, Y, Z*, and *F* are defined.

In the first instance, the model in Figure 13.5 may be treated as a kind of (quasi-)latent class model {*XB,XC,XD,XE*} with (quasi-)latent variable *X* and four indicators *B* through *E*. *X* is a joint variable having as its categories all combinations of all categories of the variables *A, W, Y, Z*, and *F*, the variables that are in the structural part of the model. The indicators *B* through *E* depend on *X*, that is, on the joint variable *AWYZF*, in such a way that *B* and *C* only depend on *W*, *D* is only determined by *Y*, and *E* only by *Z*.

If all restrictions implied by the structural part of the model in Figure 13.5 (the part between the dashed lines) are ignored, the parameters of the resulting log-linear model {*AWYZF,BW,CW,DY,EZ*} can be estimated as an ordinary one-step log-linear model with latent variables. However, the estimated expected frequencies of this one-step model obviously do not correctly reflect the hypothesized relations among *A*,

W, Y, Z, and *F:* The (estimated expected) entries of marginal table *AWYZF* ought to mirror the structural part of Figure 13.5.

Although it seems to be doing the job, the intended restrictions on marginal table *AWYZF* are not realized by setting up log-linear model $\{AY,WY,YZ,WZ,WF,ZF\}$ for this marginal table. To illustrate this point: It is assumed in Figure 13.5 that Age (*A*) and Mental Health (*W*) are independent of each other. Accordingly, no term $\{AW\}$ occurs in model $\{AY,WY,YZ,WZ,WF,ZF\}$, that is, λ_{ip}^{AW} is a priori set to zero. As log-linear parameters are generally partial coefficients, however, model $\{AY,WY, YZ,WZ,WF,ZF\}$ implies that A and W are independent of each other holding the other variables (*Y, Z,* and *F*) constant. But given the causal order of the variables in Figure 13.5 and from the adage that what is causally posterior cannot influence what is causally prior, it follows that Age (*A*) and Mental Health (*W*) should be independent of each other without holding the other variables constant. The independence model $\{A, W\}$ is assumed to hold in marginal table *AW*. If the independence model has to be rejected for marginal table *AW*, the two-variable effect λ_{ip}^{AW} in the saturated model $\{AW\}$ applied to marginal table *AW* provides the correct estimate of the effects of Age on Mental Health and not λ_{ip}^{AW} in model $\{AW,AY,WY,YZ,WZ,WF,ZF\}$ for table *AWYZF*.

Following the same kind of logic, marginal table *AWY* should be used to determine the effects of Age (*A*) and Mental Health (*W*) on Loneliness at Wave 1 (*Y*). If Figure 13.5 is a true representation of reality, model $\{AW,AY,WY\}$ should be valid for marginal table *AWY*. Note that model $\{AW,AY,WY\}$ does contain the parameter λ_{ip}^{AW}, as it follows from the collapsibility theorem (Bishop et al., 1975, p. 47), that given the postulated effects in Figure 13.5, log-linear effect λ_{ip}^{AW} will not be zero in marginal table *AWY* if it is zero in the collapsed table *AW* (see also Agresti, 1990, p. 152).

To determine the effects of Age (*A*), Mental Health (*W*), and Loneliness-Time 1 (*Y*) on Loneliness-Time 2 (*Z*), the frequencies of marginal table *AWYZ* should be in agreement with model $\{AWY,WZ,YZ\}$. Again, all parameters referring to the independent variables of this submodel are included (by means of the term $\{AWY\}$).

Finally, to determine the effects on the ultimate dependent variable Divorce (*F*) of all other variables that are part of the structural model in Figure 13.5, model $\{AWYZ,WF,ZF\}$ is postulated for marginal table *AWYZF*.

For models without latent variables, in which all variables are directly observed, Goodman (1973) has shown how to obtain the parameter estimates of all submodels and how to calculate the estimated expected frequencies for the whole model in such a manner that all subtables are in agreement with all postulated submodels. Actually, the simplest way to proceed in that case is to set up the appropriate observed subtables, apply to them the submodels concerned employing the principles outlined above, and to sum all likelihood ratio chi-square test statistics and degrees of freedom of the submodels to arrive at one overall test statistic. When there are latent variables involved, the EM-algorithm described in the next section may be used to obtain the estimated expected frequencies for the whole model.

If the total model has to be rejected, one or more of the restrictions in one or more of the submodels may be relaxed and hierarchically nested models may be compared with each other by computing the conditional test statistics. In this way, it can be determined which restriction in what submodel is responsible for the rejection of the total causal model (although all criticisms that might be leveled against repeated and ex post facto testing apply here as well).

6. Estimation Procedures and Available Computer Programs

Under the (product) multinomial sampling scheme, maximum likelihood estimates for log-linear models may be obtained by means of the Newton-Raphson or the EM algorithm (Goodman, 1974a, 1974b; Haberman, 1979, chap. 10; Little & Rubin, 1987, chap. 7). Programs for estimating log-linear models with latent variables are not yet part of packages such as BMDP, SAS, or SPSS^x. Stand-alone programs— most of which are rather easy to use—are readily available, however.

Haberman's program LAT (Haberman, 1979) and its successor NEWTON (Haberman, 1988) are completely formulated in log-linear terms rather than in terms of Lazarsfeld's parametrization using conditional response probabilities. All kinds of restrictions, including equality and (curvi)linear restrictions, may be imposed on the log-linear effects by means of the appropriate design matrix.

All log-linear models with latent variables discussed above can be routinely estimated by means of LAT and NEWTON, except modified LISREL models. Although using NEWTON, one can in principle apply the stepwise estimation approach needed in the modified LISREL models, a particular reparametrization has to be chosen for each particular causal model, which is far from easy to handle (Winship & Mare,

1989, appendix). On the other hand, as follows from the collapsibility theorem (Bishop et al., 1975, p. 47), a number of causal models that seemingly have to be estimated in a stepwise fashion may be treated as ordinary one-step log-linear models—the model in Figure 13.4 is a case in point—and no special reparametrization is required when using NEWTON.

As LAT and NEWTON make use of the scoring algorithm and a variant of the Newton-Raphson algorithm respectively, initial parameter estimates have to be rather close to the final estimates. Although much better than LAT, one still encounters difficulties, even with NEWTON, in finding the appropriate initial parameter estimates for some models and data sets.

The EM algorithm is much less sensitive to the "quality" of the initial estimates. [A more complete comparison of the (dis)advantages of Newton-Raphson and EM can be found in Hagenaars, 1990.] Because of this feature, a simple version of the EM algorithm will be discussed below after mentioning a few programs that make use of this algorithm.

One of the first programs for latent class analysis in which Goodman's version of the EM algorithm has been implemented and that uses Lazarsfeld's parametrization of the model in terms of conditional response probabilities is Clogg's MLLSA (Clogg, 1981b; Goodman, 1974a, 1974b). It is now part of Eliason's CDAS package (Department of Sociology, Pennsylvania State University). By means of MLLSA, the parameters of log-linear models with latent variables can be estimated, provided that the relations among all external and latent variables that make up the structural part of the model satisfy the saturated model. Although originally written for the analysis of (latent) Markov chains, Van de Pol and Langeheine's PANMARK can be used for many of the models mentioned above and work is still being done to enhance the program's applicability (Van de Pol & Langeheine, 1990).

LCAG is based on the same Goodman algorithm as MLLSA, but with the additional possibility of imposing unsaturated hierarchical models on the latent level (Hagenaars, 1990, 1993; Hagenaars & Luijkx, 1987). All models mentioned above, including the modified LISREL models, can be (and have been) estimated by means of LCAG. Work is in progress to add several of the desirable features of NEWTON to LCAG resulting in a new program *l*EM (Vermunt, 1993).

The EM algorithm may be seen as an extension of the Iterative Proportional Fitting (IPF) Procedure. IPF can be used to find the estimated expected frequencies $\hat{F}$ of hierarchical log-linear models without latent variables (Bishop et al., 1975). In IPF, the initial estimates of F are iteratively adapted to the sufficient statistics, that is, to the observed marginal frequencies f to be reproduced by the hierarchical model. For example, in model $\{AB,AC,BC\}$, the estimated expected frequencies $\hat{F}_{ijk}^{ABC}$ are iteratively estimated in such a way that at the end the estimated expected frequencies $\hat{F}$ of the marginal tables AB, AC, BC are exactly identical to the corresponding observed frequencies f of marginal tables AB, AC, BC respectively, that is, $\hat{F}_{ij+}^{ABC} = f_{ij+}^{ABC}$, $\hat{F}_{i+k}^{ABC} = f_{i+k}^{ABC}$, and $\hat{F}_{+jk}^{ABC} = f_{+jk}^{ABC}$. If A and B are regarded as causes of C, stepwise estimation may be necessary. For example, if it is assumed that A and B are statistically independent, submodel $\{A,B\}$ should be applied to marginal table AB. If it is further postulated that A and B both influence C, but without affecting each other's influence on C, submodel $\{AB, AC,BC\}$ should be valid for table ABC. Goodman (1973) has shown that the estimated expected frequencies $\hat{F}^*$ for the whole model, assuming that both submodels are true, can be obtained as follows:

$$\hat{F}_{ijk}^{*ABC} = \hat{F}_{ij}^{AB}(\hat{F}_{ijk}^{ABC}/\hat{F}_{ij+}^{ABC}) = \hat{F}_{ij}^{AB} \hat{\pi}_{ijk}^{AB\bar{C}}, \qquad [13.5]$$

where $\hat{F}_{ij}^{AB}$ refers to the estimated expected frequencies for model $\{A,B\}$ applied to marginal table AB and $\hat{F}_{ijk}^{ABC}$ and $\hat{F}_{ij+}^{ABC}$ to the estimated expected frequencies for model $\{AB,AC,BC\}$ for table ABC.

For hierarchical log-linear models with latent variables, the complete table including the latent variables is not an observed table and some or all of the sufficient statistics are not observed, not known. The basic idea behind the EM algorithm is very simple: try to get good estimates of the unobserved sufficient statistics and then proceed as if the resulting estimated sufficient statistics are just ordinary sufficient statistics.

The EM algorithm essentially consists of a repetition of two steps, the E- and the M-step. These steps will be exemplified using an observed table $SEABC$, in which S(ex) and E(ducation) are external variables, and A, B, and C indicators of latent variable Y. We want to fit model $\{SE,SY,EY,YA,YB,YC\}$ to table $SEABC$. Because the complete table $\{SEYABC\}$ is not observed, the sufficient statistics, the "observed" frequencies of marginal tables SY, EY, YA, YB, and YC, are not known.

In order to estimate the sufficient statistics, first, initial estimates $\hat{F}_{ijrklm}^{SEYABC}(0)$ have to be found that satisfy the restrictions implied by the postulated model. These estimates can be obtained by roughly estimating the parameters of the model. Then, in the E-step, the estimated observed frequencies $\hat{f}^{SEYABC}_{ijrklm}$ are calculated by using $\hat{F}(0)$ as estimates of $\hat{F}$:

$$\hat{f}^{SEYABC}_{ijrklm} = f^{SEABC}_{ijklm}(\hat{F}^{SEYABC}_{ijrklm}/\hat{F}^{SEYABC}_{ij+klm}) = \hat{f}^{SEABC}_{ijklm}\,\hat{\pi}^{SE\overline{Y}ABC}_{ijrklm}. \qquad [13.6]$$

In the M-step, the estimated expected frequencies $\hat{F}$ obtained so far— $\hat{F}(0)$ at the first M-step—are improved by means of IPF, treating the estimated observed frequencies $\hat{f}$ as if they were regular observed frequencies f. In this example, for model $\{SE,SY,EY,YA,YB,YC\}$, $\hat{F}^{SEYABC}_{ijrklm}$ is successively adjusted to reproduce the estimated observed marginal frequencies $\hat{f}^{SEYABC}_{ij++++}$, $\hat{f}^{SEYABC}_{i+r+++}$, $\hat{f}^{SEYABC}_{+jr+++}$, $\hat{f}^{SEYABC}_{++rk++}$, $\hat{f}^{SEYABC}_{++r+l+}$, and $\hat{f}^{SEYABC}_{++r++m}$. If a modified LISREL model is defined (which is not true in this example) and a stepwise estimation procedure is needed during the M-step, the appropriate marginal tables $\hat{f}$ and $\hat{F}$ are set up, and the postulated submodels are fitted to the estimated observed marginal tables. The estimated expected frequencies $\hat{F}$ obtained for each sub-model are combined to obtain the estimated expected frequencies $\hat{F}^*$ for the whole modified LISREL model in the manner of Equation 13.5.

The estimated expected frequencies that come out of the M-step are used in the E-step to get new and better estimates of the estimated observed frequencies $\hat{f}$, which in turn are used in the M-step to improve the estimates $\hat{F}$, and so on, until the outcomes converge.

6. Conclusions

As exemplified above, log-linear models with latent variables are extremely useful for answering a large number of questions that arise in the context of longitudinal research. However, log-linear modeling shares with all forms of categorical data analysis the problems caused by sparse tables. Even relatively "small" models like the one in Figure 13.5 require very large samples to obtain reliable and robust parameter estimates and to carry out significance tests. Many proposals have been made to solve the sparse table problem, but no really satisfying solution yet exists (Agresti, 1990; Read & Cressie, 1988). An interesting and promising approach involving a renewed interest in (Fisher's) exact tests has come up within the context of graphical models (Agresti, 1992; Whittaker, 1990). Because of this problem of small sample size, it is important to include as many cases as possible and not to waste a respondent because he or she failed to answer just one particular item. Excellent theoretical work in this area has been done by Little and Rubin (1987). Log-linear models with latent variables taking missing data into account can be handled using LCAG or NEWTON (Hagenaars, 1990, sec. 5.5.1; Winship & Mare, 1989).

Although researchers often do it to avoid sparse tables and it was done here also—mainly for reasons of simplicity of exposition—dichotomizing all variables is not really necessary. Within the context of log-linear models, polytomous manifest and/or latent variables can be handled, in principle, as easily as dichotomous variables.

An interesting class of polytomous variables form the polytomous variables whose categories are ordered. Croon (1990, 1993) has developed some interesting models taking the ordered character of the categories into account by imposing inequality restrictions on particular log-linear parameters, thus obtaining monotonically increasing or "umbrella"-like relationships between the latent and the manifest variables.

Others have assigned interval-level scores to the polytomous manifest or latent variables and restrict the log-linear parameters in such a way that linear relationships among latent and manifest variables result (Formann, 1992; Haberman, 1979, McCutcheon, Chapter 6 *this volume*). This latter development has made it clear that interesting relationships exist between latent trait and latent class models (Heinen, 1993; Heinen, Hagenaars, & Croon, 1988; Langeheine & Rost, 1988). The fusing of these two models will extend the range of applicability even more, and therewith the usefulness of log-linear models with latent variables.

References

Agresti, A. (1990). *Categorical data analysis*. New York: John Wiley.

Agresti, A. (1992). A survey of exact inference for contingency tables. *Statistical Science, 7*, 131-177.

Andersen, E. B. (1990). *The statistical analysis of categorical data*. Berlin: Springer.

Barnes, S. H. (1990). Partisanship and electoral behavior. In M. K. Jennings & J. W. van Deth (Eds.), *Continuities in political action* (pp. 235-272). Berlin: deGruyter.

Bishop, Y.M.M., Fienberg, S. E., & Holland, P. W. (1975). *Discrete multivariate analysis: Theory and practice*. Cambridge: MIT Press.

Clogg, C. C. (1981a). Latent structure models of mobility. *American Journal of Sociology, 86*, pp. 836-868.

Clogg, C. C. (1981b). New developments in latent structure analysis. In D. J. Jackson & E. F. Borgatta (Eds.), *Factor analysis and measurement in sociological research* (pp. 215-246). Beverly Hills, CA: Sage.

Collins, L. M., & Wugalter, S. E. (1992). Latent class models for stage-sequential dynamic latent variables. *Multivariate Behavioral Research, 27*, 131-157.

Croon, M. A. (1990). Latent class analysis with ordered classes. *British Journal of Mathematical and Statistical Psychology, 43*, 171-192.

Croon, M. A. (1993). Ordinal latent class analysis for single-peaked items. *Kwantitatieve Methoden, 14*, 127-142.

De Leeuw, J., Van der Heijden, P.G.M., & Verboon, P. (1990). A latent time-budget model. *Statistica Neerlandica, 44*, 1-22.

Fisher, R. A. (1990). *The design of experiments*. Oxford: Oxford University Press. (Original work published 1935)

Formann, A. K. (1992). Linear logistic latent class analysis for polytomous data. *Journal of the American Statistical Association, 87*, 476-486.

Goodman, L. A. (1968). The analysis of cross-classified data. *Journal of the American Statistical Association, 63*, 1019-1131.

Goodman, L. A. (1973). The analysis of multidimensional contingency tables when some variables are posterior to others: A modified path analysis approach. *Biometrika, 60*, 179-192.

Goodman, L. A. (1974a). The analysis of systems of qualitative variables when some of the variables are unobservable. Part I—A modified latent structure approach. *American Journal of Sociology, 79*, 1179-1259.

Goodman, L. A. (1974b). Exploratory latent structure analysis using both identifiable and unidentifiable models. *Biometrika, 61*, 215-231.

Goodman, L. A. (1991). Measures, models, and graphical displays in the analysis of cross-classified data. *Journal of the American Statistical Association, 86*, 1085-1138.

Haberman, S. J. (1978). *Analysis of qualitative data: Vol. 1. Introductory topics.* New York: Academic Press.

Haberman, S. J. (1979). *Analysis of qualitative data: Vol. 2. New developments.* New York: Academic Press.

Haberman, S. J. (1988). A stabilized Newton-Raphson algorithm for log-linear models for frequency tables derived by indirect observation. In C. C. Clogg (Ed.), *Sociological methodology 1988* (Vol. 18, pp. 193-212). Washington, DC: American Sociological Association.

Hagenaars, J. A. (1986). Symmetry, quasi-symmetry, and marginal homogeneity on the latent level. *Social Science Research, 15*, 241-255.

Hagenaars, J. A. (1988a). Latent structure models with direct effects between indicators: Local dependence models. *Sociological Methods and Research, 16*, 379-405.

Hagenaars, J. A. (1988b). LCAG—Log-linear modelling with latent variables: A modified LISREL approach. In W. E. Saris & I. N. Gallhofer (Eds.), *Sociometric research: Vol. 2. Data analysis* (pp. 111-130). London: Macmillan.

Hagenaars, J. A. (1990). *Categorical longitudinal data: Log-linear panel, trend, and cohort analysis.* Newbury Park, CA: Sage.

Hagenaars, J. A. (1993). *Loglinear models with latent variables* (Sage University Paper series on Quantitative Applications in the Social Sciences, series no. 07-094). Newbury Park, CA: Sage.

Hagenaars, J. A., & Luijkx, R. (1987). *Manual LCAG.* Working Paper Series #17, Department of Sociology, Tilburg University.

Heinen, A. G. (1993). *Discrete latent variable models.* Tilburg: Tilburg University Press.

Heinen, A. G., Hagenaars, J. A., & Croon, M. (1988, December 18-21). *Latent trait models in LCA perspective.* Paper presented at the SMABS Conference, organized by the Society for Multivariate Analysis in the Behavioral Sciences, Groningen, The Netherlands.

Langeheine, R., & Rost, J. (Eds.). (1988). *Latent trait and latent class models.* New York: Plenum.

Lazarsfeld, P. F., & Henry, N. W. (1968). *Latent structure analysis.* Boston: Houghton Mifflin.

Little, R.J.A., & Rubin, D. B. (1987). *Statistical analysis with missing data.* New York: John Wiley.

Luijkx, R. (1988). Loglinear modelling with latent variables: The case of mobility tables. In W. E. Saris & I. N. Gallhofer (Eds.), *Sociometric research: Vol. 2. Data analysis* (pp. 131-159). London: Macmillan.

Maccoby, E. E. (1956). Pitfalls in the analysis of panel data: A research note on some technical aspects of VOTING. *American Journal of Sociology, 61,* 359-362.

Marsden, P. V. (1985). Latent structure models for relationally defined social classes. *American Journal of Sociology, 90,* 1002-1021.

Mooijaart, A., & Van der Heijden, P.G.M. (1992). The EM-algorithm for latent class analysis with equality constraints. *Psychometrika, 57,* 261-269.

Moss, P., & Plewis, I. (1977). Mental distress of mothers of preschool children in inner London. *Psychological Medicine, 7,* 641-652.

Nunnally, J. C. (1978). *Psychometric theory.* New York: McGraw-Hill.

Plewis, I. (1985). *Analysing change: Measurement and explanation using longitudinal data.* Chichester, UK: John Wiley.

Read, T.R.C., & Cressie, N.A.C. (1988). *Goodness-of-fit statistics for discrete multivariate data.* New York: Springer.

Thorndike, R. L. (1942). Regression fallacies in the matched groups experiment. *Psychometrika, 7,* 85-102.

Van der Heijden, P.G.M., Mooijaart, A., & De Leeuw, J. (1992). Constrained latent budget analysis. In P. Marsden (Ed.), *Sociological methodology 1992* (Vol. 22, pp. 279-320). Oxford: Blackwell.

Van de Pol, F., & Langeheine, R. (1990). Mixed Markov latent class models. In C. C. Clogg (Ed.), *Sociological methodology 1990* (Vol. 20, pp. 213-247). Oxford: Blackwell.

Vermunt, J. K. (1993). *lEM: Loglinear and event history analysis with missing data using the EM algorithm.* WORC Paper 93.09.015/7. Tilburg University.

Wiggins, L. M. (1955). *Mathematical models for the analysis of multi-wave panels.* Doctoral Dissertation Series No. 12.481, Ann Arbor, MI (published by Elsevier, Amsterdam, 1973).

Winship, Ch., & Mare, R. D. (1989). Loglinear models with missing data: A latent class approach. In C. C. Clogg (Ed.), *Sociological methodology 1989* (Vol. 19, pp. 331-368). Oxford: Blackwell.

Whittaker, J. (1990). *Graphical models in applied multivariate statistics.* Chichester, UK: John Wiley.

14

Latent Logit Models With
Polytomous Effects Variables

ALLAN L. McCUTCHEON

The estimation of log-linear and logit models with latent variables has long interested researchers analyzing categorical data. In early work on this topic, Goodman (1974a, 1974b; see also Clogg, 1981) demonstrated how conventional latent class models can be parameterized to estimate saturated log-linear and logit models with latent variables. More recent work by Hagenaars (1988, 1990) shows how conventional latent class models can be modified to estimate nonsaturated log-linear and logit models with latent and "quasi-latent" variables. These contributions substantially extend the utility of the latent class model for causal analysis.

Both Goodman's and Hagenaars's approaches allow only models that can be estimated with Lazarsfeld's original parameterization, which treats the latent class model as a set of unobserved latent class and conditional probabilities. Although these earlier approaches permit the estimation of hierarchical (latent) log-linear models, they necessarily ignore certain kinds of information. In particular, these approaches are unable to take advantage of the linearities that are potentially present in models with ordered, polytomous effects (independent) variables. Consequently, these earlier approaches are limited to those cases in which all effects variables in the model are either nominal or dichotomous; when *ordered* polytomous variables are present, these variables are treated as nominal level and the information on order is ignored.

In this chapter, I present an alternative method for the estimation of *latent logit models*—logit models with latent dependent variables. This method is an extension and generalization of earlier work presented by Haberman (1974, 1979), Clogg (1988), and McCutcheon (1991, 1992) and permits the estimation of logit models that cannot be estimated using the earlier approaches. The present discussion focuses on models involving the analysis of ordered polytomous effects variables; these models are closely related to the linear-by-linear restricted model first presented by Haberman (1974).

Following a brief discussion of the basic latent class model, Goodman's and Hagenaars's models are presented. Next the proposed model is examined, and an empirical example of an estimated latent logit model is presented; this presentation illustrates the interpretation of the latent logit parameters as odds ratios and percentages. The example focuses on factors influencing the American public's attitudes toward legalized abortion for social reasons.

Hierarchical Log-Linear Models With Latent Variables

In two classic papers, Lazarsfeld (1950a, 1950b) presented the basic latent class model that used information from categorically scored manifest (observed) indicator variables (e.g., A_i, B_j, C_k) to characterize a single latent variable (X_t) with T classes, which are mutually exclusive and exhaustive, and within which the manifest variables are stochastically independent.[1] Thus, the probabilities for each of the cells of the latent cross-tabulation can be represented as the product of the latent class probabilities (π_t^X) and the conditional probabilities (e.g., $\pi_{i\,t}^{\bar{A}X}$, $\pi_{j\,t}^{\bar{B}X}$, $\pi_{k\,t}^{\bar{C}X}$

$$\pi_{i\,j\,k\,t}^{ABCX} = \pi_t^X \pi_{i\,t}^{\bar{A}X} \pi_{j\,t}^{\bar{B}X} \pi_{k\,t}^{\bar{C}X} . \qquad [14.1]$$

Early estimations of such models were restricted to dichotomous indicator items and were problematic in as much as these procedures could yield parameter estimates that exceeded the permissible boundaries of 0.0 and 1.0. Goodman (1974a, 1974b) made a major contribution by developing a generalizable procedure by which parameters for latent class models could be estimated, such that permissible estimates would always result (Formann, 1978; Goodman, 1979).

Goodman (1974a, 1974b) also showed that a highly restricted latent class model can be explained as a log-linear model with latent variables.[2] The procedure involved imposing an extensive set of deterministic and equality restrictions on the latent class model so that the latent variable (X) represents the joint distribution between a categorical dependent variable and one or more causal variables. Goodman used his method of iterative proportional fitting to estimate such models. Dempster, Laird, and Rubin (1977) have shown iterative proportional fitting to be a special case of the EM algorithm, and nearly all who have examined latent log-linear models have employed the EM algorithm for estimation.

Consider the example of a latent class model with three manifest indicator variables (e.g., A, B, C) and two manifest non-indicator variables (e.g., E, F). An 8-class latent variable X can be restricted to represent the joint distribution of a dichotomous latent variable Z and two dichotomous manifest variables E and F

$$\pi_1^X = \pi_{1\,1\,1}^{EFZ} \quad \pi_2^X = \pi_{1\,1\,2}^{EFZ} \quad \pi_3^X = \pi_{1\,2\,1}^{EFZ} \quad \pi_4^X = \pi_{1\,2\,2}^{EFZ}$$

$$\pi_5^X = \pi_{2\,1\,1}^{EFZ} \quad \pi_6^X = \pi_{2\,1\,2}^{EFZ} \quad \pi_7^X = \pi_{2\,2\,1}^{EFZ} \quad \pi_8^X = \pi_{2\,2\,2}^{EFZ}, \qquad [14.2]$$

with the usual condition that

$$\sum_{t=1}^{T} \pi_t^X = 1.0. \qquad [14.2.1]$$

This latent cross-tabulation is presented in Figure 14.1.

We can sum over the eight categories of the latent variable X to obtain the marginal distributions for the effects variables E and F, as well as for the dichotomous latent variable Z. For example, by summing over the appropriate cells of Figure 14.1, we can obtain the marginal probabilities of being at the first level for each of the three variables

$$\pi_1^E = \pi_{1\,1\,1}^{EFZ} + \pi_{1\,1\,2}^{EFZ} + \pi_{1\,2\,1}^{EFZ} + \pi_{1\,2\,2}^{EFZ} = \pi_1^X + \pi_2^X + \pi_3^X + \pi_4^X$$

$$\pi_1^F = \pi_{1\,1\,1}^{EFZ} + \pi_{1\,1\,2}^{EFZ} + \pi_{2\,1\,1}^{EFZ} + \pi_{2\,1\,2}^{EFZ} = \pi_1^X + \pi_2^X + \pi_5^X + \pi_6^X$$

$$\pi_1^Z = \pi_{1\,1\,1}^{EFZ} + \pi_{1\,2\,1}^{EFZ} + \pi_{2\,1\,1}^{EFZ} + \pi_{2\,2\,1}^{EFZ} = \pi_1^X + \pi_3^X + \pi_5^X + \pi_7^X. \quad [14.2.2]$$

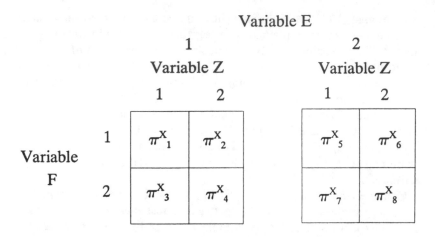

Figure 14.1. Latent E × F × Z Cross-Tabulation

To estimate the latent cross-tabulation illustrated in Figure 14.1, we must restrict the effects variables E and F, and the response variable Z, with respect to the latent X variable

$$\pi_{11}^{\bar{E}X} = \pi_{12}^{\bar{E}X} = \pi_{13}^{\bar{E}X} = \pi_{14}^{\bar{E}X} = 1.0, \quad \pi_{15}^{\bar{E}X} = \pi_{16}^{\bar{E}X} = \pi_{17}^{\bar{E}X} = \pi_{18}^{\bar{E}X} = 0.0,$$

$$\pi_{11}^{\bar{F}X} = \pi_{12}^{\bar{F}X} = \pi_{15}^{\bar{F}X} = \pi_{16}^{\bar{F}X} = 1.0, \quad \pi_{13}^{\bar{F}X} = \pi_{14}^{\bar{F}X} = \pi_{17}^{\bar{F}X} = \pi_{18}^{\bar{F}X} = 0.0,$$

$$\pi_{11}^{\bar{Z}X} = \pi_{13}^{\bar{Z}X} = \pi_{15}^{\bar{Z}X} = \pi_{17}^{\bar{Z}X} = 1.0, \quad \pi_{12}^{\bar{Z}X} = \pi_{14}^{\bar{Z}X} = \pi_{16}^{\bar{Z}X} = \pi_{18}^{\bar{Z}X} = 0.0. \quad [14.2.3]$$

Each of the indicator variables for the latent variable Z also must be restricted with respect to each of the levels of the eight classes of X. To obtain a single parameter expressing the relationship between each indicator variable and the latent variable, the usual set of restrictions (Clogg, 1981; Hagenaars, 1988) on the three dichotomous indicator variables of Equation 14.2 imposes three sets of equality restrictions, one set of equality restrictions for each of the indicator items

$$\pi_{11}^{\bar{A}X} = \pi_{13}^{\bar{A}X} = \pi_{15}^{\bar{A}X} = \pi_{17}^{\bar{A}X} = \pi_{22}^{\bar{A}X} = \pi_{24}^{\bar{A}X} = \pi_{26}^{\bar{A}X} = \pi_{28}^{\bar{A}X},$$

$$\pi_{11}^{\bar{B}X} = \pi_{13}^{\bar{B}X} = \pi_{15}^{\bar{B}X} = \pi_{17}^{\bar{B}X} = \pi_{22}^{\bar{B}X} = \pi_{24}^{\bar{B}X} = \pi_{26}^{\bar{B}X} = \pi_{28}^{\bar{B}X},$$

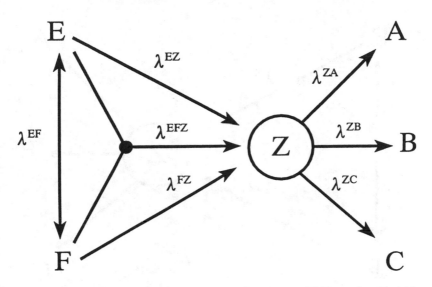

Figure 14.2. Goodman's Log-Linear Model With a Latent (Z) Dependent Variable

$$\pi_{11}^{\overline{CX}} = \pi_{13}^{\overline{CX}} = \pi_{15}^{\overline{CX}} - \pi_{1?}^{\overline{CX}} = \pi_{22}^{\overline{CX}} - \pi_{24}^{\overline{CX}} = \pi_{26}^{\overline{CX}} = \pi_{/X}^{\overline{CX}} . \qquad [14.3]$$

Models with restrictions such as these have been routinely estimated by programs implementing the EM algorithm, such as Clogg's program MLLSA (1977) and Hagenaars and Luijkx's (1987, 1990) program LCAG. These model restrictions allow the estimation of the expected frequencies for the unobserved $E \times F \times Z$ cross-tabulation by multiplying the respective π_t^X's by the sample size (N). In a second step, the expected frequencies for the latent table can then be input to widely available computer programs such as SPSS or ECTA to estimate the log-linear (λ) and logit (β) coefficients for log-linear models with latent variables.

While Goodman's restricted latent class model approach was the first to enable the estimation of log-linear models that include both latent and observed (non-indicator) variables, these restricted latent class models enable the estimation of *saturated* latent log-linear models only.[3] In the latent log-linear model restrictions presented above, for example, estimates for all 3 two-variable interactions (i.e., *EF, EZ, FZ*) as well as for the three-variable interaction (*EFZ*) must be included for the unobserved $E \times F \times Z$ cross-tabulation. Figure 14.2 illustrates

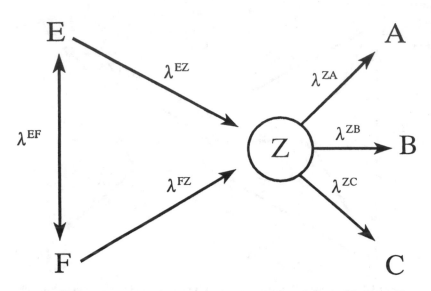

Figure 14.3a. Hagenaars' Log-Linear Model With a Latent (Z) Dependent Variable (Model 1)

models such as those considered by Goodman. Non-saturated latent log-linear models cannot be estimated by this method.

In recent work, Hagenaars (1988, 1990) has presented a new method that makes it possible to estimate nonsaturated log-linear models with latent and observed non-indicator ("quasi-latent") variables. This method modifies the EM algorithm to adjust iteratively the relevant marginals of the latent cross-tabulation at the end of each M-step (Hagenaars, 1990, p. 124). This modified EM algorithm has been implemented in the widely available program LCAG (Hagenaars & Luijkx, 1990).

Hagenaars's approach represents an important advance over the earlier methodology for estimating log-linear models with latent variables. His modification of the EM algorithm enables the extension of log-linear and logit models to include estimation of hierarchical models in which higher order terms are restricted to zero. Consequently, the range of log-linear and logit models that were once possible with models including only manifest (observed) variables has now been extended to include models with any combination of manifest and latent variables. Figures 14.3a and 14.3b illustrate two nonsaturated models that may be of empirical interest.

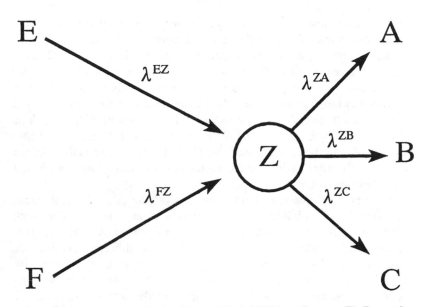

Figure 14.3b. Hagenaars' Log-Linear Model With a Latent (Z) Dependent Variable (Model 2)

Like Goodman's restricted latent class model approach, however, Hagenaars's approach is best suited to instances in which all effects variables are dichotomous; neither is able to exploit potential linearities in associations between latent response variables and effects variables that are ordered polytomies.[4] Both approaches first estimate the latent class probabilities (π_t^X) for a restricted latent class model. These estimates are then multiplied by the sample size (N) to obtain the modeled frequencies for the unobserved (e.g., $E \times F \times Z$) cross-tabulation. Like the Goodman approach, the estimates of these modeled frequencies are then used in other programs to calculate the latent log-linear and logit coefficients (Hagenaars & Luijkx, 1990, p. 8).

When all of the non-indicator variables are either dichotomies or unordered polytomies, Hagenaars's approach represents the preferred modeling strategy. When there are one or more ordered polytomous non-indicators, however, neither of the earlier approaches is capable of incorporating the information in the ordering into the model; both require the estimation of multiple parameters for each of the polytomous indicator and non-indicator parameters (e.g., $I - 1$ for the indicator variable A and $M - 1$ for the non-indicator variable E).

Finally, recent work by Mooijaart and van der Heijden (1992) suggests that the estimation of models such as those examined here may be problematic when using the EM algorithm. As they note, the EM algorithm is most problematic when equality constraints are imposed on a variable across different classes of the latent variable(s), such as those imposed by Equation 14.3. At each iteration of the EM algorithm, a system of L nonlinear equations must be solved, where L is the number of sets of different variable-class equality restrictions imposed; in the current example, $L = 3$.

The approach presented below focuses on the estimation of latent logit models and is based on the estimation of log-linear models with latent variables first presented by Haberman (1979). As will be seen, the latent logit models that can be estimated using this approach include many of those from the earlier approaches, as well as models with linear-by-linear restrictions (Haberman, 1974) which cannot be estimated with the earlier approaches. Moreover, this approach avoids the problems of the EM algorithm, using instead variants of the Newton-Raphson algorithm introduced by Haberman (1979, 1988a).

Latent Logit Models

Logit models have played an especially important role in categorical data analysis, because logit models are most directly analogous to regression analysis. Unlike the usual log-linear models, in which all of the variables have the same status, in logit models one of the variables is designated as the dependent (response) variable and the others are designated as causal (effects) variables (Agresti, 1990; Aldrich & Nelson, 1984; Bishop, Fienberg, & Holland, 1975; Haberman, 1979; Hagenaars, 1990; Hosmer & Lemeshow, 1989; Nerlove & Press, 1973). Unlike regression analysis, however, logit models have discrete, categorically scored dependent variables. Consequently, researchers who wish to investigate causal models with categorically scored dependent variables often rely on logit analysis.[5]

The latent logit model presented here, while closely related to those of Goodman and Hagenaars, derives directly from the latent class model first presented by Haberman (1979). Haberman examines the latent class model as a restricted log-linear model in which the indicator variables (e.g., *A*, *B*, *C*) are locally independent with respect to the latent variable (*X*). Thus, Haberman's basic model is analogous to Goodman's basic model presented in Equation 14.1 above:

$$\log(\hat{f}_{ijkl}) = \lambda + \lambda_t^X + \lambda_i^A + \lambda_j^B + \lambda_k^C + \lambda_{i\,t}^{AX} + \lambda_{j\,t}^{BX} + \lambda_{k\,t}^{CX}. \qquad [14.4]$$

with the usual conditions that $\Sigma_t \lambda_t^X = \Sigma_i \lambda_i^A = \Sigma_j \lambda_j^B = \Sigma_k \lambda_k^C = \Sigma_i \lambda_{i\,t}^{AX} = \Sigma_t \lambda_{i\,t}^{AX} = \Sigma_j \lambda_{j\,t}^{BX} = \Sigma_t \lambda_{j\,t}^{BX} = \Sigma_k \lambda_{k\,t}^{CX} = \Sigma_t \lambda_{k\,t}^{CX} = 0$.

Haberman's model can be extended to include observed variables (e.g., E_m, F_n) that are not indicator variables; this is the basic model of the latent logit model to be considered here

$$\log(\hat{f}_{ijktmn}) = \mu + \lambda_t^X + \lambda_i^A + \lambda_j^B + \lambda_k^C + \lambda_{i\,t}^{AX} + \lambda_{j\,t}^{BX} + \lambda_{k\,t}^{CX} + \lambda_{t\,m}^{XE} + \lambda_{t\,n}^{XF} + \lambda_{t\,mn}^{XEF},$$

$$[14.5]$$

where $\mu = \lambda + \lambda_m^E + \lambda_n^F + \lambda_{mn}^{EF}$. It is important to note that this model requires none of the equality restrictions that are so problematic with the EM algorithm used in the earlier models.[6] Only the indicator variables are restricted to having zero relationships with the variables other than the latent variable (e.g., $\lambda_{ij}^{AD} = \lambda_{im}^{AE} = 0$); the so-called *axiom of local independence* (Lazarsfeld & Henry, 1968). The observed non-indicator variables are unrestricted by the axiom of local independence and can thus have nonzero associations with each of the other variables in the model.

When one or more of the non-indicator variables in Equation 14.5 have three or more ordered categories, this latent log-linear model can be reparameterized in a manner that differs significantly from Goodman's and Hagenaars's approaches. In the saturated model, for example, when *M*, *N*, and *T* are all greater than 2, the previous approaches require the estimation of $(T-1)(M-1)$ lambda parameters for the {*X E*} relationship, $(T-1)(N-1)$ lambda parameters for the {*X F*} relationship, and $(T-1)(N-1)(M-1)$ for the {*X E F*} relationship. In contrast, linear-by-linear restrictions (Haberman, 1974) on these lambda parameters may be tested for the log-linear model in Equation 14.5.[7] Consequently, the model in 14.5 may be estimated with three linear-restricted parameters (φ) instead of the $(T-1)(MN-1)$ lambda parameters previously required for the {*X E*}, {*X F*}, and {*X E F*} associations:

$$\log(\hat{f}_{ijktmn}) = \mu + \lambda_t^X + \lambda_i^A + \lambda_j^B + \lambda_k^C + \lambda_{i\,t}^{AX} + \lambda_{j\,t}^{BX} + \lambda_{k\,t}^{CX}$$

$$+ \varphi^{XE}(u_t - \overline{u})(v_m - \overline{v}) + \varphi^{XF}(u_t - \overline{u})(w_n - \overline{w})$$

$$+ \varphi^{XEF}(u_t - \overline{u})(v_m - \overline{v})(w_n - \overline{w}) , \qquad [14.6]$$

where v_m is the score assigned to category m of the ordered polytomous variable E, u_t is the score assigned to class t of the latent variable X, and w_n is the score assigned to category n of the non-indicator variable F. Thus this approach avoids the parameter inflation problem by requiring the estimation of fewer model parameters by allowing us to incorporate into our estimation the information that may be inherent in the ordering of the polytomous effects variables.

The latent log-linear model in Equation 14.6 is analogous to several log-linear models considered by Agresti (1984, see esp. chap. 5). As Agresti notes, when Model 14.6 does not fit the data well, but Model 14.5 does, there may be intermediate models that are simpler than 14.5. For instance, if the relationship between E and X is not linear, $\varphi^{XE}(u_t - \overline{u})$ $(v_m - \overline{v})$ may be replaced by either of the more general terms λ_{tm}^{XE} or $\tau_t^{XE}(v_m - \overline{v})$, where the τ_t^{XE} effects reflect the deviation in the t levels of $\log(\hat{f}_{tm})$ from independence as a linear function of E, with slope τ_t^{XE}, and $\sum \tau_t^{XE} = 0$. If E is an ordered polytomy and X is an unordered polytomy, $\varphi^{XE}(u_t - \overline{u})(v_m - \overline{v})$ and $\varphi^{XEF}(u_t - \overline{u})(v_m - \overline{v})(w_n - \overline{w})$ would be replaced by $\tau_t^{XE}(v_m - \overline{v})$ and $\tau_t^{XEF}(v_m - \overline{v})(w_m - \overline{w})$.

Consider the case where the latent variable X is a dichotomous response (dependent) variable. Following the argument based on Bishop (1969), the latent logit model may be derived by subtracting the latent log-linear model for $\hat{f}_{ijk2mn}$ from the model for $\hat{f}_{ijk1mn}$. Thus, for Equation 14.5 we obtain

$$\log\left(\frac{\hat{f}_{ijk1mn}}{\hat{f}_{ijk2mn}}\right) = \beta_0 + \beta_i^A + \beta_j^B + \beta_k^C + \beta_m^E + \beta_n^F + \beta_{mn}^{EF} , \qquad [14.7]$$

where the β coefficients equal twice the respective lambda coefficients (e.g., $\beta_0 = 2\lambda_1^X$, $\beta_i^A = 2\lambda_{i1}^{AX}$, $\beta_m^E = 2\lambda_{1m}^{XE}$) and each of the variables is effects-coded. As we see, $M - 1$ logit parameters must be estimated for the $\{XE\}$ association, $N - 1$ logit parameters must be estimated for the $\{XF\}$ association, and $(M-1)(N-1)$ logit parameters must be estimated for the $\{XEF\}$ association; thus, a total of $MN - 1$ must be estimated for these associations in the latent logit model presented in Equation 14.7. For Equation 14.6, on the other hand, we obtain

$$\log\left(\frac{\hat{f}_{ijktmn}}{\hat{f}_{ijktmn}}\right) = \beta_0 + \beta_i^A + \beta_j^B + \beta_k^C + \beta^E(v_m - \overline{v}) + \beta_n^F(w_n - \overline{w})$$

$$+ \beta^{EF}(v_m - \overline{v})(w_n - \overline{w}), \qquad [14.8]$$

where β_0, β_i^A, β_j^B, and β_k^C are defined as in Equation 14.7, and $\beta^E(v_m - \overline{v})$, $\beta^F(w_n - \overline{w})$, and $\beta^{EF}(v_m - \overline{v})(w_n - \overline{w})$ are equal to twice their respective φ (or τ) coefficients. When $\{XE\}$, $\{XF\}$, and $\{XEF\}$ are linear-by-linear associations (i.e., when they are calculated from φ's), it is necessary to estimate only a single parameter for each of these associations; thus $MN - 4$ fewer estimated parameters are required as compared to Equation 14.7. When either E or F is an unordered polytomy, the respective β's are calculated from the estimated τ's; thus, the number of estimated parameters is greater than when all associations are linear-by-linear. For example, if E is an ordered, and F is an unordered, polytomy, then $\{XF\}$ and $\{XEF\}$ each require the estimation of $N - 1$ parameters. This model, then, would require the estimation of $2N - 1$ parameters and would result in the estimation of $MN - 2N - 2$ fewer parameters than Equation 14.7.

In the following section, we apply this new approach to an empirical example of a latent logit model with a polytomous effects variable. Models such as these may be estimated using algorithms such as those in Haberman's programs LAT (scoring algorithm) and DNEWTON (modified Newton-Raphson algorithm), thus avoiding the EM-algorithm estimation problem discussed by Mooijaart and van der Heijden (1992).[8]

Latent Logit Models With
Ordered Polytomous Effects Variables:
An Empirical Example

In previous research (McCutcheon, 1987b), I have examined the degree to which Americans' attitudes toward legalized abortion are influenced by their attitudes toward voluntaristic life-taking (euthanasia) and premarital sexuality. The present analysis extends this research to examine the impact of religion (variable E: Protestant/Catholic), attitudes regarding euthanasia (variable F: approve/disapprove), and attitudes regarding premarital sexuality (variable G: always wrong/sometimes wrong/not wrong) on the American public's latent attitudes toward legal abortion for social reasons; it is the three-level polytomous

Table 14.1 Chi-Square Values for the Logit Models With the Latent
Dependent Variable Representing Attitudes Toward
Legalized Abortion for Social Reasons

Model Description	Degrees of Freedom	Likelihood Ratio Chi-Square	Pearson Chi-Square
H₁: Saturated Latent Logit Model	66	80.89	81.60
H₂: 2-Variable Effects Latent Logit Model	68	81.86	83.03
H₃: Main Effects Latent Logit Model	73	85.18	86.55
H₄: Main Effects Latent Logit Model With Linear-by-Linear Constraint	74	85.95	87.12

premarital sexuality variables that we will examine for potential linearities with the latent logit variable. Responses to three dichotomous questions (approve/disapprove) are used as indicator variables: legal abortions for married women who are too poor to have additional children (variable A); for married women who wish to have no more children (variable B); and for single women who do not wish to marry the man (variable C). Data from the 1989, 1990, and 1991 General Social Surveys are combined in the analyses reported below.

The data in Table 14.1 include the likelihood ratio (L^2) and Pearson (χ^2) chi-square statistics for four logit models with the dichotomous latent variable reflecting attitudes toward social reasons for abortion. While we focus our attention on the L^2's, the χ^2's are also reported because they have been shown to better approximate the theoretical chi-square distribution when expected cell frequencies are small (Haberman, 1988b; Larntz, 1978; Margolin & Light, 1974; Read & Cressie, 1988).

The first model reported in Table 14.1 (H_1) represents the saturated log-linear model with a two-class latent variable characterizing attitudes toward legalized abortion for social reasons. This model, which utilizes the approach introduced by Goodman (1974a), can be estimated by several widely available programs, including MLLSA (Clogg, 1977), LCAG (Hagenaars & Luijkx, 1987, 1990), LAT (Haberman, 1979), DNEWTON (Haberman, 1988a), and *I*EM (Vermunt, 1993). As we can see from the second model, H_2, however, the four-factor $\{EFGX\}$ effect need not be included in the model, since its exclusion results in only a modest ($81.86 - 80.89 = .97$, 2df) increase in the L^2. Thus, we conclude

Table 14.2 Estimated Parameters and Asymptotic Standard Errors for Latent Logit Models H_3 and H_4

Parameter	H_3 Estimate	ASE	H_4 Estimate	ASE
λ_1^X	−.471	.309	−.494	.297
λ_1^A	−.954	.091	−.951	.092
λ_1^B	−1.163	.069	−1.163	.069
λ_1^C	−.535	.253	−.514	.239
λ_{11}^{AX}	3.296	.118	3.300	.118
λ_{11}^{BX}	2.634	.133	2.634	.133
λ_{11}^{CX}	1.787	.253	1.765	.239
λ_{11}^{XE}	.153	.039	.153	.039
λ_{11}^{XF}	.386	.044	.387	.044
λ_{11}^{XG}	−.486	.058	—	—
λ_{12}^{XG}	.044	.051	—	—
φ^{XG}	—	—	−.456	.046

that the saturated model "overfits" the observed data. Model H_2 can be estimated by programs like LCAG, LAT, DNEWTON, and *I*EM.

As the L^2's in Table 14.1 indicate, the latent logit "main effects" model (H_3) represents a considerable improvement over the two-factor effects model. As the data in Table 14.1 indicate, model H_3 results in a modest ($85.18 − 81.86 = 3.32$, 5df) increase in the model L^2 over H_2. In comparison to the two-factor effects model of H_2, the main effects model (H_3) fits five fewer parameters (i.e, λ_{111}^{XEF}, λ_{111}^{XEG}, λ_{112}^{XEG}, λ_{111}^{XFG}, λ_{112}^{XFG}) for the joint influence of the three independent variables on the latent variable. The latent logit main effects model may also be represented as the hierarchical log-linear (AX, BX, CX, EX, XF, XG, EFG) model, and may be estimated by the programs LCAG, LAT, DNEWTON, and *I*EM.

As the data in Table 14.2 indicate, however, the ordered independent variable (variable G: attitude toward premarital sex) appears to have a linear relationship with the latent dependent variable. That is, the log-linear parameter for the second level (i.e., λ_{12}^{XG}) fails to exceed its asymptotic standard error (.044 and .051, respectively). Thus, model H_4 fits a linear-by-linear restriction to the three-level variable G. As the data in Table 14.1 indicate, the modest increase ($85.95 − 85.18 = .77$, 1df) in the model L^2 indicates that H_4 is preferred to H_3. Models such

Table 14.3 Conditional Probabilities for the H$_4$ Latent Logit Model

	I	II
No More	.991	.001
Poor	.950	.001
Single	.924	.010

as H$_4$ cannot be represented as hierarchical log-linear models and have not been previously reported in the literature.

The log-linear coefficients reported in Table 14.2 can be readily translated into the conditional probabilities of the conventional latent class model. We can extend the equality first noted by Haberman (1979, pp. 551-552; see also McCutcheon, 1992) to include the latent logit model H$_4$. Thus, when there are two effects variables (e.g., E and F) and one latent variable X:

$$P(A = i \mid X = t, E = m, F = n) = \frac{\exp(\lambda_i^A + \lambda_{i\,m}^{AE} + \lambda_{i\,n}^{AF} + \lambda_{i\,mn}^{AEF} + \lambda_{i\,t}^{AX})}{\sum_i \exp(\lambda_i^A + \lambda_{i\,m}^{AE} + \lambda_{i\,n}^{AF} + \lambda_{i\,mn}^{AEF} + \lambda_{i\,t}^{AX})}$$

[14.9]

The lambda parameters between the non-indicator and indicator variables (e.g., $\lambda_{i\,m}^{AE}$, $\lambda_{i\,n}^{AF}$, $\lambda_{i\,mn}^{AEF}$) have been restricted to zero in the models and example presented here. The conditional probabilities for each of the two classes approving of abortion for each of the three reasons are reported in Table 14.3.

As the conditional probabilities in Table 14.3 indicate, Class I has a very high probability of approving of each of the three social reasons for legalized abortion. These probabilities range from a high of .991 for married women who wish to have no more children to a low of .924 for single women who do not wish to marry the man. The error rates for Classes I and II are not identical for the indicator variables, since two λ parameters (e.g., λ_i^A and $\lambda_{i\,t}^{AX}$) relate each indicator variable to the latent variable. Thus, we see that for Class I the errors range from (1.0 − .991) .009 to (1.0 − .924) .076; that is, latent "approvers" have a 0.9% likelihood of *disapproving* of legal abortions for married women wishing to have no more children, and a 7.6% likelihood of *disapproving* of legal abortions for single women who do not wish to marry the man.

Similarly, the conditional probabilities for Class II respondents indicate that Class II has a very low probability of *approval* for any of the three reasons (i.e., from .001 to .010).

We can also interpret the parameters in Table 14.2 as odds ratios. Thus, we see that the estimate for the religion variable indicates that Catholics and Protestants differ in their likelihood of approving of legal abortions for social reasons (Class I). Using Equation 14.5, we note that the estimate $\lambda_{1\bar{1}}^{XE}$ yields

$$\log \theta_{1\bar{1}}^{XE} = \lambda_{1\bar{1}}^{XE} + \lambda_{2\bar{2}}^{XE} - \lambda_{1\bar{2}}^{XE} - \lambda_{2\bar{1}}^{XE} = 4\lambda_{1\bar{1}}^{XE} = .61072, \qquad [14.10]$$

and an estimated cross-product ratio of

$$\exp(.61072) = 1.84.$$

Consequently, the estimated odds show that Protestants are 1.84 times as likely as Catholics to approve of social reasons for abortion (or, conversely, that Catholics are 1.84 times as likely to *disapprove* of social reasons for abortion). Similarly, we see that the odds of those who approve of euthanasia are estimated to be $e^{1.54892} = 4.71$ as great as those who disapprove of euthanasia to approve of social reasons for abortion.

Using Equation 14.6, we may also estimate the odds ratio of approving of abortion for the ordered polytomous premarital sex variable. When integer scores are used,

$$\theta_{o\,t}^{XG} = 2\varphi^{XG}(y_o - y_{o+1}), \qquad [14.11]$$

since the latent variable has only two latent classes (i.e., $T = 2$), which means that $\varphi^{XG}(y_o - \bar{y})(u_t - \bar{u}) = -\varphi^{XG}(y_o - \bar{y})(u_{t+1} - \bar{u})$ and that $\varphi^{XG}(y_{o+1} - \bar{y})(u_{t+1} - \bar{u}) = -\varphi^{XG}(y_{o+1} - \bar{y})(u_t - \bar{u})$. Thus, we see that the odds of those who say premarital sex is "sometimes wrong" are $e^{.91296} = 2.49$ as likely to be Class I respondents as those who say it is "always wrong." Further, when we compare those who hold polar positions with regard to the approval of premarital sex, those who say premarital sex is "not wrong" are $e^{1.82592} = 6.21$ as likely to approve of abortion for social reasons as those who say it is "always wrong."

Finally, we can also use the estimates presented in Table 14.2 to calculate the probability that a respondent with a given set of values on

Table 14.4 Latent Class Probabilities (Class I) for Each Combination of the Independent Variables

| | Protestant | | Catholic | |
| | Euthanasia | Euthanasia | Euthanasia | Euthanasia |
Premarital Sex	Approve	Disapprove	Approve	Disapprove
Always wrong	.306	.086	.193	.048
Sometimes wrong	.523	.189	.373	.112
Not wrong	.732	.367	.597	.240

the independent variables will be characterized as approving (Class I), or disapproving (Class II), of abortion for social reasons. In a manner directly analogous to the usual logit model (see e.g., Aldrich & Nelson, 1984), the coefficients for the latent logit model may also be used to calculate these assignment probabilities. The data presented in Table 14.4 represent the probabilities that respondents with each combination of the independent variables are Class I type respondents.

As the data in Table 14.4 indicate, Protestants are more likely than Catholics to approve of abortion for social reasons; those who approve of euthanasia are more likely than those who do not approve of euthanasia to approve of abortion for social reasons; and those who approve of premarital sex are more likely to approve of abortion for social reasons. These probabilities are consistent with the odds ratios (θ) discussed above—for example, $[.732/(1 - .732)]/[.306/(1 - .306)] = 6.21$.

Summary and Conclusions

In this chapter we have presented a new methodology for latent logit models with polytomous effects variables. While Goodman's (1974a) original contribution enabled the inclusion of latent variables in such models, his approach allows only the estimation of the saturated model in which all higher-order effects are included. Recent advances by Hagenaars (1988, 1990) have enabled the estimation of nonsaturated models with latent variables. Neither of these earlier approaches, however, are capable of exploiting potential linearities in associations in which one or more variables are ordered polytomies.

The approach presented here extends the earlier approaches to include the estimation of linear-by-linear effects (Haberman, 1974). The methodology presented in this chapter is appropriate for empirical problems in which the dependent variable is a set of latent categories and in which one or more of the independent variables is an ordered polytomy.

Notes

1. Good introductions to the basic latent class model can be found in Langeheine (1988), McCutcheon (1987a), and Shockey (1988).

2. See especially, Goodman (1974a) Figures 10.A.3, 10.B.3, and 10.G.3, and footnote 115, pp. 1256-1257.

3. Unlike saturated log-linear models, saturated *latent* log-linear models require certain parameters to be restricted to zero; the axiom of local independence allows indicator variables to have nonzero associations with only the latent variable(s).

4. The concern here is with models having ordered polytomous *effects* variables; Dayton and Macready (1988a, 1988b) and Formann (1992) present related models with interval covariates. For work on latent class models with polytomous *indicator* variables see Formann (1985, 1989) and Rost (1988a, 1988b); for work on latent class models in which the *latent classes* are ordered polytomies, see Clogg and Sawyer (1981); also Clogg and Goodman (1986) and Croon (1990, 1991).

5. Probit models provide an alternative to logit models (see e.g., Finney, 1971). Since these models tend to yield similar results, the relative computational ease of the logit model and the greater ease in interpretation of the logit parameters have led most researchers to prefer the logit to the probit model.

6. While the models presented here will be estimated with variants of the Newton-Raphson algorithm, no equality restrictions are necessary. Thus this approach is not subject to the problem discussed by Mooijaart and van der Heijden (1992), so the model in Equation 14.5 can be estimated with the EM algorithm (Haberman, 1976).

7. Clogg (1988) and McCutcheon (1991, 1992) have discussed linear-by-linear restrictions in latent association models in which the indicator and/or latent variables have three or more ordered categories.

8. Haberman's program LAT was used to estimate the coefficients reported here. Initial values for the LAT program were generated using an EM-algorithm GAUSS program written by the author.

References

Agresti, A. (1984). *Analysis of ordinal categorical data.* New York: John Wiley.

Agresti, A. (1990). *Categorical data analysis.* New York: John Wiley.

Aldrich, J. H., & Nelson, F. D. (1984). *Linear probability, logit, and probit models.* Sage University Paper series on Quantitative Applications in the Social Sciences, 07-045. Beverly Hills, CA: Sage.

Bishop, Y.V.V. (1969). Full contingency tables, logits, and split contingency tables. *Biometrics, 25*, 119-128.

Bishop, Y.V.V., Fienberg, S. E., & Holland, P. M. (1975). *Discrete multivariate analysis: Theory and practice.* Cambridge: MIT Press.

Clogg, C. C. (1977). Unrestricted and restricted maximum likelihood latent structure analysis: A manual for users. Working Paper 1977-09. University Park, PA: Population Issues Research Office.

Clogg, C. C. (1981). New developments in latent structure analysis. In D. J. Jackson & E. F. Borgatta (Eds.), *Factor analysis and measurement* (pp. 215-246). Beverly Hills, CA: Sage.

Clogg, C. C. (1988). Latent class models for measuring. In R. Langeheine & J. Rost (Eds.), *Latent trait and latent class models* (pp. 173-205). New York: Plenum.

Clogg, C. C., & Goodman, L. A. (1986). On scaling models applied to data from several groups. *Psychometrika, 51*, 123-135.

Clogg, C. C., & Sawyer, D. O. (1981). A comparison of alternative models for analyzing the scalability of response patterns. In S. Leinhardt (Ed.), *Sociological methodology* (pp. 240-280). San Francisco: Jossey-Bass.

Croon, M. A. (1990). Latent class analysis with ordered latent classes. *British Journal of Mathematical and Statistical Psychology, 43*, 171-192.

Croon, M. A. (1991, July). *Latent class models with ordered latent classes: An approach to nonparametric latent trait analysis.* Paper presented at the International Workshop on Statistical Modelling and Latent Variables, Trento, Italy.

Dayton, C. M., & Macready, G. B. (1988a). Concomitant-variable latent class models. *Journal of the American Statistical Association, 83*, 173-178.

Dayton, C. M., & Macready, G. B. (1988b). A latent class covariate model with applications to criterion-referenced testing. In R. Langeheine & J. Rost (Eds.), *Latent trait and latent class models* (pp. 129-143). New York: Plenum.

Dempster, A. P., Laird, N. M., & Rubin, D. B. (1977). Maximum likelihood estimation from incomplete data via the EM algorithm (with discussion). *Journal of the Royal Statistical Society, Series B, 39*, 1-38.

Finney, D. J. (1971). *Probit analysis* (3rd ed.). Cambridge: Cambridge University Press.

Formann, A. K. (1978). A note on parameter estimation for Lazarsfeld's latent class analysis. *Psychometrika, 43*, 123-126.

Formann, A. K. (1984). *Die Latent-Class-Analyse. Einfürung in Theorie und Anwendung.* Weinheim: Beltz.

Formann, A. K. (1985). Constrained latent class models: Theory and applications. *British Journal of Mathematical and Statistical Psychology, 38*, 87-111.

Formann, A. K. (1989). Constrained latent class models: Some further applications. *British Journal of Mathematical and Statistical Psychology, 42*, 37-54.

Formann, A. K. (1992). Linear logistic latent class analysis for polytomous data. *Journal of the American Statistical Association, 87*, 476-486.

Goodman, L. A. (1974a). The analysis of systems of qualitative variables when some of the variables are unobservable. Part I—A modified latent structure approach. *American Journal of Sociology, 79*, 1197-1259.

Goodman, L. A. (1974b). Exploratory latent structure analysis using both identifiable and unidentifiable models. *Biometrika, 61*, 215-231.

Goodman, L. A. (1979). On the estimation of parameters in latent structure analysis. *Psychometrika, 44*, 123-128.

Haberman, S. J. (1974). Log-linear models for frequency tables with ordered classification. *Biometrics, 30,* 589-600.

Haberman, S. J. (1976). Iterative scaling procedures for log-linear models for frequency data derived by indirect observation. *Statistical Computing Section Proceedings of the American Statistical Association, 1975,* 45-50.

Haberman, S. J. (1979). *Analysis of qualitative data: Vol. 2. New developments.* New York: Academic Press.

Haberman, S. J. (1988a). A stabilized Newton-Raphson algorithm for log-linear models for frequency tables derived by indirect observation. In C. Clogg (Ed.), *Sociological methodology* (pp. 193-212). Washington, DC: American Sociological Association.

Haberman, S. J. (1988b). A warning on the use of chi-squared statistics with frequency tables with small expected cell counts. *Journal of the American Statistical Association, 83,* 555-560.

Hagenaars, J. A. (1988). Latent structure models with direct effects between indicators: Local dependence models. *Sociological Methods and Research, 16,* 379-405.

Hagenaars, J. A. (1990). *Categorical longitudinal data.* Newbury Park, CA: Sage.

Hagenaars, J. A., & Luijkx, R. (1987). *LCAG: Latent class models and other loglinear models with latent variables.* Tilburg, The Netherlands: Tilburg University.

Hagenaars, J. A., & Luijkx, R. (1990). *LCAG: A program to estimate latent class models and other loglinear models with latent variables with and without missing data, version 2.1.* Tilburg, The Netherlands: Tilburg University.

Hosmer, D. W., & Lemeshow, S. (1989). *Applied logistic regression.* New York: John Wiley.

Langeheine, R. (1988). New developments in latent class theory. In R. Langeheine & J. Rost (Eds.), *Latent trait and latent class models* (pp. 77-108). New York: Plenum.

Larntz, K. (1978). Small sample comparisons of exact levels for chi-square goodness-of fit statistics. *Journal of the American Statistical Association, 73,* 253-263.

Lazarsfeld, P. F. (1950a). The interpretation and computation of some latent structures. In S. A. Stouffer et al. (Eds.), *Measurement and prediction* (pp. 362-412). Princeton, NJ: Princeton University Press.

Lazarsfeld, P. F. (1950b). The logical and mathematical foundations of latent structure analysis. In S. A. Stouffer, L. Guttman, E. A. Suchman, P. F. Lazarsfeld, S. A. Star, & J. A. Clausen (Eds.), *Measurement and prediction* (pp. 413-472). Princeton, NJ: Princeton University Press.

Lazarsfeld, P. F., & Henry, N. W. (1968). *Latent structure analysis.* Boston: Houghton Mifflin.

Margolin, B. H., & Light, R. J. (1974). An analysis of variance for categorical data: II. Small sample comparisons with chi-square and other competitors. *Journal of the American Statistical Association, 69,* 755-764.

McCutcheon, A. L. (1987a). *Latent class analysis.* Sage University Paper series on Quantitative Applications in the Social Sciences, 07-064. Beverly Hills, CA: Sage.

McCutcheon, A. L. (1987b). Sexual morality, pro-life values, and attitudes toward abortion. *Sociological Methods and Research, 16,* 256-275.

McCutcheon, A. L. (1991, July). *Association models with latent variables: An analysis of secular trends in abortion attitudes, 1965-1985.* Paper presented at the International Workshop on Statistical Modelling and Latent Variables, Trento, Italy.

McCutcheon, A. L. (1992). *Multiple group association models with latent variables: An analysis of secular trends in abortion attitudes, 1975-1985.* Unpublished manuscript.

Mooijaart, A., & van der Heijden, P.G.M. (1992). The EM algorithm for latent class analysis with equality constraints. *Psychometrika, 57,* 261-269.

Nerlove, M., & Press, S. J. (1973). *Univariate and multivariate log-linear and logistic models.* Tech. Re. R-1306-EDA/NIH. Santa Monica, CA: Rand.

Read, T.R.C., & Cressie, N.A.C. (1988). *Goodness-of-fit statistics for discrete multivariate data.* New York: Springer.

Rost, J. (1988a). Rating scale analysis with latent class analysis. *Psychometrika, 53,* 327-348.

Rost, J. (1988b). Test theory with qualitative and quantitative latent variables. In R. Langeheine & J. Rost (Eds.), *Latent trait and latent class models* (pp. 147-171). New York: Plenum.

Shockey, J. W. (1988). Latent class analysis: An introduction to discrete data models with unobserved variables. In J. S. Long (Ed.), *Common problems/proper solutions.* Newbury Park, CA: Sage.

Vermunt, J. K. (1993). *lEM: Loglinear and event history analysis with missing data using the EM algorithm.* WORC Paper 93.09.015/7. Tilburg, The Netherlands: Tilburg University.

15

Latent Variables Markov Models

ROLF LANGEHEINE

The focus of this chapter is on Markov models that allow us to make statements about change (progress, growth or decay, regression) and/or stability across time. These models start from categorical manifest (observed) variables assumed to be indicators of some categorical latent (unobserved) variable (construct) that may change over time. That is, in contrast to models assuming subjects' measurement on a continuous latent trait, these models assume that subjects may be classified into a few (at least 2) categories, classes, or types.

These models therefore appear to be well suited in evaluating theories of development that have been aligned with the type paradigm while, at the same time, assuming that development passes through distinct stages, each of these being qualitatively different. Such theories are especially prominent in developmental psychology. To give a few examples: Piaget (1947, 1971) and his followers postulate stages of intellectual development, as do Kohlberg (1980) and co-workers (Colby, Kohlberg, Gibbs, & Lieberman, 1983), with respect to moral development; Chall (1983) presented a 5-stage model of reading development; Freud (1940) assumes sexual development to pass through stages, as does Gesell (1966) with respect to motor behavior.

This is not to say that stage theories are confined to developmental psychology; they may play a prominent role in other contexts as well. West's (1985) five stages of understanding the development of a discipline—(1) verbal description, (2) static linear relationships, (3) linear dynamic description, (4) dynamical steady states, (5) dynamical nonlinear theory—fit well with our own discipline: social statistics. The models considered in this chapter belong with West's fifth stage.

In view of the controversy about the adequacy of stage theories and continuous growth theories (cf. Eckstein & Shemesh, 1992) it should be noted that the models considered here are so-called discrete time models. That is, statements about change refer to what happens from one point in time to the next. Researchers who are interested in what happens between consecutive points in time would argue in favor of continuous time (Markov) models (e.g., Singer & Spilerman, 1979).

The remainder of this chapter is organized as follows. Section 1 presents a hierarchy of discrete time Markov models. The focus of Section 2 is on latent Markov models, both with respect to single and multiple (manifest) indicators. In Section 3 we show applications of these models to several data sets. Section 4 concludes with emphasis on some related work of other groups of researchers.

1. A Hierarchy of Discrete Time Markov Models

Figure 15.1 presents a hierarchy of Markov chain models. Researchers interested in making statements about change across time when considering a single categorical variable very often start with the simple Markov model. This model almost never fits a given set of data, however. The most prominent reasons for this misfit are: (a) The model assumes population homogeneity, that is, the dynamics across time hold for all individuals. This restrictive assumption may be relaxed by allowing for population heterogeneity via a mixed Markov model that conceives observed response patterns as generated by a mixture of two or more Markov chains, each of which is characterized by its specific dynamics. The goal then is to unmix the observed frequency table into several unobserved subtables. The problem was attacked by several authors, but only Poulsen (1982) presented a general solution. (b) The model assumes the data to be free of measurement error, which—at least in the social sciences—is a rather unrealistic assumption in nearly all cases. The latent Markov model therefore corrects the manifest data for measurement error with the result that the (true) dynamics are now given on the latent level. The latent Markov model was first presented by Wiggins (1955, 1973). However, applications were hampered due to problems in parameter estimation. Again, Poulsen (1982) presented an efficient method for estimating the parameters of the latent Markov

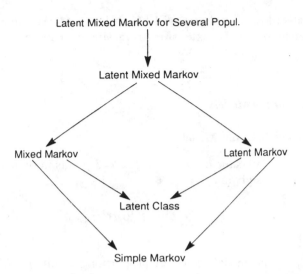

Latent Mixed Markov for Several Popul.

Latent Mixed Markov

Mixed Markov

Latent Markov

Latent Class

Simple Markov

Figure 15.1. A Hierarchy of Discrete Time Markov Models

model. It is interesting to note that the classical latent class model (Lazarsfeld, 1950) can be shown to be a special case of both the mixed and the latent Markov model (see Section 2.2).

Model fans might wonder whether there is a more general model including both the mixed and the latent Markov model as special cases. In fact, the latent mixed Markov model of Langeheine and Van de Pol (1990) does. It extends the 1-chain latent Markov model to a mixture of several latent chains. If these chains are considered to be free of measurement error this model is equal to the mixed Markov model.

On top of the hierarchy, finally, we have the latent mixed Markov model for several populations presented by Van de Pol and Langeheine (1990) that enables a simultaneous analysis of several groups defined by additional external discrete variables such as gender, socioeconomic status, or experimental versus control group.

It should be noted that the hierarchy in Figure 15.1 gives a condensed picture of the state of affairs. In fact, there is a great variety of models known from the literature that may be shown to be special cases of either one of the models included in the hierarchy. For overviews and details see Langeheine (1988a), Langeheine and Van de Pol (1990, 1992, forthcoming), and Van de Pol and Langeheine (1989, 1990).

In what follows, emphasis will be on latent Markov models with special attention to the extension from single to multiple indicator models.

2. Latent Markov Models

2.1. The Single Indicator Model

For a single indicator E measured at $T = 3$ points in time, the latent Markov model is given by

$$P_{ijk} = \sum_{abc} \delta_a^1 \rho_{i|a}^1 \tau_{b|a}^{2\,1} \rho_{j|b}^2 \tau_{c|b}^{3\,2} \rho_{k|c}^3 \qquad [15.1]$$

where P_{ijk} is the model expected proportion of cell ijk (i, j, and k referring to the categories of E at the three points in time). δ_a^1 is the proportion for class a of the latent (marginal) distribution at time $t = 1$. This distribution is characterized by conditional response probabilities $\rho_{i|a}^1$ for answering category i of E given membership in latent class a. $\tau_{b|a}^{2\,1}$ are latent transition probabilities denoting where respondents go to from $t = 1$ to $t = 2$ ($a = b = $ no change, $a \neq b = $ change). At $t = 2$ the latent distribution is characterized by conditional response probabilities $\rho_{j|b}^2$, and so on. A graphical representation of this model is given in the top panel of Figure 15.2, where E^t refer to manifest marginal probabilities, R^t refer to matrices of conditional response probabilities and $T^{t+1,t}$ refer to matrices of latent transition probabilities.

In order to identify the model, two kinds of restrictions are necessary. First, because all parameters are probabilities they have to sum to unity (e.g., $\sum_a \delta_a^1 = \sum_i \rho_{i|a}^1 = \sum_b \tau_{b|a}^{2\,1} = 1$). Second, the single indicator latent Markov model is not identified unless (at least some of the) conditional response probabilities are restricted to be time homogeneous. For three points in time only, this requires us to set $R^1 = R^2 = R^3 = R$. If, in addition, transitions are restricted to be constant in time, the result is a first-order stationary latent Markov chain.

Multiplying P_{ijk} by N (the sample size) gives frequencies expected under the model that may be compared with observed frequencies to evaluate model fit via some chi-square statistic from the so-called family of power divergence statistics (see Read & Cressie, 1988).

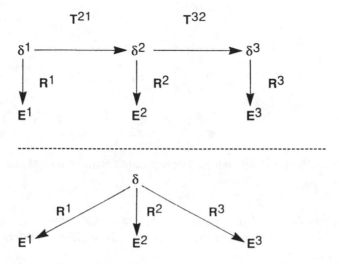

Figure 15.2. A Path Diagram for the Single Indicator Latent Markov Model (upper panel) and a Classical Latent Class Model (lower panel)

2.2. The Multiple Indicator Model

In the previous section we considered the situation where a single indicator is measured repeatedly at T points in time. A more realistic situation on the side of the data may be given by a data cube where K variables considered as indicators of some latent construct are measured at T points in time. As an example, take the path diagram in Figure 15.3 where we have $K = 2$ indicators E and F measured at $T = 3$ occasions.

Fortunately, this situation may be easily handled by formalizing the K-indicator model as a single indicator model with $K \times T$ "time points" (for details see Langeheine & Van de Pol, 1993, forthcoming). The keys to this become obvious from Figure 15.2. If indicators E^1, E^2, and E^3 (upper panel of Figure 15.2) are considered as multiple indicators of the same construct then δ^1, δ^2, and δ^3 coincide. This may be done by constraining transition matrices T^{21} and T^{32} to the identity matrix, I. The result is given by the path diagram in the lower panel of Figure 15.2, where we have a single latent distribution δ, unreliably measured

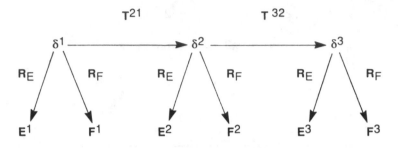

Figure 15.3. A Path Diagram for a Two-Indicator Latent Markov Model

by three indicators (time points in this case that, however, may be replaced by any categorical indicators), that is, a classical latent class model.

With respect to the situation in Figure 15.3 this simply means specifying a six-wave nonstationary latent Markov model with five transition matrices, while constraining the first, third, and fifth of these to the identity matrix. The remaining two matrices of transitions then give the ones we are interested in (T^{21} and T^{32}) that, in addition, may be specified to be time homogeneous. Formally, the respective model is given by

$$P_{ij\ ij\ ij}^{11\ 22\ 33} = \sum_{abc} \delta_a^1 \rho_{ila}^1 \rho_{jla}^1 \tau_{bla}^{21} \rho_{ilb}^2 \rho_{jlb}^2 \tau_{clb}^{32} \rho_{ilc}^3 \rho_{jlc}^3 \qquad [15.2]$$

where $P \ldots$ is the model expected proportion of cell ij ($t = 1$), ij ($t = 2$) and ij ($t = 3$) with parameters having the same meaning as in Equation 15.1.

One advantage of the multiple indicator model is that conditional response probabilities need not be restricted to be time homogeneous for model identifiability. However, allowing for both change in subjects and items may render interpretation of results difficult. In general, models of interest fall into one of the four boxes of the 2×2 classification defined by change in subjects (no, yes) and change in items (no, yes). If subjects are free to change we have a latent Markov model (with items allowed to change or not). If subjects are not allowed to change, the latent Markov model reduces to a latent class model with items allowed to change (e.g., getting easier) or not. The latter case is the most restrictive one, a model postulating no change at all.

Table 15.1 An Arithmetic Word Problem. Item C: Observed and Expected Frequencies (upper panel), Parameter Estimates (lower panel)

	1	1	1	1	2	2	2	2
$t =$	1	1	2	2	1	1	2	2
	1	2	1	2	1	2	1	2
f obs.	276	176	82	172	46	45	34	134
f exp.	278.5	171.2	76.1	177.8	47.7	47.8	35.6	130.4

	Class Prop.	Cond. Resp. Probs., ρ Cat.		Transition Probs., τ from t to $t+1$ Class		from $t = 1$ to $t = 3$ Class	
Class	δ at $t = 1$	1	2	1	2	1	2
1	.79	.87	.13	.70	.30	.50	.50
2	.21	.17	.83	.02	.98	.04	.96

3. Applications

For demonstrative purposes we start with a simple example of a dichotomous item measured at $T = 3$ points in time. Examples 2 and 3 refer to the situation of two binary items measured at two occasions. Finally, Example 4 has three 2-categorical items measured at three occasions. For ease of exposition, only dichotomous items are considered. It should be noted, however, that the methodology and software (PANMARK; Van de Pol, Langeheine, & de Jong, 1991) are not restricted with respect to number of categories.

3.1. Example 1:
An Arithmetic Word Problem

Observed and expected frequencies together with parameter estimates under the latent Markov model assuming time homogeneous transition probabilities are presented in Table 15.1 for a fail (category 1) / pass (category 2) item. This is item C from a battery of math items presented as word problems (for more details see Example 4 below).

The model gives an excellent fit (1.20 for both the likelihood ratio chi-square G^2 and the Pearson X^2 associated with df = 2—see also expected frequencies). As the parameter estimates show, this is a rather difficult item. At $t = 1$ we find 79% of the students in Class 1, which is characterized by a high probability of not solving the item (.87), whereas those having a high probability of passing the item (.83) are found in Class 2. As the transition probabilities from t to $t + 1$ show, the probability of progressing from Class 1 to Class 2 is .30 at $t = 2$ and $t = 3$. However, there also appears to be some slight decay ($\tau_{211} = .02$) across time. Transition probabilities from $t = 1$ to $t = 3$ are also given in Table 15.1 because they provide a more clear cut picture about what happens from the first to the last occasion. We thus see that 50% of those originally not mastering the item have a high probability of doing so at $t = 3$, whereas some 4% of the original masters have problems with the correct solution at the third occasion. The marginal latent distributions at $t = 2$ and $t = 3$ (which are obtained by multiplying δ^{t-1} by T) are $\delta^2 = (.56, .44)$ and $\delta^3 = (.40, .60)$, thus indicating a considerable net growth of 39%. With respect to a detailed breakdown of the total variation into proportions of true stability, true change, and error the reader is referred to Langeheine and Van de Pol (1990).

3.2. Example 2:
Sociometric Choices

Observed frequencies in Table 15.2 were generated from sociometric choice matrices where each student indicated with respect to every classmate whether he or she would choose or reject him or her as a partner in a number of sociometric choice criteria supposed to be indicators of interpersonal attractiveness. The two choice criteria considered here are A (share a table in case of a new seating arrangement) and B (share a tent if the class would go for a camping trip). We consider repeated measurements from two points in time only with a 1-week interval for a class of 36 students (19 boys, 17 girls, mean age 12.5). Observed frequencies in Table 15.2 were generated as follows: Each of the four sociometric choice matrices was written into a $36 \times 36 - 36$ (excluding self choices) vector. The four vectors were then combined in a $1,260 \times 4$ (A^1, B^1, A^2, B^2) raw data matrix from which observed frequencies were generated. The model of interest thus is a simple two-indicator model for two points in time.

Goodness-of-fit statistics for several models are given in Table 15.3. Model S1 is the no change at all model. Model S2 allows items—but not subjects—to change across time (time heterogeneous response probabilities). In Model S3 subjects are free to change while item probabilities are restricted to be time homogeneous. Model S4 allows for both item and

Table 15.2 Sociometric Choices: Observed and Expected
Frequencies Under Model S3

A^1	B^1	A^2	B^2	Obs. Freq.	Exp. Freq.	Chi-Square contribution
	Indicators					
1	1	1	1	673	668.75	.03
1	1	1	2	32	32.54	.01
1	1	2	1	27	29.80	.26
1	1	2	2	62	61.53	.01
1	2	1	1	25	27.87	.30
1	2	1	2	25	8.89	29.20
1	2	2	1	6	4.29	.68
1	2	2	2	29	43.97	5.10
2	1	1	1	24	27.91	.55
2	1	1	2	3	4.40	.45
2	1	2	1	10	2.48	22.88
2	1	2	2	17	19.31	.28
2	2	1	1	37	35.87	.04
2	2	1	2	29	43.16	4.64
2	2	2	1	12	18.34	2.19
2	2	2	2	249	230.91	1.42

NOTE. Category 1 = rejection, category 2 = choice.

subject specific change. Since Model S1 is nested in Model S2 and
Model S3 is nested in Model S4 we see that we can neglect models with
item specific change (i.e., S2 and S4). Comparison of Models S1 and
S3 shows that there is obviously some considerable latent change of
subjects from $t = 1$ to $t = 2$ (G^2 – difference = 189.2, df = 2).

Model S3, however, does not result in an acceptable fit. Structural
equation modelers who know about this problem would recommend
extending the model by including what they call "residual association
between observations over time," "correlated errors," or "direct effects
between indicators" (see Hagenaars, 1990, and Chapter 2 this volume).
Our methodology and software cannot handle such effects because the
parameters to be estimated are probabilities. The problem may be
solved, however, by reformalizing it as a log-linear latent class model
and using programs like LAT, NEWTON (Haberman, 1979, 1988) or
LCAG (Hagenaars & Luijkx, 1987). Extending Model S3 by direct
effects $A^1 A^2$ and $B^1 B^2$ in fact improves the fit considerably. But this
model is not identified.

Table 15.3 Sociometric Choices: Goodness-of-Fit Statistics

Model	Change in		df	G^2
	Items	*Subj.*		
S1	−	−	10	239.1
S2	+	−	6	228.3
S3	−	+	8	49.9
S4	+	+	4	49.7
S5	−	+,−	6	4.3

NOTE: Change in items, subjects: − = no, + = yes

It is often worthwhile to look at the residuals from a fitted model. As the last column of Table 15.2 shows, misfit of Model S3 is mainly due to two cells, both of which show consistent responses across time. Response pattern 1 2 1 2 says that someone else is rejected as a seating partner but chosen to share a tent. The opposite is true for response pattern 2 1 2 1. In view of the composition of the class this should not be surprising. We therefore extended Model S3 by two additional deterministically fixed classes. This model (S5) results in an excellent fit.

Table 15.4 contains parameter estimates that reveal the proportion of general rejection (Class 1) to be rather high, while acceptance in both indicators (Class 2) amounts to 30%. In view of the small proportion of the two deterministically fixed Classes 3 and 4, the improvement in fit of Model S5 over Model S3 is interesting to note. Substantively, latent change appears to be small. Overall, there is some shift from rejection to acceptance. The latent distribution at $t = 2$ is $\delta^2 = (.64, .33, .02, .01)$.

3.3. Example 3: Cognitive Development in the Tradition of Piaget

The data in Table 15.5 come from a project on "child development and social structure" (Schröder, 1986). At the age of 7 years, several tasks were presented to $N = 113$ children, with repeated measurements at the age of 9 years. According to Piaget (1947), children acquire the competence to master such tasks at the stage of concrete operations. While Schröder's data refer to three items given at the age of 7 and two of these given at the age of 9, we retain only the two items presented at both $t = 1$ and $t = 2$, that is, "inclusion" and "logical multiplication."

Table 15.4 Sociometric Choices: Parameter Estimates for Model S5

Class	Class Prop. δ at $t = 1$	Ind.	Cond. Resp Probs., ρ Cat. 1	2	Transition Probs., τ Class 1	2	3	4
1	.67	A	.96	.04	.91	.09	0	0
		B	.97	.03				
2	.30	A	.10	.90	.11	.89	0	0
		B	.05	.95				
3	.02	A	1	0	0	0	1	0
		B	0	1				
4	.01	A	0	1	0	0	0	1
		B	1	0				

NOTE: Parameter values of 0 and 1 are fixed by definition.

Table 15.5 Cognitive Development: Observed Frequencies

Occasion Indicator	1 I7	M7	2 I9	M9	Obs. Freq.
	1	1	1	1	13
	1	1	1	2	2
	1	1	2	1	22
	1	1	2	2	21
	1	2	1	1	0
	1	2	1	2	0
	1	2	2	1	12
	1	2	2	2	11
	2	1	1	1	0
	2	1	1	2	1
	2	1	2	1	5
	2	1	2	2	8
	2	2	1	1	0
	2	2	1	2	2
	2	2	2	1	5
	2	2	2	2	11

NOTE: Indicators inclusion (I7, I9) and logical multiplication (M7, M9) at the age of 7 and 9. Categories 1 = fail, 2 = pass.

Table 15.6 Cognitive Development: Parameter Estimates

| | | Cond. Resp. Probs., ρ | | Transition Probs., τ | | |
| | Class Prop. | Correct Resp. | | Class | | |
Class	δ at $t = 1$	I	M	1	2	3
1	.74	.06	.25	.15	.48	.37
2	.07	.94	.25	0	.22	.78
3	.19	.94	.75	0	0	1

NOTE: Conditional response probabilities are given for category 2 = correct response only. Parameter values of 0 and 1 are fixed by definition.

Since these data refer to a single stage of Piaget's theory they cannot be used to test his general theory. However, within the stage of concrete operations, Piaget postulates competencies invariance, inclusion, and logical multiplication to be acquired in this order. In addition, Piaget postulates that a competence once acquired will never be lost. These hypotheses may be translated into a multiple indicator Markov model, which (for indicators I7, M7, I9, and M9) has the following properties: (a) If competencies are acquired in the order postulated there should be three states (classes) at each time point only: children who do not have both competencies (Class 1), those who master inclusion but not logical multiplication (Class 2), and children having both competencies (Class 3). (b) Since a competence once acquired is never lost, all elements in the lower triangular of the matrix of transition probabilities have to be fixed at zero.

The first proposition is thus equivalent to postulating some Guttman-type *ordered categorical* latent variable. To complete the model definition, we decide for the so-called latent distance model with item specific error rates (cf. e.g., Langeheine, 1988b): (a) Each item has a single error rate. (b) These error rates are constant across classes. In addition, they are assumed to be time homogeneous.

Table 15.6 contains parameter estimates. The response probabilities reveal that error rates are considerably higher for logical multiplication as compared with inclusion. With respect to change we see that there is considerable growth. At the age of 7 the majority of the children are found in Class 1; 85% of these make progress to Class 2 or 3 at the age of 9, as do most of those originally in Class 2. The latent distribution at $t = 2$ is nearly reversed, $\delta^2 = (.11, .37, .52)$.

Though the model considered so far appears to be plausible, it is not without problems. First, chi-square statistics ($G^2 = 17.68$, $X^2 = 13.78$, df = 8) disagree at the 5% level. In view of the small sample size this is all the more noteworthy. Second, standard errors of parameter estimates (not in a table) pinpoint a weak part of the model: Class 2 ($t = 1$) τ's have a large standard error of .69. Formally, this problem may be attacked by fixing either $\tau_{2|2}$ or $\tau_{3|2}$ to 1. However, these models cannot be accepted either.

As a next step we have therefore relaxed the postulate of no decay by allowing for a full transition matrix. This model converges to parameter estimates of the original model. That is, the postulated model is correct with respect to no regression.

As detailed in Langeheine (1991) several different error rate models were fitted to the data, however without success with respect to test statistics.

This example was primarily included for two reasons: (a) It shows how a well-defined theory about qualitative development may be translated into a latent Markov model. (b) It demonstrates how the implicit assumption of categorical latent variables may be modified to handle ordered categorical latent variables. To save space, we therefore refrain from presenting a well-fitting model ($G^2 = 6.4$, df = 8) for these data that assumes population heterogeneity via a so-called partially latent mover-stayer model (a model with one latent mover chain and one manifest stayer chain; for details see Langeheine, 1991).

Note that both Examples 2 and 3 may be easily formalized in terms of classical latent class models lumping together latent variables at $t = 1$ and $t = 2$ into a single latent variable with as many categories as there are nonempty cells in the transition matrix. This is because only two points in time are considered. However, things become really interesting if $T \geq 3$, as in the following example.

3.4. Example 4: More About Arithmetic Word Problems

This section presents a condensed version of an example from a recent paper by Langeheine, Stern, and Van de Pol (forthcoming, to be denoted LSP) while—at the same time—presenting a rival model. From theory and research on solving arithmetic word problems, LSP derive two models that they hypothesize to describe children's progress in a set of binary fail/pass items. The case of interest here is LSP's postulated model Y that was rejected in favor of their model Va.

LSP's model Y refers to the situation of three hierarchically ordered items A, B, and C that clearly differ in their requirement of mathematical strategies. The wording of item A, the easiest one, is

Peter had seven sweets.

Then he gave two sweets to Susan.

How many sweets does Peter have now?

These items were therefore considered as indicators of an ordered categorical latent variable ("availability of mathematical strategies"). As a consequence, the measurement part of model Y was assumed to follow a four-class latent distance model with item specific error rates (single error rate per item). A no-decay model was specified for the structural part of the model (δ's and τ's).

The data used by LSP come from a large-scale longitudinal study of the Max Planck Institute of Psychological Research in Munich, Germany, with repeated measurements at $T = 3$ points in time and half-year intervals. Children's mean age at $t = 1$ was 7.5 years. The sample size, using valid responses across time, is 965.

With three binary items measured at three points in time a 2^9 contingency table with 512 cells is the point of departure. This clearly implies sparse data that cast doubt on the adequacy of chi-square statistics. LSP therefore report three statistics from the so-called family of power divergence statistics (Read & Cressie, 1988) with $\lambda = 0$ equal to G^2, $\lambda = 1$ equal to X^2, and $\lambda = 2/3$, which is the compromise statistic recommended by Read and Cressie. In addition, they give BIC (Schwarz, 1978), an information type descriptive statistic that has been shown to be a consistent estimator of model dimensionality. BIC is defined as follows: BIC $= -2 \log (L) + \log (N) k$, where L is the maximum of the likelihood function, k is the number of nonredundant estimated parameters, and N is the sample size. The smaller BIC the better.

For several reasons, LSP fitted several models to these data. First, in order not to overlook possibly simpler models, a set of two-class models, differing in whether item specific and/or subject specific change is allowed for, were evaluated. Second, all models (including four-class ones) were fitted twice by specifying (a) time homogeneous and (b) time heterogeneous transitions (with the exception of no latent change, of course).

LSP's results (based on the three power divergence statistics) may be summarized as follows: (a) All two-class models are rejected or appear at least to be questionable due to disagreement of the power divergence statistics. (b) Allowing for time heterogeneous transitions leads to only marginal improvement in fit. This also holds for four-class models. (c) Models with both item and subject specific change do not fare better than either one of these.

Table 15.7 Arithmetic Word Problems: Test Statistics for Multiple
Indicator Models

Model	# Classes	df	Power $\lambda = 0$ G^2	Diverg. 2/3	Statistics 1 χ^2	BIC
Y	4	499	469	619	958	8,262
V	4	493	311	329	386	8,146
VI	5	496	292	353	487	8,106

NOTE: Models Y and V are denoted Ya and Va in LSP.

Table 15.8 Arithmetic Word Problems: Parameter Estimates for Model V

Class	Class Prop. δ at t = 1	Cond. Resp. Probs. Correct Resp., ρ Item A	B	C	Transition Probs., τ, from t to t + 1 Class 1	2	3	4
1	.05	.04	.10	.11	.20	.40	.36	.04
2	.23	.96	.10	.11	.08	.36	.51	.05
3	.50	.96	.90	.11	.02	.14	.36	.48
4	.22	.96	.90	.89	.00	.01	.15	.84

NOTE: Conditional response probabilities are given for correct responses only.

In what follows we therefore consider models with subject specific change and time homogeneous transitions only.

Because of disagreement of the power divergence statistics (see Table 15.7), LSP rejected their hypothesized no-decay model Y in favor of model V that allows for decay. Note that model V obviously is far more adequate: (a) The deviance is reduced considerably; (b) all three statistics agree fairly well; (c) BIC also favors this model. Estimated parameter values of this model are given in Table 15.8.

In light of a rival model considered below we will not go into details of interpretation with respect to model V. Suffice it to say that the classes are well defined with relatively small error rates. A considerable number of the children make progress across time. The latent distribution at the third occasion, $\delta^3 = (.03, .13, .30, .54)$, reveals that Classes 1-3 decrease in size over time. Decay is mainly to adjacent classes (for more details and explanations for decay see LSP).

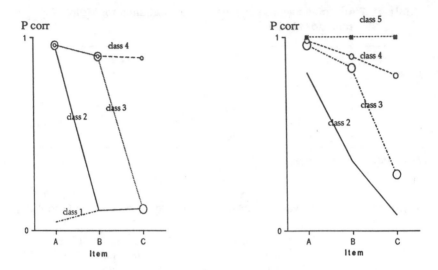

Figure 15.4. Arithmetic Word Problems. Item Profiles Under Model V (left panel) and Model VI (right panel, without class 1, see text)

Ordered classes require nonintersecting item profiles. One way to achieve orderedness is by using equality constraints such as in a latent distance model. However, as the left panel of Figure 15.4 shows, this implies putting severe strain on the response probabilities. Ordered classes may also be obtained by using inequality constraints (Croon, 1990). However, our software (PANMARK) cannot handle inequality constraints. Still another way is to let item probabilities vary freely while starting the algorithm with starting values as in the latent distance model, hopefully ending up with nonintersecting item profiles.

This is exactly what was done in model VI for Classes 2, 3, and 4 while adding two deterministically fixed classes: a class of perfect masters (Class 5) and a class of pure nonmasters (Class 1). The reason behind this is that fit is generally improved considerably when the two extreme response patterns are fitted perfectly. As the transition matrix in Table 15.9 shows, the latter two classes were specified to be stayers, as was Class 4. Finally, a one-step only growth model without decay was assumed.

According to G^2 this model fares better than model V despite a smaller number of parameters to be estimated. This is also why model VI is favored by BIC, which is a function of the log-likelihood and the number of parameters (and the sample size).

Table 15.9 Arithmetic Word Problems: Parameter Estimates for Model VI

Class	Class Prop. δ at t = 1	Cond. Resp. Probs. Correct Resp., ρ Item			Transition Probs., τ, from t to t + 1 Class				
		A	B	C	1	2	3	4	5
1	.001	0	0	0	1	0	0	0	0
2	.37	.81	.36	.08	0	.74	.26	0	0
3	.54	.96	.84	.29	0	0	.47	.53	0
4	.05	.98	.90	.80	0	0	0	1	0
5	.04	1	1	1	0	0	0	0	1

NOTE: Conditional response probabilities are given for correct responses only. Parameter values of 0 and 1 are fixed by definition.

Table 15.9 presents estimated parameter vales for model VI. Item profiles plotted in the right panel of Figure 15.4 are worth mentioning for several reasons. First, note that we have omitted Class 1 because it was estimated to be only of proportion .001. Second, classes are clearly ordered. Third, despite some differences the profiles of Classes 2, 3, and 4 in model VI match fairly well with those of Classes 2, 3, and 4 in model V. In model VI, however, we have no nonmasters (Class 1 in model V), whereas there is an additional class of perfect masters. The main differences between these two models thus are two: (a) Under model VI a higher proportion of children starts at lower levels. (b) This obviously is the reason for decay under model V. In line with this also is the considerably higher proportion of 47% net change under model VI—δ^3 = (.001, .20, .24, .52, .04)—as compared with 32% in model V.

Finally, it should be noted that model VI is well identified with standard errors of parameters (not in a table) ranging from .01 to .06 with the exception of Class 3 transitions (.11). In order to obtain an even better fit one might be tempted to remove some additional 0/1 restrictions on the transition probabilities. We have checked several versions—ending up, however, with weakly identified or not identified models all of which hardly improve deviance.

4. Conclusions

Rindskopf (1990, p. 467) starts his summary by stating that "latent class analysis gives the developmental researcher a statistically rigorous way of testing a wide variety of models." No doubt this is true. But Rindskopf—just as most other authors—considered repeated measurements from only two occasions. As has been mentioned in Section 3.3, this situation may be formally handled by a classical latent class model by equating the number of classes in the latent class model with the number of estimated τ parameters in the respective latent Markov model.

Formalizing such problems in terms of latent Markov models has several advantages, however. First, the Markov approach has more appeal because change (e.g., growth) is an integral part of the model in terms of the transition probabilities. Second, with more than two points in time it becomes impracticable and sometimes even impossible to specify latent Markov models in terms of classical latent class models. A typical case in point is the assumption of time homogeneous transition probabilities. Third, algorithms used in programs for latent class analysis usually diverge if at least one class is estimated to be empty. This causes no problems in PANMARK. Fourth, as has been shown— especially in Section 2.2—the classical latent class model turns out to be a special case of the latent Markov model. All of these considerations and additional ones (e.g., multiple chains, multiple groups) make evident that the methodology presented here is far more flexible in testing developmental hypotheses than the approach advocated by Rindskopf.

Of course, latent Markov models have much in common with latent class models. The most important extension over the latter is the incorporation of latent change. This is also why we call these models "mixed Markov latent class models" or "latent class models with latent change."

At the same time, these models share features of other classes of models. In Section 2, path diagrams were used to visualize the single and the multiple indicator model. In Section 3.2, we addressed a problem of misfit and how structural equation modelers would try to attack it. In Section 3.4 we referred to the measurement part and the structural part of a model—all of these making evident close analogies to structural equation models for continuous latent variables.

The latent distance model used in Sections 3.3 and 3.4 is but one out of a variety of scaling models. Whereas latent distance models conceive of latent variables as being ordered categorical, the Rasch model (Spiel, Chapter 14 this volume) assumes continuous latent variables, that is, traits. In analogy with the title of Spiel's chapter, we could also have entitled ours "Latent class models for measuring change." Apart from the measurement scale, however, there is at least one fundamental difference between these two classes of models. In the Rasch model, subject specific change means that a person's ability parameter increases or decreases through time. But the specific response vector of some subject contains no information in estimating that subject's ability, that is, all persons with the same *number* of items solved are estimated to have the same ability (e.g., persons with response vectors 100, 010, and 001). Often, however, the interest is in groups of persons (defined by manifest response patterns and/or latent item profiles) and how they change. This is where latent class models come into play (see also Formann, Chapter 1 this volume), which may also be called models of structural change.

The approach presented here has much in common with work of other (groups of) researchers. The work of Collins, Cliff, and Dent (1988) and Collins and Cliff (1990), extending the deterministic Guttman simplex to a methodology for measuring dynamic constructs in longitudinal panel studies, is of special interest because of theoretical issues addressed. Collins and Wugalter (1992) have extended this deterministic approach to a probabilistic one called "latent transition analysis." In principle, their approach is identical to our multiple indicator latent Markov model. We have not, however, seen any applications to data from more than two points in time so far. In addition, our approach appears to be more flexible in terms of other extensions, for example, multiple chains for modeling population heterogeneity.

Macready and Dayton (Chapter 9 this volume) are among those using a classical latent class formalization for longitudinal analysis (assessment of trait acquisition, in this case). They demonstrate how various hypotheses about what they call unconstrained, forward, and no migration may be evaluated using latent class models. Their analysis refers to several items measured at three occasions and, in addition, to several instructional groups. With respect to number of time points this clearly is a step forward. Nevertheless, several limitations become obvious with using the Clogg and Goodman (1984, 1985) simultaneous group analysis approach. First, unconstrained migration is equal to assuming a second-order latent Markov model. That is, two competing explanations for misfit of simple manifest Markov models—higher order and measurement error—are combined into one model. Our experience is, however, that either one of these (but not both) is relevant for a given set of data. Second, transition probabilities normally turn out to be time homogeneous—unless something really important happens between occasions. Unfortunately, this assumption cannot be tested using the classical latent class model when more than two points in time are considered. Third, using a traditional program for latent class analysis may become rather difficult and laborious (see below). These comments also apply to Formann (Chapter 11 this volume).

In modeling patterns of latent change Hagenaars's (Chapter 13 this volume) "modified LISREL approach" clearly has the advantage of including direct effects between indicators. Again, however, the restriction of stationary transition probabilities cannot be handled by this approach.

Most of the problems tied to one or the other approach may be easily overcome by PANMARK, a user-friendly and flexible program for latent class and Markov chain analysis. PANMARK has been used in testing all but one of the models (the one with direct effects between indicators—see Section 3.2) considered in this chapter. It may be used to test all of the hypotheses considered by Macready and Dayton (Chapter 9 this volume), part of those in Hagenaars (Chapter 13 this volume) and all but one (H_1, example 1) in Formann (Chapter 11 this volume). For $T > 2$ it allows testing hypotheses that cannot handled by programs for classical latent class analysis (e.g., stationarity of transitions), let alone that the setup of the input required by these programs may become extremely difficult, especially if T goes beyond 3. A trichotomous latent variable evaluated at $T = 4$ points in time, for example, may require up to $3^4 = 81$ classes or even more classes when assuming heterogeneous chains.

Although our methodology thus appears to be very general and flexible, it is not without problems. As we have mentioned earlier, inappropriate model fit with a multiple indicator model may be due to correlated errors across time. In contrast to other approaches, we cannot handle such effects. One way out of the problem may be to assume population heterogeneity via multiple chains. There is a limit, however, with respect to the number of chains because of identifiability, which depends on the number of time points under consideration and the number and nature of chains. Unfortunately, this is a complicated problem not allowing for clear-cut rules. But the PANMARK program offers several checks for model identification.

Another problem—shared by all latent class approaches presented in this volume—is tied to sparse data. Assume that a project refers to three 3-categorical items (assumed to tap some latent construct) repeatedly measured at $T = 3$ points in time with three groups defined by some additional external variable. This means that we start with three contingency tables with 3^9 response patterns each. That is, the total number of cells is 3 × 19,683. While such a problem may be easily handled by PANMARK (because zero observed cells are not needed for purposes of estimation) and normally causes no problems in estimating the parameters of a given model, the adequacy of popular chi-square statistics for evaluating model fit will clearly be violated. Though there are several ways out of the problem (e.g., using descriptive fit indices such as BIC), these are not without difficulty either (cf. LSP).

Still another common problem waiting to be attacked in a more general way is missing data due to panel attrition. One possible approach, also used in the examples in this chapter, is to retain subjects with (valid) responses at all points in time only. Doing so is equivalent to assuming that subjects who do not respond at some point(s) in time are a random sample of all subjects. If this assumption is not tenable—as we believe in most cases—this may lead to biased estimates.

References

Chall, J. (1983). *Stages of reading development.* New York: McGraw-Hill.

Clogg, C. C., & Goodman, L. A. (1984). Latent structure analysis of a set of multidimensional contingency tables. *Journal of the American Statistical Association, 79,* 762-771.

Clogg, C. C., & Goodman, L. A. (1985). Simultaneous latent structure analysis in several populations. In N. B. Tuma (Ed.), *Sociological methodology 1985* (pp. 81-110). San Francisco: Jossey-Bass.

Colby, A., Kohlberg, L., Gibbs, J., & Lieberman, M. (1983). A longitudinal study of moral judgement. *Monographs of the Society for Research in Child Development,* Serial No. 200, Vol. 48, Nos. 1-2.

Collins, L. M., & Cliff, N. (1990). Using the longitudinal Guttman simplex as a basis for measuring growth. *Psychological Bulletin, 108,* 128-134.

Collins, L. M., Cliff, N., & Dent, C. W. (1988). The longitudinal Guttman simplex: A new methodology for measurement of dynamic constructs in longitudinal panel studies. *Applied Psychological Measurement, 12,* 217-230.

Collins, L. M., & Wugalter, S. E. (1992). Latent class models for stage-sequential dynamic latent variables. *Multivariate Behavioral Research, 27,* 131-157.

Croon, M. (1990). Latent class analysis with ordered latent classes. *British Journal of Mathematical and Statistical Psychology, 43,* 171-192.

Eckstein, S. G., & Shemesh, M. (1992). Mathematical models of cognitive development. *British Journal of Mathematical and Statistical Psychology, 45,* 1-18.

Freud, S. (1940). *Vorlesungen zur Einführung in die Psychoanalyse.* London: Image Publishing.

Gesell, A. (1966). The ontogenesis of infant behavior. In L. Carmichael (Ed.), *Manual of child psychology*. New York: John Wiley.

Haberman, S. J. (1979). *Analysis of qualitative data: Vol. 2. New developments*. New York: Academic Press.

Haberman, S. J. (1988). A stabilized Newton-Raphson algorithm for log-linear models for frequency tables derived by indirect observation. In C. C. Clogg (Ed.), *Sociological methodology 1988* (pp. 193-211). Washington, DC: American Sociological Association.

Hagenaars, J. A. (1990). *Categorical longitudinal data. Log-linear panel, trend, and cohort analysis*. Newbury Park, CA: Sage.

Hagenaars, J. A., & Luijkx, R. (1987). *Manual LCAG*. Working Paper Series # 17. Department of Sociology, Tilburg University.

Kohlberg, L. (1980). *The meaning and measurement of moral development*. Worcester, MA: Clark University Press.

Langeheine, R. (1988a). Manifest and latent Markov chain models for categorical panel data. *Journal of Educational Statistics, 13*, 299-312.

Langeheine, R. (1988b). New developments in latent class theory. In R. Langeheine & J. Rost (Eds.), *Latent trait and latent class models* (pp. 77-108). New York: Plenum.

Langeheine, R. (1991). Latente Markov-Modelle zur Evaluation von Stufentheorien der Entwicklung. *Empirische Pädagogik, 5*, 169-189.

Langeheine, R., Stern, E., & Van de Pol, F. (forthcoming). State mastery learning: Dynamic models for longitudinal data. *Applied Psychological Measurement*.

Langeheine, R., & Van de Pol, F. (1990). A unifying framework for Markov modeling in discrete space and discrete time. *Sociological Methods and Research, 18*, 416-441.

Langeheine, R., & Van de Pol, F. (1992). Recent developments in discrete space discrete time Markov modeling. In F. Faulbaum (Ed.), *Advances in statistical software 3* (pp. 119-125). Stuttgart: Fischer.

Langeheine, R., & Van de Pol, F. (1993). Multiple indicator Markov models. In R. Steyer, K. F. Wender, & K. F. Widaman (Eds.), *Psychometric methodology*. Proceedings of the 7th European Meeting of the Psychometric Society in Trier. (pp. 248-252). Stuttgart: Fischer.

Langeheine, R. & Van de Pol, F. (forthcoming). Discrete time mixed Markov latent class models. In A. Dale & R. Davies (Eds.), *Analyzing social and political change: A handbook of research methods*. Newbury Park, CA: Sage.

Lazarsfeld, P. F. (1950). The logical and mathematical foundation of latent structure analysis. In S. A. Stouffer et al. (Eds.), *Studies in social psychology in World War II: Vol. IV. Measurement and prediction* (pp. 362-412). Princeton, NJ: Princeton University Press.

Piaget, J. (1947). *Psychologie der Intelligenz*. Zürich: Rascher.

Piaget, J. (1971). The theory of stages in cognitive development. In R. D. Green, M. P. Ford, & G. B. Flammer (Eds.), *Measurement and Piaget* (pp. 1-11). New York: McGraw-Hill.

Poulsen, C. S. (1982). *Latent structure analysis with choice modeling applications*. (PhD Dissertation, The University of Pennsylvania). Aarhus: The Aarhus School of Business Administration and Economics.

Read, T.R.C., & Cressie, N.A.C. (1988). *Goodness-of-fit statistics for discrete multivariate data*. New York: Springer.

Rindskopf, D. (1990). Testing developmental models using latent class analysis. In A. von Eye (Ed.), *Statistical methods in longitudinal research: Vol. II. Time series and categorical longitudinal data* (pp. 443-469). New York: Academic Press.

Schröder, E. (1986). *Entwicklungssequenzen konkreter Operationen: Eine empirische Untersuchung individueller Entwicklungsverläufe der Kognition. Studien und Berichte 43.* Berlin: Max-Planck-Institut für Bildungsforschung.

Schwarz, G. (1978). Estimating the dimension of a model. *Annals of Statistics, 6,* 461-464.

Singer, B., & Spilerman, S. (1979). Mathematical representations of development theories. In J. R. Nesselroade & P. B. Baltes (Eds.), *Longitudinal research in the study of behavior and development* (pp. 155-177). New York: Academic Press.

Van de Pol, F., & Langeheine, R. (1989). Mixed Markov models, mover-stayer models and the EM algorithm. With an application to labor market data from the Netherlands Socio Economic Panel. In R. Coppi & S. Bolasco (Eds.), *Multiway data analysis* (pp. 485-495). Amsterdam: North-Holland.

Van de Pol, F., & Langeheine, R. (1990). Mixed Markov latent class models. In C. C. Clogg (Ed.), *Sociological Methodology 1990* (pp. 213-247). Oxford: Blackwell.

Van de Pol, F., Langeheine, R., & de Jong, W. (1991). *PANMARK user manual. PANel analysis using MARKov chains. Version 2.2.* Voorburg: Netherlands Central Bureau of Statistics.

West, B. J. (1985). *An essay on the importance of being nonlinear.* Berlin: Springer.

Wiggins, L. M. (1955). *Mathematical models for the analysis of multi-wave panels.* (Doctoral dissertation, Columbia University). Ann Arbor, MI: University Microfilms.

Wiggins, L. M. (1973). *Panel analysis. Latent probability models for attitude and behavior processes.* Amsterdam: Elsevier.

PART 4

Testing in the Analysis of Latent Variables

16

Corrections to Test Statistics and Standard Errors in Covariance Structure Analysis

ALBERT SATORRA
PETER M. BENTLER

Introduction

In recent years a lot of attention has been given to the analysis of covariance structures, including its variants, such as confirmatory factor analysis and linear structural relation models. The major part of the statistical theory associated with the analysis of covariance structures is asymptotic (see, e.g, Anderson, 1988; Anderson & Amemiya, 1988; Bentler & Dijkstra, 1985; Browne, 1984; Fuller, 1987; Satorra, 1989; Shapiro, 1986). The major emphasis of this asymptotic theory has been on the distribution of a goodness-of-fit statistic designed to assess the adequacy of a hypothesized model and on the covariance matrix of parameter estimates. Although some alternative approaches have been used in these works, under equivalent conditions the resulting statistics are essentially agreed upon and bear strong resemblance to statistics obtained for general multivariate nonlinear models (e.g., Gallant, 1987).

AUTHORS' NOTE: The very constructive suggestions of a reviewer are highly appreciated. Work supported in part by USPHS grants DA00017 and DA01070 and by Spanish DGICYT grant PB91-0814.

399

A surprising and serious omission in these developments has been a theory for the modification of the goodness-of-fit statistic to yield distributional behavior that more closely follows a reference distribution, here, chi-square. Two variants of such modifications are quite standard in statistics. The first involves a scaling to correct the mean of the test statistic, and the second involves an adjustment to correct both mean and variance as in Satterthwaite (1941). Such corrections have been advocated, for example, in the analysis of categorical data from complex sample surveys (cf. Rao & Scott, 1981, 1984, 1987; Fay, 1985). Utilizing the classic work of Box (1954), Satorra and Bentler (1986a, 1986b, 1988a, 1988b) developed an approach to the asymptotic behavior of covariance structure statistics that rather naturally yields corrections to the goodness-of-fit statistic of the scaling and Satterthwaite types. The purpose of this chapter is to present these results and to illustrate how they improve upon the uncorrected statistics that are now implemented in the field of covariance structure analysis. It will also be shown that the proposed corrections not only encompass the ones advocated by Shapiro and Browne (1987) in case of elliptical data but do not suffer from the drawback of Browne-Shapiro's corrections of lack of robustness against deviations from the assumption of an elliptical distribution. This general approach also provides a theory for correcting the standard covariance matrix of the vector of parameter estimates.

Although no general corrections to the goodness-of-fit statistics are routinely available in covariance structure analysis, corrections based on multivariate elliptical distribution theory have been recommended (Bentler, 1983b; Browne, 1982, 1984, 1987; Browne & Shapiro, 1987; Shapiro & Browne, 1987 and, more recently, Anderson, 1993) and implemented in a public computer program (Bentler, 1989). These corrections are appropriate when the observed variables (or error components underlying these variables) are elliptically distributed. In the absence of a definitive test of an elliptical assumption, the corrections may be applied in practice when the variables appear to be elliptical, that is, are symmetric with no skew and exhibit a common degree of kurtosis. In the present chapter, it will be shown that this practice is dangerous: The correction can be so sensitive to violation of the elliptical assumption that the corrected statistic is even further off the reference distribution than the uncorrected statistic. In contrast, the statistics proposed below yield appropriate results under general types of distributions. One of the corrections is already available in EQS (Bentler, 1989; Bentler & Wu, 1993).

2. Notation and Background

Let σ be a p^* vector of population moments, s the corresponding p^* vector of sample moments, and H_0: $\sigma = \sigma(\theta)$, θ in Θ, a model for σ. Here θ is a q-vector of parameters and Θ is the corresponding parameter space, a compact subset of R^q. In this chapter, we will deal with covariance structure analysis, where σ contains the nonredundant elements of Σ, the population covariance matrix of z, a p vector of observable variables; s is the corresponding vector of sample variances and covariances, and $p^* \equiv p(p+1)/2$. We will assume that $n^{1/2}(s - \sigma)$ converges in distribution to $N(0, \Gamma)$ as n increases, where $n + 1$ is the sample size, that the function $\sigma = \sigma(\theta)$ is a continuously differentiable function of θ, and that the true parameter value θ_0 is an interior point of Θ. To make the exposition simpler, we also assume that the asymptotic covariance matrix Γ of $n^{1/2}s$ is non-singular and that the Jacobian matrix $\Delta \equiv \partial\sigma/\partial\theta'$ evaluated at the true parameter value is of full column rank. Even though we consider the case of covariance structure analysis, the theory to be described is general, and σ could be a vector on any type of population moments. For example, s could be a vector of polychoric correlations, in which case Γ would be the asymptotic variance matrix of s.

Although one type of goodness-of-fit statistic has received the dominant share of attention in covariance structure analysis, at least three types have been defined and two are in regular use. Asymptotically equivalent versions of these statistics also exist, but, since the distributional consequences are identical, these will not be discussed here. Each of these statistics can be based on a nonlinear (generalized) least squares approach (LS), or minimum chi-square analysis (see, e.g., Ferguson, 1958; Fuller, 1987, sec. 4.2). The first approach estimates θ as the value $\hat{\theta} \equiv \theta(s; V_n)$ minimizing

$$F(\theta, V_n) = [s - \sigma(\theta)]'V_n[s - \sigma(\theta)] . \qquad [16.1]$$

where V_n is a specific weight matrix that is assumed to converge with probability one to V, a positive-definite matrix. The standard goodness-of-fit statistic used to test the null hypothesis H_0: $\sigma = \sigma(\theta)$, θ in Θ, against the alternative hypothesis H_1: σ is unrestricted, is defined as

$$T_1 \equiv nF(\hat{\theta}, V_n) . \qquad [16.2]$$

Under the null hypothesis H_o and certain conditions on V to be discussed below, T_1 is asymptotically chi-square distributed with degrees of freedom (df) $r = p^* - q$.

The above approach is general and encompasses the vast majority of estimation methods used in covariance structure analysis. For instance, the analysis based on minimization of a more general discrepancy function $F^* = F^*(s, \sigma)$ of s and σ (e.g., Browne, 1984; Shapiro, 1986) is asymptotically equivalent to an LS analysis with $V = \partial^2 F^*/\partial\sigma\partial\sigma'$ evaluated at (σ, σ) (cf. Shapiro, 1985). The general distribution of (16.2) is developed in the next section.

A maximum likelihood (ML) analysis based on the assumption that the vector z of observed variables is multivariate normal distributed minimizes with respect to θ the following function:

$$F_{ML}(\theta) = \log | \Sigma(\theta) | + \text{trace}[S\Sigma(\theta)^{-1}] - \log | S | - p . \qquad [16.3]$$

It has been shown (Browne, 1974) that the ML analysis is equivalent to a LS approach with

$$V_n = 2^{-1}D'(A_n^{-1} \otimes A_n^{-1})D , \qquad [16.4]$$

where D is the $0 - 1$ "duplication" matrix (e.g., Magnus & Neudecker, 1986) and A_n is any sequence of matrices that converges to Σ with probability one. An obvious expression for A_n is just S, the sample covariance matrix of z. Any LS analysis with a weight matrix of the form (16.4) will be called normal theory LS (NTLS). We define $T_{ML} \equiv nF_{ML}(\hat{\theta})$.

The second type of estimator routinely used in a public computer program involves a linearized statistic and the associated goodness-of-fit test based on the ideas of Ferguson (1958) and others. An initial consistent estimator $\hat{\theta}_1$ is obtained by some method, for example, by minimizing (16.1) with $V_n = I$. It is then improved to yield the estimator $\tilde{\theta}$ by

$$\tilde{\theta} = \hat{\theta}_1 + (\Delta_1' V_n \Delta_1)^{-1} V_n (s - \sigma_1) \qquad [16.5]$$

where Δ_1 and σ_1 are Δ and σ evaluated at $\hat{\theta}_1$ and V_n is a weight matrix as in (16.4) (Bentler, 1983a; see also de Leeuw, 1983). The associated goodness-of-fit statistic is

$$T_2 \equiv n F(\tilde{\theta}, V_n) , \qquad [16.6]$$

which also has an asymptotic chi-square distribution under an appropriate choice of V_n as discussed further below. Bentler and Dijkstra (1985) develop the theory associated with linearized statistics and provide another goodness-of-fit statistic that is asymptotically equivalent to (16.6).

A third type of goodness-of-fit statistic can be developed based on the residual vector $n^{1/2}(s - \hat{\sigma})$ or $n^{1/2}(s - \tilde{\sigma})$. Let C_n be a $p^* \times p^*$ matrix that converges in probability to a positive definite matrix C, and let $\hat{\Delta}$ be Δ evaluated at $\hat{\theta}$. Define the modified weight matrix

$$W_n = C_n^{-1} - C_n^{-1} \hat{\Delta} (\hat{\Delta}' C_n^{-1} \hat{\Delta})^{-1} \hat{\Delta}' C_n^{-1} \qquad [16.7]$$

and the corresponding LS test statistic as

$$T_3 \equiv n F(\hat{\theta}, W_n) . \qquad [16.8]$$

When $C = \Gamma$, one obtains a statistic proposed by Browne (1982, 1984). In (16.7) and (16.8), $\hat{\theta}$ may be replaced with $\tilde{\theta}$ and $\hat{\Delta}$ with $\tilde{\Delta}$. The attractiveness of T_3 lies in the availability of the reference chi-square distribution regardless of the distribution of z and the weight matrix V_n used in the LS estimation process, providing that the model holds, the sample is large enough, and C_n is appropriately defined. In practice, T_3 may also suffer from the same drawback as the ADF method described below of lack of robustness against small to moderate sample size. The asymptotic distribution of T_3 is obtained below.

Under the null hypothesis and typical regularity conditions, LS theory gives the following asymptotic distribution for the vector $\hat{\theta}$ of parameter estimates (e.g., Bentler & Dijkstra, 1985; Fuller, 1987, appendix 4.B; Shapiro, 1986):

$$n^{1/2}(\hat{\theta} - \theta_0) \rightarrow_L N[0; (\Delta' V \Delta)^{-1} \Delta' V \Gamma V \Delta (\Delta' V \Delta)^{-1}] \qquad [16.9]$$

where θ_0 is the true parameter vector. Thus, a typical estimate of the matrix of asymptotic covariances (acov) of $\hat{\theta}$ for finite sample size n, will be

$$a\hat{c}ov(\hat{\theta}) = n^{-1}(\hat{\Delta}' V_n \hat{\Delta})^{-1} \hat{\Delta}' V_n \Gamma_n V_n \hat{\Delta} (\hat{\Delta}' V_n \hat{\Delta})^{-1} , \qquad [16.10]$$

wherein a consistent estimate Γ_n substitutes for the population Γ.

Estimators Γ_n can be obtained in a variety of ways in covariance structure analysis, and are sometimes used instead of V_n^{-1} in (16.2) and (16.6) for reasons of asymptotic efficiency. The LS analysis is said to be asymptotically optimal when the estimator $\hat{\theta}$ ($\tilde{\theta}$) is efficient (within the class of estimators that are functions of s) and the goodness-of-fit statistic T ($\equiv T_1$, T_2, or T_3) is asymptotically chi-square distributed. Conditions for this asymptotic optimality are discussed, for example, in Shapiro (1986) and Satorra (1989). From standard theory of LS estimation it follows that a choice of V that yields asymptotic optimality is

$$V^{-1} = \Gamma \equiv \text{acov}(n^{1/2}s) \,. \qquad [16.11]$$

Note that when z is normally distributed, then $\Gamma = 2D^+(\Sigma \otimes \Sigma)D^{+\prime} \equiv \Gamma^*$, where D^+ is the Moore-Penrose inverse of D, and thus both ML and NTLS analyses will be asymptotically optimal. Under very general conditions on the distribution of z, namely existence of eight order moments of z, an obviously consistent estimator of the asymptotic covariance matrix of s is given by the following matrix of sample fourth order moments:

$$\Gamma_n = n^{-1}\sum_{i=1}^{n+1} (b_i - \bar{b})(b_i - \bar{b})' \,, \qquad [16.12]$$

where $b_i = D^+\text{vec}(z_i - \bar{z})(z_i - \bar{z})'$, $\bar{b}$ and $\bar{z}$ are the mean vectors of the b_i's and z_i's respectively, and vec vectorizes a matrix columnwise. The premultiplication by D^+ suppresses the duplicated elements that arise when vectorizing a symmetric matrix. Since Γ_n of (16.12) estimates the asymptotic covariance matrix of s regardless of the distribution of z, the use of $V_n = \Gamma_n^{-1}$ gives what has been called an Asymptotically Distribution-Free (ADF) analysis, that is, it yields asymptotic optimality for any distribution of z (Browne, 1982, 1984; Chamberlain, 1982). Despite this asymptotic optimality, the ADF method is not very popular among practitioners of covariance structure analysis due to its lack of robustness against small to moderate sample size. This lack of robustness can be attributed to the need for inverting the matrix Γ_n, a matrix that involves sample fourth-order moments and hence is highly unstable in small to moderate sample sizes. In fact, the corrections proposed in the present chapter will help to robustify statistics that have been obtained using methods of analysis other than the ADF.

There are some instances, as in complex-sample surveys, where the expression of the consistent estimate of Γ differs from (16.12) (Skinner, Holt, & Smith, 1989; see also Satorra, 1992). In such cases, all the theory described in the present chapter applies by simply taking Γ_n to be the appropriate consistent estimate of Γ.

3. General Distribution of T

Although the distribution of T ($\equiv T_1$, T_2, or T_3) under the assumptions of correct model and optimal weight matrices is well known, the general distribution under misspecification of V_n or C_n (W_n) has not been described. We proceed by relating T to an asymptotic quadratic form. The usual regularity conditions are assumed, for example, that $\sigma = \sigma_0 \equiv \sigma(\theta_0)$, with θ_0 being an interior point of Θ.

It is well known (Shapiro, 1986; Satorra, 1989) that

$$T_1 \overset{a}{=} n(s - \sigma_0)'M(s - \sigma_0) , \qquad [16.13]$$

where "$\overset{a}{=}$" refers to asymptotic equality (i.e., the difference of both sides of the equality tend to zero in probability as $n \to \infty$), and where

$$M = V - V\Delta(\Delta'V\Delta)^{-1}\Delta'V . \qquad [16.14]$$

Note that asymptotically, $T_1 \overset{a}{=} T_{ML}$. Furthermore, since $n^{1/2}(\tilde{\theta} - \hat{\theta}) \overset{a}{=} 0$ (Bentler & Dijkstra, 1985, p. 16), a Taylor expansion of $F(\tilde{\theta}, V_n)$ at $\hat{\theta}$, using the fact that the derivative of F evaluated at $\hat{\theta}$ is zero, yields

$$T_1 \overset{a}{=} T_2 . \qquad [16.15]$$

Bentler and Dijkstra (1985) only considered the equality (16.15) under choice of an optimal weight matrix V_n. Since $T_3 = n(s - \hat{\sigma})'W_n(s - \hat{\sigma})$, $n^{1/2}(s - \hat{\sigma}) \overset{a}{=} n^{1/2}(s - \sigma_0) - n^{1/2}\Delta(\hat{\theta} - \theta_0)$(see Bentler & Dijkstra, 1985, eq. 1.7.2), and noting that W_n is a consistent estimator of $W = C^{-1} - C^{-1}\Delta(\Delta'C^{-1}\Delta)^{-1}\Delta'C^{-1}$, with $W\Delta = 0$, we get

$$T_1 \overset{a}{=} n(s - \sigma_0)'W(s - \sigma_0) . \qquad [16.16]$$

It will be remembered that T_3 can be used with $\hat{\theta}$ or $\tilde{\theta}$, and it may be noted that when T_3 is used with $C = \Gamma$ then $T_1 \overset{a}{=} T_2 \overset{a}{=} T_3$.

Recalling that the asymptotic covariance matrix of $n^{1/2}(s - \sigma_0)$ is Γ, theorem 2.1 of Box (1954) verifies that

$$T \overset{L}{\to} \tau = \sum_{i=1}^{r} \alpha_i \tau_i = \text{trace}\{U\Gamma\} \qquad [16.17]$$

where $\{\alpha_i\}_{i=1,2,\ldots,r}$ are the nonnull eigenvalues of $U\Gamma$, the α_i's are nonnegative numbers, $r = p^* - q$,

$$U = H - H\Delta(\Delta'H\Delta)^{-1}\Delta'H \qquad [16.18]$$

and $H = V$ (for T_1 or T_2) or $H = C^{-1}$ (for T_3). In (16.17) the τ_i's are independent chi-square variables with 1 df. The mean and variance of the asymptotic distribution of T are, respectively,

$$E(\tau) = \sum_{i=1}^{r} \alpha_i = \text{trace}\{U\Gamma\} \qquad [16.19]$$

and

$$\text{Var}(\tau) = 2\sum_{i=1}^{r} \alpha_i^2 = \text{trace}\{(U\Gamma)^2\}. \qquad [16.20]$$

Let U_n and Γ_n be consistent estimates of U and Γ respectively. Clearly, the α_i's can be consistently estimated from the latent roots of a consistent estimate of the matrix $U\Gamma$ such as $U_n\Gamma_n$. The mean and variance of the asymptotic distribution of T will be consistently estimated respectively by trace$\{U_n\Gamma_n\}$ and 2trace$\{(U_n\Gamma_n)^2\}$; see below for alternative expressions to compute these estimates.

4. Scaled and Adjusted Chi-Square Goodness-of-Fit Statistic

In this section we define two types of corrected test statistics. The first will be called the *scaled* test statistic $\bar{T}$. The second is a Satterthwaite-type and will be called the *adjusted* test statistic $\bar{T}$.

The scaled statistic is obtained by correcting T via (16.19), that is

$$\bar{T} \equiv c^{-1}T,\qquad\qquad [16.21]$$

where

$$c \equiv \text{trace}\{U_n\Gamma_n/r\}\qquad\qquad [16.22]$$

and T is referred to a chi-square distribution with r df. The rationale for using (16.21) is the following. Consider the three possible situations that may arise with respect to the dispersion of nonnull eigenvalues, α_i's, that characterize the asymptotic distribution of T:

a. all α_i's equal to one, thus $T \overset{L}{\to} \chi_r^2$
b. all α_i's equal to α, and thus $T \overset{L}{\to} \tau = \sum_1^r \alpha\,\tau_i = \alpha \sum_1^r \tau_i = \alpha\,\chi_r^2$
c. the α_i's are unequal, thus $T \overset{L}{\to} \tau = \sum_1^r \alpha_i\tau_i.$

Note that c of (16.21) estimates $\sum_1^r \alpha_i/r$, which equals 1 in case (a), and α in case (b). Thus, in contrast with T, which is only exactly chi-square distributed in case (a), $\bar{T}$ will have an asymptotically exact chi-square (df $-r$) distribution in case (a) and also in case (b). Moreover, in case (c) one is inclined to conjecture that $\bar{T}$ will be better approximated by a chi-square variate than the uncorrected statistic T. To support this conjecture, note that the asymptotic distribution of $\bar{T}$ and χ_r^2 agree in mean.

To our knowledge, the use in covariance structure analysis of the scaling correction c was first suggested by Satorra and Bentler at the *51st Annual Meeting of the Psychometric Society* (Toronto, June, 1986) and worked out in Satorra and Bentler (1986a, 1986b, 1988a, 1988b).

When the distribution of z is elliptical, Satorra and Bentler (1986a, sec. 5) show that the scaling factor c provides an estimate of the common relative kurtosis of z. Thus, when z has an elliptical distribution, $\bar{T}$ is asymptotically equivalent to the scaled-corrected chi-square statistic proposed by Browne (1984) and Shapiro and Browne (1987) (cf. Tyler, 1982, 1983). It needs to be stressed, however, that the Shapiro-Browne scaling correction is justified only when z follows an elliptical distribution. In applications, as will be shown below, the Shapiro-Browne correction can distort considerably the chi-squaredness of the statistic. In contrast, (16.21) will be seen to provide an approximately valid chi-square distribution even when the data are not elliptical.

In case (c) where the eigenvalues α_i's have high dispersion, $\overline{T}$ will only be approximately chi-square. In this case it may be worthwhile to consider Satterthwaite's (1941) adjustment, which involves a scaling as well as a degree of freedom adjustment. The adjusted test statistic $\overline{\overline{T}}$ is obtained by computing the integer d nearest to

$$d' \equiv (\text{trace}\{U_n\Gamma_n\})^2/\text{trace}\left\{(U_n\Gamma_n)^2\right\} \qquad [16.23]$$

and computing the statistic

$$\overline{\overline{T}} = (d/\text{trace}\{U_n\Gamma_n\})T. \qquad [16.24]$$

This is the standard approach that can make use of tabled chi-square values. Alternatively, when chi-square tables or programs are available for noninteger df, one would instead compute $\overline{\overline{T}} = (d'/\text{trace}\{U_n\Gamma_n\})T$ and use the fractional degrees of freedom; this method should be more precise. It follows then from the general asymptotic distribution of T (see (c) above), that, under the null hypothesis, $\overline{\overline{T}}$ is approximately distributed as chi-square variate with d degrees of freedom. See, for example, Theorem 3.1 in Box (1954). Note that now the asymptotic distribution of $\overline{\overline{T}}$ and χ_d^2 coincide not only in mean but also in variance. It can be easily seen that when the α_i's are equal, $\overline{T} \overset{a}{=} \overline{\overline{T}}$, and of course, when all the α_i's are equal to 1, then $T \overset{a}{=} \overline{T} \overset{a}{=} \overline{\overline{T}}$

Although (16.21) and (16.24) present a single-scaled statistic $\overline{T}$ and an adjusted statistic $\overline{\overline{T}}$, it will be clear that we have in fact defined a family of such statistics. First, each statistic corrects one of the three statistics T_1, T_2, or T_3, and each of these statistics in turn represents a variety of statistics depending on the choice of V_n or W_n. Related statistics such as T_{ML} are also correctable in the same way. Second, (16.21) and (16.24) can be implemented under several alternative choices of estimators of Γ. For example, Γ may be estimated via Γ_n^*, that is, as based on normal theory, or on elliptical theory, or on alternative distribution-free estimators of Γ, or on estimates of Γ that take into account the complex-sample structure of the data (Satorra, 1992). The possibility that the choice of estimator may not make much difference in some contexts is investigated in the example.

Let $\Delta_\perp$ denote the orthogonal complement of Δ (i.e., a $p^* \times (p^* - q)$ matrix of full column rank such that $\Delta_\perp' \Delta = 0$), then we can write

$$\text{trace } \{U_n \Gamma_n\} = \text{trace} \{\hat{\Delta}_\perp (\hat{\Delta}'_\perp C_n \hat{\Delta}_\perp)^{-1} \hat{\Delta}'_\perp \Gamma_n\}$$

$$= \text{trace } \{(\hat{\Delta}'_\perp C_n \hat{\Delta}_\perp)^{-1} \hat{\Delta}'_\perp \Gamma_n \hat{\Delta}_\perp\}$$

$$= \text{trace} \{(\hat{\Delta}'_\perp C_n \hat{\Delta}_\perp)^{-1} \sum_{i=1}^{n+1} d_i d_i'/n\}$$

$$= n^{-1} \sum_{i=1}^{n+1} d_i' (\hat{\Delta}'_\perp C_n \hat{\Delta}_\perp)^{-1} d_i \qquad [16.25]$$

where $d_i \equiv \hat{\Delta}'(b_i - \bar{b})$ and the well-known equality (e.g., Rao, 1965, exer. 33, p. 77)

$$C_n^{-1} - C_n^{-1} \Delta (\Delta' C_n^{-1} \Delta)^{-1} \Delta' C_n^{-1} = \Delta_\perp (\Delta'_\perp C_n \Delta_\perp)^{-1} \Delta'_\perp \qquad [16.26]$$

has been used. Note that the d_i's are r-dimensional vectors, where $r = p^* - q$ is the number of degrees of freedom of the chi-square test. Hence, in contrast to the ADF method, which requires one to store and invert the usually large $p^* \times p^*$ matrix Γ, the computation of the scale correction c will usually involve matrices of reduced dimension. Further,

$$2\text{trace } \{(U_n \Gamma_n)^2\} = 2\text{trace } \{[(\hat{\Delta}'_\perp C_n \hat{\Delta}_\perp)^{-1} \sum_{i=1}^{n+1} d_i d_i'/n]^2\}. \qquad [16.27]$$

Finally we review the scaled chi-square goodness-of-fit statistic advocated in Browne (1982, 1984) and Shapiro and Browne (1987) for z having an elliptical distribution. This statistic is

$$\dot{T} = k^{-1} T \qquad [16.28]$$

where k is a rescaled Mardia's sample measure of multivariate kurtosis (Browne, 1984, eq. 4.4), which estimates 1 when z is multivariate normal. As has been mentioned before, this scaled statistic may perform poorly when the distribution of z is not elliptical. In the theoretical case of z having an elliptical distribution, all the α_i are equal, hence we have $\overset{.}{T} \overset{a}{=} \overline{T} \overset{a}{=} \widetilde{T}$.

5. Scaling Corrections for Standard Errors

When the asymptotically exact estimates of standard errors provided by (16.10) are not available, we can apply scaling corrections to improve the standard errors provided by the "information matrix" $(\Delta'V\Delta)^{-1}$. Information matrix standard errors are computed by existing programs (Bentler, 1989; Jöreskog & Sörbom, 1988). Assume that the matrix Γ is approximated by

$$\Gamma = \alpha V^{-1} + \beta\sigma\sigma', \qquad [16.29]$$

for certain scalar values α and β. Assume also that the model is Quasi Linear (QL) (cf. Satorra & Bentler, 1986b), that is,

$$\sigma = \Delta\delta \qquad [16.30]$$

where δ is a $q \times 1$ vector. Then, inserting the approximation (16.29) into (16.10), and using the QL assumption (16.30), we easily get

$$\mathrm{avar}(\hat{\theta}) = n^{-1}[\alpha(\Delta'V\Delta)^{-1} + \beta\delta\delta']. \qquad [16.31]$$

Furthermore, the vector δ is given by

$$\delta = (\Delta'\Delta)^{-1}\Delta'\sigma. \qquad [16.32]$$

Suppose further that there exists a reordering of the parameters of the model such that $\delta\delta' \equiv P$, say, partitions as

$$P = \begin{pmatrix} P_{11} & 0 \\ 0 & 0 \end{pmatrix} \qquad [16.33]$$

This partition of P shows that for the estimates of certain parameters of the model the additive component of the variance associated with $\beta\delta\delta'$ vanishes; thus, for these specific parameters, just a scaling correction of the corresponding elements of $(\Delta'V\Delta)^{-1}$ is required. Usually the parameters requiring only a scaling correction are the parameters of major interest, such as the regression coefficients or factor loadings. The approximation requires an estimate for α. When (16.29) holds, with V being the weight matrix associated to the current estimation method, then, using (16.30) and U of (16.18) with $H = V$, we get

$$\text{trace}\{U\Gamma\} = \text{trace}\{U(\alpha V^{-1} + \beta\Delta\delta\delta'\Delta')\} = \text{trace}\{UV^{-1}\alpha\} = r\alpha, \quad [16.34]$$

which suggests the statistic given in (16.22), that is, $c = \text{trace}\{U_n\Gamma_n/r\}$, as an estimate of the scaling factor α. That is, the conventional variances provided by the typical inverse of the "information matrix" expression $(\Delta'V\Delta)^{-1}$ are simply multiplied by c. In order to know which parameters just need a scaling correction, that is, to have a zero additive correction, one simply inspects which are the parameters with zeros at the corresponding elements of (16.32) or (16.33). Note that in this development we have used the condition that the model be QL, which is implied (cf. Lemma 5.1 of Satorra & Bentler, 1986b) by the more typical condition of "invariance under a constant scaling factor" (Browne, 1984). For details and proofs of the above equalities, see Satorra and Bentler (1986a, sec. 5; 1986b, p. 553). The equalities (16.31) to (16.33) were reached also by Shapiro and Browne (1987).[1]

The corrections defined in this section are asymptotically exact when z follows an elliptical distribution (cf. Satorra & Bentler, 1986b) and the model is QL. Our approach also accommodates Tyler's (1982) maximum likelihood estimates of σ obtained under certain elliptical assumptions, in which case (16.31) is satisfied with equality, and the correction is asymptotically exact (provided of course the model is QL). However, it should be noted that the approximation (16.31) does not need to be restricted to the case of $\alpha = \beta + 1$, which holds when the distribution of z is elliptical.

6. Illustration

A four-variable one-factor model will be used to illustrate the behavior of the scaled and adjusted test statistics. Data were generated from a population having one-factor model structure in which the common factor was normally distributed with variance equal to one and each of the four error variables was distributed as power three of a standard normal distribution, conveniently scaled for the observable variables to have variance equal to one, and with all generating variates mutually independent. The size of the loadings was chosen to be 0.8. The four error variances and three factor loadings were free parameters of the model to be estimated in each sample. The factor variance was fixed at 1.0. The degrees of freedom (df) of the corresponding goodness-of-fit statistic was thus equal to 3. One thousand samples of sample size $n +$ $1 = 300$ were drawn, parameters were estimated by several methods, and test statistics were computed. The mean (standard deviation) of the skewness of the four measured variables were $-.046$ (1.60), $-.040$ (1.60), $-.047$ (1.46), and $.034$ ($.86$) across the $1,000$ replications. The variables thus showed no significant skew. They were also homogeneous in kurtosis, with a multivariate kurtosis of 3.73 (standard deviation 1.18). Thus the data appear to be elliptical and provide an interesting test of our theory as well as the results that Shapiro and Browne developed to "have definite practical applications" (1987, p. 1096).

The model estimates and statistics were computed in each sample by three methods: unweighted least squares, minimizing (16.1) with $V_n = I$; maximum likelihood, based on minimizing (16.3); and asymptotically distribution free, based on minimizing (16.1) with $V_n = \Gamma_n^{-1}$ [see 16.12]. The empirical distribution of the test statistics T_{ML}, $\bar{T}_{ML}$, $\dot{T}$, $T_1(ADF)$, $T_3(ULS)$, and $T_3^*(ULS)$ is summarized in Table 16.1. Since the model is correct, the theoretical mean and variance of chi-square distributions are 3 and 6, respectively (as in the chi-square distribution with df = 3). The bottom two rows of the Table 16.1 verify that all test statistics have empirical means and variances close to the theoretical ones, except the Browne-Shapiro statistic $\dot{T}$, which is completely off the mark. The tabled percentage points of the theoretical and empirical distribution function, in fact, are so unrelated that it is clear that $\dot{T}$ cannot be used to evaluate model adequacy. Each of the other statistics performs at close to nominal levels. It may be surprising to note that T_{ML} performs well. In fact, this is a case where the model and distribution of the generating variables guarantee robustness of T_{ML} against the misspecification of multinormality (Amemiya & Anderson, 1990; Browne & Shapiro, 1988; Satorra & Bentler, 1986b, 1990, 1991). The scaled statistic $\bar{T}_{ML}$ "recognizes" this fact and yields only a very minor adjustment that improves T_{ML}, for example, at 50% and 75%. $\bar{T}_{ML}$ is also slightly more accurate than $T_1(ADF)$ in this range. The statistics T_3 and

Table 16.1   Chi-Square Goodness-of-Fit Statistics. Simulated values of $100P[T > \chi_3^2(1 - \alpha)]$, where T denotes a goodness-of-fit statistic, and $\chi_3^2(1 - \alpha)$ is the $(1 - \alpha)$-fractile of a chi-square distribution with 3 degrees of freedom

	Type of Statistic[a]					
$\alpha\%$	T_{ML}	$\overline{T}_{ML}$	$\dot{T}$	$T_1(ADF)$	$T_3(ULS)$	$T_3^*(ULS)$
01	1.3	1.1	0.0	0.8	0.7	1.0
05	6.2	4.6	0.0	5.4	5.8	5.4
10	10.3	9.9	0.0	10.9	10.7	10.5
25	24.0	25.0	0.4	26.3	26.5	24.1
50	46.4	51.6	4.4	54.2	53.3	46.2
75	72.7	76.9	23.4	80.8	81.2	73.0
90	88.9	90.9	53.0	91.9	91.7	89.1
95	94.1	95.2	70.9	96.0	95.9	94.1
Mean	2.96	3.06	0.84	3.16	3.15	2.92
Variance	6.57	5.82	0.54	5.72	5.60	6.30

NOTES: a. T_{ML} Normal theory ML test statistic
$\overline{T}_{ML}$ Scaled ML test statistic (16.21)
$\dot{T}$ Browne-Shapiro's test statistic (16.28)
$T_1(ADF)$ Statistic T_1 of (16.2) with $V_n = \Gamma_n^{-1}$
$T_3(ULS)$ Statistic T_3 of (16.8) with $V_n = I$ and $C_n = \Gamma_n$
$T_3^*(ULS)$ Statistic T_3 of (16.8) with $V_n = I$ and $C_n = \Gamma_n^*$

T_3^* based on [16.8] using an unweighted LS estimator and C_n equal to Γ_n and Γ_n^*, respectively, perform equivalently. The correct behavior of T_3^* in this example is to be expected from the theory of asymptotic robustness (see Satorra & Bentler, 1990).

The statistic T_1 based on $V_n = I$ (unweighted least squares) is not expected to be chi-square distributed. Thus it is interesting to determine if the adjusted statistic $\overline{T}$ can yield approximate chi-square behavior. Table 16.2 provides results of this correction, using the fractional counterpart to (16.24). Since the df are adjusted, the mean and variance are not those based on a chi-square distribution with df = 3. However the variance is approximately twice the mean in each case, as expected. While both $\overline{T}$ and $\overline{T}^*$ are off at the higher percentage points, in the range .01 to .10 that is typically used to evaluate the adequacy of models, the statistics perform remarkably well.

Table 16.2 The Adjusted Fit Statistics (ULS analysis). Simulated values of $100P[T > \chi^2_{d'}(1 - \alpha)]$, where T is the adjusted statistic and $\chi^2_{d'}(1 - \alpha)$ is the $(1 - \alpha)$-fractile of a chi-square distribution with the adjusted d' degrees of freedom

	Type of statistic[a]	
$\alpha\%$	$\overline{\overline{T}}$	$\overline{\overline{T}}^*$
01	1.2	1.5
05	4.6	5.5
10	9.4	8.5
25	24.9	22.6
50	52.1	50.1
75	82.8	79.1
90	97.1	96.0
95	99.4	99.1
Mean	1.43	1.45
Variance	2.87	3.23

NOTES: a. $\overline{\overline{T}}_1$ Adjusted statistic (16.24) computed with fractional df, based on $V_n = \Gamma_n^{-1}$
$\overline{\overline{T}}_1^*$ Adjusted statistic (16.24) computed with fractional df, based on $V_n = \Gamma_n^{*-1}$

7. Conclusion

Simple corrections to the standard statistics of covariance structure analysis have been developed. The scaling and adjusting corrections to the goodness-of-fit test statistics are classical in nature and appear to behave quite well in practice. When the eigenvalues α_i's are equal, as for example when the distribution of z is elliptical, the scaling correction provides an exact asymptotic chi-square goodness-of-fit statistic. Under inequality of the α_i's, the scaling corrections yield an approximate chi-square statistic. In the case of high dispersion of the α_i's, the adjusted chi-square goodness-of-fit statistic may provide a more accurate approximation than the scaled one. It is worthwhile to note that when the corrections discussed are not needed, that is, when the distributional assumptions or conditions for asymptotic robustness hold, the corrections are automatically inactive (asymptotically). The corrections will also be inactive when applied in the case of the ADF method and T_3 with C_n equal to a consistent estimate of Γ. Using formulas (16.25) to (16.27) the corrections discussed can in fact be obtained without having to compute a consistent estimate of the usually large matrix Γ. Using formula (16.25), the matrices to be inverted in order to compute the scaling correction c are of dimension $r \times r$, with r the degrees of freedom of the test statistic.

As stated in the introduction, the theory just described is general and could apply, for instance, to structural equation models with discrete data, with appropriate replacement of s and Γ. In a brief overview of estimating and testing of structural equation models for continuous variables, Muthén (1993) describes the above scaling and adjusted statistics and applies the scaled statistic $\overline{T}$ to binary data. When giving the scaling correction in formula (25) of Muthén (1993), however, references to Satorra and Bentler (1988a, 1988b) where this formula was derived were inadvertently omitted.

Our theory for the scaling correction was also documented in the published manual for the EQS program (Bentler, 1989), where it also has been available computationally. Kano (1992) specializes the scaling correction of Satorra and Bentler (1986b, 1988a) to the test of independence and related structural equation models. Satorra (1992) considers the above corrections for the analysis of augmented moment structures with data possibly from complex samples. The scaled and adjusted corrections in the case of multiple samples are considered in Satorra (1993).

A recent study by Hu, Bentler, and Kano (1992) compared the behavior of normal theory T_{ML} and T_{LS} statistics, the elliptical statistic $\dot{T}$, a test statistic that permits heterogeneous marginal kurtoses (Kano, Berkane, & Bentler, 1990), the scaled statistic $\overline{T}$, and Browne's ADF statistic T_3 under seven different conditions on the distribution of factors and unique variates in a 15-variable confirmatory factor analysis model at each of six sample sizes. The two normal theory tests worked well under some conditions but completely broke down under other conditions. The elliptical test statistic $\dot{T}$ performed variably. The test that permits heterogeneous marginal kurtoses performed better. The presumably optimal distribution-free ADF statistic performed spectacularly badly in all conditions at all but the largest sample sizes. The scaled test statistic performed best overall. A similar result was reported by Chou, Bentler, and Satorra (1991) who compared T_{ML}, the ADF statistic T_3, and the scaled statistic $\overline{T}$ in a Monte Carlo study. They found that the scaled statistic performed better than the ML and ADF statistics.

The correction of Shapiro and Browne (1987) appears to be so sensitive to violation of assumptions that it should be used with great caution. Actually, this result is not totally unexpected, since Harlow (1985) had already reported that Browne's (1982, 1984) correction substantially overcorrected. However, overcorrection is not the only inappropriate behavior of this statistic. Hu, Bentler, and Kano (1992) found both overcorrection and undercorrection under different conditions. When factors and errors were independent, the elliptical statistic too frequently accepted the correct models at their chosen alpha levels, while when factors and errors were dependent but uncorrelated, it tended to reject the model too frequently, especially at the smaller sample sizes.

The corrections to the information matrix standard errors developed in Section 5 are practical but less important to apply in practice. They would be useful primarily when the correct covariance matrix (16.10) is not available or when it is too expensive to compute. The correct covariance matrix can be obtained in EQS (Bentler, 1989). Corrections to the ML statistics, for example, are obtained with the specification that the method should be "ML, ROBUST." Using this method, Chou, Bentler, and Satorra (1991) found that the correct standard errors as well as the ADF standard errors yielded more appropriate estimates of samp ling variability than the ML standard errors under conditions of nonnormality. However, it should be noted that when the number of variables is very large, the size of the matrices involved in the computation may be too large for the computational facilities available, and our correction to the standard errors may be worth considering. As far as we known, further studies of this correction have not yet been made.

The corrections developed above will apply also to variants of model testing situations, for example, in testing only a specific set of restrictions by means of differences between the above mentioned statistics, by Lagrange Multiplier tests, or by Wald statistics. A general review of these statistics is given in Satorra (1989), who also provides the appropriate form for the matrix U that would be used to scale and adjust the corresponding statistics.

For simplicity, we have only considered the null distributions of our statistics by assuming that the model holds, that is, $n^{1/2}(s - \sigma_0) \to N(0, \Gamma)$. Asymptotic power considerations can be introduced by simply assuming that the asymptotic mean of $n^{1/2}(s - \sigma_0)$ is nonzero. In (16.17) we would then get a mixture of noncentral chi-square distributions instead of centered ones. However, in such a case of "minimal" structural misspecification, the α_i would remain the same, and thus the scaled and adjusted statistics would have noncentral rather than central distributions.

Note

1. Recently, a technical report by Shapiro and Browne (1985) came to our attention, which is the source of the Shapiro-Browne paper; we acknowledge that their derivation of (16.31) and (16.33) predates ours. Our results were developed independently of the mentioned Shapiro-Browne work.

References

Amemiya, Y., & Anderson, T. W. (1990). Asymptotic chi-square test for a large class of factor analysis models. *The Annals of Statistics, 3,* 1453-1463.

Anderson, T. W. (1988). Multivariate linear relations. In T. Pukkila & S. Puntanen (Eds.), *Proceedings of the Second International Conference in Statistics* (pp. 9-36). Tampere, Finland.

Anderson, T. W. (1993). Nonnormal multivariate distributions: Inference based on elliptically contoured distributions. In C. R. Rao (Ed.), *Multivariate analysis: Future directions* (pp. 1-24). Amsterdam: Elsevier.

Anderson, T. W., & Amemiya, Y. (1988). The asymptotic normal distribution of estimators in factor analysis under general conditions. *Annals of Statistics, 16,* 759-771.

Bentler, P. M. (1983a). Simultaneous equation systems as moment structure models. *Journal of Econometrics, 22,* 13-42.

Bentler, P. M. (1983b). Some contributions to efficient statistics in structural models: Specification and estimation of moment structures. *Psychometrika, 48,* 493-517.

Bentler, P. M. (1989). *Theory and implementation of EQS, a structural equations program.* Los Angeles: BMDP Statistical Software.

Bentler, P. M., & Dijkstra, T. (1985). Efficient estimation via linearization in structural models. In P. R. Krishnaiah (Ed.), *Multivariate analysis VI* (pp. 9-42). Amsterdam: North-Holland.

Bentler, P. M., & Wu, E.J.C. (1993). *EQS/Windows user's guide.* Los Angeles: BMDP Statistical Software.

Box, G.E.P. (1954). Some theorems on quadratic forms applied in the study of analysis of variance problems: I. Effect of inequality of variance in the one-way classification. *Annals of Mathematical Statistics, 25,* 290-302.

Browne, M. W. (1974). Generalized least squares estimators in the analysis of covariance structures. *South African Statistical Journal, 8,* 1-24.

Browne, M. W. (1982). Covariance structures. In D. M. Hawkins (Ed.), *Topics in applied multivariate analysis* (pp. 72-141). Cambridge, MA: Cambridge University Press.

Browne, M. W. (1984). Asymptotically distribution-free methods for the analysis of covariance structures. *British Journal of Mathematical and Statistical Psychology, 37,* 62-83.

Browne, M. W. (1987). Robustness of statistical inference in factor analysis and related models. *Biometrika, 74,* 375-384.

Browne, M. W., & Shapiro, A. (1987). Adjustments for kurtosis in factor analysis with elliptically distributed errors. *Journal of the Royal Statistical Society, Series B, 49,* 346-352.

Browne, M. W., & Shapiro, A. (1988). Robustness of normal theory methods in the analysis of linear latent variate models. *British Journal of Mathematical and Statistical Psychology, 41,* 193-208.

Chamberlain, G. (1982). Multivariate regression models for panel data. *Journal of Econometrics, 18,* 5-46.

Chou, C.-P., Bentler, P. M., & Satorra, A. (1991). Scaled test statistics and robust standard errors for non-normal data in covariance structure analysis: A Monte Carlo study. *British Journal of Mathematical and Statistical Psychology, 44,* 347-357.

de Leeuw, J. (1983). Models and methods for the analysis of correlation coefficients. *Journal of Econometrics, 22,* 113-137.

Fay, R. E. (1985). A jackknifed chi-square test for complex samples. *Journal of the American Statistical Association, 80,* 148-157.

Ferguson, T. S. (1958). A method of generating best asymptotically normal estimates with application to the estimation of bacterial densities. *Annals of Mathematical Statistics, 29,* 1046-1062.

Fuller, W. A. (1987). *Measurement error models.* New York: John Wiley.

Gallant, A. R. (1987). *Nonlinear statistical models.* New York: John Wiley.

Harlow, L. L. (1985). Behavior of some elliptical theory estimators with nonnormal data in a covariance structures framework: A Monte Carlo study. Unpublished doctoral dissertation, University of California, Los Angeles.

Hu, L., Bentler, P. M., & Kano, Y. (1992). Can tests statistics in covariance structure analysis be trusted? *Psychological Bulletin, 112,* 351-362.

Jöreskog, K. G., & Sörbom, D. (1988). *LISREL 7: A guide to the program and applications.* Chicago: SPSS.

Kano, Y. (1992). Robust statistics for test-of-independence and related structural models. *Statistics & Probability Letters, 15,* 21-26.

Kano, Y., Berkane, M., & Bentler, P. M. (1990). Covariance structure analysis with heterogeneous kurtosis parameters. *Biometrika, 77,* 575-585.

Magnus, J. R., & Neudecker, H. (1986). Symmetry, 0-1 matrices and Jacobians: A review. *Econometric Theory, 2,* 157-190.

Muthén, B. (1993). Goodness of fit with categorical and other nonnormal variables. In K. A. Bollen & J. S. Long (Eds.), *Testing structural equation models* (pp. 205-234). Newbury Park, CA: Sage.

Rao, C. R. (1965). *Linear statistical inference and its applications.* New York: John Wiley.

Rao, J.N.K., & Scott, A. J. (1981). The analysis of categorical data from complex sample surveys: Chi-squared tests for goodness of fit and independence in two-way tables. *Journal of the American Statistical Association, 76,* 221-230.

Rao, J.N.K., & Scott, A. J. (1984). On chi-squared tests for multi-way contingency tables with cell proportions estimated from survey data. *The Annals of Statistics, 12,* 46-60.

Rao, J.N.K., & Scott, A. J. (1987). On simple adjustments to chi-square tests with sample survey data. *The Annals of Statistics, 15,* 385-397.

Satorra, A. (1989). Alternative test criteria in covariance structure analysis: A unified approach. *Psychometrika, 54,* 131-151.

Satorra, A. (1992). Asymptotic robust inferences in the analysis of mean and covariance structures. In P. V. Marsden (Ed.), *Sociological methodology 1992* (pp. 249-278). Oxford & Cambridge, MA: Basil Blackwell.

Satorra, A. (1993). Asymptotic robust inferences in multi-sample analysis of augmented moment structures. In C. M. Cuadras & C. R. Rao (Eds.), *Multivariate analysis: Future directions II* (pp. 211-229). Elsevier: Amsterdam.

Satorra, A., & Bentler, P. M. (1986a). Robustness properties of ML statistics in covariance structure analysis. Unpublished manuscript.

Satorra, A., & Bentler, P. M. (1986b). Some robustness issues of goodness of fit statistics in covariance structure analysis. *ASA 1986 Proceedings of the Business and Economic Statistics Section*, 549-554.

Satorra, A., & Bentler, P. M. (1988a). Scaling corrections for chi-square statistics in covariance structure analysis. *1988 Proceedings of the Business and Economic Statistics Section of the American Statistical Association*, 308-313.

Satorra, A., & Bentler, P. M. (1988b). Scaling corrections for statistics in covariance structure analysis. *UCLA Statistics Series #2*. Los Angeles: University of California.

Satorra, A., & Bentler, P. M. (1990). Model conditions for asymptotic robustness in the analysis of linear relations. *Computational Statistics & Data Analysis, 10*, 235-249.

Satorra, A., & Bentler, P. M. (1991). Goodness-of-fit test under IV estimation: Asymptotic robustness of a NT test statistic. In R. Gutiérrez & M. J. Valderrama (Eds.), *Applied stochastic models and data analysis* (pp. 557-567). Singapore: World Scientific Publishing.

Satterthwaite, F. E. (1941). Synthesis of variance. *Psychometrika, 6*, 309-316.

Shapiro, A. (1985). Asymptotic equivalence of minimum discrepancy estimators to GLS estimators. *South African Statistical Journal, 19*, 73-81.

Shapiro, A. (1986). Asymptotic theory of overparameterized structural models. *Journal of the American Statistical Association, 81*, 142-149.

Shapiro, A., & Browne, M. W. (1985). *Adjustments to normal theory for elliptical distributions in the analysis of covariance structures*. Research Report Navorsingsverslag 85/7. University of South Africa.

Shapiro, A., & Browne, M. W. (1987). Analysis of covariance structures under elliptical distributions. *Journal of the American Statistical Association, 82*, 1092-1097.

Skinner, C. J., Holt, D., & Smith, T. M. F. (1989). *Analysis of complex surveys*. New York: John Wiley.

Tyler, D. E. (1982). Radial estimates and the test for sphericity. *Biometrika, 69*, 429-436.

Tyler, D. E. (1983). Robustness and efficiency properties of scatter matrices. *Biometrika, 70*, 411-420.

17

Testing in Latent Class Models Using a Posterior Predictive Check Distribution

DONALD B. RUBIN
HAL S. STERN

Model Monitoring Using Posterior Predictive Checks

Model selection and comparison are critical issues in empirical investigations. Standard statistical models, such as linear regression, permit a variety of goodness of fit measures and, under some assumptions, simple and valid statistical tests for nested models. In more complicated models, however, the usual tests and goodness of fit measures may not be adequate. Rubin (1984) describes a general procedure for model monitoring based on the posterior predictive distribution of any test statistic that is sensitive to possible failures of the model.

To fix ideas, let $P(X|\theta)$ represent the null model specification where θ represents a (possibly multivariate) parameter with prior distribution $P(\theta)$. Denote the observed data by X_{obs}. Formal inference about the model parameters is typically obtained by considering the posterior distribution $P(\theta|X_{obs})$. Because the posterior distribution of θ assumes

AUTHORS' NOTE: This work was partially supported by National Science Foundation Grant NSF SES-8805433 and the William F. Milton Fund. The authors thank Jerome Kagan, Doreen Arcus, and Nancy Snidman for permission to use the data from the infant temperament study.

the truth of the underlying model, it contains no information about the propriety of the model. Judging the fit of a model requires comparing features of the observed data with the same features of data sets that would be expected under the model. If replications of the data generated by the probability model fail to recreate the relevant features of the observed data, then the model should be rejected. Following this definition, it is possible to reject a model even when aggregate measures of fit (e.g., F-statistics with more than one degree of freedom in the numerator) indicate no inadequacies.

Let $T(X)$ be any statistic designed to reveal lack of fit of the model; for example, $T(X)$ might be a function of the residuals or the distance from the null model to a competing larger model (e.g., the likelihood ratio statistic). The basic model monitoring approach compares $T(X_{obs})$ to the reference distribution obtained by averaging the distribution $P[T(X)|\theta]$ over the posterior distribution $P(\theta|X_{obs})$. The resulting reference distribution is the posterior predictive distribution of $T(X)$ conditional on the model $P(X|\theta)$ and the data X_{obs}, and is the distribution of $T(X)$ that would be expected in replications of the study under the model (with the same parameters that generated the original data but with an entirely new data set).

Frequently, especially in sophisticated models, the posterior predictive distribution cannot be obtained analytically. In such cases, the following technique may be used to simulate the posterior predictive distribution of $T(X)$:

1. generate a draw from the posterior distribution $\theta^* \sim P(\theta|X_{obs})$
2. generate a replicate of the data set $X^* \sim P(X|\theta^*)$
3. repeat Steps 1 and 2 to obtain R replicates
4. compare $T(X_{obs})$ to the reference distribution $T(X^*)$

The appropriate definition of the replications (Steps 1 and 2), and thus the appropriate posterior predictive distribution, depends on the context of the data, and in general might include fixing some aspects of the data in the replications or allowing the replications to involve a new setting with new values of the parameters [hence replacing the posterior distribution in (1) by the prior distribution $P(\theta)$]. This issue is discussed further in Rubin (1984) and in an example in the next section.

In the following sections, the use of a posterior predictive distribution for model monitoring is demonstrated with two examples. The first example is relatively straightforward and is used solely to illustrate ideas in a simple setting: Inferring the equality of the probability of success in two independent binomial populations using the posterior predictive distribution of the usual Pearson chi-squared and Fisher exact test statistics. Following the binomial example, a posterior predictive check distribution is used in a more sophisticated and realistic example: determining the number of classes in a latent class model for data from an infant temperament study.

The Posterior Predictive Check Distribution: A Binomial Example

Consider two binomial populations, A and B, with interest focusing on the hypothesis that the probability of success π_a in population A is the same as the probability of success π_b in population B. The preferable analysis would focus on the posterior distribution of the difference $\pi_a - \pi_b$ or ratio π_a/π_b rather than on a significance test of the hypothesis that $\pi_a = \pi_b$. We focus attention on the significance test to illustrate the use of the posterior predictive distribution for model checking.

In this example, there is no single correct binomial test because of the existence of a nuisance parameter, which can be chosen to be $(\pi_a + \pi_b)/2$, the average success level. We can, however, obtain a p value free of the nuisance parameter; three methods are: (1) condition on the margins, which implies some loss of information, and do Fisher's exact test; (2) use asymptotic arguments based on normality (i.e., variants using χ^2 tests); or (3) average the distribution of any test statistic over the posterior distribution of the nuisance parameter as described in the previous section. In practice with most reasonable sample sizes, the three methods agree fairly well, although with small samples there are differences. There is a vast literature concerning the choice between methods 1 and 2 including Berkson (1978), D'Agostino, Chase, and Belanger (1988), Little (1989), Richardson (1990), and Yates (1984).

To illustrate the use of method 3, the posterior predictive check distribution, consider the two by two table corresponding to two independent binomial samples with notation given by

Treatment	Success	Failure	Total
A	x_a	$n_a - x_a$	n_a
B	x_b	$n_b - x_b$	n_b
Total	$x_a + x_b$	$N - x_a - x_b$	N

We consider the two specific tables discussed in Little (1989):

| table T1 | $n_a = 3$ | $x_a = 3$ | $n_b = 3$ | $x_b = 0$ |
| table T2 | $n_a = 172$ | $x_a = 170$ | $n_b = 171$ | $x_b = 162$ |

Suppose that we wish to test the hypothesis that the probability of success is the same in the two populations, $\pi_a = \pi_b$, versus the one-sided alternative $\pi_a > \pi_b$. The hypothesis concerns the parameter $\pi_a - \pi_b$ that distinguishes between the null and alternative models. Assume that the nuisance parameter $\pi = (\pi_a + \pi_b)/2$ has a prior distribution $P(\pi)$ (note that under the null hypothesis $\pi_a = \pi_b = \pi$). The posterior distribution of π describes the values of π that are plausible under the null model given the data. The distribution of any test statistic (e.g., Pearson's chi-squared statistic or the p value of Fisher's exact test) can be averaged over the posterior distribution of the nuisance parameter to obtain a posterior predictive distribution of the test statistic that can be used to check the null model (i.e., the null hypothesis). This monitoring distribution describes the variability in the test statistic that would be expected in replications of the two binomial samples under the null model. The observed value of the test statistic can be compared with its posterior predictive distribution to determine if the data are consistent with the null model.

To be more specific, let $X = (X_a, X_b)$ where

$$X_a = \text{\# of successes in } n_a \text{ trials} \sim \text{Bin}(n_a, \pi_a) \qquad [17.1]$$

and

$$X_b = \text{\# of successes in } n_b \text{ trials} \sim \text{Bin}(n_b, \pi_b). \qquad [17.2]$$

Under the null model, the two binomial populations are assumed to be independent with $\pi_a = \pi_b = \pi$. When the prior distribution of π is taken to be a beta distribution,

$$\pi \mid c, d \sim \text{Beta}(c, d), \qquad [17.3]$$

the posterior distribution of π given data $X_{\text{obs}} = (x_a, x_b)$ is also a beta distribution

$$\pi \mid x_a, x_b, c, d \sim \text{Beta}(c + x_a + x_b, d + n_a - x_a + n_b - x_b). \qquad [17.4]$$

The posterior predictive distribution of new results $X^* = (x_a^*, x_b^*)$ that would be expected in replications of the study is obtained by averaging the distribution of $X^*|\pi$ over the posterior distribution of π,

$$P(x_a^*, x_b^* \mid x_a, x_b, c, d) = \int_0^1 P(X_a = x_a^*, X_b = x_b^* \mid \pi)P(\pi \mid x_a, x_b, c, d)d\pi$$

$$= \frac{\Gamma(c + x_a + x_b + x_a^* + x_b^*)\Gamma(d + n_a - x_a + n_b - x_b + n_a - x_a^* + n_b - x_b^*)}{\Gamma(c + d + 2n_a + 2n_b)}$$

$$\times \frac{\Gamma(c + d + n_a + n_b)}{\Gamma(c + x_a + x_b)\Gamma(d + n_a - x_a + n_b - x_b)}$$

$$\times \frac{\Gamma(n_a + 1)}{\Gamma(x_a^* + 1)\Gamma(n_a - x_a^* + 1)} \times \frac{\Gamma(n_b + 1)}{\Gamma(x_b^* + 1)\Gamma(n_b - x_b^* + 1)} . \qquad [17.5]$$

The posterior predictive distribution of any statistic $T(X^*)$ can be computed directly from the posterior predictive distribution for X^*. A p value for testing the hypothesis of equal probabilities is obtained by finding the probability that $T(X^*) \geq T(X_{\text{obs}})$, where $T(X)$ is any statistic that is sensitive to deviations from the null hypothesis (Pearson's chi-square statistic or Fisher's exact conditional p value, for example). This p value represents the proportion of data sets with more extreme values of T that would be expected to occur in hypothetical replications of the study under the null model.

The first two columns in Table 17.1 contain p values obtained from the posterior predictive check distributions of the Pearson and Fisher statistics for testing the hypothesis of equal success probabilities in table T1. Each row gives results for an analysis with a different prior distribution for the nuisance parameter. The results in the two columns are identical because the p value in this case is the probability of the observed 2×2 table (there are no more extreme tables) and this probability does not depend on the choice of test statistic $T(X)$. Table 17.2 gives the results for table T2. The p values indicate the probability of a result more extreme than the data, as measured by either the Pearson test statistic or the Fisher p value, under the posterior predictive check distribution of the test statistic.

Table 17.1   Posterior Predictive p Values for Table T1 (Fisher $p = 0.05$, Pearson $p = .0072$)

Parameters of Beta Prior on π	Post. Pred. p value Pearson	Post. Pred. p value Fisher	Posterior Distribution of $\pi_a - \pi_b$ Prior Distribution is Beta $(1,1)$ .01 quantile	.50 quantile	.99 quantile
$c = 0.0,\ d = 0.0*$	.0108	.0108	−.058	.574	.956
$c = 0.5,\ d = 0.5$	.0113	.0113	−.056	.587	.958
$c = 1.0,\ d = 1.0$	.0117	.0117	−.053	.598	.959
$c = 1.5,\ d = 1.5$	.0120	.0120	−.051	.608	.960
$c = 2.0,\ d = 2.0$	.0122	.0122	−.049	.616	.960
$c = 5.0,\ d = 5.0$	.0133	.0133	−.038	.649	.964

NOTE: * Calculated as limiting distribution as $c,\ d \to 0$ with $c = d$.

Table 17.2   Posterior Predictive p Values for Table T2 (Fisher $p = 0.03$, Pearson $p = .0156$)

Parameters of Beta Prior on π	Post. Pred. p value Pearson	Post. Pred. p value Fisher	Posterior Distribution of $\pi_a - \pi_b$ Prior Distribution is Beta $(1,1)$ .01 quantile	.50 quantile	.99 quantile
$c = 0.0,\ d = 0.0*$	.0145	.0150	−.004	.034	.082
$c = 0.5,\ d = 0.5$	.0147	.0152	−.004	.035	.085
$c = 1.0,\ d = 1.0$	.0149	.0155	−.004	.037	.087
$c = 1.5,\ d = 1.5$	.0150	.0157	−.004	.038	.090
$c = 2.0,\ d = 2.0$	.0151	.0159	−.004	.040	.092
$c = 5.0,\ d = 5.0$	.0153	.0168	−.005	.048	.106

NOTE: * Calculated as limiting distribution as $c,\ d \to 0$ with $c = d$.

For both tables, the p values obtained from the posterior predictive check distribution are close to the p value of the unconditional Pearson procedure. This occurs because the posterior predictive check distribution does not condition on the observed number of successes in defining the hypothetical replications, although it does fix the sample sizes n_a and n_b. In some situations, it might be reasonable to define the hypothetical replications such that the total number of successes is fixed. The posterior predictive distribution in this case is the hypergeometric distribution of the Fisher exact procedure and the model monitoring p values, for both test statistics, are identical to the Fisher exact conditional p value. Rubin (1984) discusses more fully the question of how to define replications that are relevant to a particular analysis.

Finally, it is important to remember that when an alternative model is being considered, it is preferable to focus on the posterior distribution (under the alternative) of the parameter that describes the difference between the null model and the alternative model (e.g., the posterior distribution of $\pi_a - \pi_b$ in this case). An interval estimate for $\pi_a - \pi_b$ provides more information than a p value for the null model. Accordingly, the last three columns in Tables 17.1 and 17.2 list the .01, .50, and .99 percentiles of the posterior distribution for $\pi_a - \pi_b$ under a fully Bayesian analysis. The analysis assumes that the nuisance parameter $\pi = (\pi_a + \pi_b)/2 \sim \text{Beta}(c, d)$, with values of c, d specified by the row of the table, and the conditional prior distribution of the difference $\pi_a - \pi_b$ given the value of π is assumed to be $\text{Beta}(1, 1)$ in its natural parameter space, that is, uniform on the interval $[-2\min(\pi, 1 - \pi), 2\min(\pi, 1 - \pi)]$. The marginal posterior distribution of the difference $\pi_a - \pi_b$ is obtained by numerical integration. [A Fortran program implementing Simpson's rule, based on an open formula that avoids evaluating the integrand at the endpoints, is available from the authors. See also Press, Flannery, Teukolsky, & Vetterling (1986).] This specification of the prior distribution, in terms of the average success probability and the difference of the success probabilities, allows for easy investigation of the effect of different prior distributions for the nuisance parameter. Comparing rows of the tables indicates that the results are not sensitive to the prior distribution on the nuisance parameter. An alternative analysis is obtained by placing independent prior distributions on the two success probabilities (Altham, 1969; Little, 1989). The posterior distribution of the difference in success probabilities, reported in our tables, is not very sensitive to the form of the prior. The results using independent $\text{Beta}(1,1)$ prior distributions for each success probability are quite similar to those reported in Tables 17.1 and 17.2. In fact, the row with $c = d = 2$ corresponds to a marginal prior distribution on the difference $\pi_a - \pi_b$ that is quite similar to the marginal prior distribution implied by independent $\text{Beta}(1, 1)$ priors.

Testing in Latent Class Models

A posterior predictive check distribution is more likely to be useful for monitoring sophisticated models for which simple posterior distri-

Table 17.3 Observed Data for Infant Temperament Study

M	C	#	F = 1	F = 2	F = 3
1	1	10	5	4	1
1	2	3	0	1	2
1	3	4	2	0	2
2	1	21	15	4	2
2	2	6	2	3	1
2	3	10	4	4	2
3	1	10	3	3	4
3	2	5	0	2	3
3	3	9	1	1	7
4	1	5	2	1	2
4	2	4	0	1	3
4	3	6	0	3	3

butions for parameters in alternative models are not readily available.
We apply the approach to estimating the number of classes in a latent
class model for data from an infant temperament study. Each infant is
classified according to the level of motor activity M observed at 4
months (between 1 and 4), the fret/cry (or irritability) level C observed
at 4 months (between 1 and 3), and the level of fear F observed at 14
months (between 1 and 3). Thus the data to be analyzed form a 4 × 3 ×
3 contingency table, displayed in Table 17.3.

The data indicate that infants who exhibited low levels of both motor
activity and irritability at 4 months had significantly lower fear level at
14 months than the infants who exhibited high levels of motor activity
and irritability. The remaining children, those exhibiting high levels of
motor activity with low levels of irritability or vice versa, are difficult
to categorize at 14 months. These results can be explained by the
existence of two or more distinct classes of children, resulting perhaps
from different thresholds of excitability in the amygdala or its circuits.
The classes cannot be identified directly, but rather must be inferred
indirectly from the relations among the observed variables. Additional
details concerning the psychological theory underlying the study, the
data collection and coding procedures, and the analysis can be found in
Stern, Arcus, Kagan, Rubin, and Snidman (forthcoming).

Let n_{ijk} denote the number of infants in the study with $M = i$, $C = j$,
$F = k$, and let π_{ijk} represent the probability that an infant is observed in
this cell of the table. It is assumed that there is a latent variable with T

categories (theory suggests that T is likely to be two or four). The proportion of infants belonging to the tth latent class is denoted by π_t. In addition, we define the conditional probability $\pi_{ijk|t}$ that $M = i$, $C = j$, $F = k$ given that an infant is from the tth class. The joint distribution of M, C, F is a mixture of the joint distributions within each of the classes:

$$\pi_{ijk} = \sum_{t=1}^{T} \pi_t \pi_{ijk|t} . \qquad [17.6]$$

As is common in latent class models, we assume that the three observable variables M, C, F are independent, imperfect measures of the latent variable. Let $\pi_{i|t}$, $\pi_{j|t}$, $\pi_{k|t}$, represent the conditional distributions of M, C, F for the tth class. The joint distribution can then be written

$$\pi_{ijk} = \sum_{t=1}^{T} \pi_t \pi_{i|t} \pi_{j|t} \pi_{k|t} . \qquad [17.7]$$

The general latent class model is described more fully elsewhere (Clogg, 1981a, 1981b; Goodman, 1974a, 1974b; Haberman, 1979; Lazarsfeld & Henry, 1968; McCutcheon, 1987), and is itself an example of the broader class of mixture models described in, for example, Titterington, Smith, and Makov (1985). Alternative latent class models, with additional structure on the relationship among the variables within a class, were also applied to this data but are not reported here.

Maximum likelihood estimates for the parameters of the latent class model are obtained using the EM algorithm (Dempster, Laird, & Rubin, 1977) as described by Goodman (1974a, 1974b). The results of the estimation procedure, assuming first that the population consists of two groups ($T = 2$) and then that the population consists of three groups ($T = 3$), are shown in Table 17.4. Although no standard errors are shown in Table 17.4, asymptotic standard errors can be calculated using the SEM algorithm (Meng & Rubin, 1991), which uses complete-data standard errors and the EM program itself; however, because the likelihood for mixture models may have several modes, these asymptotic standard errors may not be inferentially appropriate. Here, two different modes were found for the two-class model and 13 different modes were found for the three-class model. The results in Table 17.4 represent the

Table 17.4   Two- and Three-Class Latent Class Model Estimates

Proportion of Children	Two Class		Three Class		
	Class 1 .50	Class 2 .50	Class 1 .45	Class 2 .46	Class 3 .09
$Pr(M = 1)$	.22	.14	.25	.15	.00
$Pr(M = 2)$	.60	.19	.55	.13	1.00
$Pr(M = 3)$	.12	.40	.14	.43	.00
$Pr(M = 4)$	.06	.27	.06	.29	.00
$Pr(C = 1)$	.71	.28	.83	.26	.00
$Pr(C = 2)$	.08	.31	.00	.32	.55
$Pr(C = 3)$	.21	.41	.17	.42	.45
$Pr(F = 1)$	.74	.00	.73	.00	.41
$Pr(F = 2)$	.26	.32	.23	.29	.59
$Pr(F = 3)$	.00	.68	.04	.71	.00

solutions corresponding to the highest mode. The log-likelihood at the modes for the three-class model ranged from approximately -302.0 to -300.5. The shape of the likelihood calls into question the use of the maximum likelihood estimates and the associated standard errors as summaries of the data. Nevertheless, the parameter estimates in the two-class model indicate that children are evenly divided between Class 1 and Class 2. Class 1 children are characterized by (a) low motor activity at 4 months, (b) low irritability at 4 months, and (c) low fear at 14 months. The Class 2 children are characterized by high levels of motor activity, fretting/crying, and fear.

The first two classes in the three-class model are similar to the classes discussed above. The third class describes a group of children with intermediate levels of the three variables. Each additional latent class adds eight parameters to the model, as follows: three parameters are required to describe the distribution of M within the additional class (π_{ilt}, $i = 1, \ldots, 4$ subject to $\sum_i \pi_{ilt} = 1$), two parameters for the distribution of C in the class, two for the distribution of F, and one parameter for the size of the class. The larger three-class model is expected to provide a closer fit to the data due to the additional parameters. The added complexity introduced by the third group, however, may outweigh the benefits of the improved fit.

To determine if more than two classes are supported by the data, the likelihood ratio chi-square statistic is often considered as a goodness of fit measure:

$$L^2 = 2 \sum_{i=1}^{4} \sum_{j=1}^{3} \sum_{k=1}^{3} n_{ijk} \ln(n_{ijk} / \hat{n}_{ijk}), \qquad [17.8]$$

where ln is the natural logarithm with $0 \ln 0 = 0$ by convention, and $\hat{n}_{ijk}$ represents the number of children estimated to have $M = i$, $C = j$, $F = k$ under the model. The degrees of freedom associated with L^2 is the difference between the number of parameters in the latent class model and the number of parameters in the associated saturated model (35 in this case). In Table 17.5, the likelihood ratio statistics are presented for models having from one to four latent classes. The two-class model is the smallest model that provides an adequate fit (the chi-squared statistic is 14.1 with 20 degrees of freedom). The three- and four-class models also provide adequate fits but generate little improvement over the two-class model. For most statistical models, the difference between the likelihood statistics of two nested models can be used in a chi-squared test to determine if the smaller model provides a sufficiently good fit. In the present context of mixture models, this approach cannot be used to test validly the two-class model versus the three- or four-class alternative because, under the null hypothesis that the smaller model is sufficient, the likelihood is not asymptotically full-rank normal. To test validly a two-class model versus a larger model, an alternative reference distribution or an entirely new procedure is required. The posterior predictive distribution of the likelihood ratio statistic, conditional on a particular model and the observed data, can be used to provide an honest p value.

To test the S class model versus the $S' > S$ class model, replications drawn from the posterior predictive distribution of the data under the S class model are needed. Two steps are required for each replication: (1) draw a set of parameter values (π_t, π_{ilt}, π_{jlt}, π_{klt} for all i, j, k, t) from their joint posterior distribution and (2) create a data set (same size as the original) using random draws from multinomial distributions with the chosen parameter values. The second step is extremely straightforward since each observable (M, F, C) is drawn from an independent multinomial once the class of the infant has been determined. The first step, drawing parameter values from the posterior distribution, can be carried out using a Markov chain sampling approach, in particular a Data Augmentation algorithm (Tanner & Wong, 1987) that will be described shortly.

In the following description, the number of levels of the observed variables arc I, J, K and the number of latent classes is T. To perform

Table 17.5 Comparing Latent Class Models

Model Description	Degrees of Freedom (35 – # of params.)	Likelihood Ratio Chi-Square
Independence (= 1 class)	28	48.761
2 Latent Classes	20	14.150
3 Latent Classes	12	9.109
4 Latent Classes	4	4.718
Saturated	—	—

this analysis, a prior distribution for the parameters is needed; to simplify notation let

$$\pi = \left\{ \pi_t, (\pi_{i\,|\,t}, i=1,\ldots,I), (\pi_{j\,|\,t}, j=1,\ldots,J), \right.$$

$$\left. (\pi_{k\,|\,t}, k=1,\ldots,K), t=1,\ldots,T \right\}, \qquad [17.8.1]$$

where for the infant study $I = 4$, $J = 3$, $K = 3$. The prior distribution for each set of multinomial parameters (e.g., $\pi_{i|t}$, $i = 1, \ldots, I$) is taken to be a Dirichlet distribution. For example, the prior distribution on the probabilities of the motor activity categories in the tth class is

$$P(\pi_{i\,|\,t}, i=1,\ldots,I) = \frac{\left(\sum_{m=1}^{I} \alpha_{mt} \right)!}{\prod_{m=1}^{I} \alpha_{mt}!} \prod_{i=1}^{I} \pi_{i\,|\,t}^{\alpha_{it}-1}. \qquad [17.9]$$

The relative sizes of the α_{it} indicate the relative sizes of the means of the corresponding motor category probabilities in the tth class; the absolute sizes of the α_{it} indicate the strength of the prior belief about the values. Weak (or diffuse) prior distributions ($\sum_i \alpha_{it} = 1$) are used in this analysis. In general we ignore the constant and indicate only the part of the distribution involving $\pi_{i|t}$. The prior distributions for other sets of parameters are also Dirichlet,

$$P(\pi_{j|t}, j = 1, \ldots, J) \propto \prod_{j=1}^{J} \pi_{j|t}^{\beta_{jt} - 1}$$

$$P(\pi_{k|t}, k = 1, \ldots, K) \propto \prod_{k=1}^{K} \pi_{k|t}^{\gamma_{kt} - 1}$$

$$P(\pi_t, t = 1, \ldots, T) \propto \prod_{t=1}^{T} \pi_t^{\delta_t - 1} . \qquad [17.10]$$

The prior distribution of the entire parameter set, $P(\pi)$, is the product of the prior distributions on each component:

$$P(\pi) = \prod_{t=1}^{T} \left[\pi_t^{\delta_t - 1} \left(\prod_{i=1}^{I} \pi_{i|t}^{\alpha_{it} - 1} \prod_{j=1}^{J} \pi_{j|t}^{\beta_{jt} - 1} \prod_{k=1}^{K} \pi_{k|t}^{\gamma_{kt} - 1} \right) \right] . \qquad [17.11]$$

The posterior distribution is obtained by combining this prior distribution with the latent class likelihood,

$$P(\pi \mid n) \propto \prod_{i,j,k} \left[\sum_{t=1}^{T} \pi_{i|t} \pi_{j|t} \pi_{k|t} \pi_t \right]^{n_{ijk}} P(\pi) , \qquad [17.12]$$

where

$$n = \left\{ n_{ijk}, \ i = 1, \ldots, I, j = 1, \ldots, J, k = 1, \ldots, K \right\} \qquad [17.13]$$

represents the observed data. This posterior distribution is not in a convenient form for sampling.

An iterative Markov sampling approach (Gelfand & Smith, 1990; Tanner & Wong, 1987) is used to obtain a draw from the posterior distribution. As with maximum likelihood estimation using the EM algorithm, the data set is augmented with unobserved indicators Z_{ijkmt} where $Z_{ijkmt} = 1$ if the mth observation in the ijkth cell of the contingency table ($m = 1, \ldots, n_{ijk}$) is from latent class t and 0 otherwise. The joint distribution of the parameters π, the entire set of indicators Z and the data n is

$$P(\pi, Z, n) \propto \prod_{i, j, k} \prod_{m=1}^{n_{ijk}} \prod_{t=1}^{T} (\pi_{i\,|\,t}\,\pi_{j\,|\,t}\,\pi_{k\,|\,t}\,\pi_{t})^{Z_{ijkmt}} P(\pi) . \quad [17.14]$$

The conditional distribution of π given Z and n is a product of independent Dirichlet distributions with the prior parameters supplemented by the number of observations with observed values i, j, k, t. The conditional distribution of Z given π and n is a Bernoulli distribution, where the probability that $Z_{ijkmt} = 1$ is obtained by Bayes's rule:

$$P(Z_{ijkmt} = 1 \mid \pi, n) = \frac{\pi_t\,\pi_{i\,|\,t}\,\pi_{j\,|\,t}\,\pi_{k\,|\,t}}{\sum_t \pi_t\,\pi_{i\,|\,t}\,\pi_{j\,|\,t}\,\pi_{k\,|\,t}}. \quad [17.15]$$

Thus the two conditional distributions $P(Z|\pi,n)$ and $P(\pi|Z,n)$ are easy to sample, which leads to an iterative simulation algorithm for sampling the posterior distribution of π, $P(\pi|n)$. Specifically, to obtain a draw from the posterior distribution of π, the following algorithm is used:

1. begin by drawing an initial set of parameter values $\pi^{(0)}$ from the prior distribution $P(\pi)$, and set $i = 1$;
2. draw a sample of indicators $Z^{(i)}$ from the conditional distribution $P(Z|\pi^{(i-1)},n)$;
3. draw a sample of parameters $\pi^{(i)}$ from the conditional distribution $P(\pi|Z^{(i)},n)$;
4. let $i = i + 1$; repeat Steps 2 and 3 until convergence.

At convergence, the final values of Z and π are a sample from the joint posterior distribution $P(Z, \pi \mid n)$. We discard the last value of Z and use the final π as a draw from its marginal posterior distribution. Issues concerning convergence of the algorithm are discussed in Tanner and Wong (1987). For the results described here, convergence was assessed using multiple sequences of draws with starting values chosen from an overdispersed distribution (Gelman & Rubin, 1992). For the one-class model, Steps 2 and 3 were iterated 500 times to generate a single draw from the posterior distribution. The two-class model required 4,000 iterations to generate a single draw.

To create a replicated data set for each drawn value of the parameters, we draw a data set $X^* = (n_{ijk}^*)$ from the latent class sampling distribution using a sequence of multinomial random variables. For each replicated data set under a given prior distribution and model, the likelihood ratio statistic for testing S versus S' classes is calculated. As mentioned earlier, the latent class model likelihoods may have several modes, especially in three- or four-class models. For obtaining maximum likelihood estimates for computing the likelihood ratio statistic, 10 different starting values were used and the highest peak of the likelihood was taken to be the maximum. This difficulty suggests that a more Bayesian alternative to the likelihood ratio test statistic might be a more appropriate statistic (Gelman, Meng, & Stern, 1993). Nevertheless, the distribution of the likelihood ratio statistic provides a reference distribution to which the observed value of the corresponding likelihood ratio statistic from Table 17.5 can be compared.

For example, to test the model with one class versus the model with two classes, replicated data sets that are consistent with the observed data under the one-class model (independence model) are generated. The average value of the likelihood ratio statistic for testing one class versus two classes over 100 replicated data sets is 11.46 with a standard deviation of 4.21. Note that this mean is not consistent with the χ_8^2 distribution that would be expected under the usual asymptotic theory. The observed likelihood ratio statistic, 34.61, is larger than all 100 replicates. Thus the observed data set is not at all similar to the data sets that would be expected if the one-class model were correct. A Monte Carlo estimate of the p value is the empirical probability that a value of the test statistic larger than the observed value would occur under the model, in this case, less than 1/100.

The prior distribution that is used for the one-class model is based on the observed marginal distribution of each variable. The parameters of the Dirichlet distributions are chosen such that the means of the prior distributions match the empirical probability distributions of the observed variables. The prior distribution for models with two or more classes is based on the theory of our psychology collaborators. For example, the prior distributions for the multinomial parameters in the two-class model are chosen to reflect the belief that children in one class are likely to exhibit low levels of M, C, and F, whereas children in the other class are expected to exhibit high levels of M, C, and F. The values of the parameters in the prior distributions for the one-class and two-class models are shown in Table 17.6. In all cases the values of α are small, indicating weak or diffuse prior distributions. The posterior predictive distributions of the likelihood ratio statistics are not sensitive to the choice of prior distributions (unless the values of α are large).

Based on the data, there is little evidence that more than two classes are required. Table 17.7 gives the mean and standard deviation of the

Table 17.6 Prior Distributions for Latent Class Models—One- and Two-Class Models

Model	Model Parameter	Prior Distribution (independent factors)
1 Class	$\pi_{il\ t=1}$, $i = 1,...,4$	Dirichlet(0.18,0.40,0.26,0.16)
	$\pi_{jl\ t=1}$, $j = 1,...,3$	Dirichlet(0.50,0.19,0.31)
	$\pi_{kl\ t=1}$, $k = 1,...,3$	Dirichlet(0.37,0.29,0.34)
2 Class	π_t, $t = 1,2$	Dirichlet(0.55,0.45) = Beta(0.55,0.45)
	$\pi_{il\ t=1}$, $i = 1,...,4$	Dirichlet(0.45,0.35,0.15,0.05)
	$\pi_{jl\ t=1}$, $j = 1,...,3$	Dirichlet(0.80,0.15,0.05)
	$\pi_{kl\ t=1}$, $k = 1,...,3$	Dirichlet(0.80,0.15,0.05)
	$\pi_{il\ t=2}$, $i = 1,...,4$	Dirichlet(0.05,0.15,0.35,0.45)
	$\pi_{jl\ t=2}$, $j = 1,...,3$	Dirichlet(0.05,0.15,0.80)
	$\pi_{kl\ t=2}$, $k = 1,...,3$	Dirichlet(0.05,0.15,0.80)

posterior predictive distribution of the likelihood ratio test statistic (based on 100 draws), the observed likelihood ratio test statistic, and the Monte Carlo p value (second to last column of Table 17.7) for a sequence of hypothesis tests. The estimated p value for testing the two-class model versus the three-class model is .94. Figure 17.1 shows the posterior predictive distribution of the likelihood ratio test statistic for each test, where the dashed line indicates the likelihood ratio statistic in the observed data set (from Table 17.5). The p values for a second set of prior distributions (centered around the uniform distribution for each multinomial) are given in the last column of Table 17.7 and exhibit little difference from the previous column. Psychological theory suggests that four classes are likely to be present, although perhaps with some restrictions on the parameters. Recent power calculations using the posterior predictive check distribution indicate that a larger sample size and/or additional measurements should provide an opportunity to discover the four hypothesized classes.

Discussion and Conclusions

Tests for latent class models, or for statistical models in general, can be conducted using the posterior predictive distribution of an appropriate

Table 17.7 Posterior Predictive Tests for Latent Class Models

# Classes Null	# Classes Alternative	Observed LRT Stat.	Prior 1 Mean LRT Stat.	Prior 1 Std. Dev. LRT Stat.	Prior 1 p value	Prior 2 p value
1	2	34.61	11.46	4.21	0.00	0.00
2	3	5.04	10.00	3.50	0.98	0.94
2	4	9.43	16.42	4.61	0.98	0.94
3	4	4.39	7.75	3.49	0.87	0.88

test statistic under the null model. The p values obtained from such tests are honest in the sense that they represent the chance, given the observed data, of seeing a result more unusual than the observed result if the null model is correct. Test statistics that are sensitive to specific deviations from the null model provide more powerful testing procedures than more general test statistics.

Although we illustrated the use of the posterior predictive distribution using a two-sample binomial problem, no test is recommended in that case because a complete Bayes analysis focusing on the difference in the population proportions is clearly better. Testing in general, and specifically tests using a posterior predictive check distribution, are appropriate in situations where there is no obvious alternative model (in the binomial case, the alternative is that the difference between the two proportions is a parameter to be estimated) and/or situations where the obvious alternative model differs from the null model by many parameters. In the latent class model, when testing the S class model versus the $S' > S$ class model, there is no single parameter that distinguishes between the two models. We would have to carry out a Bayesian analysis of the larger model and then examine the posterior distribution for many sets of the parameters to determine if the posterior distribution suggests a smaller model (evidence might include the estimated size of some class being near zero, or the parameters describing the distribution of variables within two classes being similar). When the fully Bayesian analysis of the alternative model requires a great deal of effort relative to the null model, as with the three- or four-class model relative to the smaller two-class model, it is often preferable to determine via a preliminary test whether such extra model-building effort is worthwhile. The posterior predictive distribution of an appropriate test statistic can be used to help make this assessment.

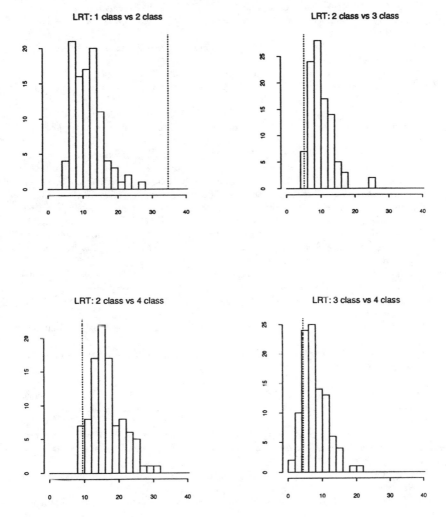

Figure 17.1.

References

Altham, P.M.E. (1969). Exact Bayesian analysis of a 2 × 2 contingency table and Fisher's "exact" significance test. *Journal of the Royal Statistical Society, B 31*, 261-269.

Berkson, J. (1978). In dispraise of the exact test. *Journal of Statistical Planning and Inference, 2*, 27-42.

Clogg, C. C. (1981a). Latent class analysis across groups. In *Proceedings of the Social Statistics Section, 1981 Annual Meeting of the American Statistical Association,* 299-304.

Clogg, C. C. (1981b). Latent structure model of mobility. *American Journal of Sociology, 86,* 838-868.

D'Agostino, R. B., Chase, W., & Belanger, A. (1988). The appropriateness of some common procedures for testing equality of two independent binomial proportions. *The American Statistician, 42,* 198-202.

Dempster, A. P., Laird, N. M., & Rubin, D. B. (1977). Maximum likelihood estimation from incomplete data via the EM algorithm (with discussion). *Journal of the Royal Statistical Society, B 39,* 1-38.

Gelfand, A. E., & Smith, A.F.M. (1990). Sampling-based approaches to calculating marginal densities. *Journal of the American Statistical Association, 85,* 398-409.

Gelman, A., Meng, X. L., & Stern, H. S. (1993). *Bayesian model invalidation using tail area probabilities.* Technical Report, Department of Statistics, Harvard University.

Gelman, A., & Rubin, D. B. (1992). Inference from iterative simulation using multiple sequences (with discussion). *Statistical Science, 7,* 457-511.

Goodman, L. A. (1974a). The analysis of a system of qualitative variables when some of the variables are unobservable: Part I. A modified latent structure approach. *American Journal of Sociology, 79,* 1179-1259.

Goodman, L. A. (1974b). Exploratory latent structure analysis using both identifiable and unidentifiable models. *Biometrika, 61,* 215-231.

Haberman, S. J. (1979). *Analysis of qualitative data* (Vol. 2, chap. 10). New York: Academic Press.

Lazarsfeld, P. F. & Henry, N. W. (1968). *Latent structure analysis.* Boston: Houghton Mifflin.

Little, R.J.A. (1989). Testing the equality of two independent binomial proportions. *The American Statistician, 43,* 283-288.

McCutcheon, A. L. (1987). *Latent class analysis.* Newbury Park, CA: Sage.

Meng, X. L., & Rubin, D. B. (1991). Using EM to obtain asymptotic variance-covariance matrices: The SEM algorithm. *Journal of the American Statistical Association, 86,* 899-909.

Press, W. H., Flannery, B. P., Teukolsky, S. A., & Vetterling, W. T. (1986). *Numerical recipes: The art of scientific computing* (pp. 102-130). Cambridge: Cambridge University Press.

Richardson, J.T.E. (1990). Variants of chi-square for 2×2 contingency tables. *British Journal of Mathematical and Statistical Psychology, 43,* 309-326.

Rubin, D. B. (1984). Bayesianly justifiable and relevant frequency calculations for the applied statistician. *The Annals of Statistics, 12,* 1151-1172.

Stern, H. S., Arcus, D., Kagan, J., Rubin, D. B., & Snidman, N. (forthcoming). Using mixture models in temperament research. *International Journal of Behavioral Development.*

Tanner, M. A., & Wong, W. H. (1987). The calculation of posterior distributions by data augmentation. *Journal of the American Statistical Association, 82,* 528-550.

Titterington, D. M., Smith, A.F.M., & Makov, U. E. (1985). *Statistical analysis of finite mixture distributions.* New York: John Wiley.

Yates, F. (1984). Tests of significance for 2×2 contingency tables (with discussion). *Journal of the Royal Statistical Society, A 147,* 426-463.

Author Index

Subject Index

445

About the Contributors

Peter M. Bentler is Professor of Psychology at the University of California, Los Angeles. His research deals with theoretical and statistical problems in psychometrics, especially structural equation models, as well as with personality and applied social psychology, especially drug use and abuse.

C. Mitchell Dayton is Professor of Measurement, Statistics, and Evaluation at the University of Maryland, where he has been a faculty member since 1964. He also earned two graduate degrees from the same institution after completing his undergraduate studies at the University of Chicago. In addition to introductory-level statistics course, his teaching interests have focused in areas of experimental design and multivariate methods. His research interest in latent class models dates from the mid-1970s, and he has published on a wide variety of theoretical and applied topics, including psychological scaling, mastery assessment, adaptive testing, and randomized-response models.

Anton K. Formann is Titular Professor of Psychology at the Institute for Psychology at the University of Vienna, Austria. He has degrees in psychology and statistics. His main research interests concern latent class analysis and Rasch models. Major works include papers on linear logistic latent class analysis in the *Biometrical Journal* and the *Journal of the American Statistical Association,* and papers on constrained latent class models in the *British Journal of Mathematical and Statistical Psychology.*

Jacques A. Hagenaars is Full Professor of Methodology of the Social Sciences at Tilburg University, the Netherlands. His current research interests center on categorical longitudinal and causal analysis. He is the author of LCAG, a program for loglinear modeling with latent variables and missing data, coeditor of a Dutch textbook on causal analysis, author of *Categorical Longitudinal Data: Loglinear Panel, Trend, and Cohort Analysis* (Sage, 1990), of *Loglinear Models With Latent Variables* (Sage, 1993), and of many articles in Dutch and international scholarly journals.

Scott L. Hershberger is an Assistant Professor of Methodology and Statistics within the Department of Psychology and Family Studies at the United States International University. His research interests include structural equation modeling, psychometric theory, and developmental behavior genetics.

Rolf Langeheine is a member of the Department of Educational and Psychological Methodology, Institute for Science Education, at the University of Kiel, Germany. Over many years, a focus of his work has been on the analysis of categorical data by loglinear and latent class models with a special interest in Markov chain models for the analysis of longitudinal categorical data in the past few years. He is editor (together with Jürgen Rost) of the *Latent Trait and Latent Class Models* volume. He shares coauthorship with Frank van de Pol on papers about Markov chain models that appeared in journals such as *Sociological Methods and Research* and *Sociological Methodology,* or edited volumes such as the forthcoming book *Analyzing Social and Political Change.*

George B. Macready is Professor of Measurement, Statistics, and Evaluation at the University of Maryland, where he has been a faculty member since 1970. He obtained his graduate training in Education at the University of Oregon, where he received an M.A. degree, and at the University of Minnesota, where he received a Ph.D. His research interests are in the area of theory and applications of latent class procedures to modeling educational and psychological phenomena. His publications in latent class modeling include such topics as mastery assessment, adaptive testing, test bias, and trait acquisition.

Allan L. McCutcheon is Associate Professor and Associate Chair of Sociology at the University of Delaware. He is the author of *Latent Class Analysis* and has authored and coauthored a number of articles using loglinear and latent class models. He has taught in the ICPSR summer program at the University of Michigan and the Spring Seminar sponsored by the Central Archive for Empirical Social Research at the

University of Cologne, Germany; he currently teaches in the European Consortium for Political Research's summer program at the University of Essex, England. In addition to his interest in categorical data analysis, his current research interests focus on the political, social, economic, and religious changes in the newly emerging democracies of Central and Eastern Europe.

Peter C. M. Molenaar graduated from the University of Utrecht, The Netherlands, in mathematical psychology, psychophysiology, and time series analysis. He is currently at the University of Amsterdam and Pennsylvania State University. He has published in the following areas: state-space modeling of developmental processes, behavior genetics, and psychophysiological signal analysis. His current interests include nonlinear dynamical approaches to epigenetics and biophysics.

John R. Nesselroade received his Ph.D. in Psychology from the University of Illinois at Urbana–Champaign. He is currently Hugh Scott Hamilton Professor of Psychology at the University of Virginia. He is a frequent guest scientist at the Max Planck Institute for Human Development and Education, Berlin. His areas of research and publication include life-span developmental research methodology, invariance and change in personality and ability dimensions, research design, and multivariate data analysis.

Michael J. Rovine received a Bachelor's Degree in Mathematics in 1971 from The University of Pennsylvania. After working as a research assistant at the Philadelphia Geriatric Center, he attended graduate school at the Pennsylvania State University where he took a Master's and Ph.D. in Educational Psychology. Since then, he has been a member of the faculty of the Department of Human Development and Family Studies in the College of Health and Human Development. Primarily a methodologist, he has done work in structural modeling and missing data estimation. He also has been looking at and comparing characteristics of different correlational and regression techniques and is currently looking at nonlinear models. More recently, he has been associated with the Center for Developmental and Health Research Methodology where he is Acting Director.

Donald B. Rubin is Professor of Statistics and Chair of the Department of Statistics at Harvard University. Previously he was Professor of

Statistics and of Education at the University of Chicago and chair of the Statistics Research Group at Educational Testing Service. His research has dealt with causal inference in experimental and observational studies, missing data and nonresponse in surveys, and applied Bayesian statistics, including computational methods. He has been coordinating and applications editor of the *Journal of the American Statistical Association* and is a past member of the Committee on National Statistics. He is a fellow of a number of professional associations, including the American Academy of Arts and Sciences, the American Association for the Advancement of Science, the Institute of Mathematical Statistics, the American Statistical Association, and the International Statistics Institute. He received an A.B. degree from Princeton University and an M.S. degree in computer science and a Ph.D. degree in statistics, both from Harvard University.

Albert Satorra is Professor of Statistics in the Department of Economics of the Universitat Pompeu Fabra in Barcelona. His area of interest is statistical methodology in social sciences, especially structural equation modeling, a topic on which he has published numerous articles in leading journals.

Thomas Schmitt studied Psychology at the University of Trier, where he earned his diploma in 1993. His thesis was on the application of causal regression models in the research on mood states. He is working as a clinical psychologist.

Michael E. Sobel is Professor of Sociology and of Applied Mathematics at the University of Arizona. In addition to his work on causal inference, he works on covariance structure models and models for the analysis of categorical data.

Christiane Spiel received her Ph.D.s in History and Psychology at the University of Vienna, Austria. She is currently Associate Professor of Psychology at the Department of Psychology, University of Vienna. She has published in the following areas: developmental research methodology, test theory, development in childhood and adolescence, children at risk, family relationships, and text processing.

Hal S. Stern is Associate Professor of Statistics at the Department of Statistics at Harvard University. His research has dealt with mixture and latent variable models, models for paired comparison and rank data, and applications of statistical methods to psychological research. He is coeditor of *Chance* magazine and is a member of the American Statistical Association, the Institute of Mathematical Statistics, and the American Association for the Advancement of Science. He received a B.S. degree from the Massachusetts Institute of Technology and M.S. and Ph.D. degrees in statistics from Stanford University.

Rolf Steyer studied Psychology at the University of Göttingen (Germany), where he received the diploma. In 1977 he began teaching statistics at the University of Frankfurt, where he got his doctor of philosophy in 1982. He then took a position at the University of Trier, where he received the *venia legendi* in Psychology in 1989. Since 1993 he has been teaching both at the University of Trier and the University of Münster. He has made major contributions in three areas of methodology: First, he published the book *Theorie kausaler Regressionsmodelle,* where he developed the mathematical foundations of causal modeling, both in experimental and nonexperimental empirical research. Second, in his book *Messen und Testen* (coauthored with Michael Eid), he explicated the relationship between representation theory of measurement and psychometric test theory. Third, in a series of papers (coauthored by several colleagues), he developed latent state-trait theory, which generalizes classical psychometric test theory taking explicitly into account that not only persons but also situations and the interaction between persons and situations may determine psychological test scores and other observations.

Hoben Thomas is Professor of Psychology at The Pennsylvania State University. His research interests focus on formal theory and methods in various areas of psychology, including cognitive development, psychometrics, genetics, and meta-analysis. He is the author of *Distributions of Correlation Coefficients* (1989) and (with A. Lohaus) of *Modeling Growth and Individual Differences in Spatial Tasks* (1993).

Alexander von Eye is Director of the Research-Outreach Methodology Program and Professor of Family and Child Ecology and Psychology at Michigan State University. He has held Assistant Professorships at the Universities of Trier and Erlangen Nürnberg and was Senior Research Scientist at the Max Planck Institute for Human Development and Education in Berlin, Germany. He was Professor of Human development and Education at The Pennsylvania State University. His main areas of interest include cognitive development and methodology and statistics in the social sciences. In the area of cognitive development, he conducts experiments investigating hypotheses concerning life-span development of memory for prose and cognitive complexity. In the areas of methodology and statistics, his main concentrations are on analysis of categorical variables in developmental contexts, classification methods, and computational statistics. His works include more than 150 articles and book chapters and six edited and three authored books, chiefly covering methodological topics.

Phillip K. Wood received his dissertation from the University of Minnesota in 1985. He is currently an Assistant Professor at the University of Missouri–Columbia. His research interests include structural equation modeling, particularly as it is related to the assessment of differential change and growth and adult cognitive development. Substantive research interests include the assessmen⁺ of college outcomes and graduate training in statistics.